D1030809

Songs of Flying Dragons

Harvard-Yenching Institute Monograph Series, Volume 22

Songs of Flying Dragons

A CRITICAL READING

PETER H. LEE

HARVARD UNIVERSITY PRESS

CAMBRIDGE, MASSACHUSETTS

1975

UNESCO COLLECTION OF REPRESENTATIVE WORKS
KOREAN SERIES

This book
has been accepted
in the Korean Series
of the Translations Collection
of the United Nations
Educational, Scientific and
Cultural Organization
(UNESCO)

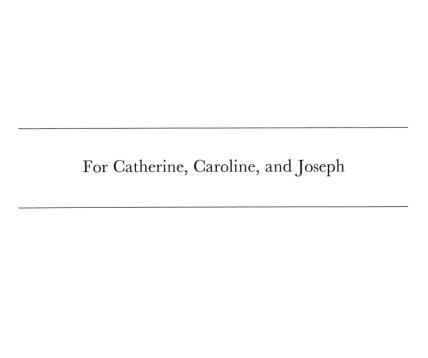

For Catherine, Caroline, and Joseph

Preface

The *Songs of Flying Dragons* is a Korean eulogy cycle in 125 cantos composed in 1445–1447 to celebrate the founding of the Yi dynasty. The work of a committee of the foremost contemporary philologists and literary men, it represents a happy collaboration of poetry and historiography. Its implied political and ideological motives notwithstanding, the *Songs*, as the title suggests, are ultimately a eulogy employing all literary devices known to the tradition. The compilers rightly traced the precedents of their work to the dynastic hyms in the *Book of Songs* in praise of the Chou founders, and 248 poems in the cycle belong, if anything, to a genre of poems of praise and fulfill what the panegyric is expected to perform. An analysis in the following pages of the *Songs'* rhetorical strategies, encomiastic topics, and stylistic devices will, I hope, demonstrate their matter and manner. As a landmark in the long eulogistic tradition in East Asia, the *Songs* is an important literary work calling for a comparative investigation of the concepts of praise, the nature and function of kingship, and the morality of revolution.

Certain basic assumptions and achievements in the *Songs* might need some clarification. One is the use of history by literature. The concern with the values and uses of history was a vital element in the eulogy, as it tries to order man's existence and experience and to establish heroic and moral beauty as worthy of admiration and emulation. The material was drawn from history, but the result is not a facile reduction of history to a paraphrase of politico-moral concepts, but a transformation of history into moving examples and a dramatization of heroic and virtuous deeds which found their fulfillment in history. The compilers, however, could not be blamed for their vague distinction between history and literature. As poets and historians, they enjoyed the poet's freedom to create fables and myths and fulfilled the historian's function of elucidating and evaluating historical phenomena. Indeed, the difference between the two, as Aristotle and Sidney seem to say, is a matter of degree.

The lessons of the *Songs*, disguised behind moving anecdotes and persuasive aphorisms, are ultimately moral, consonant with the prevailing contemporary view of literature. Every civilized society craves order and harmony, and the importance of social cohesion and cultural continuity has been a major literary concern. In the traditional view, poetry was essential to the welfare of society, as the *Songs*' encyclopedic learning and sententious elements bespeak a humanist ideal of the time. Assertive contents were as much part of poetry as dramatic enactment, and no poetic value was independent of objective truth, although modern explicatory criticism might disagree. Furthermore, the Korean poetic tradition usually did not recognize nonoral poetry, the musical aspect of poetry being its important structural and dramatic device. Poetry played a role in the education of society in its traditions, in the molding of morals and manners of listeners, and in the improvement of the art of memory. And in a handbook of the ideal education of the Confucian prince, the aim of literature and the aim of education are one. This needs no apology: the basic theory of literature for some twenty centuries in East and in the West was didactic. Literature teaches by example, moving men to love of virtue and abhorrence of vice. It is both enjoyable and instructive, as the *Songs* legitimately aver.

The multiple motives and complex structure of the *Songs* repay the closest reading. My aim in this volume is to present a sustained analysis of the *Songs* with appropriate parallels drawn from Western literature. An introductory chapter, in which I attempt to provide a short account of the Korean events to which the poems refer, is followed by an analysis of the form and structure of the work. Two chapters on "The Confucian Soldier" and "The Confucian Statesman" set the themes of the *Songs* into the framework of Confucian politico-moral thought and attempt to explore the Confucian view of man and his conduct in the world. The subject of the fifth is traditional *topoi* and symbolism as well as folklore and myth based on the macro-microcosmic correspondence employed in the creation of hero and the atmosphere of the work. In the last chapter, through an analysis of the symbolism of the "sacred" tree, I attempt to explore from yet another angle the East Asian view of man and history. This and other recurrent symbols of East Asian civilization invest the work with the timeless human dimension.

The book was initiated and completed under a grant from the Bollingen Foundation, American Council of Learned Societies, and American Philosophical Society, and I am grateful to these institutions for their support. The Center for Japanese and Korean Studies at the University of California in Berkeley and the Center for Korean Studies at the University of Hawaii have supplied funds for the preparation of the manuscript. It is a pleasure to express my thanks to Reuel Denney, L. Carrington Goodrich, Josephine Miles, Earl Miner, Leonard Nathan, Lawrence V. Ryan, Daniel Stempel, Arthur F. Wright, and Lien-sheng Yang for reading all or parts of the work and offering valuable suggestions. I wish also to thank Glen W. Baxter of the Harvard–Yenching Institute for his generous assistance.

Acknowledgments

Grateful acknowledgment is made to the following for permission to quote copyrighted material:

Cambridge University Press, for Honor Matthews, *Character & Symbol in Shakespeare's Plays*, © 1962 Cambridge University Press

Columbia University Press, for Burton Watson, *Hsün Tzu: Basic Writings*, Copyright © 1963 by Columbia University Press, and *Ssu-ma Ch'ien: Grand Historian of China*, Copyright © 1958 by Columbia University Press

George Allen and Unwin, Ltd., for Arthur Waley, *The Analects of Confucius* (1949) and *The Book of Songs* (1954)

Harcourt Brace Jovanovich, Inc., and Faber and Faber, Ltd., for Dudley Fitts, *The Birds: An English Version*, © 1957 by Harcourt, Brace and Company, Inc.

Harold Matson Company, Inc., for *The Aeneid of Virgil*, Copyright 1952 by C. Day Lewis, reprinted by permission of Harold Matson Co., Inc.

Indiana University Press, for Northrop Frye, *The Educated Imagination*, Copyright © 1964 by Indiana University Press

Penguin Books, Inc., for Dorothy L. Sayers, *The Song of Roland*, Copyright © 1957 by executors of Dorothy L. Sayers

Princeton University Press, for *A Source Book in Chinese Philosophy*, translated and compiled by Wing-tsit Chan, Copyright © 1963 by Princeton University Press, and Donald R. Howard, *The Three Temptations*, Copyright © 1966 by Princeton University Press

University of California Press, for J. S. P. Tatlock, *The Legendary History of Britain*, Copyright 1950 by The Regents of the University of California; Maynard Mack, *King Lear in Our Time*, © 1965 by the Regents of the University of California; and Joseph R. Levensen and Franz Schurmann, *China: An Interpretive History*, Copyright © 1969 by the Regents of the University of California. All originally published by the University of California Press; reprinted by permission of the Regents of the University of California

University of Chicago Press, for Richmond Lattimore, *The Iliad of Homer*, Copyright 1951 by The University of Chicago; and Smith Palmer Bovie, *Virgil's Georgics*, Copyright 1956 by The University of Chicago

Contents

Abbreviations

AHKB *Akhak kwebŏm* 樂學軌範
AM *Asia Major*
AY *Asea yŏn'gu* 亞細亞研究

BD Herbert A. Giles, *A Chinese Biographical Dictionary*
BMFEA *Bulletin of the Museum of Far Eastern Antiquities*

CG *Chōsen gakuhō* 朝鮮學報
CH *Chindan hakpo* 震檀學報
CKK Chōsen kosho kankōkai ed. 朝鮮古書刊行會
CKS *Chōsen kinseki sōran* 朝鮮金石總覽
CKT *Chung-kuo ku-chin ti-ming ta-tz'u-tien* 中國古今地名大辭典
CMP *Chŭngbo munhŏn pigo* 增補文獻備考
CS *Chou shu* 周書
CTS *Chiu T'ang shu* 舊唐書
CWTS *Chiu wu-tai shih* 舊五代史

ELH *Journal of English Literary History*

HGS *Han'guk sa* 韓國史
HHS *Hou Han shu* 後漢書
HJAS *Harvard Journal of Asiatic Studies*
HLQ *Huntington Library Quarterly*
HMN *Haedong myŏngsin nok* 海東名臣錄

HS (*Ch'ien*) *Han shu* 前漢書
HTS *Hsin T'ang shu* 新唐書
HWTS *Hsin wu-tai shih* 新五代史
HYS *Hsin Yüan shih* 新元史

JA *Journal Asiatique*
JAOS *Journal of the American Oriental Society*
JHI *Journal of the History of Ideas*

KIC *Kukcho inmul chi* 國朝人物志
KKH Kojŏn kanhaeng hoe ed. 古典刊行會
KRS *Koryŏ sa* 高麗史
KRSC *Koryŏsa chiri chi* 高麗史地理志
KRSCY *Koryŏ sa chŏryo* 高麗史節要
KSC *Kuksasang ŭi chemunje* 國史上의諸問題
KT *Kyŏngguk taejŏn* 經國大典
KTH *Kugyŏk Taejŏn hoet'ong* 國譯大典會通

LCL Loeb Classical Library (Cambridge, Mass., 1912–)
Legge James Legge, *The Chinese Classics*
LC Lucien Gilbert, *Dictionnaire historique et géographique de la Mandchourie*

MCRKH *Mansen chiri rekishi kenkyū hōkoku* (Tokyo, 1915–1926)
MH Edouard Chavannes, *Les Mémoires historiques de Se-ma Ts'ien*
MLQ *Modern Language Quarterly*
MSL *Ming shih-lu* 明實錄
MTB *Memoirs of the Research Department of the Tōyō Bunko*

PMLA *Publications of the Modern Language Association*
PS *Pei shih* 北史

SC *Shih chi* 史記
SGSG *Samguk sagi* 三國史記
SGYS *Samguk yusa* 三國遺事
SjS *Sejo sillok* 世祖實錄
SKC *San kuo chih* 三國志
SnS *Sejong sillok* 世宗實錄
SnSC *Sejong sillok chiri chi* 世宗實錄地理志
SPPY *Ssu-pu pei-yao* 四部備要
SPTK *Ssu-pu ts'ung-k'an* 四部叢刊
SR *Sewanee Review*
SS *Sŏnwŏn segye* (in *HGS*) 璿源世系
STN *Seoul taehakkyo nonmunjip* 서울大學校論文集

SZ   *Shigaku zasshi* 史學雜誌

TCTC   *Tzu-chih t'ung-chien* 資治通鑑
TG   *Tōyō gakuhō* 東洋學報
TFYK   *Ts'e-fu yüan-kuei* 冊府元龜
TnS   *T'aejong sillok* 太宗實錄
TP   *T'oung Pao*
TS   *T'aejo sillok* 太祖實錄
TSCC   *T'u-shu chi-ch'eng* 圖書集成
TT   *Tongguk t'onggam* 東國通鑑
TYS   *Sinjŭng Tongguk yŏji sŭngnam* 新增東國輿地勝覽

WYWK   *Wan-yu wen-k'u* 萬有文庫

YC   *Yongjae ch'onghwa* 慵齋叢話
YG   *Yongbi ŏch'ŏn ka* 龍飛御天歌
YH   *Yŏksa hakpo* 歷史學報
YK   *Yŏllyŏsil kisul* 燃藜室記述
YKP   *Yŏllyŏsil kisul pyŏlchip* 燃藜室記述別集
YS   *Yüan shih* 元史

The Yi Dynasty (simplified) based on *Sŏnwŏn segye*

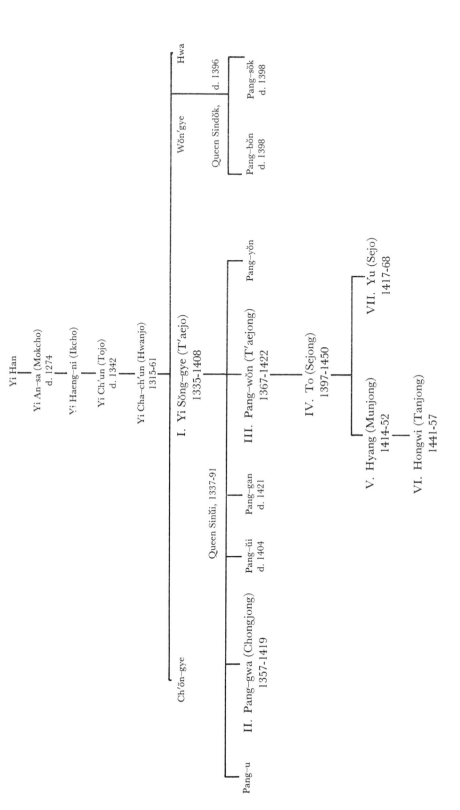

Songs of Flying Dragons

Chapter I. Introduction

On August 5, 1392, General Yi Sŏng-gye (1335–1408) ascended the Korean throne as the first monarch of the Yi dynasty. Some fifty years later, King Sejong, Yi Sŏng-gye's grandson and fourth monarch, ordered the preparation of a eulogy to celebrate the event. The result was the *Songs of Flying Dragons* (*Yongbi ŏch'ŏn ka*), a cycle of 125 cantos comprising 248 poems. The *Songs* are an important historical, philological, and literary document. Historically, they are a manifesto of the policies of the new state and a mirror for future monarchs; the Confucian concepts in their Korean application of the dynastic mandate, portents, and nature and function of the ruler are elaborated and developed. Philologically, the 248 poems are the first experimental use in verse of the Korean alphabet invented in 1443–1444. As literature, the cycle is a repository of heroic tales and foundation myths of China and Korea, replete with cosmological speculations, folk beliefs, omens and prophecies. It marks the reawakening of Korean national consciousness and a sense of national solidarity, manifested in the invention of the native alphabet and the birth of a national literature. The exposition of the heroic valor and virtue of the dynastic founder is an eloquent expression of patriotic fervor. I will examine the temper and ideal of the time as depicted by the *Songs*, which spans roughly the mid-fourteenth to the mid-fifteenth century.

In East Asia the mid-fourteenth century was an age of outward splendor and internal decay. The stupendous fabric of the Mongol government in China and its vassal states was at the point of dissolution. The dynasty was rent with disunity, the people suffered from natural catastrophes, and the nation had become the prey of warring rebel leaders. From the wreckage of the empire so assiduously built by Cinggis Qan emerged Chu Yüan-chang, who proclaimed himself emperor of the new Ming dynasty. This dramatic change in the continental political scene precipitated a shift of allegiance in the Korean court. The peace treaty signed in 1259 between the Koryŏ king and the Mongol empire had inaugurated a hundred years of Mongol domination in Korea. Royal hostages were periodically taken to Peking, the Mongol capital, and the Korean kings were required to marry Mongol princesses. Mongol resident commissioners supervised Korea's central administration, and Mongolian manners and customs, including coiffure, were adopted by the court. King Kongmin, the thirty-first Koryŏ monarch, attempted to throw off this stringent political and cultural incursion. His revolt was partly successful. He recovered territory in the north but was powerless against the desperate ills of the country. His successor, Shin U, was blamed for plunging Korea into chaos, although he was only a boy of ten when he ascended the throne. The factious nobility, devoid of any sense of national purpose, offered no solutions to the national and international problems. The country was harassed by the ruling clique's shifting allegiance to Ming or to Northern Yüan (the remnant Mongol empire after the Mongols were driven out of Peking), the coastal raids of Japanese pirates, the corruption of the nobility, and agrarian discontent. Buddhism, the national faith for eight hundred years, had lost its inspiration and vigor. Overgrown with native beliefs and practices, it no longer provided spiritual solace for the people. Koreans thirsted for a leader who would restore unity to the nation and rule a willing people as a trust of Heaven. From this chaos Yi Sŏng-gye emerged to respond to a call from the nation and people.

Yi Sŏng-gye was born in 1335 in the area of modern Yŏnghŭng, the second son of Yi Cha-ch'un. Yi's family, said to be originally from the south, had moved to the northeast in the second half of the thirteenth century. This migration was undertaken by Yi's great-great-grandfather, Yi An-sa (temple name Mokcho, died

1274), who later held a Mongol office (see the translation, cantos 3–6, 17–18). Of Yi Haeng-ni (temple name Ikcho), Yi's great-grandfather, and Yi Ch'un (temple name Tojo, died 1342), Yi's grandfather, we know little. Yi Cha-ch'un (temple name Hwanjo, 1315–1360), Yi's father, makes his first appearance in history in 1355 when, as the Chiliarch of Ssangsŏng, he arrived in the Koryŏ capital of Kaesŏng to pay homage to King Kongmin. The king, in order to free himself from the Mongol yoke and to recover the territory in the north, ordered the destruction of the Mongol commissioner's headquarters in Ssangsŏng. Yi Cha-ch'un received royal orders and participated in the successful campaign (canto 24). Thus Yi Sŏng-gye's ancestors were Koryŏ nationals who held minor Mongol offices in the northeast but felt no loyalty to Mongol overlords. By geographical proximity, they were in contact with the Mongols and the Jürched tribes and were familiar with their manners and customs. Yi Sŏng-gye was raised in these surroundings and is said to have excelled in equestrian archery from boyhood. He used the *hu* arrows (canto 27), which were widely used by the Sukchin people, the ancestors of the Jürched.

In 1361, Yi Sŏng-gye, as Myriarch of the Northeast, put down a rebellion and in early 1362 repulsed the Red Turbans, recapturing from them the capital Kaesŏng (cantos 33–34). In the seventh month of 1362, he defeated the forces of Mongol General Naɣaču on the plain of Hamhŭng (cantos 35–36, 88). In 1364, a Korean defector to the Mongols crossed the Yalu and devastated the northern province. Yi first repulsed him in the northwest and, turning his troops to the northeast, regained towns from the rebels (cantos 37, 42). For his distinguished service he was awarded the senior third rank and laudatory epithets. In January 1370, with 5,000 cavalry and 10,000 infantry, as "General of the Northeast," he marched north to destroy the Mongol garrison and sever relations with the Northern Yüan. His troops went deep into enemy territory, as far as the right bank of the T'ung-chia River, and captured an enemy stronghold there (cantos 38–41). As a consequence, his name was dreaded by Mongols and Jürched alike.

Yi's military genius also manifested itself in his campaigns against the Japanese pirates. In 1223 the Japanese began raiding Korea's southern coast; these raids became more frequent and disastrous under Shin U's reign. With their bases on the islands of

Iki, Tsushima, and Kyushu, the pirates' aims were to raid store-houses of grain, to intercept the fleets transporting tax grains to the capital, and to kidnap Korean technicians and artisans. In August 1371, the area along the Yesŏng River was pillaged, but Yi, as Regional Commander for the Western River, repulsed them. In 1377 he encountered the pirates in the south and fought a decisive battle below Mount Chii (cantos 47–48). In 1378 the Japanese landed in Sŭngch'ŏnbu (modern Kaep'ung) and battled stubbornly until Yi, with his picked cavalry, wiped out the invaders (canto 49). His most famous campaign was in 1380, when he attacked the pirates at Unbong, cornered them at Mount Hwang, and annihilated them (cantos 50–52). In 1382 he became Regional Commander for the Northeast, and the following year he fought a successful battle against the Jürched chief on the plain of Kilchu. His final engagement with Japanese pirates at Hamju in 1385 was equally successful (cantos 58–62).

Perhaps Yi Sŏng-gye's most dramatic decision before he ascended the throne was his refusal to march north to drive out Ming garrisons in Liaotung (1388). Instead, he turned his army back from Wihwa Island and thus inflicted a deadly blow to the waning Koryŏ dynasty and its pro-Mongol faction (cantos 9–14; 67–69). This was the chain of events which led to his decision. Although Sino-Korean relations immediately after the founding of the Ming were friendly, two events in 1374 muddied these relations: the assassination of King Kongmin by eunuchs (on the night of October 19),[1] and the murder of the returning Ming envoy by a Korean escort (December 28).[2] These events made the Ming founder suspicious of Korean sincerity, and he refused to receive Korean envoys.[3] On numerous occasions envoys were turned back

1. *KRS*, 44, 34a; *KRSCY*, 29, 28b-29b.
2. The Ming envoys, Lin Mi and Ts'ai Pin, arrived on May 24, 1374, to request a tribute of 2,000 horses for the northern campaign (*KRS*, 44, 23b ff.) and left the Korean capital on October 8 with 200 horses. Kim Ŭi escorted them. Upon their arrival in P'yongyang, he heard the news of the murder of the king. Kim then killed Ts'ai and fled with Lin to Naγaču (*KRS*, 131, 34a-b).
3. Already in July 1373, the Korean envoy sent to congratulate the heir apparent on his birthday could not proceed beyond Liaotung (*KRS*, 44, 4a). A dispatch from the Secretariat specifies a triennial tribute mission but prohibits missions on the occasions of the birthday of the emperor or heir apparent (*MSL*, 76, 1397, 1400-1). In April 1374, a Korean envoy left for Nanking to request the land route and an annual tribute mission (*KRS*, 44, 21b ff.; *MSL*, 89, 1574-5) but returned in July without sueccess. See Suematsu Yasukazu, *Seikyū shisō*, I (Tokyo, 1965), 328–345, and 345–361 for the question of the amount of annual tribute.

at Liaotung, and those who managed to reach Nanking were banished or imprisoned. Despite the Ming emperor's ill treatment of envoys and his exorbitant demands for tribute horses, Koryŏ continued to demonstrate its good will. The emperor, however, made further unreasonable demands, levied 5,000 Korean horses (1386),[4] and moved the Ming–Korean border far below the Yalu, between the modern Kangwŏn and Hamgyŏng provinces.[5] The moving of the border particularly disturbed the Korean court, and it consequently sent forces under Yi Sŏng-gye and other generals to destroy the Ming garrisons there. Upon reaching Wihwa Island in the middle of the Yalu, Yi Sŏng-gye and his tired Right Army refused to advance. He marched back to the capital, banished the war advocates, and took the helm of the state.

Yi Sŏng-gye's progressive pro-Ming party, comprised mainly of students of neo-Confucianism, set about to remove the sources of future problems. First, Shin U and Shin Ch'ang, the thirty-second and thirty-third rulers of Koryŏ, were accused of being the sons of an evil monk, were banished, and later executed. King Kongyang was installed in their place (1389; canto 11). Second, in 1389 Yi Sŏng-gye and his supporters enforced a land reform and burned the land registers of the old Koryŏ nobility the following year (canto 73). Third, his followers assassinated the Koryŏ minister, Chŏng Mong-ju, on the night of April 26, 1392, thereby removing the last obstacle to final victory (canto 93). On July 31, the last Koryŏ king was sent into exile, and five days later Yi Sŏng-gye ascended the throne (cantos 12, 14).

Soon after his accession, Yi Sŏng-gye sent envoys to Nanking informing the Ming of the dynastic change. He also requested the Ming founder to select a new name for Korea. The emperor chose Chosŏn ("brightness of the morning sun"; canto 85) as a most beautiful and fitting name for Korea, which was adopted on March 27, 1393. Because of Korean–Jürched difficulties and the yearly tribute, however, friendly relations were not easily estab-

---

4. *KRS*, 136, 11b.
5. *KRS*, 137, 3b-4a (*MSL*, 187, 2807-8). On February 4, 1388, the emperor ordered the Ministry of Revenue to send the message to Korea, which was brought by Sŏl Chang-su during the second month of 1388. See Suematsu, I, 361–374 and Henry Serruys, *Sino-Jürced Relations during the Yung-lo Period (1403–1424)* (Wiesbaden, 1955), p. 49.

lished. The Ming emperor accused Korea of influencing Ming border officials, of enticing the Jürched to cross the Yalu and violate Ming territory, and of sending weak horses as tribute. Several missions sent to exculpate Korea of these charges were unsuccessful until Yi's fifth son went to Nanking (1394; canto 94). Sino-Korean relations eventually normalized in 1401, when Ming envoys arrived with a proclamation of investiture and the golden seal of the "King of Korea."[6] Yi Sŏng-gye had already abdicated in favor of his second son (Yi Pang-gwa; Chŏngjong), who, in turn was succeeded by Yi's fifth son, Yi Pang-wŏn (T'aejong). Yi Pang-wŏn, born in Hamhŭng, took a *chinsa* degree in 1382 and the following year passed the final civil service examination (canto 81). After Yi's march back from Wihwa Island, Pang-wŏn worked zealously for his father's cause. A far-sighted strategist, he persuaded his father to eliminate the major opposition, Chŏng Mong-ju. Like Li Shih-min of the T'ang, to whom he is often compared, Yi Pang-wŏn played an important and decisive role in placing his father on the throne. Despite his meritorious services, one of his half-brothers, Yi's eighth and youngest son, became heir apparent in 1392. Under the pretext that some powerful ministers plotted with the heir apparent to kill the other princes, Yi Pang-wŏn initiated a coup on the night of October 6, 1398, killed the ministers, and had his half-brothers killed on their way to exile (cantos 98, 108). To avoid suspicion, he refused to be named heir apparent and instead placed his elder brother, Pang-gwa, on the throne (canto 99). Only after a second feud among the princes did Yi Pang-wŏn accept the nomination as heir apparent (cantos 102–103, 109). Nine months later he assumed rule.

In 1418 Yi Pang-wŏn abdicated in favor of his third son, Yi To (Sejong), who ascended the throne on September 9, 1418, at the age of twenty-one. Sejong's reign of thirty-two years ushered in the golden age of the Yi dynasty. His greatest concerns were the advancement of Confucian learning and the cultivation of men of ability. In 1420 he established the Academy of Worthies as a

6. *MSL*, 234, 3222–3. For Korean–Jürched problems see Sonoda Kazuki, *Mindai Kenshū Jochokushi no kenkyū* (Tokyo, 1948–53), and Wada Sei, *Tōashi kenkyū* (Tokyo, 1955). For the tribute system of the Yi dynasty see Tagawa Kōzō, *Richō kōnōsei no kenkyū* (Tokyo, 1964), *passim*.

royal research institute and assembled young scholars there.[7] At first chiefly employed in the preparation of the royal lectures, the academy was soon charged with multiple functions: the drafting of royal decrees and diplomatic messages, the reception of Chinese envoys, the administration of civil service examinations, the exegesis of the Chinese classics, and the study of Chinese institutions. As the focal point of political, cultural, and educational activities of early Yi, the academy became a symbol of enlightenment and the nation's intellectual and cultural center. Among its achievements were the exaltation of Confucianism as a unifying ideology of the literati, the invention of the Korean alphabet, and the compiling or composing of a number of significant philological, literary, and historical works, among them the *Songs*. Kindled by the king's broad learning and untiring guidance, the scholars of the academy fostered an era of Confucian learning unprecedented in Korean history. A sovereign who was "infinite in faculties" and a model of majesty, King Sejong inspired the imagination and loyalty of these dedicated men by his erudition and example, taste and tact. It was his great achievement to channel the ideals and aspirations of the age and to give diverse activities a strong sense of national purpose.

The *Songs* are imbued with the ideals and aspirations of Korea's Confucian era and with a strong sense of national purpose. In every civilization the cherished literary subjects are the heroic achievements of its people, especially its popular heroes, which it seeks to glorify and perpetuate. The greater a hero as historical figure, the richer the romantic or apocryphal legend that surrounds

---

7. The academy existed, under different names, in the Three Kingdoms and Koryŏ. In 1116 King Yejong established the Pomun Hall, but in 1136 its name was changed to Chiphyŏnchŏn. In 1400, it was renamed Pomun Hall, but, again, Chiphyŏnchŏn in 1410. On April 28, 1420, King Sejong made it the center of learning and compilation (*SnS*, 7, 30a). It was abolished in 1456 (*SjS*, 4, 14b). Before 1420 positions in the academy were honorary, held concurrently by officials, with two to three full-time members. Under the king, the membership rose to twenty or even thirty. In order to facilitate research, they were provided with books, clerks, and servants. The king not only purchased books but rewarded those who donated rare items to the academy. He also ordered the casting of new types (the so-called 1420 type). *KRS*, 76, 27b-30a; *CMP*, 221, 26a-b; *P'irwŏn chapki* (CKK, 1909), 1, 296–297; *YC*, 2, 32–33. For a comprehensive study see Ch'oe Sŭng-hŭi, "Chiphyŏnchŏn yŏn'gu," *YH*, XXXII (1966), 1–58; XXXIII (1967), 39–80.

him. This is not unusual, for fact and fiction are often inextricable and indistinguishable in heroic literature. To understand the *Songs*, which are generally accepted as the most significant and representative creation of their time and culture, it is necessary to examine the ethos which inspired them. This ethos is, of course, consistently Confucian, but a fuller appreciation of the *Songs* demands that we understand what the age believed to be their nature and purpose. Their subject matter is the history of an important national era of which I have given a brief account. But its compilers selected and interpreted the material in the light of the political and moral philosophy of the time in order to reinforce the legitimate functions of the work. Inevitably, changes were made, such as the inflation, if not fabrication, and suppression of evidence, the better to effect the political purpose of the work and to adhere to orthodox historiographical tradition. Certain principles of classical and humanist historiography in the West offer a possible parallel to the *Songs*, for the characteristic features of Greco-Roman and especially Renaissance historical writing were its nationalist, moral, and didactic purpose.[8] Like heroic poetry and history play in the West, the *Songs* went to history for inspiration,[9] but, although they drew upon the *Veritable Records*, they are ultimately, as their title suggests, a dynastic hymn cycle and employ all literary devices known to Korean and Chinese tradition. Their fulfillment of multiple functions of history, however, in no way detracts from their value as literature. Their historicity is a key to their success as a work of art. Any distinction between history and literature—as in the epics, panegyrics, heroic poetry, and historical poetry of the Renaissance and neoclassical periods[10]—is vague here; but anything approaching a genre theory, which attempts to classify every literary work with subtle critical distinctions, is a later phenomenon. When John Heming and Henry Condell took upon themselves the editorial task of Shakespeare's

---

8. See M. M. Reese, *The Cease of Majesty* (London, 1961), pp. 1–88, and E. M. W. Tillyard, *The Elizabethan World Picture* (New York, 1944).

9. For history plays see Lily B. Campbell, *Shakespeare's "Histories": Mirror of Elizabethan Policy* (San Marino, 1947); Irving Ribner, *The English History Play in the Age of Shakespeare* (Princeton, 1957), pp. 3–32; L. C. Knights, *Further Explorations* (Stanford, 1965), pp. 11–32; Geoffrey Bullough, "The Uses of History," in *Shakespeare's World* (London, 1964), pp. 96–115.

10. See O. B. Hardison, Jr., *The Enduring Monument* (Chapel Hill, 1962), and Hugh T. Swedenberg, Jr., *The Theory of the Epic in England 1650–1800* (Berkeley, 1944).

folio in 1623, for example, they classified his plays on recent British history as "histories" but grouped others as comedies and tragedies whether or not they touched on history. And when Dryden called his *Annus Mirabilis* (1667) a historical poem, when it is in fact a panegyrical propaganda piece written in answer to seditious tracts against Charles II and the church, he probably contributed to its misreading by posterity.[11]

The *Songs* are the earliest literary example in the native medium of national consciousness ignited by a Confucian era in Korean history. Buddhism had been the state religion of Korea during the preceding dynasties of Silla and Koryŏ. During eight centuries of royal and national sponsorship, it had become highly national and secular in orientation and practice. As royal chaplains and advisers, politicians and diplomats, compilers and exegetes, eminent monks played important and at times crucial roles in the development and preservation of the national tradition. Some were pilgrims who braved storm and sand to reach Serindia; some were commentators who during their stay abroad made contributions to doctrinal studies; some were astute observers of international power politics; some were spiritual advisers to the aristocracy, for example, the elite corps of knights in Silla; some took up arms to repulse foreign invaders; and some, through their research and writing, struggled to preserve the native tradition. The last work of importance by a Buddhist monk before the founding of the Yi dynasty was by the Great Master Iryŏn, the *Samguk yusa*, a treasury of *memorabilia* and *mirabilia* of Korea's past. Iryŏn—and before him Wŏn'gwang, Kyunyŏ, and Kakhun, to mention only a few—struggled to salvage the cultural remains from the Silla and Koryŏ periods. A recent critic has traced the beginnings of European nationalism to the twelfth century, citing as evidence such compilers of pseudo-history of nationalisic inspiration as Geoffrey of Monmouth, Saxo Grammaticus of Denmark, Magister Vincentius of Poland, and Snorri of Iceland.[12] Like some of the learned monks

11. Edward N. Hooker, "The Purpose of Dryden's *Annus Mirabilis*," *HLQ*, X (1946–7), 49–67, and Alan Roper, *Dryden's Poetic Kingdoms* (New York, 1965), pp. 74–87. Roper comments that it is the poet's "most ambitious poem" (p. 74) but laments that it is "too long for effective control of its panegyric themes and with insufficient narrative coherence to justify its pretensions toward historical poem" (p. 80). See also Earl Miner, *Dryden's Poetry* (Bloomington, 1967), pp. 3–35.

12. Halvdan Koht, "The Dawn of Nationalism in Europe," *American Historical Review*, LII (1947), 265–280, and Gains Post, "Two Notes on Nationalism in the Middle Ages," *Traditio*, IX (1953), 281–320.

in the West, Iryŏn and some of his predecessors were custodians of the native tradition. True, even earlier epics in Europe could be cited as expressing in varying degrees a sense of pride in their people through the praise of their heroes, notably the *Chanson de Roland* with its "dulce France." The same critic argues that often contemporary armed conflicts stimulated a sense of national unity in a people, as attested by the nationalist poets' praise of ruling family and leaders as symbols of *patria* and their concomitant contempt for the enemies. In Korea, continuous royal protection of the faith, close alliance between the ruling classes and church, monopoly of knowledge by eminent monks, and their religious fervor to create a perfect state according to Buddhist ideals are some of the factors that contributed to the unique role played by the church and its distinguished members. The compilation of the *Songs* as the embodiment of new ideals and visions of the age in the light of Confucian ritual and tradition may be termed a Confucian revenge against the Buddhist tradition, which, as heresy, the new kingdom attempted to displace.[13]

Among the sources used by the members of the Academy of Worthies were the Confucian classics and the later interpretative scheme which constantly contorted the texts to find their moral and political significance. The whole corpus of the classics was often read in this manner, using especially the "praise and blame" technique; the hymns in the *Book of Songs*, the speeches, ordinances, and documents in the *Book of Documents*, and the bare asyndetic accounts in the *Spring and Autumn Annals* were all construed to yield moral lessons for the benefit of society. The panegyrics in the *Book of Songs* in praise of the Chou founders, for example, made use of the technique of praise, especially the praise of a ruler, and various epideictic types and formulae. The *Book of Documents*, the commentaries on the *Spring and Autumn Annals*, and the histories, such as the *Historical Record* (*Shih chi*), which is modeled on the former two, further developed the method of epideictic rhetoric. With growing stress on the moral utility of praise—so reminiscent of the Greek ideal of *paideia* and the classical and Renaissance conception of poetry and history—the end of praise was considered to be chiefly didactic, the creation of patterns of virtue and vice, models of emulation and exhortation. The principal function of

13. Han U-gŭn, "Yŏmal Sŏnch'o ŭi pulgyo chŏngch'aek," *STN*, VI (1957), 3–80, esp. 18–44.

the poet and historian was therefore to create what Sidney called the "lively images of the virtues and vices," to present the traditionally typical and exemplary as enduring norms for the conduct of man. Consonant with the prevalent view of man and history, the eternal recurrence of typical events and behavior patterns encouraged imitation—for man's nature, like Nature herself, does not change—and the emulation of moral eminence in itself was held to be a liberal education.

The stylistic devices necessary to express the eminence of man's virtue (or vice) had been explored by the Confucian tradition: comparison and amplification—familiar devices in Western epideictic rhetoric—together with special vocabulary, traditional formulae and *topoi,* and the form best suited to the heightened presentation of the subject. The presentation was facilitated by a harmony of different voices, the language of the classics and histories, which relies for its metaphoric force on the implied and accepted view of the Confucian world order. The standard tropes and symbols associate the social and moral order with the cosmic (or divine), linking kingly virtue with the forces of Nature. This analogical thought based on the concepts of a triad of Heaven, Earth, and Man allowed the fullest exploration of the device of parallelism, a type of analogy.

The special vocabulary reserved for the king and his enterprise—the king's language—consists mainly of formulaic expressions, both bound (epithets) and unbound, commensurate with the power and prestige of one who has won Heaven's alliance and the people's allegiance, and who in the monarchic world order is the "origin, source, and prime exemplar" of virtue and wisdom. Analogy of king and sun, lodestar, or water is commonplace in political rhetoric. The usurper who through "by-paths and indirect crook'd ways" snatches the crown, the erring ruler who through his inefficiency dethrones himself, or the tyrant who by his disregard of degree and order ruptures order on all planes, invalidates the premise of the analogical language. The commoner cannot resort to it without provoking a thunderbolt from Heaven. When the *Songs* constantly remind the reader of the fact that the founding of the Yi dynasty was ordained and blessed by Heaven and that Yi Sŏng-gye merely fulfilled Heaven's charges, it may be well to recall Hellenistic kings or Roman emperors who were often equated with Dionysus or Romulus, or the "language of Christological exemplarism" based on the Christocratic-liturgical concept of kingship in the Middle Ages,[14] and the "preposterous identification"[15] of Elizabeth I with the Virgin, as well as with Gloriana, Belphoebe, Diana, Cynthia, Astraea, a pearl, star, phoenix, moon, unicorn, rose, and pelican,[16] and the murdered Charles I with Christ, or Cromwell with the sun, Amphion, Caesar and Hercules.[17] Restrained by Confucian decorum, such zealous allegorizing is rare in the *Songs*, and the compilers seldom attempt to "nationalize" Heaven.

The *Songs* open with the invocation of the enunciated subjects, the "six dragons": the four royal ancestors and the first and third monarchs of the new dynasty. This is followed by the main section, the account of the heroic and sagely virtues of the founder, Yi Sŏng-gye. The method of presentation follows the techniques evolved in the Chinese classics and histories, especially the biographical patterns in moral lives and eulogies of eminent men which made use of the topics of praise (or blame) to create an exemplum of virtue (or vice). Such a portrait was usually created through narration in chronological order of the subject's parentage and childhood and idealized accounts of his heroic *facta*, especially military victories. If he is renowned for martial prowess, each episode is carefully constructed to exemplify a specific martial virtue such as fortitude, magnanimity, or constancy. If he is a universal genius, a flower of valor and virtue, like Yi Sŏng-gye, his qualities as a leader of nation and people follow, again with a

14. Ernst H. Kantorowicz, *The King's Two Bodies* (Princeton, 1957), pp. 88, 93.

15. Malcolm M. Ross, *Poetry and Dogma* (New Brunswick, 1954), p. 132.

16. Elkin C. Wilson, *England's Eliza* (Cambridge, Mass., 1939), and Frances A. Yates, "Queen Elizabeth as Astraea," *Journal of the Warburg and Courtauld Institutes*, X (1947), 27–82.

17. By Marvell, Waller, Dryden, and Milton, to name only a few. He is usually praised as a delegate of Providence, Heaven's choice, master of the elements, or healer of social discord. For Marvell's treatment see John M. Wallace, "Marvell's Horatian Ode," *PMLA*, LXXVII (1962), 33–45 (for a bibliography on the poem see p. 33, n. 1), and "Andrew Marvell and Cromwell's Kingship: 'The First Anniversary,' " *ELH*, XXX (1963), 209–235; also in *Destiny His Choice* (Cambridge, 1968), pp. 69–144; Joseph A. Mazzeo, *Renaissance and Seventeenth-Century Studies* (New York, 1964), pp. 166–208; and Harold E. Toliver, *Marvell's Ironic Vision* (New Haven, 1965), *passim*. See also Ruth Nevo, *The Dial of Virtue* (Princeton, 1963), *passim*; and Ann E. Berthoff, *The Resolved Soul* (Princeton, 1970), pp. 205–207. For Waller's treatment of Cromwell see Warren L. Chernaik, *The Poetry of Limitation* (New Haven, 1968), pp. 115–171 *passim*.

series of episodes illustrating diverse aspects of civil virtues in action. As O. B. Hardison has pointed out, these topics of ancestry, of physical endowment and character (nature) are the familiar topics of epideictic oratory and rhetoric.[18] In the classics and histories, the composite formula of soldier and statesman is usually reserved for the dynastic founder, beginning with King Wu of Chou, since the ultimate end of martial valor and prowess is to found a state, which restores and safeguards order on all planes— social, political, and moral.

The Iliadic cantos of the *Songs* present Yi Sŏng-gye as possessing unusual gifts of body and character. Set apart from ordinary men in childhood, he possessed splendid appearance (cantos 28–29), superhuman strength (canto 87), and wielded huge bows and arrows (canto 27). He was a supreme archer (cantos 32, 40, 43 45–47, 63, 86–89), a master horseman (cantos 31, 34, 65, 70, 86–87), and a divine tactician (cantos 35–36, 51, 60). With these unusual qualities, he pacified the Red Turbans (canto 33), the Jürched (canto 38), the Mongols (cantos 35–37, 39, 40–41, 54), and subjugated the Japanese pirates (cantos 47–52, 58, 60–62). Commending his selfless deeds for the country and the people, Heaven not only sends down auspicious omens and portents (cantos 13, 39, 42, 50, 67–68, 83–84), but comes to his succor (cantos 30, 34, 37). He was kind to his men (cantos 66, 78–79), magnanimous (cantos 54, 67, 77), humble (64, 81), and consistent (79). He is compared to a number of Chinese paragons, only to emerge as surpassing them in moral excellence. Admiration and emulation are further stimulated by elements of the marvelous, with Heaven as his ally and with omens and portents to underscore the inevitability of the divine plan over the accidents of mere fortune or virtù. If there are no astronomical or meteorological phenomena for the enemy, we may be reminded that "when beggars die there are no comets seen" (*Julius Caesar*, II, ii, 30). There is, however, in the *Songs* no counterpart to a fiery sword, a bleeding spear, or a magic talisman like Gawain's green silk girdle that saves the wearer from being slain. Yi's talisman is his virtue, strengthened by his belief in his mission and in the ultimate triumph of Heaven's will.

Many episodes are historic, if chroniclers are to be trusted,

18. Hardison, pp. 30, 74–76.

and the tradition sanctioned the use of history by poetry in order to heighten the authenticity of the contents as well as to vindicate poetry's social role. Such forms of praise as hymns, epics, heroic poems, especially the Renaissance epics with their theme of deliverance,[19] are often held to be capable of conferring immortality on the subject and his nation. The celebration of Yi Sŏng-gye is thus also the celebration of Korea. Armed with philosophy and history, precepts and exempla, the compilers succeeded not only in conferring glory but in creating an image of ideal virtue, discharging their twofold duty as Confucians and encomiasts. "Every conqueror creates a muse," exclaims Waller. Through the creation of an enduring literary monument, the compilers assured themselves fame in posterity.

Eminence in arms, however, is not enough if Yi Sŏng-gye is to be portrayed as the prototype of a leader of nation and people, as a possessor of higher civil virtues for the good of society. His heroic prowess must have meaning in terms of Confucian ethical and political tradition. Thus Yi emerges as the embodiment of both martial and moral virtues, the former tempered and finally transformed by reason and piety, wisdom and love. The cheering people rush to him like those hastening to market and claim him as champion of their rights (cantos 10, 38, 41, 72). Aware of the heavy duties of the ruler, he declines to answer the people's wishes. Heaven finally intervenes and sends him a dream urging him to respond to its charge (canto 83). Discerning the will of Heaven, he at last ascends the throne and founds the House of Yi, thus avenging the sins of the "wicked last ruler" of Koryŏ and reasserting order and harmony.

The composite formula of action and contemplation, valor and wisdom, enjoyed a long tradition.[20] Like Aeneas, heroes of the national epic, Christ, and other biblical figures in the Christian epic who were often held up as exempla, so the sage emperors, culture heroes, and virtuous founders and rulers in Chinese history were looked upon as paradigms of moral virtue. Awareness of the inadequacy of the heroic code probably led to the reassessment and redefinition of the heroic ethos. The emergence of a great man in history is often a product of the happy conjunction of virtue and

19. Hardison, p. 51; John M. Steadman, *Milton and the Renaissance Hero* (Oxford, 1967), p. 96.
20. Steadman, pp. 10 ff., 162–163.

fortune, but the ideals and needs of the time require the transformation of Machiavellian virtù into classical and Christian virtue in the West,[21] and into Confucian virtue in the East. One who rose to power on the strength of merits often was an explorer of circumstances and political advantages, a manipulator of passions and weaknesses, or an agitator of contemporary instability with precedents and precepts in history. The mere energies and efficiency of the hero, without the sanction of Heaven, would finally lead to his downfall and self-destruction. A plaything of scythe-flourishing Fortune, the embodiment of such overweening ambition and lust for domination is usually reserved for the loser, the overreacher and overstepper mercilessly felled, the unheroic hero. By the inevitable requirements of the heroic-panegyric tradition, the victor must be portrayed differently. He must possess Heaven's blessing and moral virtue; these alone entitle him to establish his own rule. The conferment of the right to rule, the supreme reward for the victor (or the best), is generally known as the winning of the mandate of Heaven, the vindication of the morality of revolution, the supreme myth of Confucian political rhetoric.

This transformation of virtù into virtue and its subsequent glorification was often ascribed to the rationalist and humanist strains in the Confucian tradition characterized by conversion of myth into history, and mythical figures into moral paragons. Maurice Bowra, for example, cites the intellectuality of the Chinese as the chief reason for the lack of epic and comments that "Chinese . . . fashioned their own remarkable culture by other means."[22] A recent critic of Chinese culture comments that "when a prince was censured for listening to warriors . . . and not turning to the elders," this meant the "virtual suppression of the epic strain in Confucian . . . literature, for the courage of an epic hero was not the quality Confucianists preferred."[23] The Confucian term, *chün tzu* (princely man or gentleman), with its emphasis on virtue and learning, the same critic argues, suggests the irrelevance

21. For the discussion of virtù see Leonardo Olschki, *Machiavelli the Scientist* (Berkeley, 1945), pp. 35–40; Harry Levin, *The Overreacher* (Cambridge, Mass., 1952), pp. 179–183; and Joseph A. Mazzeo, *Rennaissance and Seventeenth-Century Studies*, p. 94, n. 1, and 156.

22. C. M. Bowra, *Heroic Poetry* (London, 1952), p. 47.

23. Joseph R. Levenson and Franz Schurmann, *China* (Berkeley, 1969), p. 53. Here the reference should be to *Shang shu*, 13, 4b–5a (Legge, III, 627–628).

of the feudal form of hierarchy.[24] The statement has a certain validity but seems to be a partial answer. If Chinese rationalizing and humanizing tendencies—hitherto reserved for the gods—accorded prime importance to man, focused attention on his actions, and recognized his extraordinary achievements in this world, how does one account for the lack of epic and tragedy in the tradition? What is the meaning of the Confucian insistence on the espousal of the world, with overriding emphasis on politics? These matters, together with the nature and function of Confucian heroism, are discussed in Chapter III.

The remaining cantos, the celebration of the statesmanship of Yi Sŏng-gye and Yi Pang-wŏn, explore the nature and function of kingship, the relation of power and justice, the role of mercy and remonstrance, the importance of learning and orthodoxy and culminate in the admonitory cantos that conclude the cycle. The rhetorical and dramatic devices are the same as those employed in the "arms" cantos—comparison and amplification—with constant allusion to historical events and persons. Each canto comprises, as in the "arms" section, parallel studies, the subjects of which are known examples from Chinese history, a universal history in the Confucian ecumene, much in the same manner as seventeenth-century English poetry turned to sacred history for metaphorical amplification. Some metaphorical vehicles were chosen in order to elevate their tenors or to drive home the implied contrast. In both instances, the purpose of parallels is chiefly to aggrandize the Korean tenor with historical sanction or even to demonstrate its superiority over the Chinese vehicle. To the first belong a comparison of Tan-fu to Yi Sŏng-gye's ancestors, or that of the founder of the Shang, Chou, or T'ang to Yi Sŏng-gye himself. An example of the second includes a sustained contrast between Liu Pang (Han Kao-tsu) and Yi Sŏng-gye, Liu Pang's disrespect of scholars, his habit of reviling his men, and his inconsistency and suspicion which triggered the rebellions of his erstwhile comrades in arms.

The compilers attempt to probe objectively a number of cardinal issues in statecraft, where neither the vehicle nor the tenor seems to furnish an ideal example. These are overt propaganda pieces. Liu Pang orders execution of his erstwhile saver of life (canto 105),

24. Levenson and Schurmann, p. 74.

invoking a Chinese version of the doctrine of the king's two bodies, his body natural and his body politic. For our peace of mind, however, the concept of the king's two bodies was never clearly formulated by the tradition, except in sporadic attempts by later historians to justify certain irreconcilable acts in the name of orthodoxy. Yi Pang-wŏn staged a series of murders and assassinations including the murder of the last loyal minister of Koryŏ, one of the architects of the new dynasty (canto 98), and his own half-brothers. But later Yi Pang-wŏn is made to confer a posthumous epithet on the first (canto 106), display magnanimity to his elder brother who attempted a coup (canto 103) as well as to supporters of his other rebelling brothers (canto 106), or even summon for praise a Koryŏ scholar in retirement for his unswerving loyalty to the vanquished state (canto 105). The crimes committed against the members of the ruling house of Koryŏ were many, but like all similar acts they are justified as an inevitable process of history, of the transference of legitimacy. The thirty-second and thirty-third Koryŏ kings were murdered and given a different surname; the last Koryŏ king was strangled; and finally all members of the Wang family were methodically sought out and cast into the raging waves. There was no Korean *Eikon Basilike* for the martyred: but a more powerful and lasting vengeance took the form of apocryphal stories, by which posterity avenged the innocent victims (see Chapter V).

As they scrutinize acts from multiple perspectives and investigate motives, the compilers not only illuminate the moral reverberations of every private and public act but recognize the difficulty, not to say impossibility, of attaining the Confucian ideal in a worldly kingdom. As they repeat the ritual required by tradition and claim divine sanction for their subjects, they nevertheless are able to register their dilemma concerning the traditional version of the change of mandate and the validity of official ideology which, in order to maintain the crown at all costs, imposes restraint on acts of dissent. Keenly aware of the gulf that separates the ideal from the actual, they obliquely reveal the difference between ideology and spirit. History illustrates how an attempt to realize Confucianism as a spirit, a way of life, was checked and finally defeated by upholders of official ideology, a propaganda to buttress monarchy and bureaucracy. It attests, I believe, to the compilers' moral dignity and honesty to have voiced this timeless truth, and to the dedicatee's to have comprehended it.

The vision of society that provides unity to the *Songs* is essentially moral; society is conceived as an intricate moral network, the *sine qua non* of human relations and the sphere of man's fulfillment. This moral vision of society determines the meaning of action, the dimensions of motives, choices, acts, and results that affect complex relations. Shakespearean criticism in recent decades has dealt with the poet's concept of political and social order in the history plays and tragedies and emphasized his concern with "mutuality," "relations," "human relatedness," as a "web of ties commutual."[25] Such vision of human reality is familiar to students of East Asian culture, for there the basis of social order and harmony is in the relationships between ruler and subject, father and son, husband and wife (Three Bonds), brother and brother, friend and friend. Called variously the "five universal ways" or "five universal paths in the world" (*The Mean*, 20), these relationships based on mutual moral obligations serve as the foundation of Confucian moral and political thought. And these relationships, among others, also probably account for the perennial appeal of Shakespeare's plays to East Asian sensibility, in spite of the difference of their referential world. In his recent discussion of *King Lear*, Maynard Mack has written: "Existence is tragic in *King Lear* because existence is inseparable from relation; we are born from and to it; it envelops us in our loves and lives as parents, children, sisters, brothers, husbands, wives, servants, masters, rulers, subjects—the web is seamless and unending. When we talk of virtue, patience, courage, joy, we talk of what supports it. When we talk of tyranny, lust, and treason, we talk of what destroys it."[26]

The traditional symbolism in political rhetoric—order–disorder, harmony–chaos—and materials drawn from folklore and myth which shaped the *Songs* will be discussed in Chapter V. The symbolism is based on the correspondence between man and Nature: dark clouds or thick mist that suddenly obscure the sun; unbridled sea or overflowing river that threatens the earth; or the uprooted tree or unweeded garden. Supernatural mechanisms, signs and portents, and aberrations of Nature, often fill the annals of the intemperate or tyrannous reign, especially the years attend-

25. Maynard Mack, *King Lear in Our Time* (Berkeley, 1965), p. 100.
26. Mack, p. 110.

ing the fall of a state, a miniature *Pharsalia* crowding out other accounts. The elements of folklore and archetype are, however, best employed for the creation of the hero, thus providing a version of the patterns of all heroes in literature. These common features shape the stories of his birth, growth, and maturity, and his exploits and trials are adorned with motifs in the folk tradition, magical or helpful animals, divine intervention, prophecy and dreams, and popular beliefs. In addition there is the topos of war; certain large formulas are used to describe especially righteous war, when Nature, the greatest witness and ally, takes a part. A tyrant is a murderer of Nature, and the emergence of a restorer of order is heralded by regeneration on all planes. Thus, when a dead tree puts forth green leaves immediately before the founding of the Yi dynasty, such a fable (or parable) has a long pedigree in the imagination of man.

The convention of identifying the king with the beneficent powers of Nature probably underlies the poems in the proem (canto 2). The poems invoke the tree and water, the static and the dynamic, as the emblems of the new dynasty. Both symbols are familiar enough, but what are their ancestors in the context? Does the tree, for example, invoke one that stood in the altar of soil, a presence that claimed the awe of ancient people? Is it a royal tree, like the sacred oak, or the great-rooted blossomer that inspired Yeats? What is the significance of the hieroglyphic of the river that winds safely to the sea? Is it a symbol of mutability or of undifferentiated Nature? Or is it one that "By his old Sire to his embraces runs,/ Hastening to pay his tribute to the Sea,/ Like mortal life to meet Eternity?"[27] Or an emblem of mortal life, of man's world of life, or of kingly power? These are the questions I will attempt to delineate in Chapter VI.

This essay is not primarily an historical investigation; it is more a critical reading, an attempt to analyze and illuminate the norms that constitute the *Songs*. I am aware that it is, like any analysis of literature, necessarily a partial reading, reflecting my intellectual and aesthetic predilections. I have devoted considerable space to the discussion of Confucian political and moral thought because the knowledge of cultural assumptions, which the poems reflect, is essential to their understanding and also because the problems that

27. Denham, *Coopers Hill*, ll. 162–164.

the poems raise are universal human problems, relevant to the preservation of any civilized society. Commenting on *Troilus and Criseyde*, Donald R. Howard said, "If *Troilus and Criseyde* is anything more than a chessboard of scriptural allegories designed to teach a moral lesson, then the psychological language of Christian morality is used in it . . . primarily . . . because it was the only psychological explanation which the Middle Ages had for demonstrating a moral act."[28] Equally, the full significance of the *Songs* cannot be appreciated without accounting for the Confucian view of the meaning of experience, its multifarious ramifications, and of man's nature and destiny.

28. *The Three Temptations* (Princeton, 1966), p. 122.

Chapter II. Compilation, Structure, and Form

"Do not exceed four attacks, five attacks, six attacks, seven attacks, then stop and adjust your ranks. Exert yourselves, officers! May you be martial. Be like tigers, like leopards, like black bears, like brown-and-white bears. In the suburbs of Shang, do not stop and [do not] crush those who flee, so that they can do service in the Western land. Exert yourselves, officers! In so far as you do not exert yourselves, on your persons there will be capital punishment."[1] Wielding the yellow battle-axe in the left hand and waving high the white oxtail flag with the right, King Wu marshaled his hosts and uttered this harangue one winter morning at the suburbs of the Shang capital. In his emphasis on heroic prowess and in his comparison of warriors to beasts of prey, we glimpse the fragments or, more correctly, the aftermaths, of the Chinese heroic age. But here, as elsewhere in Chinese literature, the emphasis is not so much on individual glory and honor as on the effect of one's acts on later generations, the profound, permanent change the event has brought to the Chinese people.

In the West, epic tradition was inspired by such occasions as migrations, conquests, disintegration of political systems, or even psychological changes attendant upon the introduction of a new

---

1. *Shang shu*, 6, 7b (Karlgren, *The Book of Documents* [Stockholm, 1960], p. 29; Legge, III, 304).

religion.[2] China does not lack such dramatic moments in her history. The incursions of the Huns, Turks, Khitans, Jürcheds, Mongols, and the Manchu, the unification of the country by Ch'in, the heroic expeditions to the north, west, and east, however, did not stir the bards to celebrate and versify these events. The situation was no better in Korea as far as oral literature was concerned. The Koreans' struggles against alien peoples, the wars of unification, the dynastic changes and cultural configurations failed to inspire the bards. On the other hand, heroic myths and legends, traditions of royal families, or stirring deeds of men were the credits given to culture heroes, sage kings, and dynastic founders.[3] Characteristically, they were romances, inflated versions of the adventures of a hero, or were incorporated into official histories which, like all partisan compilations, were notorious for ruthless distortion and suppression of episodes and details, facts and legends. What remains is nothing but partisan manifestoes, interspersed with bits of folklore and fable. It is therefore difficult to determine what truly happened to the oral heroic tradition, if any, of the East Asian peoples, especially the Chinese and Koreans.

In China, writing was introduced long before the onset of the Bronze Age. Whereas in Greece, Russia, and Yugoslavia oral heroic literature flourished during and after the introduction of letters, in China writing killed it or drove it underground, into narrow alleys and countrysides. The classics in their present form demonstrate that the Chinese did not conceive of their past as their heroic age. Although the declarations and narratives in the *Book of Documents* and the *Tso Commentary* may be said to reflect the narrative tradition of earlier times, the heroic age proper vanished behind semidivine culture heroes and hoary sage kings. What little heroic tradition there was in the Chou and subsequent dynasties was distorted beyond recognition. Myth and saga, which elsewhere are a reflection of life and actuality of a people's formative period, in China became instead paradigms of ruling

2. C. M. Bowra, "The Meaning of a Heroic Age," in *The Language and Background of Homer*, ed. G. S. Kirk (Cambridge, 1964), pp. 34–41 (also in *In General and Particular* [Cleveland and New York, 1964], pp. 73–80); Hector M. Chadwick, *The Heroic Age* (Cambridge, 1912); Jan de Vries, *Heroic Song and Heroic Legend* (London, 1963), pp. 180–193.
3. Henri Maspero, "Légendes mythologiques dans le Chou king," *JA*, CCIV (1924), 1–100; Jaroslav Průšek, "History and Epics in China and in the West," *Diogenes*, XLII (1963), 20–43.

families in a civilized society. Consequently, we have no record of the infancy and growth but only of the maturity of a people.

On the other hand, the compact, lapidary style of the classics is unassailable proof of the reflection of oral culture. Eric A. Havelock, in his *Preface to Plato*, convincingly showed that the formulaic technique of the Homeric epics was a poetic mechanism to compose the orally preserved word "as a compendium of matters to be memorized, of tradition to be maintained, of a *paideia* to be transmitted."[4] Plato conceived of Homer as "a sort of tribal encyclopedia," comprising examples of *nomos* and *ethos*, with typical examples of acts, attitudes, judgments, and procedures to be recalled and memorized.[5] Equally, the lapidary style in the Chinese classics—or the rhymed riddles, aphorisms, and proverbs in the *Tao-te ching*,[6] for example—were devices to rescue and preserve ancient cultural tradition. Realizing that oral memory is fallible and the human heart a most perishable vehicle for preserving tradition, the Chinese compilers resorted to the formulaic style to facilitate memory and to ensure transmission and preservation of tradition. In China the tradition was largely Confucian, emphasizing moral and political education, and the formulaic style was a fitting vehicle to express ideals and to ensure their survival and transmission. The Chinese fondness for reducing characters, situations, and episodes into archetypes, categories, and topics, must be explained in this light. As instruments for the preservation and perpetuation of tradition so vital to the survival of culture, the classics not only set the thought patterns of Confucian culture but described and prescribed "a community of forms and ideals."[7] Their overriding emphasis on politics bespeaks their intellectual and social nature and function. Describing the function of the Homeric epic, especially the first book of the *Iliad*, Havelock comments:

If the saga is functional, if its purpose is to conserve the group mores, then the men who act in it must be the kind of men whose actions would involve the public law and the family law of the group. They must therefore be "political" men in the most general sense of that

4. Eric A. Havelock, *Preface to Plato* (Cambridge, Mass., 1963), p. 49.
5. Havelock, p. 87.
6. Paul Demiéville, "Enigmes taoïstes," in *Silver Jubilee Volume of the Zinbun Kagaku Kenkyūsho* (Kyoto, 1954), pp. 54–60.
7. Werner Jaeger, *Paideia*, tr. Gilbert Highet, I (New York, 1939), xv.

term, men whose acts, passions, and thoughts will affect the behavior and the fate of the society in which they live so that the things they do will send out vibrations into the farthest confines of this society, and the whole apparatus becomes alive and performs motions which are paradigmatic. . . . In sum, the saga, in order to do its job for the community and offer an effective paradigm of social law and custom, must deal with those acts which are conspicuous and political.[8]

Perhaps no culture can boast a more brilliant gallery of types and typologies than the Chinese with its "good first" and "bad last," its sages and tyrants, virtuous heroes and villains, who are held up as paradigms of the moral and political norms in order to reinforce ideals so essential to cultural continuity. Indeed the classics and histories constitute a body of reference whose values provide the universal norms of behavior.

History, however, is the sister of epic. In China the lack of epics was made up by the abundance of historical writings. Working with a great collection of documents, the task of court historians was to impose a pattern on a welter of chroniclers' details and to discern a design in the past. With their perennial concern for the ordering and preservation of the state, the past was a prototype, an exemplar, a guide, and a mirror to the historians. History, conceived as a collection of examples, was not only an inspiration but a warning. In the accounts of the rise and fall of dynasties and great men, one must discern history's inexorable pattern, the principles which control the destinies of states and men. Their ideal of the nature and purpose of history was reinforced by historical examples, for lessons could best be taught by historical parallels. The use of analogy, the standard medium of presenting moral lessons, was based on the concept of universal parallelism, a correspondence in macrocosm and microcosm. This concept stressed the interdependence of Heaven, Earth, and Man, the order and degree in the natural, human, and political planes. The rupture of order in one plane is a reflection of rupture in another. Like the humanist historians of the Renaissance, who emphasized order and degree based on classical didacticism and medieval belief in providence, the historians of East Asia wrote and used history chiefly for moral and political reasons. The Confucian historical tradition—Confucian because this didactic form was perfected and perpetuated by Confucian literati—was the only vital

8. Havelock, pp. 167–168.

tradition upon which the compilers of our eulogy cycle could draw. There was no prototype for the *Songs* except the Chinese classics and histories, when in 1437, forty-five years after Yi Sŏng-gye founded the dynasty, the preparation for their compilation began.

The first step was to inspect the sacred places connected with the rise of royal ancestors and to collect and confirm the *facta* of the founder. We do not know whether there were unlettered bards who preserved and narrated certain episodes during the turbulent years before and after the founding of the dynasty. Nevertheless, attempts were made on a national scale. On August 30, 1437, the governor of Hamgil province, apparently at the court's order, presented names of the birthplaces and places of residence of the four dynastic ancestors, as if to prove archaeologically the historicity of dynastic myth.[9] The next day, he was further instructed to locate Chŏk Island where Yi Haeng-ni (Ikcho), Yi Sŏng-gye's great-grandfather, escaped the treachery of the Jürched chiefs.[10] On February 21, 1438, the *Veritable Record of the Grand Progenitor* was transferred to the palace from the Bureau of State Records to which it was returned on March 25.[11] On March 27, King Sejong wished to see the *Veritable Record of T'aejong* as well, but was stopped by his ministers.[12] Four years later, on April 11, 1442, the king ordered the governors of Kyŏngsang and Chŏlla provinces to gather from local elders facts and anecdotes concerning Yi Sŏng-gye's exploits during his campaign against the Japanese pirates at Unbong (1380).[13] The following day, the king ordered An Chi and Nam Su-mun to collect the tales of Yi's heroism which were not recorded in the official annals, and to confirm their authenticity by checking with surviving friends and veterans of Yi Sŏng-gye's campaigns.[14] On one occasion, a banished man was even recalled and consulted; Yi Suk-pŏn was brought to Seoul from his place of exile.[15] By this method, the compilers gathered both the deeds preserved in the annals and the popular traditions

9. *SnS*, 78, 17b.
10. *SnS*, 78, 18a.
11. *SnS*, 80, 17b, 24b.
12. *SnS*, 80, 25a–26a (stopped by Hwang Hŭi and Shin Kae).
13. *SnS*, 95, 26b.
14. *SnS*, 95, 27a.
15. *YK*, 2, 141–142; *CMP*, 127, 11b (Kim Ton was bribed to shelter him, but the king ordered his return). He was recalled October 13, 1438, arrived in the capital and questioned December 28 (*SnS*, 83, 21b–22b, 23a–b); on September 7, 1439, the Censorate requested his return (*SnS*, 86, 15a).

circulating among the people.

Finally, on May 11, 1445, Kwŏn Che, An Chi, and Chŏng In-ji presented the manuscript of the collection in ten chapters, consisting perhaps only of the Chinese verses.[16] That this copy was imcomplete is attested by the entry in the *Veritable Record of Sejong*, of December 3, 1445, in which the king expressed displeasure with the Chinese verses and suggested additions and improvements.[17] Furthermore, the entry of November 26, 1446, states that the king had the *Veritable Record of the Grand Progenitor* transferred to the *Ŏnmunch'ŏng*, the Institute of the Korean Language, in order to add more information to the sections dealing with his ancestors.[18] In all likelihood the work undertaken there was chiefly concerned with commentaries, mostly quotations from the veritable records and other sources to illustrate the events and episodes sung in the main texts. This is clear from the postscript of Ch'oe Hang: "In ten books we have, therefore, discussed the cause and effect of the contents in simple terms, added the pronuciation and meaning of difficult words to make them easily comprehensible."[19] The completed annotations, together with the Chinese and Korean verses, were presented to the throne in the second month of 1447.

When were the Korean verses in the *Songs* composed? A once popular view, now in decline, though originating in no less an authority than the Preface, dated May 11, 1445, by Chŏng In-ji, would ascribe the authorship of the Korean verses to Kwŏn Che, An Chi, and Chŏng himself.[20] It is difficult to assume this view because even the Chinese verses were incomplete by December 1445. Most important, we must not forget the fact that the Korean verses in the cycle could not have been composed without the new alphabet. The Korean verses, which are the first experimental use in verse of the new letters and which faithfully follow the rules set forth in the *Explanatory Notes and Examples of Usages* (dated ninth month of 1446)[21] could only be composed by those who knew the rules. A committee of eight scholars worked for the *Notes*; and the same committee, except for Chŏng In-ji, and two new mem-

16. *SnS*, 108, 5b-6a; Yi Sung-nyŏng, *AY*, I (1958), 61–67.

17. *SnS*, 110, 9a.

18. *SnS*, 114, 18b; *AY*, I (1958), 63–64; Kang Sin-hang, *Mullidae hakpo*, VI (1958), 147–151.

19. Postscript, 1b-2a, esp. 2b for the date.

20. Preface, 5a, esp. 4a-b.

21. *SnS*, 113, 36a-37b.

bers, compiled the *Tongguk chŏngun* (Correct rhymes of the Eastern Country; in the ninth month of 1448).[22] The standing members of this philological committee who participated in the compilation of the *Notes* as well as in four major research projects in Chinese rhyme books, were seven: Ch'oe Hang (1409–1474), Pak P'aeng-nyŏn (1417–1456), Shin Suk-chu (1417–1475), Sŏng Sam-mun (1418–1456), Yi Sŏl-lo (d. 1453), Yi Kae (1417–1456) and Kang Hŭi-an (1419–1464).[23] It was the foremost philologists of their day who brought the *Songs* to completion. The Korean verses were therefore composed by these seven between the ninth month of 1446 and the second month of 1447.

The beginning of the 1445 Preface eloquently sets out the purpose of the compilation:

Your Majesty's subject ventures to observe that the Way of Heaven and Earth is extensive and deep, high and brilliant; therefore Heaven that overshadows us and Earth that sustains us are infinite and lasting; many are the virtues of your royal ancestors, accumulated and deep, and their work of foundation is, therefore, infinite and lasting. Now the people merely see the expanse of mountains and seas, the growth of animals and plants, the change of winds, rain and thunder, the course of sun and moon, and the alternation of cold and heat. They do not see that all these are due to the Way of Heaven and Earth, extensive and deep, high and brilliant, that never ceases to operate. They see only the admirable beauty of royal ancestral halls and palaces, the wealth of prefectures and districts, and culture brought about by rites and music, by laws and government, and the abundance of benevolence, and the far-reaching effects of education. They do not see that all these are due to the firm foundation laid by the accumulated and deep virtues of your royal ancestors.[24]

As the harmonious alternation of Nature's process is the Way of Heaven and Earth, so the material welfare, political stability, and cultural excellence the age enjoys under the great King Sejong are the works of accumulated virtues of royal ancestors. The current peace is the reward of the royal labor and suffering that culminated in the founding of the new dynasty. Consider, the preface argues, the dynasty's remote origin, accumulated virtues of royal ancestors—their military might and cultural accomplishments—the

---

22. *SnS*, 117, 22a-23b (ninth month of 1447).
23. For these scholars see notes to the Postscript.
24. *YG*, 1, 1a-b.

willing allegiance of the people, and the auspicious omens. Their great work is not a fortuitous thing, but a divinely ordained process. Hence their work is coterminous with Heaven and Earth, and their glory is established firmly by high praise in song.

In order to relate the moral excellence of the rulers to the Way of Nature and to insist on the harmony of man and Nature as the realization of man's dynamic moral principles, the compilers turned to *The Mean* for vocabulary and metaphysical sanction. And *The Mean* is the right place, for it provides the essential virtues of Confucian politics and metaphysics upon which the value and greatness of the new dynasty depends.

The Way of Heaven and Earth may be completely described in one sentence: They are without any doubleness and so they produce things in an unfathomable way. The Way of Heaven and Earth is extensive, deep, high, brilliant, infinite, and lasting. The heaven now before us is only this bright, shining mass; but when viewed in its unlimited extent, the sun, moon, stars, and constellations are suspended in it and all things are covered by it. The earth before us is but a handful of soil; but in its breadth and depth, it sustains mountains like Hua and Yüeh without feeling their weight, contains the rivers and seas without letting them leak away, and sustains all things. The mountain before us is only a fistful of straw; but in all the vastness of its size, grass and trees grow upon it, birds and beasts dwell on it, and stores of precious things are discovered in it. The water before us is but a spoonful of liquid, but in all its unfathomable depth, the monsters, dragons, fishes, and turtles are produced in them, and wealth becomes abundant because of it. The *Book of Odes* says, "The Mandate of Heaven, how beautiful and unceasing." This is to say, this is what makes Heaven to be Heaven. Again, it says, "How shining is it, the purity of King Wen's virtue!" This is to say, this is what makes King Wen what he was. Purity likewise is unceasing.[25]

Thus, at the very outset of the book, we are reminded of the timelessness of the tradition that invests the story with antiquity and grandeur, conferring upon the event a universal significance.

The compilers are anxious to recount, in subsequent passages of the same preface and in the presentation letter and postscript, the

25. *The Mean*, 26 (Wing-tsit Chan, *A Source Book in Chinese Philosophy* [Princeton, 1963], pp. 109–110). Compare this and other passages in *The Mean* with the Elizabethan *Homilies*, esp. the tenth in the last series, "Sermon on Obedience" (1547). The emphasis of this homily is on the role of providence and the importance of obedience, as it was with all *Homilies*. Remove but the Christian frame, the two speak with equal force of the way of man, the nature of kingship, and the importance of order and degree.

distinguished pedigree of the House of Yi, the working of cause and effect, the continuity of the heritage of virtue, and the difficulties and circumstances of royal works. "The deep-rooted tree is luxuriant even to the end of its branches," declare the presentation letter and the proem (canto 2), "and the deep-sourced river flows longer in its courses." The compilers cite as their reference a number of poems in the *Book of Songs*,[26] chiefly for their ostensible symbolism, if not for their form. They all deal with the rise of Chou, their rise to power as the result of their founders' labor and virtue, which culminated in the exemplary reward: the mandate of Heaven. Hence the poems were read not only as panegyrics to the memory of great kings, but to provide necessary sanction. The introduction of Kings Wen and Wu is meant to equate the 1392 revolution with the chastisement of Shang by the Chou founders. By including the ideal rulers of the Confucian political and moral tradition and by holding them up as mirrors and parallels, the compilers attempt not only to justify the revolution but to inculcate in contemporaries and posterity what to follow and what to eschew.

We can easily understand the particular concern of the age. Less than a decade after the founding of the dynasty, the reigning house disputed succession by fratricidal feuds (1398, 1400).[27] The fear of dynastic rebellion and civil disorder that might plague the nation made the writers turn to history for lessons. True, as history illustrates, no nation is invulnerable to such ills, but it was the duty of the writers to point out that such dreadful examples are contrary to the wishes of the founder and should not recur. If the poems are to serve their function, they should not only celebrate national greatness but provide lessons, the postscript states: "When your heirs read these songs, they will inquire into the origin of current prosperity, strive to continue unfailingly the glorious line of our dynasty, and dare not change the norms of preserving the past. When your subjects read them, they will trace in them the cause of the current peace, will resolve to perpetuate it to posterity, and the irresistible sense of loyalty and admiration will never be ended."[28]

As a mirror for kingship and a treatise on the education of the prince, one might compare the *Songs* with a whole tradition of

26. *Book of Songs*, 154, 237, 241, 245, 270, 303.
27. See cantos 98, 99, 102, 103, 108, and 109.
28. Cf. Edwin B. Benjamin, "Fame, Poetry, and the Order of History in the Literature of the English Renaissance," *Studies in the Ranaissance*, VI (1959), 64–84.

Western political and moral tracts on the same subject, beginning
with Isocrates and Xenophon, down to medieval and Renaissance
writings, such as the series of tracts *De Regimine Principum*,[29] *De
Casibus Virorum Illustrium* (ca. 1358), *The Falls of Princes* (ca. 1430–
1438), *The Education of a Christian Prince* (1516), *the Governour* (1531),
Mirror for Magistrates (1559–1563), and other courtesy and emblem books.[30] In their emphasis on the fundamental principles of
education of the prince and his moral excellence as a sole source
for peace and order, the *Songs* share much that is common with
the "governance/mirror for princes" literature of antiquity and
the Middle Ages. They do not, however, deal exclusively, as do
the ascetic *De Casibus* and the schematic *Mirror*, with the tragedies
of illustrious men, their sins of ambition and pride and condign
punishments; nor are they, like the *Mirror*, which is a handbook of
the orthodox Tudor political doctrine, solely a mouthpiece of the
policies of the new dynasty. Perhaps not in terms of coverage of
time, for *De Casibus* begins with Adam and Eve—and we cannot
quarrel with their antiquity—but in their magnificence of scope
and intricacy of design, the *Songs* stand out as a unique literary
work. Expounding the nature and function of kingship in the light
of Confucian political and moral doctrine, the *Songs'* characters
are chosen not only as examples but for their historical importance, often revaluating, or casting new light on, a number of
cardinal issues vital to orthodox Confucian tradition. A convenient
division into cantos, eye-catching headings for the verses, citations
from the classics, ample glosses on difficult terms, and the use of
cross-references[31] give them character. Hardly a book one reads

29. Lester K. Born, "The Perfect Prince: A Study in 13th and 14th Century
Ideals," *Speculum*, III (1938), 470–504.

30. For Boccaccio see Louis B. Hall, *The Fates of Illustrious Men* (New York, 1965);
for *The Falls of Princes*, Walter F. Schirmer, *John Lydgate* (London, 1961); for Erasmus,
Lester K. Born, *The Education of a Christian Prince* (New York, 1936); for Elyot, Stanford E. Lehmberg, *Sir Thomas Elyot* (Austin, 1960); for the *Mirror*, Lily B. Campbell,
ed. *The Mirror for Magistrates* (Cambridge, 1938); for emblem books, Robert J. Clemens, "Pen and Sword in Renaissance Emblem Literature," *MLQ*, V (1944), 131–
141, and "Prince and Literature: A Theme of Renaissance Emblem Books," *MLQ*,
XVI (1955), 114–123.

31. The book relies heavily on the method of cross reference, "see above," which
is explained at the first occurrence in canto 4 (1, 7a): "If a cross reference refers to all
the incidents enumerated in the commentary, the first line of the Chinese verse is
quoted, followed by 'see above' as in canto 4; otherwise, only the appropriate event
referred to is quoted, followed by 'see above' " (as in canto 13 where it refers only to a
single event touched by the first of the four-line verse).

while waiting for the bus, the *Songs* are rather a handbook for the aspiring prince and his preceptors to meditate, an encyclopedia of statecraft and orthodoxy for inspiration. The book, therefore, ends with sixteen cantos of admonition, urging the reigning and successive kings to shun as far as they can the occupational diseases peculiar to monarchs.

In addition to these motives and purposes, perhaps the most urgent problem confronting the philologists in the Academy of Worthies was the practicability of the Korean alphabet they had just invented (1443–1444). Korea had no writing system of its own until that time. Instead, Chinese had been the written language of the lettered class. But the difference in rhythm, euphony, and syntax between the two languages made the Chinese graphs inadequate for the spoken language of Korea. A number of distinguished men of letters learned to write in Chinese using Chinese literary forms, but few mastered both the written and the spoken language. What they read were words, words from the classics and literature, but hardly the everyday colloquial speech of contemporary China. Buddhist pilgrims who went to China and India in search of the law painfully learned their linguistic shortcomings. Only a handful of writers, like Ch'oe Ch'i-wŏn (857–?) and Yi Che-hyŏn (1287–1367),[32] because of their prolonged sojourn in China, attained perfection at both levels. Even erudite Yi Saek, who served a long apprenticeship at the Mongol capital, was publicly ridiculed for his accent. When Yi Saek went to the Ming capital to request the audience of the Koryŏ heir apparent, the founder of Ming sarcastically remarked in his usual paranoiac manner, "You speak Chinese like Nayaču,"[33] hardly a compliment to one who had all his life pored over Confucian and neo-

32. For Ch'oe Ch'i-wŏn see n. 313 to my *Lives of Eminent Korean Monks* (Cambridge, Mass., 1969), p. 67. Yi Che-hyŏn passed the examination at the age of fifteen (1301). Summoned by King Ch'ungsŏn (Ijir-puqa) who opened the Hall of Myriad Volumes in Peking, Yi joined the king and befriended Yao Sui, Yen Fu, and Chao Meng-fu. King Ch'ungmok (Batura-Dorji, 1337–1345–1348) enfeoffed him as the Lord of Kyerim, and King Kongmin made him Chancellor (*Munha sijung*). Yi was one of the compilers of the *Samjo sillok*, which is no longer extant (*CMP*, 244, 5a). His collected works, the *Ikchae chip* (or *Ikchae nan'go*) was first printed in 1363, with a preface by Yi Saek; it was reprinted in 1432, 1601, 1693, and 1814 (*CMP*, 247, 4b). See *KRS*, 41, 16b and 110, 21a-42a, and *Ikchae sŏnsaeng yŏnbo*, 1a-7a, in the *Yŏgye myŏnghyŏn chip* (1959). For his activities at the Mongol capital see Kim Sang-gi, "Yi Ikchae ŭi chae-Wŏn saengae e .aehayŏ," *Taedong munhwa yŏn'gu*, I (1963), 219–244.

33. *TS*, 1, 25a; *YG*, 8, 29a.

Confucian texts. But the emperor was right. Unofficial histories and miscellaneous records are replete with episodes on the difficulty of communication between the two peoples.[34] Much of diplomatic misunderstanding, we presume, rose from political rhetoric and diplomatic expediency, but the inadequacy of interpreters and the ignorance of current Chinese usages contributed to the difficulty. The urgency of this state of affairs was one of the reasons that prompted King Sejong to initiate large-scale research into East Asian languages. When the alphabet was finally complete, the king, perfectionist that he was, wished to test its practicability in official and literary writings, to study the conduct of vowels and consonants, and to demonstrate finally the capabilities of vernacular poetry. The Korean verses in the *Songs* marked the first attempt of its application in poetry. It is no accident that the first and last encomia of the Yi dynasty, which set out to awaken the memory of the nation's great founders and to celebrate its past and present, were written in the new alphabet.

Finally, in order to perpetuate the new ideals and visions of the dynasty as a moral and educational institution, the poems were set to music to be used at court, in the ancestral temple, and for official occasions.[35] King Sejong, in so many ways a true humanist, was not only a scholar and philologist, but an accomplished musician versed in the pitches and harmony of ancient music. Deeply concerned over the current state of music, especially the lack of musicians and musical instruments, he ordered the regulation of all aspects of court music, especially the manufacturing of such instruments as bells and chimes (1423–1431) and the composition of verses for the pieces performed on various national and international occasions (1435–1444).[36] Upon completion of the *Songs*, the king had the first four and the last cantos set to music.

The proclamation of great deeds of royal ancestors must echo to the skies with the splendor and majesty of verse and song. The paradigm for posterity demands music in order to produce a patterned sense of order and harmony. Music which embodies harmony and rhythm at once reflects the cosmic and political harmony, as manifested in "the glorious and peaceful reign that the

34. E.g., *P'aegwan chapki* (CKK, 1909), chaps. 1 and 2.
35. *SnS*, 109, 31b.
36. Ch'oe Chŏng-yŏ, "Sejong taewang ŭi munhwa saŏpchung ak chŏngni ko," *Ch'ŏngju taehakkyo nonmunjip*, II (1958), 1–54; III (1960), 9–73.

age was enjoying." Glory should not only be preserved, but per-petuated and increased. These poems, like the "hymns" in the *Book of Songs*, register "the feelings of commemoration and admira-tion and thereby demonstrate the way future generations should take" (postscript).[37] Music therefore enhances the intellectual and moral appeal of the poems, facilitating both the transmission and contemplation of the examples of great deeds. It is for these reasons that the sage kings of olden times "made poetry a part of education, set it up in rhymes, and used it throughout the country in order to enlighten the world" (postscript).[38] Former kings used music to "adorn the transforming influence of instruction, and transformed manners and customs."[39] The "hymns" in the *Book of Songs*, particularly, "praise the embodied forms of complete virtue, and announce to gods its grand achievements."[40] King Sejong wished to stress the paedeutic effect of poetry and music so that their beauty would stir listeners to contemplate the ethical and symbolic content. On each performance, the ritual would provide an occasion to re-enact, however briefly, the state myth: the best way to perpetuate the memory of royal ancestors. Thus with the compositions of the poems to be the most important repertory of court music, King Sejong laid the last cornerstone—the others being the alphabet, the king's greatest gift to the Korean people, and the *Songs*, the first and last encomia of the monarchy—of a Yi dynasty culture that was to last five hundred years.

The first canto, which together with the second forms the proem, clearly sets the theme, mood, and purpose of the book: praise of the four ancestors and the first and third kings of the dynasty. The six dragons flying high in the land of the Eastern Sea are Mokcho (died 1274), Ikcho, Tojo (died 1342), Hwanjo (1315-1361), Yi Sŏng-gye (1335-1408), and Yi Pang-wŏn (1367-1422). The cen-tral part of the book covers cantos 3 to 124, subdivided into two sections: the first, cantos 3-109, praises the cultural and military accomplishments of the six dragons; the second, cantos 110-124, consists of admonitions to future monarchs. Canto 125 is a conclu-sion. Each canto, except for cantos 1, 2, and 125, consists of two

37. Postscript, 1a.
38. Postscript, 2a.
39. Great Preface, 5 (Legge, IV, 34).
40. Great Preface, 14 (Legge, IV, 36).

poems, the first relating generally the great deeds of Chinese sovereigns and the second those of the Yi kings. Both poems in cantos 110–124 deal with the Yi kings. In cantos 86–89, which are exceptions to the general scheme, both poems in each canto celebrate the deeds of the founder, except for the first verse in canto 83. Also, cantos 108 and 109, the only cantos assigned to women, praise the heroic deeds of the wife of King Wen, Queen Sinhye of Wang Kŏn, founder of Koryŏ, and Queen Wŏn'gyŏng (1365–1420) of Yi Pang-wŏn. The compilers assigned five cantos to Mokcho, nine to Ikcho, four to Tojo, six to Hwanjo, eighty-one to Yi Sŏng-gye, and twenty-three to Yi Pang-wŏn.

The stanzaic scheme characteristic of the Korean verse may be seen in the first verse in canto 2. Each quatrain in cantos 2–124 follows the same scheme, the total number of syllables varying from eighteen to thirty, but commonly twenty-four to twenty-eight. Canto 1 is a single tercet; canto 125, a single ten-line stanza. The Chinese verses, on the other hand, demonstrate more variety in form. While canto 1 has three irregular lines, canto 125 has ten such lines. Cantos 2–109 use consistently four four-word verses, and cantos 110–124 introduce another form, that of three five-word verses. No wonder this first literary work of the Yi dynasty, the creation of the best minds of the enlightened era, shows an unerringly controlled and perfected form.

The number of cantos of each book varies according to the volume of commentary that follows each canto. Book 2, for example, comprises only three cantos (10–12), for canto 11 is followed by fourteen sheets of narrative (2, 2a-15b), and canto 12 by thirty sheets (2, 16a-46a). Book 10, on the other hand, has twenty-eight cantos (98–125), for most of its contents have by then appeared in the previous books. At some points one can see the compilers' deliberate attempt to inflate the details, often irrelevantly. Canto 11, for example, which deals with the restoration of the House of Wang, is followed by King Kongyang's edict (2, 4a-15b), apparently to bolster Yi Sŏng-gye's role in setting him up as the last ruler of Koryŏ. Canto 13, which is thematically concerned with dream allegory, is followed by three memorials submitted by Yi Sŏng-gye to request leave (3, 1b-12a) and three replies by King Kongyang urging him to stay on. Three battle rounds of words, replete with traditional rhetorical *topoi*, are used undoubtedly to underscore Yi Sŏng-gye's virtue of modesty, if not his cunning and hypocrisy. The compilers' attempt to build a verbal monument to Yi Sŏng-gye fails to convince the modern reader, for the virtue of modesty cannot be conveyed by such a barrage of words. The scene, however, has a profound purport. The king's words show him as a pitiable figure, because he denies himself his royal prerogatives, the "magical" nature of his office. The scene therefore portrays the figure of a king who unkings himself, who performs the ritual of deposition, as he surrenders kingly responsibilities to the future usurper, Yi Sŏng-gye. Cunningly contrived to underscore the gulf between substance and appearance and the meaninglessness of ceremony, the king's rhetoric is fit material for future "mirror" literature, as a weak ruler rehearses the impending loss of the trust.

Another lapse is the tendency to lump details at the first mention of a person or theme. Canto 22 refers the reader for information to canto 18: canto 22 praises Liu Pang's slaying of the serpent, the White God in metamorphosis, while canto 18 recounts how he returned alone after losing his men on his way to Mount Li, but that Heaven moved the hearts of ten men to follow him. The commentary relevant to canto 22 occurs in canto 18, apparently because the subject of the two verses is the same. In canto 38, which deals with Yi Sŏng-gye's campaign against his cousins, the reader is erroneously referred to canto 35, which concerns his battle against the Mongol chief Naɣačʉ. Two years divide the incidents, and this can hardly be said to be a good cross-reference. The third example occurs in cantos 53 and 55. Canto 53 praises how the Liu-ch'iu and Siam sent tributes to pledge allegiance to the general, and canto 55, how the Jürched chiefs served him loyally. True, in terms of the theme of his far-reaching influence, other cantos such as 55, 56, and 75 might be grouped together. But canto 53 (7, 20a-26b) is hardly the right place for the narrative for canto 55 (7, 29a).

The technique of repetition and cross-reference is used not only in the commentary but in the verse proper. The first instance of a thematic repetition and interrelation in verse occurs in canto 5, which repeats canto 4, suggesting a link between the two for an obvious reason: to emphasize the difficulty of royal works. A more sophisticated device in the same system is not immediate repetition, as in canto 5, but reiteration from a different angle of the theme in antecedent cantos. This echoing device occurs in cantos 19 and 20, which repeat the theme of canto 4, for the purpose of amplification and illumination. The integrating device points to the continuity and interrelation of the flying parts of the book to shed more light on the implication and function of certain themes and motifs.

In fact, several cantos form a group by virtue of repetitive associations in order to summarize or amplify certain aspects of persons or episodes in antecedent groups of cantos. Mokcho is dealt with in canto 3 but figures again in cantos 17 and 18; Ikcho's deeds are the theme of cantos 4 to 6 as well as 19 and 20. Cantos 9 to 11 are connected by theme to cantos 67 to 69, all six dealing with the general's return from Wihwa Island, a persuasive means of associative characterization. Cantos 33–42 form one major section dealing with the general's campaign against the Red Turbans, Naɣaču, the Ki family, and the Northern Yüan. So do the themes in cantos 47–52, and 58–62, another major section about the subjugation of the Japanese pirates. The general's warlike prowess is the theme of cantos 27–32, 43–46, and culminates in a third group, cantos 86–89. One may find other examples of balance and reinforcement in other parts of the cycle.

The device of balancing or reinforcing one group of cantos by another is reminiscent of the epic technique in the West—ring-composition and *hysteron proteron*, "a vast system of *hysteron proteron* of scenes, in which episodes, and even whole books, balance each other through similarity or opposition."[41] Although the emphasis on structural symmetry in the Homeric songs has recently been challenged by G. S. Kirk,[42] it is an important technique of the *Songs* and adds much to their unity and coherence. This technique, like other devices to be discussed later, is necessitated by the subject matter and purpose of the book and is dictated by the intellectual and cultural need of the time.

The use of formulaic phrases and epithets is a time-honored practice of the Confucian classics and subsequent literature. As

41. Cedric H. Whitman, *Homer and the Heroic Tradition* (Cambridge, Mass., 1958), p. 235.

42. G. S. Kirk, *The Songs of Homer* (Cambridge, 1960), pp. 261 f.

narrative oral poets worked with formulas[43] and established themes, so our compilers skillfully used these devices at all levels. Ranging from exact quotations to variations inspired by analogy, formula phrases, characterized by a high degree of frequency, complexity, and economy, they attest a continuous pedigree ascending to remote antiquity. Unlike the formula technique of oral composition in the Homeric songs, traditional phraseology in East Asia was not composed in the mind and preserved in the memory, but transmitted by writing. Associated with kingship and surrounded by cumulative allusions to the Confucian ethical and political tradition, this formal diction helped · create the dignified and majestic tone. Two graphs, "reckless and oppressive," chosen to describe the tyranny of Shin U (canto 10), for example, are drawn from the *Book of Documents* in a speech by King Wu to his hosts before the sack of the Shang capital. As Chou. the last Shang king, was "reckless and oppressive"—reason enough for his chastisement—so Shin U was pushed aside for that very reason by Yi Sŏng-gye. The phrase at once refers the reader to the classical *locus* and summarizes classical incident, rendering dignity and majesty to Yi Sŏng-gye's deed. This is what Kirk calls "abbreviated reference style," where "brevity was dictated by the poet's desire to summarize too much in too short a phrase."[44]

The formulaic language consists of two to four graphs, placed where they sound important, often occupying the whole or part of a line, producing a slow and solemn effect like a succession of spondees. Chosen always for orotundity, they stand out amidst the Korean letters, at least visually, calling for an educated response. This kind of dramatic shift in tone effected by the linguistic elements can perhaps be illustrated by the use of Latinate elements in

43. Albert B. Lord, *The Singer of Tales* (Cambridge, Mass., 1960), pp. 4, 30 ff. Parry defines the formula as "a group of words which is regularly employed under the same metrical conditions to express a given essential idea," in *Harvard Studies in Classical Philology*, XLI (1930), 80. See Denys L. Paige, *History and the Homeric Iliad* (Berkeley, 1959), pp. 229 and *passim*; Bowra, *Heroic Poetry* (London, 1952), pp. 222–253; and J. B. Hainsworth, *The Flexibility of the Homeric Formula* (Oxford, 1968), pp. 33–45. For a revaluation and extension of the concept of formula in Japanese and Western poetry see Earl Miner, "Formula: Japanese and Western Evidence Compared," in *Proceedings of the Vth Congress of the International Comparative Literature Association* (Amsterdam, 1969), pp. 405–417.

44. Kirk, p. 164.

English poetry.[45] Left alone while Lady Macbeth went out to return the blood-stained daggers to Duncan's chamber, Macbeth feels the enormity of his crime. There is enough blood in his hands. He fears his hand would make red the vast limitless seas.

> No, this my hand will rather
> The multitudinous seas incarnadine,
> Making the green one red.
> (*Macbeth*, II, ii, 61–63)

Consider the role of two Latin words surrounded by thirteen Anglo-Saxon words. Or Wordsworth's simple lyric, "A slumber did my spirit seal," the fifth Lucy poem. "Diurnal" in the third line of the second stanza has precisely the same effect:

> No motion has she now, no force;
> She neither hears nor sees,
> Rolled round in earth's diurnal course,
> With rocks, and stones, and trees.

True, in the *Songs*, these allusion-packed formulas from the classics were used for poetic economy and convenience. But at the same time they are a tribute to the powerful ideals of the Korean renaissance which under King Sejong inaugurated resurgence and revaluation of classical learning. Used for the effects of great condensation, the formulas compel us to recall the original context in which they occur and to add a new dimension and new light to them.

The formulas are best employed in the summary of characters. The single epithet, "paltry fellow" or "mere fellow" sums up the last Shang king. A more complex one is "the king of the virtue of fire" (canto 22), which refers to Liu Pang, the founder of the Han, because he, the son of the Red God (fire), slew the White God metamorphosed into a serpent (metal), thus portending the victory of the element of fire over that of metal. "A peerless general" is enough to designate Li K'o-yung of the Later T'ang at a given moment of action (canto 23). Yi Sŏng-gye has more than one such character epithet to reinforce the reader's moral response, such as "one whose genius astounded the world" (canto 27), "a lord of myriad leagues" (canto 31), "natural genius" (canto 43), "a man of august power" (canto 62) or "big-eared minister" (canto 29),

---

45. John C. Ransom, "On Shakespeare's Language," *SR*, LV (1947), 181–198. For Milton's style see Christopher Ricks, *Milton's Grand Style* (London, 1963).

the last one in the tradition of the physiognomy prevalent in folk-lore.

The affective overtones generated by stock phrases describing moral and occasionally physical characteristics facilitate the comprehension of convention on a higher level. These metonymical terms are introduced not for metrical convenience, but for affective significance in order to project and heighten the implicit meaning of the story.[46] A tyrant is always a "mere fellow" to emphasize his moral and cosmic isolation; for the Confucian tradition has accepted the last Shang king as archetype, and anyone who disrupts the moral and social order deserves such epithet. Coriolanus[47] and Richard III, for example, are "alone," for their attempts to assert their will or impose their policy inevitably result in their isolation from the community of men. Equally, the restorer of order, be he a virtuous ruler or a dynastic founder, is said to be possessor of all the virtues in the same tradition. These affective associations, common to all heroes, are stable and are seldom complicated by additional epithets. Hence Shin U poisoned the people with murderous tyranny, like Richard Crookback who is compared to the venomous toad, rooting hog, foul devil, or bottle spider. Enemies are always "ferocious" (canto 35), "insular barbarians" or "island savages" (canto 47), or "thieves" (canto 61). Thus the compilers give their subjects emotional and moral color, and so the complexity of the character or situation is already interpreted in the light of the desired tone. There is no intentional fallacy in pointing out that the poets wished to present the typical, not the particular, for this is in accord with the epic technique so familiar to East and West alike.

Other devices of emphasis are special endings. In contrast to such normal narrative or declarative endings as *-ida*, the ending *-ni* (and *-myŏ* which occurs only once in canto 87) does not indicate an end of the line or stanza: instead, it suggests an urge to go on, in order to move the reader forward and to advance the theme. This rhetorical principle creates an atmosphere of suspense and anticipation, compelling the reader to read the next canto and ultimately reach the intended end. I would guess it is to forewarn the reader at the very beginning of the book, as it first appears in

46. Wayne Shumaker, *Unpremeditated Verse* (Princeton, 1967), pp. 91–103.
47. Harry Levin's introduction to the Pelican Shakespeare (Baltimore, 1956), p. 24.

canto 1, that each canto is not an isolated unit and that the significance of the book as a whole is only attainable after it has been completely read.

A version of the rhetorical question, the ending -*ri* (literally, "probably would"), for example, occurs in canto 16, marking the intrusion of authorial conjecture on a given situation. It entices the reader to accept the argument or implied answer, which is often the only answer possible in the context. The second verse of the same canto, which lists two foolish deeds committed by superstitious rulers of Koryŏ, offers an instance of the technique of retrospection: one of them built the second capital and the other chose as mayor of Hanyang a man with the surname Yi. These are the acts of muddle-headed kings who listened to the fallacious preachings of geomancers. Despite these alleged efforts to stop the rise of a man with the surname Yi, who was prophesied to over-throw the reigning dynasty, General Yi Sŏng-gye became the ruler of Korea. Hence "Is all their fuss not ludicrous?"

The proper rhetorical question is usually introduced by such endings as -*ikka*, -*ikko*, or simply -*ka* as in cantos 72 and 88. After narrating in canto 51 how Yi Sŏng-gye marshaled his hosts unlike others and thus annihilated the Japanese pirates at Unbong in 1380, the poets ask:

> Had they retreated,
> Would they have survived after all?

The second verse of canto 72 is an instance of the -*ikko* type. Heaven abandoned a "mere fellow" Shin U, and even the Chinese praised the general's great deed.

> Heaven abandoned a mere fellow.
> Even the Han people praised his merits.
> How much more so did
> Our people?

In the Confucian ecumene, to be known in China and celebrated there is the greatest fame. In Latin literature, to be known in India is synonymous with being known in the whole world, "the India topos" of Curtius,[48] might be called "the Chinese topos" for our purpose, as it figures often in this and other literary works.

---

48. Ernst Robert Curtius *European Literature and the Latin Middle Ages*, tr. Willard R. Trask (London, 1953), pp. 160–162.

Again, in the second verse of canto 87, after enumerating the general's heroic prowess, the compilers ask:

> How could we relate all
> The divine power of this inspired man?

This is the panegyric topos of inexpressibility,[49] explained by Curtius with rich illustrations from Latin literature, namely, that the compilers tell only a small part of the general's *facta*, and that they could not possibly recount, much less exhaust, all his deeds. Even a simple declarative ending *-ida* is charged with hortatory overtones. For example, in canto 50 the first verse sings of Li Lung-chi's (T'ang Hsüan-tsung) chastisement of the wicked empress Wei and her family, and the second of General Yi's campaign against the Japanese pirates. In the first, Heaven, in approval of the righteous ruler, hurled stars like snowflakes in a storm; in the second, a white rainbow cut across the sun. These forebodings, based on traditional omens, underline the symbolic importance of what is to come but are conveyed by a deceptive, unobtrusive sentence ending. There is more to it than meets the eye: the elements of Nature will side with the virtuous and there is no escape from the mysterious designs of Heaven.

A more striking structural device is parallelism. The objectives of the compilation were to celebrate great deeds and to provide exempla to be taught the prince. The subject demanded the analogical mode of presentation to convey the lessons by illustrations, a repertory of exempla. The primary method therefore is the use of parallelism, a selection of significant characters and incidents in Chinese and Korean history for comparison and contrast. In addition to the general stanzaic and syntactical parallelism in canto 3, there is a correspondence in the reciprocal relations between the two verses, in the subject, place names, and object: "the great ruler of Chou" (Tan-fu) matches "our founder" (Yi Sŏng-gye); "valley of Pin," "city of Kyŏnghŭng;" and "imperial works," "royal works." In addition, the identical structure is reinforced by the repetition of identical verbs, "lived" and "began," in the second and fourth lines of the two verses. The implicit parallel is of course that between Tan-fu and Yi Sŏng-gye, placed as they are in the beginning of the verses, emphasizing the correspondence: the works begun by Yi Sŏng-gye are as difficult

49. Curtius, pp. 159–160.

and glorious as those begun by Tan-fu. On the other hand, each stanza in canto 4 is interwoven with the repetition of the same subject at the beginning of the first and second lines, in the first, "Ti barbarians," and in the second, "barbarians" (here the Jürcheds are meant), thus constituting an instance of synonymous parallelism.[50]

Cantos 86–89, the climax in the enumeration of the general's martial prowess, are parallel not only in construction but in the repetition of the key phrases in the fourth line of the second verse of each canto. The phrase begins with *sŏngin* (literally, "sage"), but the first component of the formula that follows begins with *shin* ("divine" or "august") the second differing as *yŏk* (canto 87), *mu* (canto 88), and *kong* (canto 89). In order to avoid monotony in English, I have rendered them as "divine power," "peerless gallantry," and "eminent deeds" respectively; although this hardly does justice to the construction in the original, where a sudden emphasis is placed on the newly introduced graph to differentiate the three forms of the formula. Contextually, the effect of partial repetition of the significant phrases with subtle variation not only reinforces the parallel structure but generates a disciplined sense of unity and harmony. We know of similar kinds of repetition and parallelism in English poetry, for example in the ballads in Percy's *Reliques*, Shakespeare's *Venus and Adonis* and *Lucrece*, and, perhaps to excess, in Poe and Swinburne.

The first line of the first and second verses in canto 20 is a rhetorical question, "Could . . . be yielded to others?" In the second line, except for the same verb ("is not") and the synonymous pronouns *nyŏnŭ* ("others") and *nam* ("others"), the paired antonyms are "Three Han" and "Four Seas." In the third line the contrast is between *karam* ("river") and *paral* ("sea"), thus creating the grammatical rhythm, and in the fourth line between the verbs "melt" and "fill" (literally, "make it deep"). Thus the corresponding elements in the two verses are arranged to highlight the recurrence of parallelism both in rhythm and thought. In canto 26, the semantic parallel is subtly introduced in the third line by a contrast between "here and there" and "going and

50. James A. Notopoulos, "Continuity and Interconnexion in Homeric Oral Composition," *Transactions and Proceedings of the American Philological Association,* LXXXII (1951), 81–101; Nicholas Poppe, "Der Parallelismus in der epischen Dichtung der Mongolen," *Ural-Altaische Jahrbücher,* XXX (1958), 195–228.

coming," "here" against "going" and "there" against "coming." Literally, the lines read, "whether he stayed here or went there" and "whether he went there or came (stayed) here." By avoiding the usual practice of paired antonyms, this variation contributes to the austere style of the poems.

Contrast in the parallel structure also occurs in canto 66, which is designed to augment and illuminate the exemplary character of Yi Sŏng-gye. The first two lines of the verses praise the way Liu Pang and Yi Sŏng-gye won the willing allegiance of princes (Liu Pang), and people (Yi Sŏng-gye). But there is a difference. Liu Pang was notoriously disrespectful to his princes (he was "good at reviling"), while Yi Sŏng-gye stabilized the feelings of people by his munificence and affability. Hence, "despised" and "reviled" are set against "polite" and "kind." The repetition of "princes" and "people" in the second and fourth lines in each verse underscores the emphasis.

The foregoing analysis points to some of the techniques peculiar to the *Songs*: the studied development of verbal endings, the dignified and unadorned vocabulary, the audacity of the syntax, the rapidity of thought, and a symmetry engendered by parallelism. The language is simple and solemn, stripped of rhetorical embellishment or verbalism, as if to match or to equate it with kingly virtue and integrity. A normative recurrence of formulas and themes is intended to evoke a strong sense of stability and permanence in a world otherwise transient and changeable. Compressed to the point of aphorism, the language is mnemonic, and that is probably as the compilers intended it. The devices of emphasis and variation are consistent with the underlying mode of thinking and world view, which saw parallels everywhere, in nature as well as in history, thus creating a cumulative effect. The principles underlying the devices, therefore, are formality, structure, and function. Within a formal unit of the quatrain is a symmetrically balanced set of identities or opposites that determines the movement of thought and the rhythm of poetry. Each episode, boldly and briefly recounted, illuminates and drives home the cosmic, moral, and political norm so dear to classical tradition. All these devices are in accord with the nature and function of poetry, and it is their skillful employment that enabled the compilers to control the vast range of materials.

Chapter III. The Confucian Soldier

The story of the *Songs*, simply told, is the story of the rise of a family, whose ancestors suffered some great humiliation, had to abandon their alleged ancestral home in the south and move to the less civilized north, were they bode their time like "hibernating dragons," until one of the sons triumphantly returned as dynastic founder. It shares a number of motifs and themes with Western epics like the *Odyssey* and the *Aeneid*: with the *Odyssey* it shares the trials of a hero, and with the *Aeneid*, the formation and victory of a hero as he becomes the Augustan ideal, the builder of Rome. Throughout the cycle, great emphasis is placed upon the labor and suffering of the royal ancestors (cantos 4, 17–20, 24), and especially Yi Sŏng-gye himself. On him a heavy burden is laid, to chastise evil, vindicate the moral order, and bring about permanent change in a nation and people.

What strikes the reader throughout, however, is the emphasis on valor and prowess as essential parts of the founder's *facta*, almost an identification of the soldier with the statesman. The result is the creation of a universal genius who is proficient in both arms and letters, a synthesis of prowess and virtue, courage and wisdom. This emphasis probably reflects the compilers' attempt to elevate their subject in all possible ways, following the Confucian ethical and historiographical convention, if not the temper of the time, which demanded in a hero both martial and intellectual virtues, which was also one of their patron's most deeply felt convictions. The tendency is visible in dynastic histories of China and Korea, especially in the accounts of dynastic founders or restorers of dwindling imperial power, whose posthumous epithets often carry the graph *wu* (warrior, martial) as if to highlight the heroic deeds necessary for a successful revolution or restoration of imperial power.

Undoubtedly Yi Sŏng-gye was such a man, whose posthumous epithets contain the formula *shen-wu*,[1] a symbol of royal greatness, a pattern of soldierly valor, of a model hero. Perhaps no one deserves such resplendent majesty more than Yi Sŏng-gye, who was looked upon as the embodiment of a long native military tradition. The name of Chumong, the founder of Koguryŏ, which rose from a wide plain on the middle reaches of the Sungari, that cradle of Northeast Asian peoples, was interpreted to mean "excellent archer" by the Chinese.[2] Koguryŏ murals illustrate the virile and valorous character of Koguryŏ riders and archers who were widely feared by her neighboring peoples. Puyŏ, which had customs and manners similar to those of Koguryŏ, produced good horses and good horsemen.[3] Another northern tribe, Ŭmnu (Sukchin) was said to have excelled in archery;[4] Okchŏ and Ye, in foot soldiery.[5] Even Paekche, one of the southern kingdoms, is said to have excelled in equestrian archery.[6] The Mongols and Jürched of the fourteenth century with whom Yi Sŏng-gye's ancestors had close contacts, were equally proficient in this military art. Yi Sŏng-gye, therefore, was born and raised in these surroundings, and had ample time to study and master the art of the horse and bow.

The bow is Yi Sŏng-gye's characteristic weapon and a number of cantos celebrate his marksmanship. While sitting by the river on a summer afternoon, he detected a sable breaking cover from a nearby bush. He shot it and others that followed, a total of twenty, with twenty arrows (canto 32). On a hunting trip in 1372, he shot two fleeing roebucks with a single arrow (canto 43), an example of

1. *TnS*, 16, 7a.
2. *Wei shu*, 100, 2123a (*SGYS*, 1, 41, and n. 192 to the *Lives of Eminent Korean Monks*).
3. *HHS*, 115, 0896b; for the horse see *Wei chih*, 30, 1004b.
4. *HHS*, 115, 0896b-c.
5. For Okchŏ see *HHS*, 115, 0896d; for Ye, *HHS*, 115, 0897a.
6. *Sui shu*, 81, 2532b4; *PS*, 94, 3033c.

improved skill. Li Lung-chi, when he shot two wild boars at the Hsüan-wu Gate, had Wei Wu-t'ien paint the scene; but in the case of Yi Sŏng-gye, his fame and name being universally known, there is no need to depict such prowess to show the people. Hence the compilers ask:

> Must we paint
> This natural genius?

A more striking feat occurs in canto 86, where he is said to have shot six roebucks and five crows perched on a wall, with a single arrow. Canto 88 praises him for hitting always the back of the deer, apparently a feat that deserves special mention. Another time, he did not use arrowheads but simply wished to manifest his marksmanship by toppling, without hurting them, three mice from the eaves of his home (1387). This marksmanship was a means to win new followers, as was the case with Han Ch'ung and Kim In-ch'an (canto 57). Both witnessed the general's divine skill when he shot two larks perched on a mulberry tree. Awed by it, they abandoned farming, followed the great man, and later rendered conspicuous service in the founding of the dynasty.

Like Achilles' ashen spear, a wedding gift of the centaur Chiron to the hero's father, which no other mortal could wield, or Odysseus' huge bow, or Beowulf's victory-blessed blade (*sigeeadig bil*), Yi Sŏng-gye's bow was characterized by its unusual size, a fitting symbol of sheer strength and physical prowess. He cut his own arrows made of the *hu* tree, instead of the usual bamboo, which, like whistling-head arrows, made a whirring noise as they flew through the air. Upon seeing the size of the bow and arrow, his own father remarked that they were not only impractical but, in fact, incapable of being used by man. But Yi Sŏng-gye startled his father by skillfully manipulating the superhuman weapon and killed seven roebucks (canto 27). Canto 87, again highlighting prowess, introduces two episodes: one, when he with bare hands struck down a raging tiger that had jumped his horse, and another when he unlocked the horns of two fighting bulls (1389).

Like that of so many heroes, the general's animal in peace and war was the horse. "No animal invites," Bowra comments, "so technical or so discriminating a knowledge or excites stronger affection and admiration" than the horse.[7] It is the hero's trusted

7. Bowra, *Heroic Poetry*, pp. 157–170, esp. 157.

friend, to whom he usually appeals for generous help and utmost effort. The immortal steeds of Achilles mourned the impending doom of their master, and were pitied by Zeus for serving the mortal man (*Iliad*, XVII, 424–450). Liu Pei, when trapped by his adversary, attempted to flee on horseback. At that time the animal Ti-lu (White Forehead) fell in the water of T'an Creek and struggled. Addressed by the master to exert itself, the horse jumped up thirty feet and out of the water (canto 37). Like King Mu's eight bayards or Li Shih-min's six bayards that came at appropriate time to render service,[8] Yi Sŏng-gye had eight stalwart steeds, all of which performed miracles of one sort or another (canto 70):

> Heaven gave him courage and wisdom
> Who was to bring order to the country.
> Hence eight steeds
> Appeared at the proper time.

In peace time, hunting trips provided him with occasions to practice and perfect his horsemanship. Once, while chasing a boar, he suddenly found himself before a precipice. He quickly jumped off the horse, and both horse and boar plunged over the precipice (canto 31). In 1385, when two roebucks broke cover near an abyss, he shot one, stopping the horse just a few steps before the precipice (canto 31). A similar feat occurs in the first verse of canto 86. When a deer tried to escape below a slanting tree, he jumped over the tree, while his horse ran under it; he landed in the saddle on the other side of the tree and then shot down the fleeing animal. That he was thoroughly familiar with the manipulation of the horse in times of crisis is the theme of the second verse of canto 87. When his horse slipped on the bridge over a gaping abyss, hanging only by the saddle caught on a projection, he quickly jumped down and grabbed the animal's ears and mane. Although the animal was suspended in the air, he cut off the saddle and freed the horse. This episode inspired the compilers to pose a rhetorical question:

> How could we relate all
> The divine power of this inspired man?

Another opportunity for Yi to display his courage and dexterity

---

8. For a polysyndetic praise of a horse see *Song of Roland*, 1491–5; *Venus and Adonis*, 295–298; and *1 Henry IV*, IV, i, 104–110.

was in contests and games. It was the custom of the Koryŏ court to hold a polo match on the fifth day of the fifth month, usually in front of the palace. The spectators included both the king and the court, and this national event was an occasion to test the fitness and aptitude of the elite military corps, and to foster certain martial virtues. This match, together with other contests that will be discussed, was a kind of miniature warfare, an exercise in strategy and tactics, a battle in play, a noble tournament. In a match held in the year 1356, the general was among those selected for it. When the ball was hit into play, he charged very fast with his horse and completed his "graceful hang" shot. The ball caromed off a stone, bounced back through the forelegs and the hindlegs of his horse. Yi, looking up and leaning back on his side, pushed the horse's tail out of the way and hit the ball which then bounced back between the forelegs and he hit it again, making a score. The compilers called it the "pushed-back tail" play.

On another occasion when the ball had been hit into play, he again completed his "graceful hang" shot, but the ball bounced off the goal post and came back on the horse's left. The general shook off the right stirrup and turned his body around in such a way that his right foot reached down almost to the ground. He hit the ball cleanly, then back astride his mount, he hit it again and scored. The compilers called it the "sideway block" technique. "It amazed and stunned the whole country," historians tell us, "and was regarded as something unheard of even in the past" (canto 44).[9] Hence the contrast in the two verses of the canto: Li Shen's skill was admired *only* by the players in the two parties, while General Yi's by "people on nine state roads."

In 1372, King Kongmin held an archery contest, east of the capital. The contestants were requested to hit the targets 150 paces away. The famous archer, Hwang Sang, whose feats were admired even by the Mongol emperor, Shun-ti, arrived late, and could not score the mark every time he sent an arrow. General Yi was the only one who never missed the mark (canto 45). In the same year, at another contest, the targets were ten small silver mirrors placed eighty paces away (canto 46). And before his enthronement, the general sponsored a contest, where the target was a pear tree laden with scores of ripe pears. He loosed an arrow

9. *YG*, 6, 39b–40b.

from a hundred paces away and all the pears fell to the ground (canto 63).

In Western epics, the death of a hero called for an athletic contest in his honor.[10] During the funeral games for Patroclus, in the twenty-third book of the *Iliad*, as in the games for Anchises, in the fifth book of the *Aeneid*, the mark in the archery contest was a dove tied by a cord to the top of a mast. In the twenty-first book of the *Odyssey*, in the trial of Odysseus' bow, the feat required was a shot through the iron heads of twelve axes lined up in a row. These belong to the ludic tradition whose function in the total cultural pattern has already been elucidated by Huizinga.[11] But there are differences between the athletic contests in Western epics and Korean contest. First, the funeral games were in honor of the dead, a tribute to the past. Second, the target, like a dove hanging by a cord from the ship's mast, had ritualistic (and ironic, for victory is won by sacrifice) overtones of sacrifice and fulfillment. However, to bind a living bird or beast as a target even in a game is quite contrary to the Confucian tradition of fair play and humanity. Confucius is said to have "fished with a line but not with a net; when fowling he did not aim at a roosting bird" (*Analects*, VII, 26).[12] Hence in the second verse of canto 88 Yi was sure to have his attendant flush the birds into flight before shooting them down. This, the compilers argue, is a sign of "the peerless gallantry of the inspired man." Third, unlike the Greek games, the Korean contests, at least according to our sources, did not entail material prizes. This last aspect is probably least important in our context, for, as the subjects of the parallel lives in the cantos show, the purport of these episodes lies elsewhere. The general's huge bow, like Li Shih-min's, was the sign of a man "who was to save the world" (canto 27). The contests were actually provided by Heaven or Heaven induced someone to provide them in order to manifest "his august power" (canto 46) as well as to convince the king and the people and to inspire awe (cantos 31–32, 46). Indeed,

> Many could shoot an arrow:
> But he was aware of his heroic virtue.

10. William H. Willis, "Athletic Contests in the Epic," *Transactions and Proceedings of the American Philological Association*, LXXII (1941), 392–417; Kenneth Quinn, *Virgil's Aeneid* (Ann Arbor, 1968), pp. 153–156.

11. Johan Huizinga *Homo Ludens* (Boston, 1964).

12. Arthur Waley, *The Analects of Confucius* (London, 1949), p. 128.

> With his heroic virtue
> He saved many.   (canto 45)

Marksmanship alone, therefore, is not the subject of these poems: they are cited as evidence of the general's heroic virtue, indispensable for the mission he was to perform, as in the cases of Li Shih-min (canto 65), Aguda (canto 57), and Li K'o-yung of the Later T'ang (canto 63).[13] The contests were occasions for the clarification of his destiny, for him to become aware of the heavy burden the nation had laid on him. As instances of the hero's trials on a small scale, they mark the points of self-knowledge and progress he had to make for a clear understanding of Heaven's plan.

With his supreme physical and spiritual qualities, Yi Sŏng-gye responded to a call to bring order and peace to a nation harassed by foreign invaders. People therefore awaited his advent, a dazzling, royal dragon, Heaven's deputy on earth. In 1361, the Red Turbans crossed the frozen Yalu with 200,000 men and seized the Koryŏ capital; King Kongmin had to flee (canto 33). Captain of a force 2,000 strong, Yi Sŏng-gye rallied his men while they were trying to trap the rebels who attempted to flee the capital under cover of night. At that moment, a rebel struck him with a spear from behind, wounding his right ear. The situation being urgent, Yi Sŏng-gye beheaded a number of the rebels and flew across the fortress wall on horseback. This episode is similar to a story attributed to Aguda, the founder of the Chin, when he and his men successfully crossed the Amur without boats. These were instances of heavenly assistance, the compilers argue, in Aguda's case the river became a ferry, and in Yi's his unfaltering animal was a divine gift.

In 1362, as Commander of the Northeast, General Yi was in charge of a campaign against the Mongol minister Naɣaču. The commentary to canto 35 (5, 33b–37b), whose topic is the following single episode, is replete with stories of the general's divinely inspired tactics and endless feats: his sudden and swift night assault on the unsuspecting enemy and his marvelous ways of evading the enemy's arrows and spears. Canto 35, together with canto 44, are therefore the *loci* of his generalship, to illustrate his correct

---

13. For the topos of how great warrior's arms are treasured as relics see, for example, Chadwick, *The Heroic Age* (Cambridge, 1912), p. 340, where he cites *Beowulf*, 2613 ff. and 2985 f.

assessment of the situations, his creative imagination aimed at deceiving and overawing the enemy commanders' morale[14] and thus to create situations favorable for decisive actions. These are all in accord with Master Sun in his book on the military art, which preached a victory with the least possible casualties on both sides.[15] Thus, when the general rode forward alone into the enemy's ranks, it was to entice their commanders.[16] When they dashed out, the general feigned to flee but quickly drew rein and turned the horse around to the right. The Mongols could hardly imitate this feat, their momentum carried them past him, and they became the victims of the general's deadly arrows sent from behind (cantos 35–36). The importance attached to this single feat can be measured by the compilers' assignment of two cantos as parallels, two episodes from Li Shih-min's military career. One, his encounter in 626 with the Turkish khan Hsieh-li, when Li Shih-min rode forward attended only by six horsemen to display his courage and influence, culminating in the conclusion of peace at the Pien Bridge; another, the 617 campaign against the Sui contingents under Sung Lao-sheng, when upon his elder brother's fall from his horse, Li broke through the enemy ranks, furiously brandishing his weapon, "until two sword blades were nicked," and his sleeves ran with blood (canto 36). Here, as elsewhere, the general's single combat is made to carry the total action of battle; and this called for Li Shih-min, the Chinese model of heroism, but whose two similar acts of prowess could only match the weight of Yi Sŏng-gye's single performance. The motive for assigning two cantos to describe Yi's feat was precisely to augment and illuminate his exemplary heroism, for the temper of the season required a bold and fearless general.

The extraordinary tactics employed by Yi Sŏng-gye and Li Shih-min, known as the *ch'i* operation, are the topic of discussion between Li Shih-min and his general Li Ching (571–649) in the *Li Wei-kung wen-tui*,[17] an imaginary dialogue between the two on various topics of strategy and statesmanship. The book portrays them as deliberating the nature, function, and correlation of the

14. *Sun Tzu (SPPY)*, 1, 15a-24b (Samuel B. Griffith, *Sun Tzu* [Oxford, 1963], pp. 66–69).

15. *Sun Tzu*, 2, 2b-3a (Griffith, p. 77).

16. *Sun Tzu*, 1, 17a-18a (Griffith, p. 66).

17. (In the *Wu-ching ch'i-shu*; Taipei, 1965), 1, 1–5.

cheng and *ch'i* operations in warfare. Li first asks about a battle with Sung Lao-sheng in 617 (canto 36) when his righteous army made a slight retreat and he, leading the cavalry to the south, made an unexpected attack on the flanks, thus cutting off the enemy's columns. Li Ching answers that one must first employ the *cheng* and then the *ch'i*; first, the benevolent and righteous method, then the indirect method. Thus, at the battle of Ho-i, a retreat of the right flank upon the fall of his elder brother Chien-ch'eng from the horse is a *ch'i* tactic. Thereupon, Li Shih-min counters by saying that were it not for this extraordinary operation, the Great Undertaking of the Li family (the founding of the T'ang) would have been in danger. Hence he could not consider it a *ch'i*. Li Ching then explains that to advance and confront the foe is a *cheng*, but to retreat is *ch'i*. Because Li, without the retreat of the right flank, could not have elicited a sortie from Sung, who, ignorant of the art of war, dashed forward only to be captured, Li's tactics transformed the *ch'i* operation into the *cheng*. Thus, the *cheng* and *ch'i* are reciprocal and possess mutuality, often turning a calamity into advantage and final victory. Hence it is difficult to determine where one ends and the other begins. The two episodes related to Yi Sŏng-gye and Li Shih-min illustrate how the astute general could engage the foe with the *cheng* but win with the *ch'i* maneuver.[18] Confucius endorsed this operation, when he said "The man who was ready to 'beard a tiger or rush a river' without caring whether he lived or died—that sort of man I should not take. I should certainly take someone who approached difficulties with due caution and who preferred to succeed by strategy."[19]

The subjugation of the Northern Yüan, especially its stronghold Tongnyŏngbu, modern K'ai-yüan in Northwest Manchuria, was significant not only in Yi's career but in Koryŏ's struggle to assert her independence in the north and to regain the northern territory. When the general's army crossed the frozen Yalu on or about February 10, 1370, the purple mist, "the general's emanation," stretched across the sky, an indication of cosmic encouragement, presaging for the enemy an impending defeat. As a parallel to this episode, which illustrates the analogy that exists between the cosmic and human planes, a similar emanation is cited: the emanation of the Son of Heaven that hovered above the mountains and

18. *Sun Tzu*, 4, 4a, 6a, 6b (Griffith, pp. 34, 43, 91–93).
19. Waley, pp. 124–125.

marshes, the hiding places of Liu Pang before he founded the Han. Upon Yi's forward march, the Mongol vice-prefect (*t'ung-chih*) fled to the mountain fortress Ura (Wu-la), surrounded by insurmountable walls of immense height; when the general's army reached Yat'un village, he came out to fight but surrendered with 300 households. His superior stubbornly held out in the mountain fortress, however. Thus brought to bay, the Korean army laid siege and charged probably from the west side, the only place that could be scaled. There they rained down arrows, and the general's always landed on the rebels' faces (cantos 39–40).

The final series of campaigns that brought lasting fame to Yi Sŏng-gye as the nation's hope was that against the Japanese pirates. In the 1377 campaign, when the enemy occupied a position on the summit of Mount Chii, one pirate insulted the general by insolent gestures. He was felled by a single arrow shot by the general, but others appeared undaunted. While his colonel and his own son Yi Pang-wŏn were unable to gain an advantageous position, the general inspired courage in the hearts of his men by scaling the cliff himself with his horsemen. The single arrow that felled the insolent "island savages" was enough to inspire terror in the enemy (canto 47). The compilers assigned several cantos to the 1380 campaign to highlight its military and historical significance. Two factors are emphasized in connection with the decisive battle at Mount Hwang where the Korean army won the single most important victory in the war (cantos 50–51): one was his battle array, a puzzle to the enemy (canto 51):

> He marshaled troops unlike others,
> They noticed it but came forward.
> Had they retreated,
> Would they have survived after all?

Advance or retreat, the outcome of the battle to the enemy would have been the same. Another was his humanism and strong sense of justice, tempered with timely mercy. When the brave enemy captain, known as Agi-batur ("young hero"), galloped forward, the general, moved by his courage and recognizing the admirable quality in the enemy, wished to spare him and ordered his men to capture him alive. But his men argued that he was a danger to the Korean side. The general therefore first shot down his helmet (canto 52), and his archers then sent deadly arrows into his face.

This single incident is the subject of the second verse in canto 52, where the compilers ask:

> Had he not unmasked his helmet,
> Would he have saved
> The people of his country?

In 1382, in the last battles fought against the pirates in the northeast, the general rode on with a hundred horsemen until he was within a short distance of the enemy camp and ordered his men to unsaddle their horses (cantos 58, 60). Confounded by this strategy, the enemy dared not make a sortie, but they were finally decoyed to a place where an ambush was laid and were routed in the ninth month of the year. At that time, he had the conch blown, whose sound was enough to strike terror in the enemy (canto 59). His name was the magic of war, to his men a kind of talisman to ward off fear, and to the enemy a warning not to dare engage in battle (canto 61). Therefore, whenever the Japanese caught a Korean soldier, they asked him the whereabouts of the general (canto 62):

> Pirates asked where he was,
> They dreaded his name.
> A Heaven-sent,
> They would not dare come near.

As Li Shih-min's single bellow to the scouts of Tou Chien-te's army initiated a successful campaign, so when the general raised a war cry, identifying himself, the pirates began to waver.

This was the kind of service he gave his country when its safety and survival were at stake. As an ideal of martial valor, he was valiant and resourceful, confident and provident, generous and merciful. He did not parade his valorous deeds before the people; rather, he enjoyed a warm fellowship with them. Attentive to the army's safety and morale, "with cheerful semblance and sweet majesty," he always tried to inspire courage and confidence in his men (canto 89). The strength and cruelty of the enemy were therefore the measure of his heroism. The terror or grandeur of the events is augmented by strange eruptions that portent or attend victory to Korea and disaster to the enemy, such as a red halo, the mist, or a white rainbow that suddenly fills the sky. These signs of spiritual companionship not only inspire his deeds but reinforce the consciously ethical heroic standard that he stands for. But he is man after all, and he is painfully aware of the transience of human achievements that are as perishable as leaves. He has mastered the fear of death, but as he contemplates the dead bodies of men who so gallantly had served the nation's cause, he at once comprehends the limitations and finality of man's deeds.

> Pitying his own people,
> He passed by Changdan.
> At the time a white rainbow
> Cut across the sun.   (canto 50)

On his way to a decisive battle on Mount Hwang, he could not bear to look at the killed. As he, a mortal man destined to serve immortal causes, passes through the dead bodies that cover the hills and plains, he comprehends the timeless truth.

Consider the vast expanse, the deadly stillness under the burning sun, contrasted with the hoofbeats of the general's horse; or the highly motivated soldier, carrier of the nation's destiny, pitted against the impersonal, naturalistic cosmos. This scene is the main symbol of the book, replete with moral, historical, and symbolic associations. It seems to define man's place in Nature as well as his relationships to Fate. The greater the human achievement, the deeper the vision of human impermanence. The futility of man's effort to conquer time has often been the subject of literature. "Time is a child at play,"

> As when a little boy piles sand by the sea-shore
> When in his innocent play he makes sand towers
>   to amuse him
> and then, still playing, with hands and feet ruins
>   and wrecks them.   (*Iliad*, XV, 361–364)[20]

Can death be exchanged for immortal glory? East Asian tradition seems to answer negatively, for the *aristeiai* of Western epic heroes in themselves have little meaning. Already Homer in the *Odyssey* and Virgil in the *Aeneid* showed the inadequacy of the heroic code, how it "destroys more than it creates," and how heroic

20. Richmond Lattimore, *The Iliad of Homer* (Chicago, 1951), p. 319. The *Iliad* and the *Odyssey* cited here are from the Lattimore translations. Also in Heraclitus ("Time is a child moving counters in a game"), for which see Philip Wheelwright, *Heraclitus* (Princeton, 1959), pp. 29, 139–140. See also Ovid, *Metamorphosis*, XV, 234–236, and Shelley, "Ozymandias."

deeds are often "motivated by greed, accomplished with terror, and indistinguishable from piracy."[21]

The episode, designed to produce cumulative effects, shows a series of implied contrasts: a just war for the love and pity of people versus outrageous banditry in defiance of all accepted norms; a patriotic hero, an image of virtue and humanity versus unsophisticated villains, examples of violence and cupidity. One is the embodiment of present and past as well as a hope for the future; the other has no past, nor any future. From the divine viewpoint, therefore, the outcome of the battle has already been decided, for Fate (Heaven) is always on the moral side. The enemy, in the compilers' eyes, is doomed; this is the meaning of the strange cosmic manifestation which the furious bandits will misread, another cause of their imminent destruction. Here free will and Fate are inextricably interwoven, for the general's response to a call in defence of the just cause tallies with the divine plan. In this lies the general's pre-eminence. To one it is a necessary war, an instrument of peace; to the other, a game for the lust of murder and plunder. Hence, his trials and sufferings have moral and symbolic meanings, as we shall soon see. Canto 50 is therefore the scene of recognition by the hero of his own mortality, as all such scenes in the epic are. This is not submission to, but rather clarification of, his fate.

As an embodiment of the struggles of his nation and people, Yi's heroic career played out in the foreground is at once authentic, real, and of profound significance. In this national and patriotic meaning lies the unity of his struggles. As in the *Mahabharata*, *Aeneid*, *Beowulf*, *Volsunga Saga*, or *Nibelungenlied*, the trials of Yi Sŏng-gye as hero should be viewed as the incarnation of his people.[22] And as such it was fully sanctioned by Confucian orthodoxy. "When Heaven is about to confer a great responsibility on any man," Mencius said, "it will exercise his mind with suffering, subject his sinews and bones to hard work, expose his body to hunger, put him to poverty, place obstacles in the paths of his deeds, so as to stimulate his mind, harden his nature, and improve wherever he is incompetent" (6B, 15).[23] This is how Heaven prepares

21. George de F. Lord, "The Odyssey and the Western World," *SR*, LXII (1954), 423, 420.

22. Peter F. Fisher, "The Trials of the Epic Hero in Beowulf," *PMLA*, LXXIII (1958), 171–183.

23. Wing-tsit Chan, *A Source Book in Chinese Philosophy*, p. 78.

man for great tasks, as was the case of Shun, Fu Yüeh, Chiao-ko, Kuan I-wu, and other ideals of Confucian tradition. And they succeeded because they were able to take obstacles as a challenge, as a necessary step for their development. And Heaven, through signs and portents, constantly reminds them of the moral significance of their deeds. The scope of the trials—which correspond to the adventures of the hero in the mythological cycle—is the measure of their greatness. The bestowal of service on his fellow men as the hero of tried valor and virtue corresponds to the return of the mythological hero,[24] the only justification of such trials. This, then, is a process in which the hero recognizes not only his limitations, but his true mission in society. And the recognition has to be an achievement, the fruit of his heroic ordeals. In accord with the Confucian conception of a man who, by great endurance and action, raises himself to heroic status, the compilers were able to confer on the general's facta a moral and political significance, that renderd them public and ecumenical.

What, then, is the nature of war? In the Confucian tradition, war is never glorified. The sage-kings of remote antiquity had no use for such violent measures, for "a good ruler will have no enemy" (*Mencius*, 2A, 5) and "a man of humanity has no enemy in the world" (7B, 1). There is, however, a just and righteous war, which is chastisement rather than invasion. "He who injures humanity is a bandit," Mencius states. "He who injures righteeousness is a destructive person. Such a person is a mere fellow. I've heard of killing a mere fellow Chou, but not murdering him as the ruler" (1B, 8).[25] Thus the overthrow of a wicked ruler was sanctioned, as in the case of King T'ang the Completer's punishment of eleven corrupt states (canto 38) and the overthrow of Shang by the Chou founders. Indeed, "King Wu by one display of his anger gave repose to all the people of the kingdom" (canto 14).

War, however, should not be pursued for personal glory or territorial aggrandizement. The commentary to canto 17 (3, 32a–51a), which lauds the chastisement of the Sui by T'ang founders, delights in enumerating the Sui emperor's grandiose plans of Koguryŏ invasions (612–614), which were held to be the

24. Cf. Joseph Campbell, *The Hero with a Thousand Faces* (New York, 1961), pp. 97 ff.
25. Chan, p. 62.

principal cause of Sui's downfall.[26] The commentary to the first verse of canto 41 (6, 1b–31a), which praises Li Shih-min's humanity and justice in his handling of Koguryŏ prisoners of war, presents also the historians' evaluation of his Koguryŏ campaign. In 645 Li Shih-min personally marshaled a huge army and marched to Liaotung. Although initially the war was successful, his siege of the impregnable fortress of Ansi, perched on a rocky eminence, was a resounding failure. The whole population united in a heroic resolve to defend the small fortress and did not consent to any terms. In the ninth month of 645, therefore, Li Shih-min was compelled to withdraw after an unsuccessful siege of some sixty days. The moral effect of this failure was immense, and the compilers of the present cycle were anxious to point out the evil consequence of a war waged out of ambition and covetousness, for personal glory and display of influence. The compilers, therefore, resorted to the method of indirection, by citing the estimates of Chinese historians on the subject.

Fan Tsu-yü (1041–1098), in his *T'ang chien*, argues that one should not underestimate a country for its size.[27] For even a small nation like Koguryŏ has resourceful citizens who endlessly map out stratagems and brave citizens who are willing to die for their country. A large country with a large army alone, therefore, could not expect to win. The initial Chinese victory was a result of the Koguryŏ failure to cut off the T'ang supply line, as proposed by Ko Chŏng-ŭi, and of the impetuous general Ko Yŏn-su's imprudent advance.[28] The T'ang troops were thus able to ambush and decimate them, but the emperor's boastful glee, especially in a message to the heir apparent, betrayed his hidden motive for the Liaotung campaign. Despite the vast T'ang military prestige, the historian continues, Li Shih-min's delight in warfare and his personal charge of the campaign were responsible for the debacle. The only difference between him and Sui Yang-ti is that he did not ruin his own dynasty. Fan exonerates him, however, because upon encountering dangers he recalled the admonitions of honest ministers and, realizing his mistakes, tried to mend his ways.

26. For the Chinese view of war see Lien-sheng Yang, "Historical Notes on Chinese World Order," in *The Chinese World Order*, ed. John K. Fairbank (Cambridge, Mass., 1968), pp. 24 ff. For the Sui's downfall, see Michael C. Rogers, *The Chronicle of Fu Chien* (Berkeley, 1968), pp. 46–51.

27. *T'ang chien* (*TSCC*), 6, 47–49 (*YG*, 6, 18a-b, 28a-b).

28. See *CTS*, 199A, 3615c-d; *SGSG*, 21, 5–8 (*YG*, 6, 17b-18a).

Hu Yin (1098–1156), on the other hand, ascribes the cause of the Liaotung debacle to a remark made by Li Shih-chi who, when the defenders mounted the ramparts amid drums and clamor as if to mock the invaders, requested the emperor to bury alive all men inside the fortress after their capitulation. The remarks, according to Hu Yin, stiffened the will of the defenders who fought to the death. According to the Sung historian, the emperor's siege of the fortress, contrary to the heir apparent's plan to attack the Koguryŏ capital, sprang from his ambition and pride. Intent on defeating Koguryŏ, he suddenly forgot about clever tactics, and thus invited disaster.[29] As a coda to his criticism, Hu Yin quotes the aphorisms from the *Book of Rites*: "Pride should not be allowed to grow; the desires should not be indulged; the will should not be gratified to the full; pleasure should not be carried to excess."[30]

Thus Li Shih-min incurred the imputation of pride and ambition and was criticized for waging war purely for agonistic purposes, for envy of power and lust of conquest. This is a serious charge, and reminiscent of the *De Casibus* tradition. The evil which arises from a sovereign's personal motives in the execution of international politics had to be emphasized. Perhaps in order to absolve him of his less-than-ideal behavior, or perhaps out of sheer necessity of having to find a historical parallel to the second verse, the first verse pictures him as representative of the "benevolent and righteous soldier." The theme of twin studies in canto 41, the benevolent and righteous war, is a topic of discussion between Ch'en Hsiao and Hsün Tzu. Asked to elucidate his thesis that war must be based on benevolence and righteousness, Hsün Tzu answers: "The benevolent man does indeed love others, and because he loves others, he hates to see man do them harm. The righteous man acts in accordance with what is right, and for that reason he hates to see man do wrong. He takes up arms in order to put an end to violence and to do away with harm, not in order to contend with others for spoil. Therefore, where the soldiers of the benevolent man encamp they command a godlike respect. And where they pass, they transform the people. They are like the seasonable rain in whose falling all men rejoice. . . . Those nearby were won by their goodness, and those far off were filled with longing

29. *Tu-shih kuan-chien*, 18, 9a (*YG*, 6, 24a-b); 9b, 10a (*YG*, 6, 30a-b).

30. *Li chi* (*SPPY*), 1, 1a (Legge, *Sacred Books of the East*, XXVIII [Oxford, 1926], 62); *Yen-shih chia-hsün* (*SPTK*), B, 6a.

by their virtue. They did not stain their swords with blood, and yet near and far alike submitted; their virtue flourished in the center and spread to the four quarters."[31]

In Shakespeare's *Henry V*, as a reprisal for the treacherous assault on the undefended English camp at Agincourt, which resulted in a massacre of English boys, Henry orders his soldiers to kill all their prisoners:

> But, hark! what new alarum is this same?
> The French have reinforc'd their scatter'd men.
> Then every soldier kill his prisoner:
> Give the word through.   (IV, vi, 35–38)

Shortly thereafter, in the following scene, the king exclaims again:

> Besides, we'll cut the throats of those we have,
> And not a man of them that we shall take
> Shall taste our mercy.   (IV, vii, 62–65)

This rather unchivalrous act of the king, who was looked upon by Elizabethan audience as a model of king- and generalship, "the mirror of all Christian kings," is hard to justify. One commentator defends his action on the grounds that it was a military tactic necessary for the security of the English force, for the English were then surrounded by the French who outnumbered them five to one. The incident was supposed to convey the impression, not of brutality, but of "a great commander's strength, decision, and presence of mind in the crisis of . . . battle."[32]

Although we must evaluate Henry's action in terms of contemporary standards and ideals and by the poet's design and purpose of the play, the Confucian tradition would hardly call it gallantry, as Gower interprets it. Gower's comment is probably "ironic," as one critic points out,[33] for what is emphasized are not simply the evils of war, but the perennial historical issue of the Renaissance: the contradiction between ideal and reality, "rights and limits of monarchy," and ambiguities as well as validity of individual acts in the name of historical necessity.[34] Henry could have saved the

31. *Hsün Tzu (SPTK)*, 10, 7b, 13b-14b (Burton Watson, *Hsün Tzu* [New York, 1963], pp. 69–70). *YG*, 6, 1a-b.

32. *King Henry V* (Cambridge ed., 1955), introduction by J. Dover Wilson, pp. xxxiii, xxxvii (also xxxv).

33. D. A. Traversi, *An Approach to Shakespeare* (Garden City, 1956), pp. 46–47.

34. Ronald Berman, ed. *Twentieth Century Interpretations of Henry V* (Englewood Cliffs, 1968), pp. 6–9.

prisoners as a gesture of Christian mercy, which he often invokes, but at that moment his ire and hubris prompted him to choose a less Christian but, to popular taste, perhaps more heroic and partiotic alternative. The Chinese critics are painfully aware of the same double standards, of crimes and atrocities committed in the name of history and patriotism, which lay bare the terrible distance between the ideal and the human. Sun Tzu demanded of the general five qualities: wisdom, sincerity, humanity, courage, and strictness.[35] It is humanity, especially in relation to prisoners of war, that has elicited the portrayal of Yi Sŏng-gye and Li Shih-min as soldiers of benevolence and righteousness. Slaughter of prisoners of war, therefore, can hardly be reconciled with the higher goals of war in the Confucian tradition, which entails the restoration of order and the transformation by moral principles of the defeated and humbled as the potential subjects of Confucian universalism.

Consequently, canto 41 portrays both Li Shih-min and Yi Sŏng-gye as emblems of humanity and justice whose purpose in war was not spoil or pillage but the restoration of order and peace. The same theme recurs in canto 54, where the subjects of twin studies are Liu Pang (Han Kao-tsu) and Yi Sŏng-gye. Liu Pang wanted no bloodshed in the state of Lu, known for its decorum and righteousness. Hence he adopted the policy of persuasion, pleading Lu's surrender (202 B.C.). Yi, on the other hand, wishing to save the dauntless Mongol general Chao Wu, did not use arrowheads (canto 54) but awed him into surrender (1364). Like the English *curtana* (or *curteyn*),[36] the blunted sword of mercy and peace, Yi Sŏng-gye's "wooden arrowhead" (*paktu*), a substitute for the deadly arrowhead, manifests his refusal to wound and destroy, his zeal for mercy and peace. Again, following the thesis of Hsün Tzu, the righteous army was followed by a mass of people in adoration of the commander's virtue (canto 6), a crowd large enough to serve as a tribute to his prestige and magnificence. Yi Sŏng-gye's influence was enough to win the allegiance of the Jürched (cantos 9, 55, 75), of the southern barbarians (canto 53), and of his people (canto 11).

This partly explains the historians' justification of the general's return from Wihwa Island in 1388, whose importance can be com-

35. *Sun Tzu*, 1, 9a-b (Griffith, p. 65).
36. Samuel C. Chew, *The Virtues Reconciled* (Toronto, 1947), pp. 119–122.

pared to Caesar's decision to cross the Rubicon in January, 49 B.C. The general's objections, reminiscent again of Master Sun's thesis in the *Art of War*,[37] pointed out the reckless nature of the expedition, the problem of weather, and its danger to the nation's security. If carried out, the Liaotung expedition would have plunged the nation into chaos, taxing its resources and disrupting the social and moral order. Thus the state, which exists for the benefit of the common people, would have forfeited its very reason for existence. He was therefore determined to prevent the campaign rather than execute and win it. And as the "minister of people's fate" and "arbiter of the nation's destiny,"[38] he piloted the state on the right course and brought it safely through a storm. Thus when he "upheld right and marched back," "They [the people] therefore awaited his banner of justice." The willing people came out of their own accord "With rice in baskets, wine in bottles" (canto 10). The auspicious omen appeared too, as Heaven caused the Yalu not to overflow after three days of copious rains (cantos 67–68):

> Heaven did not stop a copious rain,
> But kept the tide away from him.
> Blue Heaven
> Showed its wishes on purpose.

A historical parallel to this event (cantos 9, 11–14) is the act of King Wu of Chou who chastised the wicked last ruler of Shang and who had been accepted by orthodox Confucian tradition as archetype of the representative of Heaven and the man destined to wreak vengeance on a wicked king. The compilers wish to inculcate here the legitimacy and justification of the general's move. Whether the subject should obey the wicked ruler rather than Heaven, if the ruler was in opposition to Heaven's wishes, was one of the timeless questions of Confucian historiography. That such a ruler could be deposed either by a passive or active measure had already been expounded by the classics. Although the difference between one who has failed and one who has succeeded in his attempt to act as Heaven's deputy is paper-thin, the successful one, like King Wu or Yi Sŏng-gye, always could claim the mandate of Heaven. His was not an act of insurrection or rebellion but a chas-

37. *Sun Tzu*, 1, 2b-9b (Griffith, pp. 63–65).
38. *Sun Tzu*, 2, 14b-15a (Griffith, p. 76).

tisement in Heaven's name, as Heaven's vicegerent, of the sin of the wicked king. Thus the tradition firmly established and expounded the pattern of sin and punishment, the supreme moral and political pattern in history: that Heaven withdraws its mandate from the unjust, wicked ruler; that Heaven sees as the people see; and that Heaven's deputy and the people's representative is justified in carrying out the divine plan.[39] Thus history's iterative pattern was the mirror by which the present was explained by reference to the past. Or, more correctly, Yi Sŏng-gye's act can be magnified as a parallel to King Wu's, for here the image of Yi rather than that of King Wu needs reinforcing.

> May you never shame your ancestors,
> But rather tend their inward power,
> That forever you may be linked to Heaven's charge
> And bring to yourselves many blessings.
> Before Yin lost its army
> It was well linked to God above.
> In Yin you should see as in a mirror
> That Heaven's high charge is hard to keep.[40]

King Wu's example teaches the political and moral lessons appropriate to the understanding of Yi Sŏng-gye's act. These cantos, therefore, plead the example of King Wu to convince posterity of the righteousness and the necessity of the general's return.

The compilers found it necessary to develop the argument of the people's right to choose their own ruler, and in their search in history they found in the Chou founders the supreme mirrors for the present. Upon his return from the north, the general deposed the illegitimate boy-king, whose true identity is shrouded in mystery—because the chronicles for the last years of Koryŏ were written by Yi partisan politicians—and installed and served the legitimate one from the House of Wang (canto 11). But almost as soon as he came to the throne, the last Koryŏ ruler "succumbed to slander,/and his wickedness raged every day" (canto 12). The Yi historians paint him as a small man who disliked the general's growing reputation, and when, because of the land reform, powerful families harbored grudges against, and falsely accused, the general, the ineffectual king listened to their clamor and sided with

39. *Shang shu*, 6, 4a (Legge, III, 292) (also in 2, 8a): *Mencius*, 7B, 14 (Legge, II, 483–484).

40. *Book of Songs*, 235 (Wealey, no. 241, p. 251).

them rather than with him. The historical king Kongyang, however, was hardly an impediment in the general's path to the throne.
He was a mere puppet, placed on the throne by the Yi party to
serve as pawn in their deadly power struggle. The narrative to
these cantos, lifted mostly from the dynastic histories to bolster the
claims of the Yi party, plead Chinese precedents to convince the
reader of the necessity of the revolution. But when Yi Sŏng-gye
took upon himself the task of public avenger of wrongs done by the
last Koryŏ kings to state and people, their public sins were chiefly
political. King Wu therefore had to be brought in to furnish the
moral justification—so necessary to the defenders of the revolution—to show how the sins of the last rulers of Koryŏ were direct
cause of their downfall. The details had to be altered to make them
more reminiscent of the past, and that was in accord with the
practice of Confucian historiography to make the story serve as
mirror, a political mirror for those in authority. History must
present the judgment of Heaven and people, and the justice visited
on the house of Koryŏ had to be presented as the same that determined the destruction of the Shang and later dynasties.

In spite of "a wicked plan" against him, Yi Sŏng-gye, like
Kings Wen and Wu, doubted Heaven's bidding and continued to
serve the inadequate sovereign.[41] Although the plan for the revolution was already made at the time of the army's return from
Wihwa Island, the unconvinced general refused to initiate a coup.
Heaven then manifested its will through an auspicious dream
(canto 13) and the willing allegiance of the people. The memorial
of Pae Kŭng-nyŏm urging him to "accede to the throne and fulfill
the expectations of gods and people" (canto 12)[42] finally convinced him. Thus, the fact that his revolution as not an act of
usurpation but "a gift of Heaven" (*Mencius*, 5A, 5) had finally been
expounded.

Consequently, the heroic achievements of a Confucian soldier
do not lie so much in his great feats on the battlefield, as in his
correct interpretation of his duty, by setting a new standard of
moral excellence. The end of the righteous war, reminds Hsün
Tzu, is "to put an end to violence."[43] The Confucian soldier is
the upholder of justice and humanity, one who scorns violence

41. This is another topos in Confucian historical writing.
42. *YG*, 2, 33a-35a, esp. 35a.
43. *Hsün Tzu*, 10, 13b (Watson, p. 69).

64

and irrationality by subordinating his passions and desires to a higher purpose, the fulfillment of his responsibilities. What endows him with his strength and purpose is therefore his sense of duty, his trust in his mission as a carrier of civilization, his ability to discharge the mandate in the restoration of harmony and order at all planes. "A drowning empire," Mencius expounds, "must be rescued with moral principles."[44] He must be able to look forward to the future, the unified nation and the willing people, and the dynasty that will stand as a symbol of peace and stability. In the sixth book of the *Aeneid*, Aeneas and his father Anchises meet in the underworld; and as they proceed to the upper world, Anchises points out to his son the long line of his descendants, foretells the greatness of Roman rule, and expounds Rome's great mission:

> tu regere imperio populos, Romane, memento
> (hae tibi erunt artes), pacisque imponere morem,
> parcere subiectis et debellare superbos.

> But Romans, never forget that government is your medium,
> Be this your art:—to practice men in the habit of peace,
> Generosity to the conquered, and firmness against aggressors.[45]
> (VI, 851–853)

In such terms, the Yi dynasty is the triumph of moderation over hatred, of order over disintegration, and of history and culture over human frailty. It must be able to embrace the humbled and defeated under a single society and culture, imposing on them the virtues of peace and order so vital to the establishment and maintenance of the dynasty.[46]

---

44. *Mencius*, 4A, 17 (Legge, II, 307).
45. C. Day Lewis, *The Aeneid of Virgil* (New York, 1952), p. 141.
46. Bowra, "Virgil and the Ideal of Rome," in *From Virgil to Milton* (London, 1945), pp. 33–85, esp. 60 ff.; Viktor Pöschl, *Dichtkunst Virgils*, tr. Gerda Seligson (Ann Arbor, 1962), pp. 34–60; Michael C. J. Putnam, *The Poetry of Aeneid* (Cambridge, Mass., 1965), p. 193; Brooks Otis, *Virgil: A Study in Civilized Poetry* (Oxford, 1963), pp. 313–314; Kenneth Quinn, *Virgil's Aeneid* (Ann Arbor, 1968), p. 173.

Chapter IV. The Confucian Statesman

We have seen how Yi Sŏng-gye fulfilled the function of a Confucian soldier by withstanding the trials and by responding to the demands of destiny willed by Heaven. Through trials and sufferings he became master of himself and his circumstances, thus fulfilling the highest standards set by Confucian tradition. As I have shown, he distinguished himself not by individual prowess or glory, but by identification of his own destiny with that of the nation. The ultimate justification of such trials in the tradition is the maintenance and preservation of order, best manifested in good government.

We know the overriding emphasis in the classics is politics, according to which the ideal government must be built upon the harmonious relations of men, whereby ruler and subjects work together. A ruler is a vital link in the universal order, a guardian of the harmony between Heaven, Earth, and Man. As a link in cosmic harmony, his position in the trinity is to ensure and safeguard order. The duty of a ruler or prince is awesome, for he is to maintain the necessary social harmony which is the only defense against disruption and chaos. As a father of the people and embodiment of Confucian ideals, he rules not by law and punishment, but by virtue and guides by personal examples.[1] "If a ruler

1. Waley, p. 88.

66

sets himself right, he will be followed without his command" (*Analects*, XIII, 6).[2] Having attained goodness in himself, his job is to develop the good in his subjects.

> For princes are the glass, the school, the book,
> Where subjects' eyes do learn, do read, do look.
> (*The Rape of Lucrece*, 615–616)

In his famous simile of the wind, Confucius expounded his idea of the ruler to Chi K'ang Tzu, the *de facto* duke of the state of Lu: "If you desire what is good, the people will be good. The character of a ruler is like wind and that of the people like grass. In whatever direction the wind blows, the grass always bends" (XII, 19).[3]

An extant Old Korean poem (765) by master Ch'ungdam develops the theme of degree in a favorite analogy between the structure of the family and that of the state:

> The King is father,
> And Ministers are loving mothers.
> Subjects are foolish children;
> They only receive what love brings.
>
> The people are slow, often they live idly;
> But once feed them love, and they thrive.
> No one will desert the familiar land,
> This is the way to govern a country.
>
> Peace and prosperity will prevail if each—
> King, minister, subject—live as he should.[4]

That the ruler, a counterpart of Heaven,[5] is the "father and mother of his people"[6] is a very old idea. "What is a king," asks Erasmus echoing Seneca, "if not the father to a great multitude?"[7] The organic analogy between the state and family,[8] beehive,[9]

2. Chan, p. 41 (cf. Waley, p. 173).
3. Chan, p. 40 (cf. Waley, p. 168).
4. See my *Anthology of Korean Poetry* (New York, 1964), pp. 39–40.
5. *The Mean*, 31 (Chan, p. 112).
6. *Book of Songs*, 172/3 (Karlgren, *The Book of Odes*, p. 116: Waley, no. 170, p. 179).
7. *The Education of a Christian Prince*, I, ed. Born, p. 170. Also in Claudian, *Panegyric on the Fourth Consulship of Honorius*, 294, tr. Maurice Platnauer (LCL, 1922), II, 309.
8. Aristotle, *De Motu Animalium*, 703a31; Jean Bodin, *République*, I, 2 (tr. Richard Knolles, *The Six Bookes of a Commonweale*, ed. Kenneth D. McRae [Cambridge, Mass., 1962], p. 8); Erasmus, I (Born, p. 170).
9. Virgil, *Georgics*, IV, 149–227 (Otis, *Virgil*, pp. 150–151 for the outline and pp. 181–189 for analysis); Elyot, *The Governour*, I, 2 (Everyman's Library ed., New York, 1937), p. 9; *Henry V*, I, ii, 182–213.

ship,[10] is a commonplace in East and West. The first formulation of the organic analogy may be in the *Book of Documents*, in "Kao Yao mo," where ministers are compared to the "legs and arms, ears and eyes"[11] of an emperor, which Mencius reiterates when he compares ministers to the "hands and feet" of a ruler, who is in turn "their heart and mind" (4B, 3).[12]

The didactic functions of these analogies are the same in both cultures, for the emphasis is on the interrelation of macrocosm and microcosm, the health of a nation depending on the moral health of a ruler, necessary for the maintenance of the order and degree which is often identified with musical harmony:

> For government, though high and low and lower,
> Put into parts, doth keep in one consent,
> Congreeing in a full and natural close,
> Like music.
>   (*Henry V*, I, ii, 180–183)

Contrarily, the storm (or tempest) is a traditional epic simile of fury and violence, and, as pointed out by G. Wilson Knight,[13] the recurrent symbol in Shakespeare's tragedies. The symbol of storm, emblematic of the disturbances in man and the state, highlights the correspondences of man and Nature. This concept is neatly charted in the *Great Learning* (7–10):[14] that the cultivation of a personal life is essential to the regulation of the family, which is in turn essential to the order in the state, which ultimately brings peace to the world. That the ruler or prince occupies the key in this scheme, Confucianism (and Christian humanism) emphasizes. In the Confucian context, the end of learning is the acquisition of moral standards, which are often compared to squares and com-

---

10. Plato, *Republic*, VI, 488–489 (Francis M. Cornford, *The Republic of Plato* [New York, 1959], pp. 195–196); Horace, *Odes*, I, 14 (tr. C. E. Bennett, *The Odes and Epodes* [LCL, 1964], pp. 42–43). See James E. Phillips, Jr., *The State in Shakespeare's Greek and Roman Plays* (New York, 1940), pp. 61–75.

11. *Shang shu*, 2, 10a (Legge, III, 79).

12. Legge, II, 318 (cf. *The Faerie Queene*, II, xi, ii),

13. *Myth and Miracle* (London, n.d.), pp. 23 ff.; *The Imperial Theme* (London, 1931), pp. 6, 29 ff.; for criticism of Knight's method see Maurice Charney, *Shakespeare's Roman Plays* (Cambridge, Mass., 1961), p. 204, and Roland M. Frye, *Shakespeare and Christian Doctrine* (Princeton, 1963), pp. 19–42.

14. *Great Learning*, 7–10 (Chan, pp. 90–94).

passes.[15] A sage, an exemplar of ultimate standards of human relations, the conferer of shape and the interpreter of direction, is
therefore likened to a compass or square, to clinch the view that
the ruler is the "standard" of the ruled.

Indeed, the cultivation of moral standards is the root and
foundation of cosmic and social harmony, the basis of universal
parallelism. What binds a hierarchical organism is moral virtue,
especially the Confucian *jen*, which is termed "a peaceful abode of
man."[16] Perhaps nowhere are the rights of the common people so
much emphasized as in Confucian political philosophy. For to
know man is to know Heaven (*The Mean*, 20). It is through people
that Heaven manifests its approval or disapproval of a ruler, as in
the *Book of Documents*, the *locus classicus* of the concept: "Heaven
sees as my people see, Heaven hears as my people hear."[17] The
people are the ruler's children (*The Mean*, 20/6), not a many-
headed monster Hydra, and it is love, the distinguishing characteristic of man, that binds the diverse elements in a realm. Hence in
a state, as Mencius declares, "the people are the most important . . . to gain the hearts of the peasantry is the way to become an emperor" (7B, 14).[18] If the king fails, the people owe him
no allegiance; they may have the right to oppose him or even
remove him forcibly. This was the verdict of some Christian and
Renaissance political thinkers[19] and the judgment of Confucian
historians; even the Tudor Homilies did not endorse a tyrant.
Tudor orthodoxy demanded a passive toleration of the tyranny of
a lawful hereditary king (Cambises; Soliman in Greville's
Mustapha) but condemned a usurping tyrant who seized the crown
(for example, Richard III, Macbeth, and Alaham).[20] The tyrant

15. *Shang shu*, 5, 9b (Legge III, 253); *Mencius*, 4A, 2 (Legge, II, 292), 6A, 20
(421); *Hsün Tzu*, 1, 7a (Dubs, *The Works of Hsüntze* [London, 1928], p. 31); *Han Fei
Tzu* (*SPPY*), 2, 5a (Watson, *Han Fei Tzu* [New York, 1964], p. 28); *Huai-nan Tzu*
(*SPTK*), 9, 8b-9a.

16. *Mencius*, 4A, 10 (Legge, II, 302; Chan, p. 74).

17. *Shang shu*, 6, 7b (Legge, III, 292) cf. *Mencius*, 5A, 5; also *Mencius*, 1B, 7; 4B,
3; 5A, 5; 7B, 14.

18. Legge, II, 483; Chan, p. 81.

19. John of Salisbury, *Policraticus*, VIII, 20–21 (John Dickinson, *The Statesman's
Book of John of Salisbury* [New York, 1927], pp. 367 ff.); St. Thomas Aquinas, "On
Princely Government," *Selected Political Writings*, tr. J. G. Dawson (Oxford, 1948), I,
6 (p. 31).

20. W. A. Armstrong, "The Elizabethan Conception of the Tyrant," *The Review
of English Studies*, XXII (1946), 161–181. David Bevington, *Tudor Drama and Politics*
(Cambridge, Mass., 1968), pp. 156–167.

is usually described as the embodiment of most of the seven deadly sins, and Malcolm's description of Macbeth may be cited as a typical example:

> . . . bloody,
> Luxurious, avaricious, false, deceitful,
> Sudden, malicious, smacking of every sin
> That has a name.
> (IV, iii, 57–60)

Tormented by fear and the threat of damnation, these tyrants die unnaturally, punished by God for their sin against Him, against their own soul, and against the commonweal.[21] The Confucian classics sanction the removal of the tyrant, whether he is legitimate ruler or usurper, if he perpetuates an absolute, cruel, unjust rule. Portrayed as an incarnation of evil, the traditional behavior of such a ruler does not differ much from that of the Western archetype.[22] The tyrannicide is therefore justified as the punisher of a murderer, a robber, a paltry fellow; the last underscores the loneliness of evil the tyrant embodies. Banishment, one of the cruelest punishments, is seen as monstrous isolation, as a cutoff from all human ties and the community of men, for a disrupter of harmony, a slave of ambition, and a perpetrator of evil deserves the desolation of loneliness.

This pervasive, ethical view of kingship runs through the cantos that deal with the nature and function of kingship, the subject of investigation in this chapter. The idea that political act is at once a moral act, "a moral encounter with the universe," and that the personal cannot be divorced from the political, recalls much of medieval political philosophy and Christian humanism of the Renaissance, especially Shakespeare's great plays. William Baldwin, in his dedication of the *Mirror for Magistrates*, remarks: "The goodness or badness of any realm lieth in the goodness or badness of the ruler."[23] Max M. Reese, in *The Cease of Majesty* (London,

---

21. L. A. Cormican, "Medieval Idiom in Shakespeare," *Scrutiny*, XVII (1950), 186–202, 298–317, and Michael Quinn, "Providence in Shakespeare's Yorkist Plays," *Shakespeare Quarterly*, X (1959), 45–52.

22. Arthur F. Wright, "Sui Yang-ti: Personality and Stereotype," in *The Confucian Persuasion* (Stanford, 1960), pp. 47–76, esp. 62.

23. Ed. Lily B. Campbell (Cambridge, 1938), p. 64. Also in Claudian, *Panegyric on the Fourth Consulship of Honorius*, 302: "mobile mutatur semper cum principe vulgus," which is "the most widely quoted line in all Claudian." See Alan Cameron, *Claudian* (Oxford, 1970), p. 432.

1961), a study of Shakespeare's histories, defines "majesty" as "a recognition of mutual duty."[24] Shakespeare meant by majesty "that instinct in mankind that unites them not just for their own preservation but for the attainment of virtue,"[25] "a common awareness, on all levels of society, of the worth and integrity of the whole community and the responsibilities of citizenship."[26] As Shakespeare skillfully explores in his great plays "the nature of mutuality and its opposites,"[27] so our compilers attempt in the cantos to explore some fundamental concepts and ideals of the tradition. Political problems therefore are presented in terms of social and human relationships, for society, itself a moral idea, depends upon the quality and nature of those relationships.

The problem of rendering a specific virtue or moral problem in dramatic terms was the first the compilers had to solve. They did this by the characteristic techniques employed in the cantos, by presenting certain human situations with the utmost economy of statement and objectivity. Although the verses present only the essentials distilled from vast materials in the chronicles, often an entire career reduced to a few lines, the utmost economy and concretization were possible, because the communal values to which they refer are familiar to every schoolboy. As usual, the subjects of parallel studies in these cantos are chiefly drawn from Chinese history. In the cantos devoted to Yi Sŏng-gye, they include, in chronological order: Liu Pang (cantos 66, 76, 78–79), Liu Pei of Shu Han (canto 80), Li Shih-min (canto 77), Kuo Jung (Shih-tsung of the Later Chou; canto 73), Chao K'uang-yin (Sung T'ai-tsu; canto 81), and Qubilai (canto 82). In the cantos assigned to Yi Pang-wŏn, they comprise: Liu Pang (cantos 97, 105), Liu Heng (Han Wen-ti; canto 96), Li Yüan (canto 107), Li Shih-min (cantos 91–92, 104), Li Lung-chi (T'ang Hsüan-tsung; canto 99), Kuo Jung (canto 93), Chao K'uang-yin (canto 106), and A-pao-chi (Liao T'ai-tsu; canto 103). These are all familiar figures in Chinese history, some have often been the subjects of Confucian "mirror" literature, and their accomplishments and shortcomings as rulers were widely known. However, in their selection and emphasis of specific situations and conducts as dramatic materials, the com-

24. P. vii.
25. P. viii.
26. P. 109.
27. L. C. Knights, *Further Explorations* (Stanford, 1965), p. 22.

pilers not only reflected the attitudes and anxieties of the age, but obliquely implied judgment on the relative values of these situations. Thus their choice not only voiced the attitudes and interests of the age but underscored the vast reverberations of every action of these men. The ramifications and implications of every political act are vast in relation to the moral and cosmic order, for political problems cannot be divorced from social and human problems. And in an age when the moral nature of man was the only context, this method of presentation enabled the reader to explore and contemplate the moral reverberations of political acts.

Structurally, these cantos may be divided into two sections: (1) those in the main body of the cycle related to Yi Sŏng-gye and Yi Pang-wŏn; and (2) those in the final section (cantos 110–125), which are admonitions to Sejong and his successors. The difference in the two lies in the method of presentation. In the first, the subjects of twin studies in each canto are generally Chinese emperors, implying comparison and contrast; in the second, they are four royal ancestors, Yi Sŏng-gye, and Yi Pang-wŏn. Thus, in the first, whose main purpose is to recount and glorify the brilliant deeds chiefly of Yi Sŏng-gye and Yi Pang-wŏn, some of their cardinal virtues are presented as embodiments of their *facta*; in the second, however, King Sejong, for the first time, is addressed directly in an earnest, impassioned plea charged with hortatory overtones. The compilers' emphasis is the Renaissance theme of nurture, that their patron, Sejong, and his successors should study and emulate the right examples of their ancestors. Let us examine the first section.

The dominant theme of the cantos in the first section is *jen*, benevolence, goodness, or love, perhaps the most important single concept in Chinese philosophy. Master K'ung not only revaluated but expanded this concept as the central theme in his teaching. One who embodies the supreme virtue is a perfect man, a man among men, a guardian of social and cosmic harmony, an unalterable principle upon which a nation stands. The virtue of *jen*, the master said, is to love man (*Analects*, XII, 22).

This supreme virtue in the Confucian tradition is amply manifested by both Yi Sŏng-gye and Yi Pang-wŏn. Yi Sŏng-gye was "polite with his men, kind in words," and therefore able to stabilize the hearts of his subordinates (canto 66). He loved his stepbrother who once rose in revolt (canto 76) and his former rivals and enemies (canto 77) and showed a consistent concern for the welfare of meritorious subjects even after his enthronement, thus winning their lasting loyalty (cantos 78–79). Equally, Yi Pang-wŏn continued to love his elder brother in spite of the latter's attempt to kill him (canto 103), the scope of his magnanimity being compared to that of Aguda's leniency toward his rebelling brothers: "A benevolent man does not lay up anger," Mencius said, "nor cherish resentment against his brother, but only regards him with affection and love" (5A, 3).[28] By setting such lofty examples, they

> Inspired beautiful customs
> Which were to endure myriad years.   (canto 103)

It is, therefore up to the ruler through his virtuous deeds to demonstrate "humane manners and customs" (canto 76). The ruler is a bulwark of the state and a rampart of the realm, delegated by Heaven "to conserve that in which the people may be deficient." The mores and ethos, "humane manners and customs," embodied in the perfect ruler are therefore compared to a dike[29] which not only conserves virtue but serves as a barrier against evil. Unbound water or unbridled sea, emblems of sheer energy and power, the mutiny of appetite and will, must be confined and diverted.

Cantos 66 and 79 present contrasting examples of kingship. When Hsiang Yü, in 206 B.C., banished and murdered the King Yi of Ch'u, Liu Pang proclaimed mourning for the dead emperor. Hsiang Yü's motive, in Hu Yin's judgment,[30] was to avenge personal grievances and his murder of the emperor was a deed which Heaven and Earth could not forgive. Hence, the empire fell to Liu Pang who was able to plan strategies in his room. Hsiang Yü's inhuman deed caused the nobles to gather around Liu Pang, enabling him to found a dynasty. He is rightly praised for upholding the cause of justice but blamed for his notoriously disrespectful attitude toward his men, some of whom were finally compelled to revolt. They were, among others, Wei Pao, King of Wei, and Kuan Kao, chancellor of Chao.

---

28. Legge, II, 349.

29. *Li chi*, 15, 14a (Legge, *Sacred Books of the East*, XXVIII, 284). The same image occurs in *HS*, 56, 0496b.

30. *Tu-shih kuan-chien*, 1, 20a-b (*YG*, 8, 9b-10a).

The theme of canto 79 is the inevitable result of Liu Pang's inconsistency, which was held responsible for a series of revolts against him by Han Hsin, P'eng Yüeh, and Ch'ing Pu. In the *Li Wei-kung wen-tui*,[31] Li Shih-min asks Li Ching (571–649) why Liu Pang executed Han Hsin (196 B.C.) and P'eng Yüeh and imprisoned the prime minister Hsiao Ho. Li replies that although the success of Liu Pang was largely due to the strategy of Chang Liang and the supplies Han Hsin sent by land and water, Liu Pang, like Hsiang Yü, was unable to secure the permanent loyalty of his generals. Chang Liang, for instance, wanted to avenge the state of Han, and Ch'en P'ing and Han Hsin harbored a grudge against the state of Ch'u for not employing them. As for Han Hsin, Ts'ao Ts'an, Fan K'uai, and Kuan Ying, they all once had fled and for this reason Liu Pang later exploited them. Each had his own personal motives and accordingly Liu Pang was incapable of winning them over. Li Shih-min then asks whether Liu Hsiu (Emperor Kuang-wu) could be considered a better ruler. Li Ching concurs and goes on to argue that although Liu Hsiu's generals were not as brilliant as those of Liu Pang, Liu Hsiu was able to rally them to his cause, rely on their loyalty, and thus retain meritorious subjects. In Li Ching's estimate, therefore, Liu Hsiu was a far better ruler than Liu Pang.

Their personal motives notwithstanding, the cause of the Han generals' revolts was the emperor's suspicion and inconsistency. Unable to generate in his men a sense of complete loyalty to the state, he caused them to harbor fear and distrust. By failing to recognize his moral duty and royal responsibilities, he failed to reconcile the conflicting passions of men and to bind them ultimately with love. As the sole cause of imbalance in society, he was responsible for the rupture of order and harmony. What is underscored here is not that the emperor was able to quell the rebellions once dissension arose but that such rebellions were provoked by his mistrust (canto 66) and inconsistency (canto 79). Thus he failed the test of a good king, which Yi Sŏng-gye amply passes.

Contrarily, Liu Pang was cited for his magnanimity (canto 76) and for his capacity to inspire courage (canto 78). The apparent contradiction to find in the life of one man both good and bad qualities was a result of the didactic reading of history in order to seek whatever norms of behavior the occasion demanded. Liu

31. Quoted in *YG*, 9, 18a-20b.

P'i, nephew of the emperor's cousin Liu Chia, was made king of Wu, despite his "look of a rebel." The emperor saved him, and his magnanimity was praised by the Sung poet Su Shih.[32] The emperor was also known for his unexpected way of treating his generals, his peculiar way of inspiring courage. Lü Tsu-ch'ien cites as examples his reception of Ch'ing Pu and the four brave men of Chao.[33] He would first administer an unexpected humiliation, to be followed by unexpected honor. That he was able to win such a man as Ch'ing Pu was not enough, for he was unable to secure his lasting loyalty. By exploring the emperor's character from diverse angles, therefore, the compilers subtly show how defects in the ruler's moral nature inevitably lead to evils. The compilers' sympathy lies neither with the miscreants Han Hsin and Ch'ing Pu, for rebellion cannot be endorsed under any circumstances, nor with the emperor, for moral defect in the ruler has the widest repercussions in the empire.

Important in any inquiry into the nature of power is its justification and limits. The Confucian ruler should never be absolute, ideally at least, for he has been delegated to rule by Heaven which sees as the people see. The virtuous ruler has the opportunity to inspire and guide the people to the good by his moral example, not by arbitrary law or policy. Such moral stewardship inevitably transforms the mores and ethos, for the grass bends when the virtuous wind blows. Unselfish magnanimity, the impartial administration of justice, is the *sine qua non* of a humane government. Clemency, Seneca holds, is sovereignty's ornament and higher safety.[34] To save innocent life is the prerogative of high estate,[35] for clemency succors not only innocence but also virtue. Indeed, power must be beneficent, for frequent punishment provokes only the hatred of all.[36] With clemency, an impregnable fortress of the ruler,[37] spontaneous and unprodded innocence becomes a rule, a public good.[38]

At the same time amnesty should not be granted easily. The

32. *Tung-p'o hsü-chi* (*SPPY*), 8, 16a-b.
33. Quoted in *YG*, 9, 5b.
34. *De Clementia*, 11 (Moses Hadas, tr. *The Stoic Philosophy of Seneca* [Gloucester, 1965], p. 151).
35. *Ibid.*, 5 (Hadas, p. 144).
36. *Ibid.*, 8 (Hadas, p. 146).
37. *Ibid.*, 19 (Hadas, p. 159).
38. *Ibid.*, 23–24 (Hadas, pp. 162–163).

compilers quote the *Hua-yang kuo-chih* (canto 80) to illustrate the point. When in the sixth month of 246 an amnesty was granted, Meng Kuang reproved Fei I at a gathering: "Amnesty is a more or less worn-out thing, not proper to an age of enlightened rule. It is granted only when decadence has gone beyound remedy, under extreme circumstances when there is no other choice. Our present sovereign is good and capable, and the hundred officials are fulfilling their functions. What imminent urgency is there that such an extraordinary favor should be repeated, only to benefit the wilfully wicked?" The same source cites the remarks of Chuko Liang (181–234), who believed that the empire should be governed by great virtue, not petty kindness. Quoting the precedents of K'uang Heng in 42 B.C. and Wu Han in A.D. 44, Chu-ko Liang cites Liu Pei who once remarked, "When I studied under Ch'en Chi and Cheng Hsüan, at each instruction they taught me how to govern, but they never mentioned amnesties." In accordance with the belief in the interdependency of man and Nature, natural calamities were thought to be symbolic of misrule and injustice. Solar eclipses and other disorders in the stars and planets, earthquakes and fires, droughts and floods were construed as Heaven's warning against the rupture of the norm and occasioned the reinvestigation of cases, resulting in the reduction of punishment and granting of pardon. At times the ruler himself investigated prisoners and vindicated the innocent. The grievances of the innocently killed, argued those opposing amnesty, will offset the harmony of Nature, if offenders are freed and killers are pardoned. "Mercy but murders, pardoning those that kill" (*Romeo and Juliet*, III, i, 202). A more convincing argument is that an enlightened rule does not require "petty kindness," for if the sovereign rules by virtue and *li*, his transforming power, like the flow of a stream, will lead the people to goodness. Such ruler, therefore, has no need of punishment or amnesty.[39]

A number of cantos illustrate the ideals of justice and magnanimity of Yi Pang-wŏn, while only canto 77 is assigned to Yi Sŏng-gye. When, after his enthronement, someone proposed to kill a few Koryŏ loyalists who, dictated by their persuasion, refused to serve the new ruler, Yi Sŏng-gye is said to have spared them and

---

39. Hsü Shih-kuei, *Chung-kuo ta-she k'ao* (Shanghai, 1934), pp. 6–10; T'ung-tsu Ch'ü, *Law and Society in Traditional China* (Paris, 1961), pp. 214–218; and Derk Bodde and Clarence Morris, *Law in Imperial China* (Cambridge, Mass., 1967), pp. 19 ff.

restored them to their former rank. Yi Pang-wŏn, too, is praised for tempering justice with mercy, especially with those who were loyal to their lord (cantos 105–106). Kil Chae (1353–1415), a famous Koryŏ loyalist and Yi's schoolmate, withdrew from the world upon the collapse of the Koryŏ dynasty and, when summoned by Yi, refused to take office on the grounds that he could not serve two dynasties. But Yi understood and praised him. He granted a posthumous epithet to Chŏng Mong-ju, another Koryŏ loyalist, whom he earlier had managed to assassinate. These and other acts of magnanimity, to his erstwhile enemies, are no doubt propaganda pieces, but they are in complete accord with the Confucian tradition. That one should serve when the Way prevails but should retire when it does not is a commonplace (*Analects*, VIII, 13; XII, 10).[40] Although the master was gently ridiculed for his over-seriousness by "a man carrying a basket who passed by the house where he and his disciples were lodging in Wei" (XIV, 42),[41] both he and Mencius (2B, 5)[42] upheld the unswerving loyalty of the subject to his lord and his moral principles as the highest goal of a virtuous man. On the other hand, the master praised King Wu as having "summoned lost subjects back to prominence," thus winning the willing allegiance of the people (XX, 1).[43] Hence the tradition praised not only one who withdrew from the world for his uncompromising moral principles but also one who was big enough to summon to office those who had retired into obscurity.

The subject of parallel studies in canto 105 is Liu Pang and his dealing with Lord Ting. Once, in a battle, Lord Ting allowed Liu Pang to escape when the latter was in dire straits. At the lord's visit, however, Liu Pang ordered his execution, for by saving Liu Pang's life, Lord Ting was disloyal to his own master, causing him to lose the battle. Liu Pang doubtless wished to set an example, if not to have a sobering effect on sentimental courtiers who may have anticipated mercy, or to breed loyalty in others, as Ssu-ma Kuang seems to interpret it. The Sung historian condones the emperor's act as one of justice, a warning which elicited fear among many people, thus enabling the house of Han to secure

40. Waley, pp. 135, 165–166.
41. Waley, pp. 190–191.
42. Legge, II, 219.
43. Waley, p. 232.

Heaven's blessings for four hundred years.[44] This raises the cruel question that in some situations the impartial act of love and mercy could be interpreted as an act of disloyalty or even treason. The compilers are fully aware of the fact that the emperor here is obviously playing a propaganda part. But what are we to make of the story? Are we disposed to applaud Liu Pang who does not seem to understand the truth that the most extreme justice is the greatest injustice? The questions the compilers raise, however, concern the human validity of the emperor's excessive severity and his inability to understand the complexity of the human situation. A strong ruler is undoubtedly vital as a deterrent to probable disunity or rebellion, "For what doth cherish weeds but gentle air?" (*3 Henry VI*, II, vi, 21). But Liu Pang by his act seems to dissociate the private man from the public. A private favor done him can, he seems to imply, hardly be a deterrent to the execution of his royal occupation. Or perhaps the emphasis here is on the correct interpretation of the different duty required of a king and of his subject. The emperor's act recalls Henry V's execution in Southampton, shortly before his sail to Harfleur, of three English noblemen who have taken French gold to assassinate him:

> You have conspir'd against our royal person,
> Join'd with an enemy proclaim'd, and from his coffers
> Receiv'd the golden earnest of our death;
> Wherein you would have sold your king to slaughter,
> His princes and his peers to servitude,
> His subjects to oppression and contempt,
> And his whole kingdom into desolation.
> Touching our person seek we no revenge;
> But we our kingdom's safety must so tender,
> Whose ruin you [have] sought, that to her laws
> We do deliver you.
> (II, ii, 167–177)

Henry's verdict seems to echo Liu Pang's that a crime against the state is a most grave crime. The audiences at the Globe must have concurred with the king's decision for, as a symbol of the perfect English king, he was expected to discharge his royal profession with steely authority.

Contrarily, the reckless murder of an enemy who was discharging his duty to his lord is a deed far short of the ideal soldier, the

44. *TCTC*, 11, 360–361 (*YG*, 10, 29b–30a).

theme of the first verse of canto 106. Han T'ung, vice-general of the Later Chou army, was killed by Wang Yen-sheng, when he attempted to check the advance of the Sung army to K'ai-feng. Chao K'uang-yin, the founder of the Sung, therefore praised Han's loyalty but censured his own man's senseless fury. A soldier who does not comprehend the complexity of loyalty due one's lord is hardly qualified to lead men; he is dangerous and merciless, for he fails to understand the fact that the loyalty he expects of his subordinates is equally expected of his opponents by their commander. Indeed, one must be willing to recognize a good quality even in the enemy, if one wishes to be recognized for it by others.

The compilers drew Yi Pang-wŏn as a symbol of justice and mercy and assign no fewer than five cantos (96, 103–106) as illustrations. Here perhaps it is not unfair to see through their intention, for the picture one is likely to get from official annals is not exactly what the compilers attempt to portray him to be. He was merciless; anyone who stood in his path to success was cruelly felled. It is not surprising, therefore, that some episodes were altered to better delineate him as an example, for such changes are entirely in line with the practice of Confucian historians. In 1397 Pak Cha-an unwittingly divulged a military secret to the Japanese pirates and was sentenced to death. His son, Pak Shil, came to Yi Pang-wŏn's mansion and entreated him to pardon his father. Yi Pang-wŏn intervened on Pak's behalf and saved his life. Pak Shil was later enrolled in the palace guard as a reward for his filial piety. What moved Yi Pang-wŏn, it seems, was the son's virtue, in which he, too, was supposed to have excelled (cantos 91–93). Thus he helped perpetuate "the humane state begun by his father," as Liu Heng (Han Wen-ti), the subject of parallel study, did by saving the life of Ch'un-yü I. Again, in 1400, Cho Chun, a meritorious subject, was imprisoned on a false charge. Yi Pang-wŏn saved Cho so that he could clear his name (canto 104). The subject of parallel study for this canto is Liu Wen-ching (568–619) who, in spite of Li Shih-min's desperate plea to his father, was beheaded as a victim of his former concubine's slander and his colleague P'ei Chi's animosity. The complexity of the situation was elucidated by Hu Yin, who argues that Li Shih-min could, but dared not, save Liu's life. Liu was *his* close friend, but P'ei Chi was his father's; he could not go against his father's wishes.[45]

45. *Tu-shih kuan-chien*, 16, 40a (*YG*, 10, 26a-b omits two lines).

This brings us to a discussion of filial piety, for which Yi Pang-wŏn was distinguished. Although later ages distorted the true nature of filial piety to bolster authoritarianism, it is, according to Confucius, the "root of humanity (*jen*)" (I, 2). Family is the training ground to learn, practice, and develop not only piety to one's parents but other virtues vital to public service, which is the ultimate to be aspired to. As the basis of social cohesion, therefore, the family not only determined the norms of behavior but was an ideal place to realize the Confucian way in daily life. The subject of the first verse in cantos 91 and 92 is Li Shih-min; but canto 91 not only matches Yi Pang-wŏn and Li Shih-min for their piety but contrasts the attitudes of their fathers to their sons' filial conduct. While Li Shih-min's shedding of secret tears over his deceased mother was the cause of Li Yüan's anger (4, 27a-b), Yi Pang-wŏn's same act evoked an irresistible sympathy in Yi Sŏng-gye and his attendants. This is probably meant to be a censure partly because Chinese historians often depict Li Yüan as a vacillating and irresolute character and also because his disapproval of the son's conduct is said to have been caused by the slanderous tongues of his second wife and her attendants. Li Shih-min's piety is again revealed in the remark he made on his birthday: "How can I enjoy myself on this day when my parents toiled to rear me!"

The theme of canto 93 is the son's duty to remonstrate with his father, if necessary, and the importance of judicious interpretation of ritual observance. In 954, Kuo Wei, the founder of the Later Chou, died; Liu Ch'ung (later Min) of the Later (or Eastern) Han enticed the Khitans and invaded the Later Chou. Kuo Jung of the Later Chou then asked Feng Tao to entomb the royal coffin, but himself went to Kao-p'ing to punish the invaders. Although normally one was not to attend to other matters during the mourning, if the fate of a state was at stake, one should act expediently. As Po-ch'in[46] who, during the mourning for his father, marched against the Yi of the Huai and the Jung of the Hsü to secure the state of Lu, so Kuo Jung fought the Khitan invaders at close quarters so as to solidify the imperial works of the Later Chou. Thus he won the approval of Hu An-kuo (1074–1138) for

---

46. *Shang shu*, 13, 2b (Legge, III, 621). The information, however, appears in canto 24 (*YG*, 4, 15b). *SC*, 33, 0127c.

having carefully weighed the gravity of the matter.[47] To Yi Pang-wŏn is attributed the same judiciousness and acumen when, in spite of his father's insistence that he return to the side of his mother's grave to complete the period of mourning,[48] he retreated to his quarters to plan the murder of Chŏng Mong-ju. Had he not done so, the compilers ask,

> Could he have achieved
> The merits of the foundation?

Probably not, for had Chŏng Mong-ju lived, he might have culled enough strength to block their path to success. By disobeying his father's wishes, he helped found the new kingdom. No canto is assigned to Yi Sŏng-gye's filial conduct, partly because by being true to the memory of his ancestors and by continuing the royal work initiated by them, he had singularly performed the acts of filial piety.

When the compilers took the trouble to interpret Yi Pang-wŏn's seemingly unfilial act as a vital service for the foundation of the dynasty, it is not surprising that they devote two cantos to a woman, Yi Pang-wŏn's wife, for her political sagacity, courage, and determination. While Socrates—and later the Stoics—taught that women had the same nature and virtue as men, which Plato interpreted to mean women must become as much like men as possible, "even serving in the army," Aristotle maintained women were by nature inferior to men,[49] and so did Confucius (*Analects*, XVII, 25)[50] and his commentators. On the other hand, the Confucian tradition inspired many moral anecdotes about women, like the *Lieh-nü chuan* (*Lives of Famous Women*) stories designed to illustrate and emulate such virtues as chastity, constancy, obedience, or piety. Popular literature often contains accounts of similar deeds by women, sometimes their heroic acts, resembling Plutarch's *Mulierum Virtutes* or the exemplary lives of female worthies in Elizabethan England. Like the heroines in Plutarch's lives (Telessila of Argos [4] and Cloelia of Rome [14]) or the Bible (Judith, Deborah, Esther) or historical personages (Isabella of

---

47. Quoted in *YG*, 4, 15a-b.
48. Arthur Waley, *Three Ways of Thought in Ancient China* (London, 1946), pp. 129–134.
49. Philip A Stadter, *Plutarch's Historical Methods: An Analysis of the Mulierum Virtutes* (Cambridge, Mass., 1965), pp. 3–4.
50. Waley, pp. 216–217.

Spain, Joanna of Naples, Joan of Arc, Mary Stuart) in Renaissance moral lives[51]—all embodiments of martial prowess, magnificence, chastity, temperance, or wisdom—the subjects of cantos 108 and 109 are cited for their role in moments of national crisis. In 1398 Chŏng To-jŏn invited the princes to the palace to massacre them. Yi Pang-wŏn's wife feigned illness, sent for him, and devised with him a strategy which eventually caught the evil Chŏng by surprise. In the same canto this account is matched with a similar deed performed by the wife of Wang Kŏn, the founder of Koryŏ, whose cogent argument and encouragement were held to be responsible for Wang's decision to oppose his tyrannous master and found his own kingdom. The theme of parallel lives in canto 109, actually, is a woman's heroic resolve to follow her husband to death. Here Lady Min, Yi Pang-wŏn's wife, is compared in her resolve to the wife of King Wen of Chou, the putative author of the third poem[52] in the *Book of Songs*, from which the compilers derived much of the vocabulary. Upon seeing a horse that belonged to her husband's stable returning with an arrow in its flank during a princely feud in 1400, Lady Min thought her husband had lost the battle and resolved to follow him into death. The wife of a great man is equally great, the poems seem to say, but the compilers' intention was no doubt to honor the mother of Sejong, their patron, as a great queen and mother.

No Confucian mirror for the perfect prince is complete without illustration of the importance of learning. The *Analects* begin with the famous sentence every schoolboy knows by heart, "Is it not a pleasure to learn and to repeat or practice from time to time what has been learned?" Again, the master said to Tsu-lu, "One who loves humanity but not learning will be obscured by ignorance. One who loves wisdom but not learning will be obscured by lack of principle" (XVII, 8).[53] Therefore, Yi Sŏng-gye, fully accoutered in armor, read books between battles in order to learn the art of government (canto 80), as Liu Pei of Shu Han did by receiving instruction from Ch'en Chi and Cheng Hsüan. Regretting that his family had hitherto not produced any scholar, Yi

51. *Mulierum Virtutes*, 4 (Stadter, pp. 45–53), 14 (pp. 80–84); Celeste T. Wright, "The Elizabethan Female Worthies," *Studies in Philology*, XLIII (1946), 628–643. See also Bowra, *Heroic Poetry*, pp. 480–492, for the treatment of women in heroic poetry.

52. Legge, IV, 8–9; Karlgren, pp. 3–4; Waley, no. 40, p. 45.

53. Chan, p. 47.

Sŏng-gye also urged his son to pursue classical learning. Yi Pang-wŏn eventually passed the final civil service examination in 1383. Yi Sŏng-gye's respect for scholarship is also manifested in his courteous reception of Yi Saek, when the latter returned from his banishment in 1391:

> Upon receiving an old scholar
> He knelt down with due politeness.   (canto 82)

This account is matched in the first verse by Qubilai's equally polite and reverential reception accorded two Koryŏ scholars in 1290 who accompanied the Koryŏ heir apparent to the Mongol capital. While Qubilai received the heir apparent, a grandson by his daughter (future King Ch'ungsŏn), leant against a stool, but before interviewing the two learned men, he donned his cap and paid them the respect due Confucian scholars. No doubt, Yi Sŏng-gye and Qubilai were setting examples required by accepted decorum, but their respect for scholars as transmitters of Confucian tradition was double tribute to the tradition which furnished the political and moral ideology so vital to the maintenance of order and to the values and ideals which are timeless in Confucian universalism.

Yet another theme vital to any inquiry into the nature of kingship, which occurs particularly in canto 107, is that of Confucian orthodoxy. This concept is in the form of a suppression of heresy, in this case Buddhism, which was proscribed by Yi Pang-wŏn for the same reasons by which other monarchs justified their measures. The advocates of anti-Buddhist propaganda during the reign of Emperor Wu of the Northern Wei (446) and the southern dynasties, for example, justified their phobia in nationalist terms: that Buddhism, a foreign religion, is alien, inferior, barbaric, seditious, or impractical, or a combination of all these vices. Worst of all, it is subversive of public morality, for it disturbs the five relations upon which social harmony depends. Instigated by Fu I (554–639), Li Yüan reduced the number of monasteries and monks in his realm, the subject of the first verse. Han Yü's anti-Buddhist memorial on the Buddha's bone[54] and the Hui-ch'ang persecution of 845 by Wu-tsung were chiefly nationalist and practical in their

---

54. For Han Yü's anti-Buddhist memorial on relics, see "Memorial on the Bone of Buddha," *Sources of Chinese Tradition* (New York, 1960), pp. 427–429.

motives.[55] Sung neo-Confucianists attacked the doctrine of *sunyata*, elevated instead the concept of *jen* as all-embracing principle, and urged the monks to return to normal life as members of society.

In Korea, Buddhism had been the state religion for almost eight hundred years before it was branded as a heterodoxy by the Yi founders. All that is admirable in Silla culture, we must admit, is chiefly Buddhist; and this to a great extent is also true of Koryŏ culture. And it would not surprise us, if Yi Sŏng-gye's ancestors also practiced some form of Buddhism. This is likely at least in a birth story of Yi's grandfather, Tojo (d. 1342), who according to canto 21 was born as a miraculous response from Avalokiteśvara to Ikcho and his wife's prayers at the cave of Avalokiteśvara on Mount Nak. Before the birth of Tojo, Ikcho dreamt of a monk who foretold the birth of a son and asked him to name the child Sŏllae, the childhood name of Tojo. Sŏllae, a Chinese version of Sanskrit *Svāgata* meaning "Well come" or "welcome,"[56] is the name of an attendant of Buddha, one of 12,000 monks present at the Vulture Peak where the Buddha preached. But his great-grandson, Yi Pang-wŏn, espoused Confucianism, at least officially, and rejected Buddhism as a voice of the state, not his own voice. King Sejong, however, to whom the *Songs* are dedicated, was devout in the religion. What startles the modern reader approaching the subject from the vantage of modern perspective is the compilers' inconsistencies, in one place extolling the Buddha's miracle, or at least the divine nature of one of the royal ancestors, and in another condemning with equal conviction the very faith that all the Yi kings privately espoused. Neither the compilers nor their age detected this incongruity, for what they preach here is the fact that the test of an ideal king is his ability and courage to uphold orthodoxy. By siding with Yi Pang-wŏn, their patron's father, the compilers probably intended to imply an indirect criticism of King Sejong's private practices. We might add that such inconsistencies are characteristic not only of the *Songs* but of most compilations of this kind, whose material is drawn both from history and legend, official political philosophy and popular tradition.

---

55. Kenneth K. S. Ch'en, "Anti-Buddhist Propaganda during the Nan-ch'ao," *HJAS*, XV (1952), 166–192 (for bibliography see his *Buddhism in China* [Princeton, 1964], pp. 517–518); "Economic Background of the Hui-ch'ang Persecution," *HJAS*, XIX (1956), 67–105 (*Buddhism in China*, p. 522).

56. *HJAS*, IX (1947), 223–224.

We recall that in the history of the Koryŏ dynasty, the most frequent charge brought against the third last ruler, Shin U, is that he was an offspring of the corrupt monk Shin Ton (d. 1371). Shin U and his heir were therefore branded "rebels" and their accounts are relegated to the very last sections of the history (chaps. 132–137), instead of the annals section (*sega*). Shin Ton was also the tempter and seducer of King Kongmin. As a rebel and perpetrator of evil, he was painted in the darkest hues, so that posterity would view him with fascination and horrified revulsion as he was brought to his doom. This accomplished, it was easy to ascribe the fall of Koryŏ to the "teachings of a crafty wizard of the Western barbarians": Buddhism.[57] The ritualistic portrayal of the evils and crimes suffered by the nation at the hands of the rebels is a favorite device of Confucian historiography. The ritual is usually enacted at the end of each dynasty, when the nation is torn between good and evil forces, but always emerges victoriously in the end. The restoration of divinely willed order is the work of a dynastic founder, a chastiser of evil. And the celebration of the reassertion of order through the deeds of such a founder is a parallel ritual. That is the scheme of rewards and punishments in a planned universe. And the dramatists (official historians) who created protagonists and antagonists in their versions of official history delighted in inflicting terrible punishment upon an evildoer. The moral and political purposes of this ritual are stressed in all dynastic histories. The emphasis is not only on the inevitable fall from weal to woe, the usual material of tragedy in the Middle Ages and the Renaissance,[58] but on the validity of re-volution, elevated by divine, moral sanction. The proscription of Buddhism as a heterodoxy is therefore one of the shrewdest, and in our context possibly the only, means of fostering Confucian orthodoxy, the ideology upon which the new dynasty was built.

In the final section of the *Songs*, the compilers address King Sejong directly. This is the right place to do so, because the compilers' creative power was kindled by their very subject, which demanded not only praise but admonition, and was inspired by their patron, whom they often compared to Yao and Shun and to whom the cycle is dedicated. The compilers came a

---

57. *JHI*, XII (1951), 42–43.
58. Clifford Leech, *Shakespeare's Tragedies* (New York, 1950), pp. 3–20, and Willard Farnham, *The Medieval Heritage of Elizabethan Tragedy* (Berkeley, 1936).

long way to utter the earnest, impassioned exclamation, *nimgŭmha*, "O king," but also "who will wear the crown," namely future monarchs. The House of Yi would continue without end, so they believed, and by the dramatic use of this phrase of three syllables, they were able to insist that their work, though the product of a particular time, would convey timeless truths: *Ittŭdŭl nitti marŭsyŏsyo* is therefore repeated no less than fifteen times (cantos 110–124), triumphantly observing decorum, culminating in canto 125. *Ttŭt* is one of those ambiguous and complex words in Korean, and the latest Korean-English dictionary lists no fewer than sixteen meanings.[59] In ordinary contexts, the probable range of meaning includes "a latent meaning," "a hidden purport," "a symbolic significance," or "an earnest wish." But here, the word embraces at once the allegorical and moral meanings. This is the contextual sense of the word, the primacy given properly to the moral implications with enhancing suggestions.

Shakespeare, in *Macbeth*, presented his list of "king-becoming graces":

> . . . justice, verity, temp'rance, stableness,
> Bounty, perseverance, mercy, lowliness,
> Devotion, patience, courage, fortitude, . . .
> (IV, iii, 92–94)

These twelve qualities are present in Malcolm, son of Duncan, king of Scotland, who represents Shakespeare's final portrait of the ideal king.[60] After celebrating Korea's greatness through the deeds of four royal ancestors and the first and third monarchs of the dynasty, it is therefore most fitting for the *Songs* to enumerate what the age considered to be the most important virtues expected of a king, the sole defender of the established order.

The theme of cantos 110–113 is the evil of ease and luxury. Some royal ancestors, chased and humiliated, had to move from place to place, seeking a safer place to settle. Ikcho, for example, suffered the treachery of the Jürched chiefs (cantos 4–5) and bore hardships in a clay hut, reminiscent of Tan-fu:

59. Samuel E. Martin *et al.*, eds. *A Korean-English Dictionary* (New Haven, 1967), pp. 544b-545a.
60. Irving Ribner, *The English History Play in the Age of Shakespeare* (Princeton, 1957), p. 256; repeated in *Patterns in Shakespearean Tragedy* (London, 1960), p. 160.

> Of old Tan-fu the duke
> Scraped shelters, scraped holes;
> As yet they had no houses.[61]

In halcyon days, one who lived in a "deep sumptuous palace," a "large carpeted hall" and sat on the "richly embroidered throne" was likely to forget the toils of his ancestors and his people. Yi Sŏng-gye, Sejong's grandfather, responded to the nation's challenge and spent much of his life in repulsing the invaders and subjugating the rebels. He had no time to doff his armor (canto 112), nor to have food and drink (canto 113). Wrapped in royal robe and girt with a belt of precious gems, when you sup "northern viands and southern dainties" or "when you drink superb wine," think twice, our king, the compilers plead. These outer trappings are in accord with the convention and decorum demanded of a monarch, but he should not be blinded by external pomp:

> . . . a prince's delicates,
> His viands sparkling in a golden cup,
> His body couched in a curious bed, . . .
> (*3 Henry VI*, II, v, 51–53)

As a model for the people, a ruler must not indulge himself but establish a pattern of modesty and humility. In the histories, one of the most frequent charges against a tyrant, like the last Shang king Chou or Sui Yang-ti, is his self-indulgence and licentiousness. The compilers are not warning King Sejong, a sage king who was looked upon by the age as the "courtier's, soldier's, scholar's, eye, tongue, sword," but his successors who, through a period of continuous peace and prosperity, might be content to rest in "great chairs of ease," oblivious of royal responsibilities. The compilers' anxiety is fully justified, for the later periods witnessed Yŏnsan'gun, who viewed his office as the source of personal gratification and who consequently was depicted by chroniclers as a Confucian tyrant.

Peace is "a quiet Nurse of Idleness" in Fulke Greville's words,[62] and that decadence and excessive civilization eventually lead to decline have been amply attested by historians, East and West. Renaissance thinkers, especially Elizabethan writers, deftly de-

---

61. *Book of Songs*, 237 (Waley, p. 248).
62. Quoted in Paul A. Jorgensen, *Shakespeare's Military World* (Berkeley, 1956), p. 186 (sonnet 108 to Caelica, lines 7–8).

scribed in morbid imagery the "peace-bred imperfections of a state," finally leading to a decline in heroic aptitude.[63] War, especially a foreign war, is often a test of national unity and a cure for civil dissension.[64] Alcibiades, in *Timon of Athens*, criticizes the senatorial corruption, a disease bred by peace, plenty, and pride:

> Now breathless Wrong
> Shall sit and pant in your great chairs of ease,
> And pursy Insolence shall break his wind
> With fear and horrid flight.
> (V, iv, 10–13)

The blessings of peace often breed falsehood, deceit, licentiousness, and injustice. Only some fifty years ago the nation withstood successfully rebellions and invasions, and the northern borders are still harassed by barbarian incursions. Peace should not breed evil but heroic courage and resolve so desperately needed for national independence and stability. It must heal the cleavage between the court and the castle, and emulate the supreme example of the dynastic founder, the ideal of the complete Confucian soldier and statesman. The compilers, like their exalted patron, are fully aware of the ills peace might breed. Sejong's heirs must therefore be aroused to see in Yi Sŏng-gye an ideal mirror of a complete ruler versed in war and peace. This was the age's concern, which found expression in the *Songs*.

The following cantos, 114 and 115, amplify the theme from differing viewpoints with different meanings. The trials suffered and withstood by the dynastic founder have already been discussed. When the "wolves" (canto 111), the Red Turbans, and the Japanese pirates, wrought havoc, Yi Sŏng-gye suffered wounds and scars (canto 114). The dynasty is the fruit of such trials and pains. When a ruler, protected by stately guards, rules the kingdom effortlessly with "dangling robes and folded hands," he should ask himself whether he truly deserves the office, whether he is equal to royal responsibilities. Again, the blessings of peace should only make the ruler resolve to exercise his ordained duty, "specialty of rule," with justice and mercy.

> When you have men at your beck and call,
> When you punish men and sentence men,

63. Jorgensen, p. 188.
64. *2 Henry IV*, IV, v, 213–216 (Reese, p. 315).

Remember, my Lord,
His mercy and temperance. (canto 115)

"When all your ministers say that a man should be executed, do not listen to them," Mencius warned King Hsüan of Ch'i. "When all your great officers say so, do not listen to them. When all your people say so, look into the case, and if you find that the person should be executed, then execute him. It is therefore said that the people executed him. Only in this way can a ruler become parent of the people" (1B, 7).[65] The statutes of a benevolent ruler tally with the will of Heaven and of the people, the unchanging law, and if a ruler is truly virtuous, there is no need for the statutes at all. "Under a true king, the people feel magnificent and at ease with themselves," Mencius again expounded. "Though he punishes them by death, they do not complain" (7A, 13).[66] These are King Sejong's measures to humanize the penal code: sentencing of a criminal only after three deliberations; prohibition of flogging with the bamboo on the buttock (1430); punishment of those who willfully killed their slaves without a prior appeal to the government (1444); or a thorough investigation of disputable cases in the light of the precedents.[67] Seneca, in *De Clementia* (I, 2),[68] preached that punishment should be graded to the offense, in the famous simile of a physician who applies simple remedies first and grave measures only as a last resort. Dio Chrysostom (40–?117) compared a benevolent king to a shepherd, and a cruel master like Xerxes or Darius to a butcher.[69]

Consequently, one of the severest charges against a tyrant is his butchery of the loyal and good. Every civilization has an archetype for such a butcher. In Chinese, it is the last Shang king, Chou, who not only imprisoned and enslaved but burned and roasted the loyal and good. He cut out the heart of worthy people, much as Thomas Preston's tyrant, Cambises, inspired by Herodotus, sent a deadly arrow through the heart of Praxaspes' young son for the minister's remonstrance against drunkenness.[70] Chou

65. Legge, II, 166.
66. Legge, II, 455.
67. See *HGS*, III, 89, 264, and *SnS*, 50, 20b-21a; 105, 24b-25a (*KT*, 5, 3).
68. Hadas, p. 140.
69. "On Kingship," IV, 44, tr. J. W. Cohoon, I (LCL, 1949), 189.
70. Ribner, pp. 54–55 and Armstrong's article cited above. See also Plutarch, "Brotherly Love," in *Moralia*, VI, 311–312; Herodotus, III, 30.

murdered his own son, Pi-kan, Cambises, his virtuous younger brother Smirdnis, and Greville's Alaham, his father and brother. But there is no immediate vengeance of Heaven upon the transgressor's caprice and defiance. Evil must run its full course, if history is to accomplish its purpose. It is the enigma of Heaven's mysterious design. Heaven's wrath could not stir the conscience of a despot to "a moral victory in the midst of ruin"; it is the work of Heaven's deputy to wreak vengeance and reassert moral order. Such is the scheme of rewards and punishments in an ordained universe, and the convention of Confucian historiography.

The perfect king is one versed in the human heart. Upon seeing the dead bodies that covered the hills and plains during the 1380 campaign against the Japanese, Yi Sŏng-gye could neither sleep nor eat (canto 116). He saw as the compassionate Heaven saw, for "a government that cannot bear to see the suffering of the people is conducted [by] a mind that cannot bear to see the suffering of others" (*Mencius*, 2A, 6).[71] The man of humanity is naturally at ease with humanity (*Analects*, IV, 2), for only he "knows how to love people" (IV, 3) and "be free from evil" (IV, 4). Once a ruler rules with the transforming power of love, "all within the four seas are brothers" (XII, 5). We recall that Mencius branded Chieh of Hsia and Chou of Shang as "bandits" because they injured humanity (1B, 8).[72] If a ruler observes the golden rule (*Analects*, XII, 2), his only question would be: "Is this to the advantage of all my subjects?"[73] Such a ruler could hardly burden the people:

If you are unaware of people's sorrow,
Heaven will abandon you.
Remember, my Lord,
His labor and love.   (canto 116)

One such burden is taxation, the theme of cantos 73 and 120. The first singles out Yi Sŏng-gye for his land reform in 1391:

Because robbers poisoned the people,
He initiated a land reform.   (canto 73)

Here "robbers" are powerful families who monopolize land, poisoning the people's welfare. The event is matched in the first verse

71. Legge, II, 201–204.
72. Legge, II, 167.
73. Erasmus, *The Education of a Christian Prince*, I (Born, p. 161).

by that of Kuo Jung, Shih-tsung of the Later Chou (951–960), who distributed in 958 a "well-field" chart to military governors and magistrates and, together with local authorities, carried out land reform over the entire area of Honan and part of Hopei. Canto 120 reiterates the deed celebrated in canto 73. "To a king the people are 'heaven,' " exclaimed Li I-chi, "and to the people food is heaven."[74] To burden the people, "the root of a country," is to uproot the nation's foundation. Hence,

> If a ruler taxes his people without measure,
> The basis of the state will crumble.   (canto 120)

The next topic is modesty (canto 117), and its counterpart, pride. The compilers have correctly seen the evil of flattery, common to all historical and political literature in East and West. Asked what animal was the most dangerous of all, Plutarch, in *How to Tell a Flatterer from a Friend* (19), answered: "If you mean among the wild beast, I will say the tyrant; if among the tamed ones, the flatterer."[75] With a pleasing poison, this despicable and dangerous beast says and does what will give pleasure, a pander to his master's passions of self-esteem and pride, a fawning dog begging for sweetmeats. Plutarch's similes brilliantly characterize the flatterers: a bore-worm, vermin, cuttle-fish, gadfly, ape, and a crab,

> Whose body is all belly; eyes that look
> All ways; a beast that travels on it teeth.[76]

We can best protect ourselves against him when we remember that our soul has two sides; truthfulness and irrationality, love of the honorable and of falsehood.[77] *King Lear* comes readily to mind. In order to avenge the injury done to his self-love and to demonstrate his power, he banishes Cordelia for her outspoken sincerity and refusal to offer flattering vows and promises. The play has been described variously: a tragedy of wrath in old age, a study in Christian patience, a process of self-discovery, or a study in

74. *SC*, 97, 0228c (Watson, I, 271).
75. *Moralia*, I (LCL, 1949), 327.
76. "How to Tell a Flatterer from a Friend," 1 (*Moralia*, I, 267), 8 (I, 285), 12 (I, 299), 23 (I, 345), 9 (I, 291), respectively.
77. *Ibid.*, 20 (*Moralia*, I, 327).

human relation as the ultimate reality of human being;[78] it might as well be a tragedy of lack of family piety, caused by Lear's pride. Once the basis of society, the family, crumbles, its reverberations will inevitably affect not only the social but the moral and cosmic order as well. These implications of a planned universe of rewards and punishments notwithstanding, Lear succumbs to flattery and cannot accept faithful reprimands. He does not understand Kent's righteous anger at his injustice. Only

> Time shall unfold what plighted cunning hides;
> Who covers faults, at last shame [them] derides.
> (I, i, 283–284)

Flatterers are equally slanderers. The *Book of Songs* already compared them to "shell-brocades"[79] for their fabrication, and their pretensions and artful words to a "reed organ."[80]

> Jibber-jabber, blither-blather!
> Their idea of "counsel" is to slander men.[81]

They are best served as offerings to "jackals and tigers." These ancient songs anticipated Plutarch's description of the flatterer (and slanderer) when he compared him to "an extravagant wrought picture, which by means of gaudy pigments, irregular folds in the garments, wrinkles, and sharp angles, strives to produce an impression of vividness."[82] Lucian defines slander as a "clandestine accusation, made without the cognizance of the accused and sustained by the uncontradicted assertion of one side."[83] The slanderer is a soldier in ambush, whose drives are deceit, falsehood, perjury, insistence, impudence, and a thousand other unprincipled means. He flourishes where envy is great, suspicions are countless, occasions for flattery and slander are frequent, such as at court. Man succumbs to it partly because of his fondness for novelty and

78. *Shakespeare's Tragic Heroes* (New York, 1961), pp. 175–207. John F. Danby, *Poets on Fortune's Hill* (London, 1952), p. 105 and *Shakespeare's Doctrine of Nature* (London, 1961); Maynard Mack, *King Lear in Our Time* (Berkeley, 1965), p. 102. Cf. Ribner, pp. 249–250; Honor Matthews, *Character and Symbol in Shakespeare's Plays* (Cambridge, 1962), pp. 138–162, 200; and Paul A. Jorgensen, *Lear's Self-Discovery* (Berkeley, 1967).

79. *Book of Songs*, 200 (Waley, pp. 315–316). Philip Wheelwright, *The Burning Fountain* (Bloomington, 1954), pp. 117–118, for the symbolism of "weaving."

80. *Book of Songs*, 198 (Karlgren, p. 148; Waley does not translate this poem).

81. *Book of Songs*, 200 (Waley, p. 315).

82. "How to Tell a Flatterer from a Friend," 22 (*Moralia*, I, 235).

83. "Slander," Lucian, I (LCL, 1953), 367.

his ennui and weakness to be attracted by rumors, slyly whispered stories, packed with innuendo.[84] Canto 123 emphasizes the saving of the innocent, the victims of the acrid tongue and treacherous design. The compilers cite as example Yi Pang-wŏn's ability to penetrate intrigue, the sign of a strong and astute king. The broadsides against those who succumbed to calumny probably are a most edifying part of histories and popular literature. Hence a tirade against the last Koryŏ king, Kongyang, who succumbed to that "vice very ugly and monstrous."[85]

The minister's job is, among others, to warn his ruler of the danger of flatterers and slanderers. The less-than-ideal ruler given to self-love is certain to construe every honest admonition as an attack on his person rather than on his deed, an injury to his self-esteem and pride. The upright minister who risks life to admonish the transgressing ruler has had a long history in East (characters of Confucian martyrology) and West. As the *raison d'état*, the minister should not be afraid of "denouncing people to their faces" or "wrangle before his master." The episodes cited in canto 121 deal with Liu Pang and Yi Pang-wŏn. The former concerns Chi Pu, who as a commander of Hsiang Yü's army several times made serious trouble for Liu Pang. After the destruction of Hsiang Yü, Liu Pang mercilessly hunted down Chi Pu in order to avenge him. Persuaded by Lord T'eng that such pettiness because of some private resentment is dangerous to the state, the emperor finally pardoned Chi Pu. The second verse cites how Yi Pang-wŏn forgave the rebels who joined his younger brother's revolt to claim the throne in 1398 (cantos 98, 106). In fact, the first episode, in the form of an interlinear gloss (10, 49b), is introduced only to reinforce the message, for the general scheme in the last section of the *Songs* does not call for parallel lives. The occasion however offered the compilers a chance to uphold past examples as the characteristics of a wise sovereign.

The minister's honest criticism should be a frank admonition, friendly, modest, and noble, but not faultfinding. The ruler should therefore not be stirred to anger, like Lear and Chu Yüan-chang (Ming T'ai-tsu), for example, but search his mind to discover his shortcomings. The compilers did not assign a separate canto to anger, but it is implied throughout the section. *The Mean*

84. Lucian, I, 379, 383.
85. Elyot, *The Governour*, III, 27 (Everyman's Library ed., p. 288).

(20) enjoined the ruler to be respectful to the great ministers as one of the nine standards by which to administer the state. Because ideally every word the superior man utters becomes the pattern of the world (*The Mean*, 29), he does not resort to anger and the people are awed (*The Mean*, 33). Isocrates, in *To Nicocles*, urged the ruler never to act in anger but to be careful to govern himself so that his control may be an example to his people.[86] Marcus Aurelius recommended that the man in power should be slow to take vengeance.[87] After comparing a quiet, deliberate reign to a serene, shining sky, Seneca argues that for a king even a raised voice and intemperate language are a degradation of majesty, for his fierce temper is the insatiable bane of a nation.[88] According to the *Policraticus* (1129) of John of Salisbury, the good prince should "accept with patience the words of free speaking."[89] After mentioning the frank, tempered advice offered by Solon to Croesus, Socrates to Alcibiades, Cyrus to Cyaxares, Plato to Dion, and Demaratus to Philip, Plutarch recommends that the true friend should not offer advice in the manner of a schoolmaster.[90] Unwholesome seasonings of free speech as arrogance, ridicule, scoffing, and scurrility must be eliminated. Plutarch disapproves of public censure, citing the unfortunate examples of Plato and Pythagoras, and goes on to illustrate the point: "For error should be treated as a foul disease, and all admonition and disclosure should be in secret, with nothing of show or display in it to attract a crowd of witnesses and spectators. For it is not like friendship, but sophistry, to seek for glory in other men's faults, and to make a fair show before the spectators, like the physicians who perform operations in the theatres with an eye to attracting patients."[91] However, the more despotic and capricious the ruler becomes, the louder becomes his minister's remonstrance. As the conscience of the state, the censorial organs played an important part in the Confucian bureaucracy, and the histories are replete with examples of loyal ministers who scorned axe and sword.

Ministerial service is in general a thankless job. Some were

86. Isocrates, I, tr. George Norlin (LCL, 1961), 57–59.
87. VI, 6 (tr. C. R. Haines [LCL, 1961], p. 133). See also, XI, 14 (p. 311) on anger and flattery.
88. I, 7 (Hadas, p. 145); I, 26 (Hadas, p. 165).
89. VII, 25 (Dickinson, p. 324).
90. "How to Tell a Flatterer from a Friend," 34 (*Moralia*, I, 387).
91. *Ibid.*, 27 (*Moralia*, I, 359); 32 (I, 377).

parasites of a credulous and vacillating king, susceptible to influence and prompt in disavowal. Some fraudulently exploited the Confucian code of morality, interpreting every popular outcry as the voice of Heaven in order to further their own petty prestige. Some vigilant ones, however, in an attempt to bridge the terrible distance between ideal and reality, sought to censure a ruler who exploited that same doctrine for despotic purposes. Enough has been said about the conflict latent in Confucian ideology between monarchy and bureaucracy, action and knowledge, ideal and reality, convention and protest.[92] History demonstrates unmistakably both the virtues and vices of the censorial organs in the Yi dynasty. In their eagerness for upholding traditional norms and values and their literal interpretations of the classics, they often were an instrument, rather than restraint, of despotism.[93] The complexity of man and motive notwithstanding, we would do injustice to the compilers if we did not recognize the honesty and urgency of the problem of the age. It is more appropriate, if not easier, to believe in the compilers' honesty than to read into their plan an insinuation of their self-aggrandizement. As spokesmen and guardians of Confucian mores and ethos, it is their duty to point out the place of honest criticism and disinterested opinion required of the minister. For if they wrangle before a king, it is only to "assist and secure the throne" (canto 121).

Canto 118 celebrates the transforming power of virtue as the bulwark of order, the only means to conquer separatism. We should recall here our discussion about cantos 9, 53, 55, 56, and 75, how Yi Sŏng-gye's majesty and humanity attracted the Jürched into submission. Transformed by his good government, Jürched chiefs stopped their dispute and composed their differences (canto 75), just as King Wen's bright virtue caused the rulers of Yü and Jui to feel shame for their petty squabbling (canto 11; cf. *Book of Songs*, 237; *The Great Learning*, 3). We should also recall the motif that characterizes a hero: the willing allegiance of the people. When Tan-fu, great grandson of Hou Chi, left Pin and settled below Mount Ch'i, the young and old followed him like people flocking to market (canto 6). Similarly, the willing people fol-

92. David S. Nivison and Arthur F. Wright, eds. *Confucianism in Action* (Stanford, 1959), pp. 1–24; Arthur F. Wright, ed. *The Confucian Persuasion* (Stanford, 1960), pp. 177–201.

93. Charles O. Hucker, *The Censorial System in Ming China* (Stanford, 1966).

lowed the course of Ikcho's migration (cantos 4, 6). Hence, Yi
Sŏng-gye is praised here as having "won the support of everyone
under Heaven," an unmistakable sign of a great man according to
Mencius (2B, 1).[94] When the virtuous king reigns, even the
tundra comes under census (canto 56).

> He opened the four borders,
> Men on islands had no more fear of pirates.
> Southern barbarians beyond our waters,
> How could they not come to him?
> (canto 53)

The first verse of the same canto sings the authority and prestige
of Li Shih-min:

> He pacified the four seas,
> Travelers need not take packed rice.

At the christening of Princess Elizabeth in *Henry VIII*, Cranmer,
Archbishop of Canterbury, utters an eloquent prophecy of the
glory the infant will bring to England:

> In her days every man shall eat in safety
> Under his own vine what he plants, and sing
> The merry songs of peace to all his neighbours.
> (V, v, 34-36)

Such is the picture of a golden era literature presents.

Therefore, "even his kin will rebel" against a ruler unmindful of
the cultivation of moral virtue—the inward power. One who cannot set his household in order is hardly expected to act as defender
of national mores and custodian of the way of the Former Kings.
How regulation of the family is necessary to public order is illustrated in canto 119, by one of the Five Relationships, brotherly
love. I have already discussed how Yi Sŏng-gye and Yi Pang-wŏn
are pictured as norms of the five universal ways, especially in their
relations with their brothers. In spite of fraternal rebellions in 1371
against Yi Sŏng-gye and in 1398 and 1400 against Yi Pang-wŏn,
both rulers loved the ambitious malcontents and their ties
remained firm.

> If brothers are split,
> A villain will enter and sow discord.
> (canto 119)

94. Legge, II, 210.

Good brothers are "generous and indulgent," while bad ones "mutually do harm to each other."[95] A separatism caused by brotherly rivalry, which almost plunged the dynasty into chaos, was still strong in the compilers' memory. Hence their earnest plea.

The theme of canto 122 is the importance of learning. Confucius already declared the superiority of learning over meditation (*Analects*, XV, 30) and went on to remark that "love of learning is akin to wisdom" (*The Mean*, 20). Wisdom is among the most important qualities required of the perfect prince in East and West. Plato, in the *Republic*, expounded that "the true lover of learning will be absorbed in the delight of the spirit," for a philosopher-ruler is able to penetrate the shadow into the realities.[96] Plutarch compared a prince without education to a golden statue filled with clay, stone, and lead.[97] Synesius (?370–413) also recommended study of philosophy as a means to regulate the prince's life.[98] Indeed, no one can be a good prince who is not also a philosopher.[99] Believing that learning is better than riches, Sir Thomas Elyot, in the *Governour*, writes of wisdom as "that parte of Sapience that of necessitie must be in euery gouernour of a iuste or perfeyte publike weale" (III, 23).

That the prince must remain watchful at night (Plato, *Laws*, VI, 758),[100] although in a different context, is echoed in *The Mean* to the effect that the superior man is watchful over himself when he is alone, examining his own heart (1, 20).[101] One who is able to bring man and Nature into harmony is an embodiment of the Way of Heaven, sincerity (*ch'eng*), and such a ruler is one with Heaven. Indeed, the ruler must be able to impose moral order on the world of history. The compilers therefore went to *The Mean* for inspiration, the religious and mystical tractate on human nature, the way of Heaven, harmony between man and Nature, and sincerity. By identifying the dynastic founder as a "counter-

95. *Book of Songs*, 223 (Karlgren, p. 177). Cf. Plutarch, "Brotherly Love," *Moralia*, VI, 246–325, esp. 275 ff.

96. *Republic*, X, 581–582; VII, 529; Francis M. Cornford, *The Republic of Plato* (New York, 1959), pp. 308–309 and 223.

97. "To an Uneducated Ruler," 1 (*Moralia*, X, 55).

98. "On Kingship" (Born, p. 89).

99. Erasmus, *The Education of a Christian Prince*, I (Born, p. 150).

100. The *Collected Dialogues of Plato*, ed. Edith Hamilton and Huntington Cairns (New York, 1961), p. 1337.

101. *The Mean*, 1, 20 (Chan, pp. 98, 107).

part of Heaven,"[102] he who "hits upon what is right without effort and apprehends without thinking,"[103] the compilers were able to elevate Yi Sŏng-gye to the level of a sage, a supreme exemplum for future monarchs. Hence

> If a small man wishes to curry favor
> And preaches, "No leisure for culture,"

as Ch'iu Shih-liang is said to have done when he remarked, "The Son of Heaven should not be allowed to have leisure; you should always regale his eyes and ears with luxurious pageantry,"[104] the right book to open is *The Mean*. "If you will only think of the great task you have undertaken," enjoins Erasmus, "you will never be at a loss for something to do. If you are accustomed to take your pleasure in the progress of your people, you will never be at a loss for a source of enjoyment. In this way there is no chance for ennui to trick you with the gay pleasure of leisure."[105]

> Delicately fashioned is my lord,
> As thing cut, as thing filed,
> As thing chiselled, as thing polished,
> Oh, the grace, the elegance!
> Oh, the lustre, oh, the light![106]

The Great Learning interprets the second line as referring to the pursuit of learning and the third line to self-cultivation. The entire third chapter of *The Great Learning*, in Chu Hsi's words, explains abiding in the highest good. As the beginning of moral life, the importance attached to learning (investigation of things) reflects the age's pedagogic emphasis, its earnest and energetic pursuit of learning by rulers and all who are destined to govern characteristic of a period of renaissance in any civilization.[107]

The final canto ends not only with the prophecy of national greatness but with an allusive rhetorical question. The compilers assert again that the security of the throne depends entirely upon

---

102. *The Mean*, 31 (Chan, p. 112).
103. *The Mean*, 20 (Chan, p. 107).
104. *TCTC*, 247, 7985; *HTS*, 207, 4113b-c.
105. *The Education of a Christian Prince*, I (Born, p. 184).
106. *Book of Songs*, 55 (Waley, p. 46).
107. Harry Levin, *Refractions* (New York, 1966), p. 88; Lawrence V. Ryan, *Roger Ascham* (Stanford, 1963), pp. 251–265; Ascham's *The Schoolmaster*, ed. Lawrence V. Ryan (Ithaca, 1967), pp. xxv, xxiv; J. H. Hexter, "The Education of the Aristocracy in the Renaissance," *The Journal of Modern History*, XXII (1950), 1–20.

the ruler's worship of Heaven and toil for the people. They then bring in the figure of T'ai K'ang of Hsia, whose remoteness is enough to protect them from the displeasure of the authorities, and ask:

> Could you depend upon your ancestors
> When you go hunting by the waters of Lo?

On his way from a hunting trip to the south of the Lo River, T'ai K'ang is said to have been ambushed by I who subsequently seized the throne. Hence the ruler should not rely upon his ancestors' glorious deeds and virtue. Power is a grievous burden, and only by superior moral nature can one hope to maintain and secure it. This awesome responsibility cannot be exchanged for a smug concept of authority or sentimental reliance upon Heavenly protection. The test of the good ruler is his ability to maintain order on all planes as Heaven's deputy and the people's father. T'ai K'ang's loss of the crown by his indulging in pleasure should be lesson enough for the successive rulers of the dynasty.

More important in terms of the total symbolic structure probably is the significance of the hunt, a "political metaphor for tyranny."[108] The traditional associations of the hunt with war and game are familiar enough, but here is emphasized the rapacity of the sportive tyrant, whose prey was not only beast but man. The love of the chase was often an attribute of the evil ruler: Shin U was pictured as hunting in the streets of the capital, both beast and men. So was Yŏnsan'gun, the tenth ruler of Yi (1495–1506), who turning the palace into a hunting ground went through a catalogue of outrages. History reveals the fate of the tyrannous hunter after men: he is in turn hunted, deposed, banished, and often killed, a condign punishment for the transgressor against Heaven, Earth, and Man. Except for the ritualistic game in accord with the law of Nature or the pursuit of the nation's enemy to restore order, the hunt is therefore a metaphor for the unbound, unchanneled energy of the tyrant in disregard of the ideal political and moral order. This was probably the meaning of the final canto, for upon the ruler, the custodian of Confucian values and ideals, depend the survival of society and the maintenance of harmony.

108. Earl R. Wasserman, *The Subtler Language* (Baltimore, 1959), p. 120. In the following paragraph I am indebted to his interpretation of the motif (see pp. 113 ff.); see also *Paradise Lost*, XII, 30.

This was the picture of the ideal prince from the standpoint of Confucianism as it was understood in fifteenth century Korea. As transmitters of the tradition, the compilers did not create a new philosophy, but attempted to interpret Confucian orthodoxy with added emphasis and refinement. Absorbed by an intense interest in a practical morality, norms of private and public behavior, they reflected upon the motives and deeds of emperors and kings, the materials for which they ransacked the classics and histories. Their strength lies in their insight into human problems, their passion for sincerity, and their ability to discriminate among values and ideals as guiding principles of state and society. They clung to the traditional values not because of pedantry but because the values had proved to be essential in any state and for any ruler. Viewed from a modern perspective, however, their presentation, dictated by didactic impulse, makes them appear prejudiced. The modern reader may disapprove of vituperation, the introduction and exaggeration of irrelevant faults, the imputation of mean motives, the apparent show of impartiality by juxtaposing faults and virtues in a single character. More relevant in the context, however, is whether they succeeded in their moral and political objectives. They lived in an age which believed in the interdependence of Heaven, Earth, and Man, and in the past as a repository of lessons of admonition and inspiration. This use of history was not unique to the age. That their choice of episodes reflected a definite contemporary purpose and particular need does not surprise us. But we would do injustice to the compilers, if we demanded more than what they intended to accomplish. True, the modern world has lost the patience and ability to appreciate any long literary work with moral overtones, such as the *Aeneid* and *Paradise Lost*,[109] for they demand an educated sensibility, a strong sense of discipline and order as well as ability to respond to all that was once permanent in a long-enduring culture. The loss of moral vision is serious in an age which let the great lamps that illuminated the Confucian universe flicker and die. One plausible defense for taking up the *Songs* in an age which is "pathologically mistrustful of heroism,"[110] and incapable of viewing society as a moral community of men may be the encour-

109. Thomas M. Greene, *The Descent from Heaven* (New Haven, 1963), pp. 74–77, and Christopher Ricks, *Milton's Grand Style* (London, 1963), pp. 1–21.
110. Mack, p. 84.

agement of tolerance. "In the imagination," Northrop Frye writes, "our own beliefs are . . . only possibilities, but we can also see the possibilities in the beliefs of others."[111] "It [the language of human nature] never speaks unless we take the time to listen in leisure, and it speaks only in a voice too quiet for panic to hear. And then all it has to tell us . . . is that we are not getting any nearer heaven, and that it is time to return to the earth."[112]

111. *The Educated Imagination* (Bloomington, 1965), p. 77.
112. *Ibid.*, p. 156.

Chapter V. Folklore, Fiction, and Myth

It is a truism to say that heroes from all parts of the world have common features.[1] The common biographical patterns of heroic lives have been seen in terms of traditional narrative formula (Hahn), human psychology (Rank, Campbell), myth and ritual (Frazer, Raglan, the myth-and-ritual-school), and monomyth (Campbell), an elaboration of the three stages of Van Gennep's *rites de passage*. Though diverse in their approach and scope, students of myth and folklore nevertheless discern in the plot structure the archetypal patterns that are universal and fundamental.[2] Useful as these approaches are for students of literary history, human psychology, cultural anthropology, and mythology, the study of the importance of archetypal patterns and symbols in traditional narrative has, in Archer Taylor's estimate, only begun.[3]

Heroes in East Asian history and literature also tend to conform to a type or types. There are culture heroes, mythic emperors, dynastic founders, sage kings, loyal ministers, villains, martyrs,

1. Jan de Vries, *Heroic Song and Heroic Legend* (London, 1963), p. 218.

2. Orrin E. Klapp, "The Folk Hero," *Journal of American Folklore*, LXII, no. 243 (1949), 17–25; Archer Taylor, "The Biographical Pattern in Traditional Narrative," *Journal of Indiana University Folklore Institute*, I (1964), 114–129; Stanley Hyman, "Myth, Ritual, and Nonsense," *Kenyon Review*, XI (1949), 455–475.

3. Taylor, p. 129.

brave soldiers, devoted sons, and chaste wives—to name but a few. And we discern in their portrayal, in official and unofficial writings, a set of motifs and patterns, the same categories and elements found in myth and folklore elsewhere. But the subject is yet to receive systematic study. It is questionable whether we can ever unravel the intricate relation between myth and folklore or lines of descent in the stories about the beginnings of Chinese civilization as recorded in the *Historical Record*, or heroic anecdotes during the Warring States period as in the *Tso Commentary*. The task is made more difficult by the fact that in China, "where the humanistic, moralizing force of Confucianism has fairly emptied the old myth forms of their primal grandeur," the official mythology today is "a clutter of anecdotes" about Confucian heroes and heroines.[4] Some however may originally have been myths of the seasonal cycle based on ritual recurrence, others localized and humanized versions of stories first attributed to ancestral heroes and then to historical figures as they were popularly conceived and then made consistent with their heroic character. The growth of legends about public personages often follows the pattern of myth and folklore. But research at its current state has not yet been able to determine the origins of these stories, their evolution, diffusion, and displacement, and their importance in the literary and intellectual history of East Asia.

The concept of the unity of man and Nature, one critic insists, may well characterize the entire history of Chinese philosophy.[5] Perhaps in no major civilization has the unity of man and Nature been more stressed than in East Asia, where the view of life and the world has been solidly based on the concept of the uniformity of macrocosm and microcosm. The Shang people believed in the mysterious powers of Nature, in the parallels that exist between the human cycles and natural processes. They believed in the magical, procreative powers of ancestral spirits, whose approval or disapproval of every important deed was sought by divination and sacrifice. Theirs was a chthonic religion, which emphasized ancestor worship and fertility cults.[6] With the founding of the

4. Joseph Campbell, *The Hero with a Thousand Faces* (New York, 1949), p. 249.
5. Chan, p. 3.
6. D. Howard Smith, "Chinese Religion in the Shang Dynasty," *Numen*, VIII, (1961), 142–150; Homer H. Dubs, "The Archaic Royal Jou Religion," *TP*, XLVI (1958), 217–259; Bernhard Karlgren, "Some Fecundity Symbols in Ancient China," *BMFEA*, II (1930), 1–54, esp. 3–20.

Chou a number of significant developments in Chinese belief were initiated: the concept or Heaven as "a self-existent moral law" and supreme spiritual reality, the doctrine of the mandate of Heaven, and the dependence of man's destiny on virtue rather than on ancestral power or Heaven's capricious will.[7] As a vital link in the cosmic order, the primary duty of the king was to maintain harmony between Heaven, Earth, and Man through moral examples and proper rituals. The ruler was vested with the awesome role of a vicegerent of Heaven and father to his people. It has been pointed out—by way of refuting the hypothetical myth and ritual patterns in the ancient Near East as propounded by the myth-and-ritual-school—that in ancient China, where civilized life was based on agriculture and where similar environmental conditions prevailed, that there is no trace of the elements fundamental to the Near Eastern ritual patterns: the concept of the "dying-rising god," ritual combat, the sacred marriage, triumphal procession in which the king played the role of a god, or a pantheon of celestial deities.[8] Indeed, the Chinese imagination singularly lacked the inclination to anthropomorphize gods or to create myths to explain the origin of the universe or of human life.[9] There is no cosmic clash between order and disorder, cosmos and chaos, good and evil, or love and death. The duality of the *yin* and *yang* is a duality of equally necessary, complementary forces, working toward, and culminating in, cosmic harmony.

In place of stories about gods and divine heroes were those of venerated human rulers, around whom legends gathered, and whose heroic deeds in line with culture and society were held up as paradigms of moral values. Vested with cynosural potency, these stories are designed to be inspirational, memorable, educational, or integrational.[10] Legendary and folkloristic elements in the lives of Confucian soldier-statesmen, however, do not always represent the stuff of Chinese or Korean folk tradition. Inventors or welders of heroic tales were official historians, not myth-makers,

7. Chan, pp. 3–4.

8. S. H. Hooke, ed. *Myth, Ritual and Kingship* (Oxford, 1958), p. 273; for the criticism of the myth-and-ritual-school, see Clyde Kluckhohn, "Myths and Rituals," *Harvard Theological Review*, XXXV (1942), 45–79. See also D. Howard Smith, "Divine Kingship in Ancient China," *Numen*, IV (1957), 173.

9. *Numen*, IV (1957), 194.

10. Henry A. Murray, "Definitions of Myth," in *The Making of Myth* (New York, 1962), pp. 7–37.

at least when they were aware of their function. The extent of expurgation of the more primitive aspects in these tales may be difficult to assess, but older material may still remain embedded in them. This however requires a separate study. For our purpose, we will trace those elements in our subject that follow the generally recognized patterns and motifs in hero tales.

Every schoolboy in East Asia is familiar with the stories of miraculous conception imputed to many great figures in history and hagiography: impregnation by the sun and other planets and comets or the mysterious emanation that fills the room at the time of birth. The ancestor of the Shang, for example, was born from a swallow's egg and that of the Chou after his mother stepped into the footprint of a deity. The father of the Chumong, the founder of Koguryŏ, was a heavenly deity and his mother a daughter of the Earl of River. When the egg to which his mother gave birth was cast into the wilderness, the beasts protected it. The founder of one of the ruling clans of Silla was born from a purple egg descended from Heaven, and that of another clan (Kim), from a golden casket dangling from a purple cord. Often such remarkable begettings are foretold in a dream vision or by a diviner.[11] But no such story is assigned to the founder of the Yi dynasty or his son, two of the principal characters in the *Songs*, except for Tojo, Yi Sŏng-gye's grandfather, who was born as a miraculous gift from Avalokiteśvara (canto 21). We know little about Yi Sŏng-gye's infancy or boyhood. However, endowed with extraordinary strength and exceptional gifts, "a prominent nose and dragon face" (cantos 28, 97) and "large ears" (canto 29),[12] he was already set apart from ordinary man. A prophecy of his future greatness, that he will be "mightier than his father" (canto 38), recalls the same prophecy told to Thetis about her son Achilles.

Born in a remote, uncivilized part of the country into a family persecuted and living in exile, he conquers misfortune, bides his

11. See the inscription to the King Kwanggaet'o monument in *SGYS*, appendix, p. 3, and *SGSG*, 1, 40–41 and 13, 1. For the origin of the Pak clan see *SGYS*, 1, 44 and *SGSG*, 1, 1; for that of the Kim clan see *SGYS*, 1, 48–49 and *SGSG*, 12, 7 and 28, 7. See Mishina Shōei, "Kodai Chōsen ni okeru ōja shutsugen no shinwa to girei ni tsuite," *Shirin*, XVIII (1933), 67–96, 328–372, 453–480; Suematsu Yasukazu, *Seikyū shisō*, I, 29–62; *Chōsen no semboku to yogen* (Keijō, 1933), pp. 7 ff.; for Chinese stories see Izushi Yoshihiko, *Shina shinwa densetsu no kenkyū* (Tokyo, 1943), pp. 139–161, 491–556.
12. Yi Pang-wŏn had the same features (cantos 90, 95–96); cf. Hian-lin Dschi's article in *Studia Serica* VIII (Chengtu, 1949) 96–102.

time, and returns as a superhuman archer and horseman to respond to a call from his people. In Chapter III I have already discussed the importance attached to the sufferings and trials of Yi Sŏng-gye as a human hero in the light of the Confucian concept of heroism. His extraordinary courage and might, the ideal attributes of the hero, are often manifest in feats and contests. He wields a huge bow which no other mortal can manipulate, and his deadly war cry in the thick of the battle is enough to worst the enemy. But it is emphasized throughout the cycle that only his unwavering allegiance to his mission and firmness of purpose made him worthy of wielding his invincible bow. His adversaries are not giants, ogres, or dangerous beasts, but foreign invaders that threaten the sovereignty of the nation, and villains and traitors who disrupt internal political and moral harmony. Heaven therefore not only exacts from him *constantia* and *pietas*, but rewards him with constant manifestation of companionship and encouragement. The incessant intimations of a compassionate, merciful Heaven dominate the cantos dealing with his trials and his quest for a unified nation and people. The presence of Heaven often allays the monotony of sound and fury of battle scenes, but its chief function is to objectify his state of mind at a crucial moment, his confidence in his mission, imbuing an episode with a sense of inevitability and urgency. Also it tacitly underscores the terrible distance between individual excellence, however mighty and marvelous, and mortal limitation. Our hero earns Heavenly assistance, but only after he has proved his devotion and fortitude: for he seeks not personal fame and honor but a dynasty that will last many years. Hence his every act is interpreted to be that of imposition of order on chaos, of civilization on crudity and barbarism, and of wisdom on ignorance.

During one of his hunting trips, when he found himself between a ferocious leopard and a gaping pond, Heaven covered the surface of the pond with ice for him to flee (canto 30). During a battle against the Red Turbans, when he was cornered and outnumbered, Heaven came to succor him and he was able to fly across the fortress walls on horseback (canto 34). In 1364 his horse fell into the mud in the midst of a campaign against the Mongol invaders; Heaven hardened the ground so that he and his horse could escape (canto 37). On his return from Wihwa Island, the Yalu refused to swell in spite of a torrential rain (cantos 67–68).

This episode has its pedigree probably in a similar miracle that occurred on the waters of the Ch'ien-t'ang river to the Mongol prince Bayan and his host. Here the miracle is underpinned by the actual bore in the river which did not rush in for three days, enabling the Mongol army to cross it. To the initiated in Confucian political and moral doctrine, such abstract nouns as mandate, harmony, and justice may be charged with force and awe: only the marvelous will dazzle unlettered but credulous minds. Great deeds, if unsung in popular terms, may and will perish from memory. Mnemosyne, the Greek goddess of memory, was the goddess of myth, not of history. But nowhere does Heaven intervene as Apollo does in the *Iliad* where his hand strikes Patroclus' back and broad shoulders (XVI, 791).[13]

The correspondence between man and Nature is often illustrated by portents and strange eruptions, divine instruments of fear and warning, encouragement and solace. The skillful employment of the concept of universal parallelism afforded the identification of Heaven's purposes with those of the Yi founders. As the emanation of an emperor hovers above the hiding place of the founder of the Han, so that of a great general in the form of purple mist—reminiscent of the "hero's moon" in the West—singles out Yi Sŏng-gye (canto 39). While the punishment of the ambitious and greedy who disrupt the cosmic order is accompanied by a storm of stars (canto 50), a white rainbow piercing the sun is a sign of victory (canto 50/2). On the other hand, the appearance of "a red light" above the general's camps, in a campaign against the Ki family, was a warning to evacuate his position (cantos 37, 42). Equally, a comet (canto 71) or a red halo (canto 101) portends the enthronement of a virtuous man. In one episode, Heaven sends a messenger in the form of an old woman, and the Korean sibyl, envisioned as a typical folklore character, warns Ikcho against the treacherous designs of the Jürched chiefs (cantos 4, 19). In another episode, it causes Yi Pang-wŏn to fall sick in order that he may escape an assassination plot (canto 102). These stories may very well have been patterned after the parallels cited: in the first, of an old man who pointed the road to the wayward Liu Hsiu, and in the second, of Liu Pang's astute interpretation of the place name which eventually saved his life.

The motif of magical animals, especially helpful and prophetic

13. Lattimore, p. 351.

ones, is frequent in folklore. Gods often transform themselves into animals, or culture heroes are born of a union of animal and man, and animals are endowed with human intelligence and speech. Achilles' horse Xanthus, with drooping mane, foretells his master's doom,[14] so does Marko's horse, Sarac.[15] Woodpeckers warn Sigurd against the designs of Regin, Fafnir's brother.[16] In Apollonius' *Argonautica* (III, 927–937), a crow advises Mopsus to leave Jason alone.[17] A red bird (or red crows in another version) which came to King Wu with a message did not utter a word, yet fulfilled its mission by revealing the blessings of Heaven (canto 7). The only speaking animal is the fabulous *chüeh-tuan*, a green unicorn in the shape of a deer with the tail of a horse, which appeared on Buzgala Pass in Uzbekistan. Yeh-lü Ch'u-ts'ai (1189–1243), one of Cinggis Qan's advisers, comprehends its speech, to the benefit of the Mongol army in the southern expedition (canto 42). A curious example of unnatural animal behavior, undoubtedly induced by divine power, occurs in the allegorical tale of snake and magpies (canto 7). Instead of devouring the birds felled by Tojo, the snake carried and hung them on the bough of a tree, which was interpreted to portend the rise of the Yi family. The motif of the animal nurse, often associated with the motif of "exposed child,"[18] comes readily to mind, and ours may be a disguised or corrupt version of it. Related to the prophetic animal motif as well as oneiromancy is the dragon, which usually manifests itself in a dream and occasionally in broad daylight. Tojo first doubted the plea of the White Dragon to do away with his adversary, the Black Dragon. But its second appearance in a dream prompted him to go to the described place, where he witnessed the duel of the dragons and successfully shot the black one. This is hardly a story of the struggle between order and chaos, in attenuated form, but, as a parallel in the first verse in the same canto demonstrates, a fiction based on the pseudo-scientific theory of the five elements.[19] It is also reminiscent

14. *Iliad*, XIX, 399 ff. (Lattimore, p. 403).

15. Jan de Vries, p. 135.

16. William Morris, tr. *Volsunga Saga* (New York, 1962), pp. 145–148.

17. Tr. R. C. Seaton (LCL, 1955), p. 259.

18. Donald B. Redford, "The Literary Motif of the Exposed Child," *Numen*, XIV (1967), 209–228.

19. In Ch'a Ch'ŏl-lo's version, Mokcho replaces Tojo, and the color of the adversary of the White Dragon is not black, but yellow. Chang Tŏk-sun, *Tonga munhwa*, V (1966), 56–57; for the five elements see Karlgren, "Legends and Cults in Ancient China," *BMFEA*, XVIII (1946), 222–224.

of the duel of the red (British) and the white (Saxons) dragons of the pool beneath Vortigern's castle in Nennius and Geoffrey of Monmouth.

As a thematic symbol for royalty and magnificence the dragon imagery[20] provides unity in the work. The Western and Near Eastern dragons have been interpreted variously. The Babylonian Tiamat, the Hittite Illuyankas, or the Hebrew Rahab (Behemoth) are symbolic of chaos. Yahweh conquered the "rebellious waters of primeval chaos, split it asunder and created cosmos out of chaos."[21] Even today, the overflowing river is often thought of as a dragon.[22] In the Judeo-Christian context, the dragon (or serpent) is an embodiment of evil, which, Bodkin proposes, is "descended from the ancient myth of a serpent or dragon, denizen of deep earth or sea."[23] In heroic tales, dragons are guardians of the sacred well, the Golden Fleece, the golden apples of the Hesperides, the Rheingold, the honey of eternal life in the Himalayas, or simply hoards of gold. Playing an important role in the initiation ritual, they have proved to be formidable adversaries to all-daring, mighty epic heroes: Beowulf, and Ortnit, fight the fiery drake in the primeval forest and die. But Wolfdietrich, Siegfried, and Sigurd emerge unscathed and victorious from their encounters.[24]

In China and Korea, the dragon is none of these. The guardian of mountains and waters (Dragon King), it is beneficent to man and, to Buddhists, a friend and servant to Buddha. Symbolic of clouds, thunder, lightning, and rain, it represents fecundating elements in Nature. It is variously described, but as monarch of the animal kingdom, it became a symbol of royalty and greatness, furnishing recurrent motifs for imperial insignia, regalia, robes,

20. Mary Barnard, *The Mythmakers* (Athens, Ohio, 1966), pp. 62–70; for her delightful description of the dragon see p. 69.

21. Hooke, p. 170. According to J. R. R. Tolkien, Beowulf's dragon is a "personification of malice, greed, destruction (the evil side of heroic life), and of the undiscriminating cruelty of fortune that distinguishes not good or bad (the evil aspect of all life)." See "Beowulf: The Monsters and Critics," in *An Anthology of Beowulf Criticism*, ed. Lewis E. Nicholson (Notre Dame, 1963), p. 66.

22. Theodor H. Gaster, *The Oldest Stories in the World* (New York, 1952), p. 141.

23. Maud Bodkin, *Studies of Type-Images in Poetry, Religion and Philosophy* (Oxford, 1951), p. 106 (cf. Revelation 12: 9; *Paradise Lost*, IV, 3).

24. Jan de Vries, pp. 222–224. For Sigurd's slaying of the dragon Fafnir, see *Volsunga Saga* (New York, 1962), pp. 141–144; Dobrynya, in the Slavonic folk epic, slays the twelve-clawed dragon (Jan de Vries, pp. 122–125).

and furniture.[25] Upon its return from Wihwa Island, Yi Sŏng-gye's army pressed toward the Koryŏ capital. The defenders under the command of Ch'oe Yŏng put up a strong resistance. Yi Sŏng-gye then set up his standard of the yellow dragon, took a position on the southern slope of Mount Nam, and rallied his men to victory (1, 47a). The appearance of birds and beasts of prey in the military standard is a commonplace, but the yellow dragon motif in Yi's standard is a fitting symbol of his future greatness. This recalls the use of the royal dragon ensign by various peoples in the West (the Romans, Uther Pendragon, Arthur, Richard I, Harold, Owen Glendower, and the Tudors). "With a gold solid head and a flexible body, set on top of a staff," the royal dragon ensign's chief function was to "mark the king's position in the rear of battle to which the wounded and weary may resort."[26]

The association of dragon with kingship is very old, at least in East Asia, as attested by its occurrence in some of the earliest texts. In the *Book of Changes*, a manual of divination, the workings of the universe are presented in terms of the hexagrams, consisting of unbroken (strong) and broken (weak) lines. Caused by the interaction of two forces, *yin* and *yang*, the universe is viewed as a process of constant flux and transformation. The arcane nature of the eight basic trigrams are elucidated on the analogy of elements of Nature (heaven, earth, thunder, water, mountain, wind, fire, and marsh),[27] attributes (strong, yielding, movement, dangerous, standstill, penetrating, dependent, and joyous),[28] and family (father, mother, the eldest son, middle son, the youngest son, the eldest daughter, middle daughter, the youngest daughter),[29] all of these epiphors serving as vehicles for a single tenor (trigram).[30]

25. E. T. C. Werner, *A Dictionary of Chinese Mythology* (Shanghai, 1932), pp. 284–297; Izushi, pp. 91–109; Karlgren, "Some Fecundity Symbols in Ancient China," *BMFEA*, II, 47.

26. Uther Pendragon carried to his wars a dragon fashioned in gold (*The History of the Kings of Britain*, VIII, 17). At the Battle of Bath, Arthur wore a golden helmet, "with a crest carved in the shape of a dragon" (IX, 4) and in his campaign against Lucius Hiberius at Saussy, he set up the Golden Dragon standard (X, 6). See J. S. P. Tatlock, *The Legendary History of Britain* (Berkeley, 1950), pp. 37–38, 329–330, and Lewis Thorpe, tr. (Harmondsworth, 1966), pp. 202, 217, 248.

27. Shuo kua, 2 (Wilhelm, I, 284–285); Joseph Needham, *Science and Civilization in China*, II (Cambridge, 1956), 273 ff., and a chart on page 313.

28. Shuo kua, 7 (Wilhelm, I, 293).

29. Shuo kua, 10 (Wilhelm, I, 294).

30. Philip Wheelwright, *Metaphor and Reality* (Bloomington, 1962), pp. 87–88.

In addition, there are corresponding animals, parts of the body, and additional symbols. By doubling the trigram, each line of which stands for Heaven, Earth, and Man respectively, the hexagram is born.[31] The first hexagram, *ch'ien*, consisting of six unbroken strong lines, represents the *yang*, whose attributes are energy, power, motion, and duration. The *T'uan-chuan* (Commentary on the decision) comments: "*Ch'ien* at all times rides the six dragons (*ch'i*; six lines) and controls all things under heaven. The way of *ch'ien* is to change and transform so that everything will obtain its correct nature and destiny and the great harmony will be self-proficient. There the result will be the advantage [derived from the harmony of all things] and firmness [throughout their existence]."[32] The *Wen-yen* (Commentary on the word of the text) further expounds the analogy between the great ruler and the workings of Heaven and Earth: "The character of the great man is identical with that of Heaven and Earth; his brilliance is identical with that of the sun and the moon; his order is identical with that of the four seasons, and his good and evil fortunes are identical with those of spiritual beings."[33] The oracle on "Nine on the fifth place (line)" reads:

> Flying dragons in the heavens.
> It furthers one to see the great man.[34]

Here, the emphasis falling on the strong place (fifth line) on the strong line (all lines in this hexagram are strong) is taken to symbolize the rise of a virtuous man from relative obscurity who, on the strength of his moral power, bides his time, successfully undergoes the trials, becomes a ruler, benefits mankind, bringing peace and security to his people. He has therefore attained a position where he can exercise his power and virtue, an object of universal adoration and emulation. This is the background of the dragon symbol charged with "metaphoric potencies and metaphysical overtones," when it is employed to designate the ruler. As the most majestic similitude of political rhetoric, the dragon represents the ideal pattern of withdrawal and emergence, the art of biding time, cultivation of the self, discovery of creative energy,

31. Shuo kua, 2 (Wilhelm, I, 283).
32. Chan, p. 264.
33. *Ibid.*
34. Wilhelm, I, 8; II, 15; Hellmut Wilhelm, *Change* (New York, 1960), pp. 39–40, 48–63 for the *ch'ien* and *k'an* symbolism.

and the triumphant emergence of an ideal man. The image of "the flying dragons in the heaven," so astutely chosen as the title of the cycle, reverberates with the sublimity and success, creativity and sovereignty, of a great man.

Popular lore and tradition might have been enchanted by the dragon's constant rejuvenation as it sloughs its skin and renews itself in its alleged immortality. Dragons are still favorite characters in Korean folklore and festive mythology: both the lettered and unlettered delight to speculate on their fate as they soar skyward in the teeth of a summer storm; for their ascent to Heaven is tabu to the mortal eye. But sometimes the dragon manifests itself to the credulous historians and encomiasts,[35] or even to plain people, as in canto 100 where the glistening sheen of the auspicious animal was viewed by Yi Pang-wŏn's household staff. Sage kings and great heroes often emerge like a dragon. The Duke of Gloucester, in his speech on Henry V, compares the deceased king to a dazzling, royal dragon:

> England ne'er had a king until his time.
> Virtue he had, deserving to command.
> His brandish'd sword did blind men with his beams;
> His arms spread wider than a dragon's wings;
> His sparkling eyes, replete with wrathful fire,
> More dazzled and drove back his enemies
> Than mid-day sun fierce bent against their faces.
>   (*1 Henry VI*, I, i, 8–14)

Coriolanus, too, is a dragon, a lonely one (IV, i, 30), and fights dragon-like (IV, vii, 23).

The dragon-king equation was worked to fantastic length in the stories about the origin of the Wang House of Koryŏ. The grandfather of the founder of Koryŏ was married to the eldest daughter of the Dragon King as a reward for destroying the dragon's adversary, the old fox. When the dynasty changed hands, the Yi founders mercilessly killed Shin U and Shin Ch'ang under the pretext that they were not of the legitimate Wang line. Stories circulated later to mourn the innocent deaths attest to popular belief that they, after all, were legitimate kings. Shortly before his

---

35. According to the *Tso Commentary* (Legge, V, 731a-b), a dragon appeared in 512 B.C. in the suburbs of Chiang, which occasioned a lengthy digression on the nature of the beast. The Saxon Chronicle reports, for the year 793, that fiery dragons were seen in the air (Chadwick, *The Heroic Age*, p. 128).

execution, Shin U declared that he was a descendant of the Dragon King and that, like his forebears, he had three golden dragon scales under his left armpit. When he bared his shoulders, people saw the scales were the size of a coin.[36]

Gold is perhaps related to dragon symbolism, "the king of metals and the metal of kings," another symbol of royalty. Although it properly belongs to the realm of oneiromancy, a heavenly messenger's bestowal of a golden ruler[37] upon Yi Sŏng-gye in a dream (canto 13) is rightly interpreted by the compilers:

> He was to map the norms with a ruler:
> So wishing to charge him with a good government,
> Heaven sent down
> A gold ruler. (canto 83)

The founder of Koryŏ, Wang Kŏn's ascent in a dream to the top of a nine-storied golden pagoda on the sea prognosticated his future greatness (canto 83). In both cases, gold also presages a golden age to come, *aurea saecula*, as in the *Aeneid* (IV, 792–793).[38]

Another symbol of the crown is the stag (canto 55). The *Historical Record* contains a remark made by K'uai T'ung to Liu Pang: "When Ch'in lost its stag, the whole empire pursued it. Thereupon one of great ability and nimble feet got there first."[39] The allegory of the stag as the royal beast, the symbol of power and liberty, according to one source, existed already during the Spring and Autumn period (722–481 B.C.).[40] The entry under the year 558 B.C. in the *Tso Commentary* attributes the following story to the viscount of the Jung: "As in the pursuit of a stag, the people of Chin took Ch'in by the horns, and we took it by the feet, and along with the Chin, we laid it prostrate on the ground."[41] Also in Denham's *Coopers Hill*, the struggle for power is presented in a fable of the stag hunt (lines 241–322), the leader of "that noble heard" (line 237), symbolic of the "king's continuous and controlled energy":[42]

36. *YK*, 1, 31 (*Tonga munhwa*, V, 43–59).

37. *Tonggyŏng chapki* (CKK, 1910), 3, 589, reports the same story related to the founder of Silla.

38. Albert C. Cook, *The Classic Line* (Bloomington, 1966), p. 209.

39. *SC*, 92, 0222d29–30 (*HJAS*, X [1947], 214); also in *HS*, 45, 0469c.

40. *Yen-fan-lu hsü-chi* (*Hsüeh-chin t'ao-yüan* ed.), 5, 9a.

41. *Tso chuan*, Duke Hsiang 14 (Legge, V, 464a).

42. Earl R. Wasserman, *The Subtler Language*, pp. 73–78; Brendan OHehir, *Expans'd Hieroglyphicks* (Berkeley, 1969), pp. 32, 35, 224, 244–251.

> There *Faunus* and *Sylvanus* keep their Courts,
> And thither all the horned hoast resorts,
> To graze the ranker mead, that noble heard
> On whose sublime and shady fronts is rear'd
> Natures great Master-piece; to shew how soon
> Great things are made, but sooner are undone. (235–240)

Critics recognize in this episode of feigned history, which contains a moral (line 240), an allegory of the trial and execution of Thomas Wentworth, Earl of Strafford, on May 12, 1641, and in the revised, expanded version of 1655, the execution of Charles I on January 30, 1649 ("Prince of the soyl," line 280). Also, in Robert Howard's *The Duell of the Stags* (1668), a struggle for power between Clarendon and Buckingham is allegorized in the figures of contending stags, with a moral that power eventually corrupts its possessor.[43]

The recurrent motif of "prophecy fulfilled" betrays not only the encomiastic nature of the *Songs*, but drives home the propaganda that the rise of Yi Sŏng-gye marked the culmination of a historical process. Prophecies that reinforce the revolution as the divinely ordered and blessed mission were grist for the compilers' mill. We have already alluded to the significance of motivating dreams. Dream visions, like other "prophetic flashbacks," however, often fail to foreshadow the climax or to create suspense: the event is stated before giving the significance of the dream which foretold the event. We are seldom told of the sender of a dream, its time and manner of approach, its sex, its position with regard to the sleeper, or what form of dialogue, if any, was held. It is scarcely developed as an artistic device, but we are asked to accept the fact that the sender was Heaven, as the compilers took pains to explain. It is sent to dispel doubts, as in the case of King Wu, but he makes certain that his dream and divinations coincide before launching his subjugation of the Shang (canto 3). We may point to the dream of the dragon duel as an allegorical dream, reminiscent of Penelope's dream of geese and eagle (*Odyssey*, XIX, 509–581),[44] Charlemagne's dream of such animal symbols as boar, hound,

---

43. John M. Wallace, "Dryden and History: A Problem in Allegorical Reading," *ELH*, XXXVI (1969), 283.

44. *Odyssey*, XIX, 536 ff. (Lattimore, *The Odyssey of Homer* [New York, 1965], p. 296). For the dream in the Greek epics see Eric R. Dodd, *The Greeks and the Irrational* (Berkeley, 1951), pp. 102–134.

leopard, and bear (717–736; 2525–69),[45] or Arthur's dream of bear and dragon (X, ii). The contending dragons are symbols of warring elements, the White one probably standing for the element favorable to the Yi dynasty (canto 22).

Befitting the valor and courage of Yi Sŏng-gye whose exploits constitute a major theme of the work, he often divined the outcome of expeditions by arrow. In 1377, before charging the Japanese pirates, he placed a helmet 150 paces away and hit the target three times (canto 88–89); on his return from Wihwa Island in 1388, he felled with a single arrow a pine tree from one hundred paces away, a feat which strengthened the resolution of his men to help him determine his course of actions. A similar story is told of Chao Kou (Sung Kao-tsung) during his struggles against the Jürched invaders (canto 32).

Prophecy by gnomic charts and oracles of the rise of the Yi family forms another theme in several cantos. These stories are usually connected with the solving of the hidden meaning of certain characters in one's name. An amphibological text discovered by a monk among the stones of Mount Chii read: "A tree son (child) rides on the pig and will bring order to the Three Han." A combination of tree and child makes up the logograph *Yi*, and he rides on the pig because the year Yi Sŏng-gye was born was the year of the Pig (canto 86). A variation of the theme is celebrated in cantos 13 and 69, where the logograph Yi was divided into its three components, ten, eight, and son. The meaning of the diagram replete with proverbial obscurity was said to coincide with the new name chosen by the Ming emperor for the House of Yi, Chosŏn, which means "the brightness of the morning sun" (canto 85). Another instance of prophecy by name, this time referring to Li Shih-min, occurs in canto 90, where his given name, Shih-min, was interpreted by a trained exegete to mean *chi-shih an-min*, "to benefit the age and soothe the people," a fitting motto for the great emperor. Belief in onomancy sprang from ancient conviction that a nomen contained a mystic omen (Nomen Omen).[46]

45. A. H. Krappe, "The Dream of Charlemagne in the Chanson de Roland," *PMLA*, XXXVI (1921), 131–141; Karl-Josef Steinmeyer, *Untersuchungen zur allegorischen Bedeutung der Träume im altfranzësischen Rolandslied* (Munich, 1963).

46. W. Bedell Stanford, *Greek Metaphor* (Oxford, 1936), pp. 18, 147; Edward Clodd, *Magic in Names* (London, 1920), pp. 36 ff. See, for example, *Richard III*, I, i, 46 ff.

The logographs that constitute a given name of a living sovereign were tabu, and even today, the lettered Korean does not utter his father's given name. If one's father's first name was, for example, Henry, one would respond by saying, "My father's name consists of the letters, *h, e, n, r,* and *y,*" rather than pronouncing it as a disyllabic word.

Occasionally, however, the less fortunate ones tend to interpret signs and prophecies as referring to themselves only to discover belatedly how Heaven (and people) have misled them. The impolitic Li Mi, for example, believed in the popular ballad that foretold the rise of a man surnamed Li (canto 16) only to learn that it referred to T'ang founders. A similar prophecy supposedly of long standing in Korea, like the Trojan legend which was applied at various times to suit contemporary political needs, was seized upon by the Establishment in order to present Yi Sŏng-gye as its ordained fulfiller. Rebels and enemies are usually presented as incapable of understanding the inscrutable operation of providence. Ultimately, however, it is only the victor who can afford to enlist all the supernatural sanction on his side. The aberrations of Nature, concocted and directed against him by his rivals, could easily be made to apply to himself in order to buttress his claims; his followers would busily evolve a series of *ex posto facto* prophecies to surround him with mystery and grandeur. The following lines by Alexander Brome, a Cavalier poet during the Commonwealth, summarize the truth:

> That side is always right that's strong
> And that that's beaten must be wrong.[47]

In *Annus Mirabilis,* written to counter the anti-monarchical propaganda, Dryden twisted the very arguments the rebels used to the advantage of the throne. The plague of 1665 and the great fire of 1666, construed by the dissenters as forebodings of the impending punishment of the erring monarch, were reinterpreted as trials sent by God to strengthen the bond between throne and people and to "heighten the people's loyalty to their king." Who but dusty scholars would read the *Mirabilis Annus* tracts as fabricated by the rebels? Dryden's poem is still read if not as a great work of art, at least as "a piece of inspired journalism." Were it

---

47. Quoted in C. V. Wedgwood, *Poetry and Politics under the Stuarts* (Cambridge, 1961), p. 108.

not for the poet in the service of the royal cause—for he was subsequently appointed poet laureate (1668) and historiographer-royal (1670)—probably no one would have thought of Charles II as a heavenly deputy whose prayer (lines 1045–80) was enough to halt the raging fire in London. The crown needs the pen to exalt his person and deeds. Truth should be mixed with fiction, the credible with the surprising, for Pope (as Davenant, Hobbes, and Dryden before him) seems to say, that is the art of poetry, especially of public and political poetry.[48]

Another popular belief that exerted great influence was geomancy, a pseudo-science of the Yin-yang school. The founder of Koryŏ, in the eighth article of his Ten Injunctions (943), warned his heirs never to employ a man from the south, chiefly because the inauspicious orographic formation would breed ambition and rebellion (canto 15). In 1096, a geomancer memorialized the throne by recommending the transfer of the capital further south to Hanyang (modern Seoul). When the new subsidiary capital was established, the mayor elected bore the surname Yi, in order to suppress the prophecy that a man with the same surname would rise to power (canto 16). All the fuss notwithstanding, the putative origin of Yi Sŏng-gye, the founder of the new dynasty, was in the south, and his surname was Yi. The rise of the Yi family was therefore predetermined ages ago, and there is no way of circumventing Heaven's intention. The selection of the site for the capital of the Yi dynasty was equally influenced by geomancy. After an intensive survey of orography near Mount Kyeryong and Muak, the founder finally decided on Hanyang (1394), swayed by a recommendation of the National Preceptor (canto 14). Hence

> A millennium ago,
> Heaven chose the north of the Han.
> There they accumulated goodness and founded the state.
> Oracles foretold: myriad years.   (canto 125)

The supernatural mechanisms discussed thus far were drawn from a common stock of motifs and traits which enjoyed popularity in history and literature. They emphasize the accepted moral

---

48. The discussion in this paragraph is based on Edward N. Hooker's article in *HLQ*, X (1946–1947), 49–67, and *The Works of John Dryden*, ed. Hooker *et al.*, I (Berkeley, 1961), 256–320. See also Albert Ball, "Charles II: Dryden's Christian Hero," *Modern Philology*, LIX (1961), 25–35.

standards and values, especially the correspondences between Heaven, Earth, and Man. Polysemous in intention and accumulative in effect, these symbols and motifs possess "ancestral vitality,"[49] equipped with a rhetorical and intellectual background of their own. As an example of the thematic usage of the traditional yet hidden meaning, we may point to the symbol of the dragon which, occurring in the title and in the first canto, serves as an early foreshadowing of the theme. The skillful use of omens and portents not only relates kingship to nature and order in accordance with the analogical mode of thinking but drives home the lesson that merit, not chance, determines the courses of action. The interpreter of the mandate, the conferer of order, and upholder of moral norms—such roles of kingship could not but be presented by examples rather than by rule, as Spenser in his letter to Ralegh declared ("So much more profitable and gratious is doctrine by ensample, then by rule."). The thematic repetition of didactic and moral values is perhaps best illustrated in the account of war, the typological scenes and motifs in the description of a righteous war undertaken in the name of Heaven.

Cedric H. Whitman has convincingly shown the skillful deployment of nature imagery by the poet in battle scenes in the *Iliad*.[50] The flight of missiles in the thick of the battle at the wall is compared to a great snowstorm (XII, 278–289),[51] and the defending Greeks against the onslaught of the Trojans, to a "high sea-cliff that lies close along the great salt waters,/ and stand[s] up against the screaming winds and their sudden directions,/ and against the waves that grow to bigness and burst up against it" (XV, 618–621).[52] The sound and fury of the battle are likened to breakers on the shore, bellowing fire in mountain glens, and "the crying of the wind in the deep-haired oaks" (XIII, 398–399),[53] and the flight of the Trojans, to hurricane winds which "rip all the hillsides/ and dash whirling in huge noise down to the blue sea" (XVI, 390–391).[54] A combination of such elementary images as wind, lightning, seastorm, snowstorm, clouds, and dust occurs especially when the battle is still contested, raging on both sides as

---

49. Wheelwright, *Metaphor and Reality*, p. 105.
50. *Homer and the Heroic Tradition* (Cambridge, Mass., 1958), pp. 128–153.
51. Lattimore, pp. 265–266.
52. *Ibid.*, pp. 327–328.
53. *Ibid.*, p. 292.
54. *Ibid.*, p. 340.

at the end of Book XIII (795 ff.).[55] In the *Song of Roland*, the tragedy at Roncesvalles is forecast by a formulaic description of nature:

> High are the hills, the valleys dark and deep,
> Grisly the rocks, and wondrous grim the steeps.   (814–815)[56]

Before the encounter of the Franks and Saracens, a similar description foreshadows the catastrophe that awaits Roland, especially in the last two lines:

> Throughout all France terrific tempests rise,
> Thunder is heard, the stormy winds blow high,
> Unmeasured rain and hail from the sky,
> While thick and fast flashes the levin bright,
> And true it is the earth quakes far and wide . . .
> Right at high noon a darkness falls like night,
> Save for the lightning there's not a gleam of light; (1423–32)[57]

Pausanias (10, 23/2) describes the war between the Gauls, under their chief Brennus, and the Greeks in a similar manner: the whole ground occupied by the Gallic army shook violently, with continuous thunder and lightning. The bolts from Heaven set on fire whatever objects they struck, their armors and themselves. They saw the ghosts of the Greek heroes around them, finally suffering a fatal disaster at Delphi (279 B.C.).[58] According to Gregory of Tours (IV, 22), Sigibert's nervous and frightened army, in their encounter with the Huns, saw spectres which they believed to have been caused by magic and fled affrighted before engaging the invaders.[59] The invocation of demonic assistance by magic was often attributed to the enemy, and in Christian epics to the infidels, who attempt to thwart the inevitable victory of the righteous or Christian host. O. M. Dalton, the translator of the *History of the Franks* (Oxford, 1927), comments: "The possession of [such] magical powers was commonly attributed to peoples coming from little-known regions, whether in east or north."[60]

---

55. Whitman, p. 151; Lattimore, p. 292. See also Roger A. Hornsby, *Patterns of Action in the Aeneid* (Iowa City, 1970).

56. Bowra, *Heroic Poetry*, p. 139; A. C. Cook, pp. 41–42; Dorothy L. Sayers, *The Song of Roland* (Harmondsworth, 1957), p. 28. The quotation is from Sayers, p. 83.

57. Sayers, p. 107.

58. *Description of Greece*, tr. W. H. S. Jones, IV (LCL, 1965), 499–501.

59. *The History of the Franks*, II, 138.

60. *Ibid.*, II, 525–526; Mircea Eliade, *Images and Symbols*, tr. Philip Mairet (New York, 1961), p. 38.

Likewise, the grandiose design of the ambitious emperor of the Former Ch'in, Fu Chien, was shattered in the battle of the Fei River (383) by elements of Nature which conspired to his defeat:

> Aspiring to dynastic legitimacy,
> He opposed the advice of his men.
> Hence the trees and grass on the mountain
> Turned into a host of horsemen.   (canto 98)

The retreating Ch'in army feared ambush in every tree and tuft of grass and was scared by the sound of wind and the whoop of cranes, a caricature of demoralization and defeat, the fitting metaphor of the state of mind of the frightened army, who were condemned to dogs and vultures. In *Macbeth*, Malcolm, Prince of Cumberland, in order to camouflage the size of his advancing army to Dunsinane and thereby to deceive Macbeth's scouts, orders his men:

> Let every soldier hew him down a bough
> And bear 't before him; thereby shall we shadow
> The numbers of our host and make discovery
> Err in report of us.   (V, iv, 4–7)

This time-honored military tactic at the disposal of any commander as natural, helpful means of maneuver has turned into a marching forest, summoning the tyrant to repent:

> Mess. As I did stand my watch upon the hill,
>   I look'd toward Birnam, and anon, methought,
>   The wood began to move.
> Macbeth. Liar and slave!
> Mess. Let me endure your wrath, if 't be not so.
>   Within this three miles may you see it coming;
>
>   I say, a moving grove.
> Mecbeth. . . . "Fear not, till Birnam wood
>   Do come to Dunsinane;" and now a wood
>   Comes toward Dunsinane. Arm, arm, and out!
>   (V, v, 33–46)[61]

Like the trees in Birnam Wood that rose against Macbeth,[62]

---

61. G. Wilson Knight, *The Imperial Theme* (London, 1931), p. 145; George R. Elliott, *Dramatic Providence in Macbeth* (Princeton, 1958), p. 209.

62. For the symbolism of green boughs and leafy screens see Elliott, pp. 209–221. Angus Fletcher, in *Allegory* (Ithaca, 1964), p. 92, n. 3, comments: "The imagery of trees and forests produces a type of natural banner or flag."

"Hell-hound" and "Butcher," the adversary of Fu Chien is not only a human army of the Eastern Chin, but Nature herself.

Cloaked in a subdued, matter-of-fact style shown in the narrative ending in line 4 of the original, the four-line stanza in canto 98 is made to carry the allegory and symbolism implicit in the event. The educated reader has his copy of the *Chin shu* at his elbow, the *Chronicle* of Fu Chien (chaps. 113–114) to be precise,[63] in order fully to comprehend the circumstances and to contemplate the implicit moral comment. He might find pleasure in the manner in which Confucian historians debunked Fu Chien, his blind ambition to cut a better figure in Chinese history and his disregard of honest advice to the detriment of his own dynasty. These are, the first two lines seem to say, the ostensible reasons for his military defeat. On second reading, the same reader will probably be struck by the compilers' psychological acuity in their study of parallel destinies that swept Fu Chien and Yi Pang-gan away. It is not chance alone that brought destruction upon them, but rather the interplay of their personality and circumstances. Fu Chien displayed blind will swayed by ambition, crowned by despair and ultimate destruction. He is surely not the only thief of a throne and misuser of power. Chinese history, like any other history, is besmirched with preposterous acts of bloodshed, often in the name of the righteous cause. But Fu Chien is singled out because of the contemporary relevance his downfall contains. It is the historians' purpose to hold up a polished mirror to one of the great events in Chinese history. That a man who surrenders himself to pride and ambition will eventually incur the wrath of Nature is a Confucian (and Christian) myth. Such myth was concocted when a similar representational scheme was adopted by the compilers in their account of a princely feud in 1398 from which Yi Pang-wŏn emerged victorious.

> They opposed the royal order,
> Rudely insulting the royal heir.
> Hence the empty streets of the capital
> Were filled with a host of horsemen.

The rebels saw, so the story goes, a line of cavalrymen stretching from South Mountain to Kwanghwa Gate inspiring terror in their hearts. By branding the rebels as miscreants and by imputing war

---

63.   Michael C. Rogers, *The Chronicle of Fu Chien* (Berkeley, 1968).

hysteria and hallucination to the opponents, Yi Pang-wŏn was able to claim supernatural sanction for his move. Like fiction suffused in an epic aura, the story of Li Shih-min's murder of his two brothers, Yi Pang-wŏn's similar ruthless act had to be justified and glorified.

In the battle of Badr, Muhammed (567/9–632), with 319 followers, routed 1,000 Meccans (February 624 = Anno Hegirae 2). The *Koran*, in Surah III, 11, recounts the story: "The one host fought in the cause of God, and the other was infidel. To their own eyesight, the infidels saw you twice as many as themselves, and God aided with his succor whom he would. And in this truly was a lesson for men endowed with discernment."[64]

Did these war myths arise from "the unconscious depths of the human psyche," from propaganda concocted by the Establishment, or from simple wish fantasies? Like the motif of the scapegoat, it may have had various functions, one may have been the denial and deflation of the enemy's strength and the mastery of fear.[65] That the enemy is out of favor with God or Heaven and that Nature, the supreme witness, will league with the righteous army is a well-known motif. So was Scotland ransomed,[66] as were the dynasty of Eastern Chin and, later, the Yi dynasty. Frequent snatches of jingles performed a profoundly psychological effect (cantos 13, 16). A song current before General Yi's return from Wihwa Island, like the "ch'ih-fu oracle" that prophesied the rise of Liu Hsiu, foretold both the rise of a man with the surname Yi (canto 69) and his triumphant return in order to lodge a deadly coup to his opponents at court:

> The fire rages beyond P'yongyang,
> The smoke rises over the Anju fortress.
> General Yi passes through this turbulence—
> May he save the young and old.

64. Richard Bell, *The Qur'ān* (Edinburgh, 1937), I, 45, and *Introduction to the Qur'ān* (Edinburgh, 1953), p. 23. The quotation is from J. M. Rodwell, *The Koran* (London, 1950), p. 386.

65. Marie Bonaparte, *Myths of War*, tr. John Rodker (London, 1947), pp. 64 ff. Lucan, in *Pharsalia*, I, 484–486, remarks: "Thus fear does half the work of lying fame,/ And cowards thus their own misfortunes frame;/ By their own feigning fancies are betray'd,/And groan beneath those ills themselves have made" (in Nicholas Rowe's version, in *The Works of the English Poets*, ed. Chalmers, XX [London, 1810], 23b).

66. Geoffrey Bush, *Shakespeare and the Natural Condition* (Cambridge, Mass., 1956), p. 70; Northrop Frye, *Fools of Time* (Toronto, 1967), pp. 20 *passim*.

Fire is a common symbol of destruction and purgation, that destroys the evil of tyranny and restores the politico-cosmic order. Epic heroes, in one way or another, are associated with fire, to underscore their fiery temper, their energy and *aristeiai*, and ultimately their acceptance of an ineluctable, inexorable Fate.[67] In our context, however, fire is unnatural and brutal, and can be employed only in the last resort. Once cosmic order and harmony prevail, Nature will sing again, the tree of dynasty striking deep roots and burgeoning myriad leaves.

67. For the image of fire in Shakespeare's Roman plays, see Maurice Charney, *Shakespeare's Roman Plays* (Cambridge, Mass., 1961), pp. 42–62. For the flame symbolism in the *Aeneid*, II, see Bernard M. W. Knox, "The Serpent and the Flame," *American Journal of Philology*, LXXI (1950), 279–300, and Viktor Pöschl, *Die Dichtkunst Virgils*, p. 62, for his comment on the Iliadic heroes.

Chapter VI. The Tree of Dynasty

> By trees the nations may be told apart.
> India grows her jet black ebony
> And Arabia Felix boughs of frankincense.
> Shall I tell of fragrant, gum-soaked balsams,
> Of evergreen acacia?   The soft white cotton
> In Ethiopian groves?   Or how the Chinese
> Comb their silk from leaves, or the tangled groves
> Of India's seacoast, earth's remotest fold
> Whose lofty trees no arrow can surmount
> (Although the race is famed for archery?)
> *(Georgics,* II, 116–125)[1]

Every valley and hill, every clan and tribe, every kingdom and nation has its sacred trees. From time immemorial, the tree was suffused with mythological and symbolic associations, providing the recurrent motifs and images for the arts and letters. As the embodiment of life principle, fecundity and regeneration, the tree, like springs and rivers to which it is closely allied, was regarded as the abode of a god, a symbol of supernatural power, an object of veneration and worship. It was a symbol of various

---

1.   *Virgil's Georgics,* tr. Smith Palmer Bovie (Chicago, 1956), pp. 34–35. For Dryden's version see *The Poems of John Dryden,* ed. James Kinsley, II (Oxford, 1958), 940–941.

things: of life, and knowledge of good and evil (the tree of Eden;[2]
the Irish hazel); of cosmos (the Vedic Asvatha tree; the Scandina-
vian Yggdrasil; the Chaldaean cedar; the Northern European
oak; the Celtic rowan tree); of immortality by communion with
its fruit or juice (the Vedic soma; the Iranian hoama; the Olym-
pian ambrosia),[3] and of kingdoms, temporal and eternal,[4] or of the
deathless liberation from Nature's cycle (the bodhi tree; the
"tree" of the cross). As the source and sustenance of life, the sacred
tree and its cult embraced "the highest rites in life and death,"[5]
and the health and prosperity of the community were thought to
depend on the ritual renewal by the sacral king, the custodian of
the cosmic and social order, in order to establish and maintain
harmony at all planes.[6] The theme of the tree of life and the water
of life has been the favorite subject of cultural anthropologists and
the myth-and-ritual-school. The pursuit of the mythopoeic lore
of the tree is invigorating but at times bewildering as when a
sensitive poet like Robert Graves transports us to the primeval
pagan world of the Celtic tradition.[7]

In ancient China, a sacred grove or tree was associated with the
earthmound (altar of soil), a symbol of Holy Ground (*she*), often
appearing in earlier texts with the millet (*chi*), a symbol of the
fruits of the soil and the harmonious influence of *yin* and *yang*.
T'ang the Completer, the founder of Shang, offered himself as a
victim at a sacred grove of Sang in order to alleviate a drought
that lasted for five years. Lord on High, pitying his devotion, sent
down an abundant rain.[8] Tan-fu, grandfather of King Wen, the
first king of the Chou, raised the grand earth-altar in order to
announce his punitive expedition before his troops marched off
(*Book of Songs*, 237/7).[9] What, then, are the trees associated with

2.   Genesis 2: 9.
3.   Edwin O. James, *The Tree of Life* (Leiden, 1966), pp. 257 ff.
4.   Nebuchadnezzar's vision of his empire as a tree (Daniel 4: 10–12) and *Paradise Regained*, IV, 146–151 (Daniel 2: 34–35).
5.   "Trees and plants " in Hastings' *Encyclopedia of Religion and Ethics*, XII, 454b.
6.   E. O. James, pp. 93–128, and Hooke, *Myth, Ritual and Kingship*, p. 169.
7.   *The White Goddess* (New York, 1960).
8.   Édouard Chavannes, "Le Dieu du Sol dans la Chine antique," in *Le T'ai Chan* (Paris, 1910), pp. 473–474; Karlgren, "Some Fecundity Symbols in Ancient China," *BMFEA*, II (1930), 9 ff.; "Some Sacrifices in Chou China," *BMFEA*, XL (1968), 19–25.
9.   Karlgren, *The Book of Odes* (Stockholm, 1950), p. 190, and Waley, *The Book of Songs* (London, 1954), p. 249.

the altar of soil (*she*) of the earliest dynasties? Tsai Yü, in his reply to Duke Ai, observes that the Hsia marked their Holy Ground with a pine, the Yin (Shang) with a cypress, the Chou with a chestnut tree (*Analects*, III, 21).[10] According to another source, the great altar of soil was represented by a pine, the altars of soil of the east by a cypress, those of the west by a chestnut, those of the south by a catalpa, and those of the north by an acacia.[11] Whatever its inherent qualities, a tree that sprang from the Holy Ground was a living symbol of the creative power of the fruitful earth, claiming the worshiper's awe, inviting him to contemplate the earth's bestowing power and the secret of life.

Because the establishment of altars of soil and grain was closely allied to that of a state, kingdom, or dynasty, the sacred tree—a symbol of the altars—was at once a monument to glorious works of the state's foundation, and a metaphor of the ancestral house, the native land, or the nation. Hence a group of metonymical formulas with the binoms *she-chi* (altars of soil and grain): a ruler was a "servant of the altars of soil and grain"[12]; a minister, "one who seeks the peace of the altars,"[13] or a "bulwark to the altars";[14] and a national crisis, a "tragedy to the altars."[15] That such tragedy was not merely metaphor was shown by the practice of covering the altars of a vanquished state with a shelter, severing its communication with the bright influences of Heaven and Earth.[16]

Equally, the Holy Ground and the sacred tree bear a number of resemblances to the Western counterpart. In cases of drought, caused by the imbalance of *yang*, one dug a hole at the earthmound (earth being *yin*) to connect it with an irrigation canal outside the village.[17] Moistening of the Holy Ground was expected to stimulate fructifying rain. On similar occasions in Greece, when the priest went to a shrine of Zeus on the Lycaean mountain of Arcadia and touched the water with a sprig of oak, a vapor was expected to rise and to spread in fruitful showers over the land.[18]

10. Waley, *The Analects of Confucius* (London, 1949), p. 99.
11. Chavannes, p. 467, and Tjan Tjoe Som, *Po Hu T'ung*, II (Leiden, 1952), 284–285.
12. *Analects*, XVI, 4 (Waley, p. 202).
13. *Mencius*, 7A, 19 (Legge, II, 458).
14. *Tso chuan*, Duke Hsüan 12 (Legge, V, 315).
15. *Tso chuan*, Duke Ting 10 (Legge, V, 778a).
16. Tjan, II, 384; Chavannes, pp. 459–466.
17. Chavannes, pp. 495–496.
18. *Encyclopaedia of Religion and Ethics*, XII, 453a.

Although the Chinese ritual does not provide an exact parallel, the invocation of rain was connected, in the first case, with the Holy Ground, and in the second, with the oak, the tree of Zeus the raingod. Like the palm tree of Deborah where Deborah dwelt and judged the children of Israel (Judges 4: 5), the altar of soil was the seat of judgments over punishments and death.[19] Both punitive and hunting expeditions were, as in the case of Tan-fu, announced with the *i* sacrifice,[20] and victorious campaigns usually ended at the altar with offerings. King Wu is said to have announced the crimes of the last Shang king Chou at the altar by rubbing the Holy Ground with the victims' blood.[21] In 640 B.C., the Duke of Sung sacrified the viscount of Tseng at an altar on the waters of Sui in order to awe and intimidate the wild tribes of the east.[22]

The comparison of tree and state is probably behind the common motif of the tree as a symbol of life for man or race. The poems about the blessings and boons in the *Book of Songs* usually introduce or amplify the motif with a delineation of trees and plants, in order to reinforce the correspondence between man and Nature.

> In the south is a tree with drooping boughs;
> The cloth-creeper binds it.
> Oh, happy is our lord;
> Blessings and boons secure him![23]

> On the southern hills grows the nutgrass;
> On the northern hills the goosefoot.
> Happiness to our lord
> That is the groundwork of land and home![24]

> Look at the foothills of Mount Han
> With hazel and red thorn so thick.
> Here's happiness to my lord,
> A happy quest for blessings.[25]

But in the poems of dynastic legends the motif fully exhibits, at

19. Chavannes, pp. 507–510.
20. Chavannes, p. 510; Tjan, II, 448 and 499.
21. *SC*, 33, 0216d (Chavannes, p. 507).
22. *Tso chuan*, Duke Hsi 19 (Legge, V, 177a); Chavannes, pp. 507–508.
23. No. 4 (Karlgren, p. 4; Waley, no. 163, p. 173).
24. No. 172 (Karlgren, p. 116; Waley, no. 170, pp. 179).
25. No. 239 (Karlgren, p. 191; Waley, no. 201, pp. 213–214).

least in the traditional reading, the intended symbolism—family descent, its unbroken line and future continuity, in short, the source of greatness of royal works: the spreading of young gourd stems and its long vines, the thick oak clumps, or the extended boughs.[26] Homer already compared the generation of men to those of leaves underscoring the brevity of human life:

> As is the generation of leaves, so is that of humanity.
> The wind scatters the leaves on the ground, but the
>   live timber
> burgeons with leaves again in the season of spring returning.
> So our generation of men will grow while another
> Dies.
>   (*Iliad*, VI, 146–150)[27]

The same simile occurs in the *Parabasis*, in *The Birds* of Aristophanes:

> Come now, let us consider the generation of Man,
> Compounded of dust and clay, strengthless,
> Tentative, passing away as leaves in autumn
> Pass, shadows wingless, forlorn
> Phantoms deathbound, a dream.
>   (685–689)[28]

The tree metaphor grew from the Confucian paedeutic tradition, and the formulas and clichés render it more meaningful and memorable. That is the poetic background of the first verse in canto 2, the supreme proem of the *Songs*:

> The tree that strikes deep root
> Is firm amidst the winds.
> Its flowers are good,
> Its fruit abundant.

The compilers' propensity for searching out an allegorical meaning in the realm of Nature invites the reader to contemplate the conceit that the tree of dynasty, on account of the mighty works of royal ancestors, scorns winds and all other vicissitudes. The agony of the Yi family's initial quest, its private griefs and hard-

---

26. Nos. 237, 238, 154.

27. Lattimore, p. 157; Robert Fitzgerald, "Generation of Leaves," *Perspectives USA*, no. 8 (1954), 68–85.

28. Dudley Fitts, tr. (New York, 1957), p. 61.

ships, was finally made public in the symbol of the unshakeable tree, with abundant flowers and fruits.

The second verse in the same proem introduces the theme of the water of dynasty, again in the allegorical mode:

> The stream whose source is deep
> Gushes forth even in a drought.
> It forms a river
> And gains the sea.

The tree and the stream, in the service of the *Songs'* moral message, demonstrate that nothing is achieved by chance. The stream not only becomes a river, but its tributaries grow in volume by mighty, inner movements of their own. Its gathered strength moves forward, finally reaching the ocean. Indeed, it was neither by accident, nor by luck, nor by military might alone that Yi Sŏng-gye founded the state. He was able to do so because of the accumulated virtues, "merits produced constantly by the lofty and intelligent work" of royal ancestors, as much as of his innate regal qualities.

The Heraclitean river stands for a flow of all things that come into being by conflict of opposites.[29] Denham's Thames, symbolic of "a political harmony of discord," is an emblem of life and kingship generally, and revolution and political chaos in particular.[30] The *aristeia* of an epic hero, as in the *Iliad*, V, 87-92, is aptly described by the image of a "winter-swollen river," destroying the strong-compacted dikes and mounded banks of the blossoming vineyards.[31] The moral and cosmic reverberations of a political act are often illustrated by the symbol of a overflowing river, to show that an act of transgression of the ways of Nature inevitably destroys man. The Po overflowed sweeping through woods and barns in order to lament the disasters of the civil war;[32] the river that flows backward (IV, 24) and the sea or river that rises beyond its usual bounds (V, 15) in the *History of the Franks* portend death and disaster.[33] The antithetical symbols of tempest and music in

---

29. Philip Wheelwright, *Heraclitus* (Princeton, 1959), pp. 29 ff.; G. S. Kirk, *Heraclitus* (Cambridge, 1954), pp. 369-380.

30. Wasserman, pp. 69, 80, 83; OHehir, pp. 20, 37, 196, 209, 242, 252.

31. Lattimore, p. 130.

32. Smith Palmer Bovie, p. 25.

33. Gregory of Tours, *The History of the Franks*, tr. O. M. Dalton, II (Oxford, 1927), 140, 198.

Shakespeare dramatize disorder and order, conflict and reconciliation. The use of this symbolism in political verse and ritual eulogies is too numerous to mention. In addition to the Confucian river that stands for the law of change (*Analects*, IX, 16)[34] or the original goodness of human nature, the symbol has another metaphysical value. It is a simile for the power of humanity subduing inhumanity (*Mencius*, 6A, 18),[35] the turning of people to the ruler's humanity (4A, 9),[36] or the way spiritual beings display their power (*The Mean*, 15).[37] The Mencian parable of two kinds of stream (4B, 18),[38] one that gushes out unceasingly day and night, filling every hole and flowing on to the four seas, and another which relies for its supply solely on the summer rain to be dried up again, is based on whether they have a source (spring) or not. The moral here is that the modesty required of a gentleman is held to be analogous to a stream with a source. This and other proverbial expressions with similar contents, are probably also behind the second verse of the proem, reminiscent of the river imagery in eighteenth century English didactic nature poetry.[39]

In addition to a commonplace association of life with a sea, the unceasingly rolling sea (*Iliad*, I, 348) and the rushing sea (*Odyssey*, V, 151) are probably symbols of destiny. The storm scene in the *Aeneid* (I, 8–296) marks, in Pöschl's estimate,[40] an early foreshadowing of the poem's thought and mood, especially the Odysseian half of the epic, serving as a symbol of destiny. The river in the *Songs* is a symbol of the destiny of the ruling house of Yi. It is, like the dragon, a symbol of the pattern of withdrawal and emergence, of the good qualities of an ideal ruler, as he successfully endures trials and hardships in order finally to emerge triumphant. The dynastic river, continuous and beneficent, transformed by precepts and examples and transforming mores and ethos, is a mirror

34. Waley, p. 142.
35. Legge, II, 420.
36. Legge, II, 300.
37. Chan, p. 102.
38. Legge, II, 324–325.
39. Earl R. Wasserman, "Nature Moralized: the Divine Analogy in the 18th Century," *ELH*, XX (1953), 39–76. For more on water see "Water and Watergods," in *Encyclopaedia of Religion and Ethics*, XII, 704–719; for a symbolism of sea see W. H. Auden, *The Enchafèd Flood* (New York, 1950), and Gaston Bachelard, *L'Eau et les Rêves* (Paris, 1942). For the religious symbolism of water see Eliade, *Images and Symbols*, pp. 151 ff.
40. Pöschl, *Die Dichtkunst Virgils*, pp. 13–33 and 183, n. 14.

which reflects the blessings of Heaven and the allegiance of people. By virtue of its orderly course it generates and reinforces the pattern of order and harmony, at once a symbol of the *modus vivendi* of the new dynasty and an allegory of the ideal state. In an attempt to trace to a common source the majestic flow of the virtues of royal ancestors, the compilers rightly chose the archetypal symbol of the river, probably the most ancient symbol of life and a supreme emblem of political rhetoric. Think of the course, the compilers argue, of a threatening, turbulent river whose end is not the sea of timelessness, but the destruction of the earth, man's abode. Only the temperate river can guarantee the stability and continuity of society. To the virtuous, it represents the dynamic movement of life; to the mutinous, a disastrous weapon of death. Like the crown, it is an emblem of continuing society, man's attunement to the law of Nature, his conformity to Heaven's purpose.

Let us return to the tree. Edmund Dudley (?1462–1510), in his *The Tree of Commonwealth*,[41] written during his imprisonment in the Tower, compares the commonwealth of England to a "faire and mighte tree." This tree cannot stand firm or grow upright in the realm without strong roots, the principal one being the love of God. Other roots are those of Iustice, Fydelite (truth), Vnytie (concord), and Peax. He then goes on to enumerate the fruits, the most delicate and best being honor of God ("first and most excellent fruit"). Other fruits must be used by discretion, with the "sauce of the dread of God." The following diagram summarizes his argument:

Roots	Fruit	Paring	Poisonous Core
Love of God			
Justice	Fruit of honorable dignity (king)	Compassion/pity	Unreasonable elation
Peace	Fruit of good example (clergy)	Increase of virtue/conning	Glorification
Truth	Fruit of wordly prosperity (chivalry)	True defense	Vain delectation
Concord	Fruit of profitable tranquility (commoners)	Timely exercise	Lewd enterprise

41. Ed. D. M. Brodie (Cambridge, 1948). See also James Howell, *Dendrologia* (London, 1644), pp. 134–135 for the allegory of the oak.

A similar chart can perhaps be drawn based on our discussion in Chapter IV. The various roots of the tree of dynasty might be the five cardinal principles of Confucian moral philosophy—humanity, righteousness, decorum, wisdom, and good faith. As in Dudley, the Confucian tree must be tended by the king and by his good moral examples, for it is from him that such tree grows.

The growth and decay of the tree of a royal house whose members are boughs, leaves, and fruits are elaborated in canto 84:

> The emperor was wise,
> But his heir was not yet born.
> Then the dead willow
> Grew again.

During the reign of the Han emperor Chao, a large stone in Mount T'ai stood up (79 B.C.), and in Shang-lin Park a dead willow grew again. The stone and the willow, Kuei Hung interpreted, alluded to the people, portending the rise of a commoner. As was expected, since the emperor had no heir, Liu Hsün (Emperor Hsüan), a commoner, became successor. The second verse, which traces its pedigree to the first, echoes the same theme:

> The country had a long history,
> But it was about to lose Heaven's charge.
> Then a withered tree
> Put forth green leaves.

The dead willow in the Shang-lin Park and the withered tree in Tŏgwŏn stand for the royal house, the Liu family in the first, and in the second the Wang house of the Koryŏ dynasty. The dead tree symbolizes the impending discontinuity of the Han dynasty caused by the barrenness of the emperor and the loss of mandate of Koryŏ respectively. Nature rallies against its destroyer, the last Koryŏ kings whose misrule disrupted cosmic harmony, but equally rallies with a providential sign for its reasserter or restorer. The re-growth of the dead tree therefore intimates Heaven's plan, the imminent reestablishment of cosmic and moral order, a ray of hope in the midst of darkness, and emblem of the victory of life over death.

In *Cymbeline*, Jupiter descends and visits in prison the sleeping Posthumus Leonatus, husband of Imogen, and leaves him a prophetic tablet which reads:

Whenas a lion's whelp shall, to himself unknown, without seeking find, and be embrac'd by a piece of tender air; and when from a stately cedar shall be lopp'd branches, which, being dead many years, shall after revive, be jointed to the old stock and freshly grow; then shall Posthumus end his miseries, Britain be fortunate and flourish in peace and plenty.

> (V, iv, 138–145)

The prophecy was interpreted by a soothsayer that Posthumus Leonatus is the lion's whelp; the "piece of tender air" (*mollis aer*) is *mulier*, the king's daughter (Imogen), and continues:[42]

> The lofty cedar, royal Cymbeline,
> Personates thee; and thy lopp'd branches point
> Thy two sons forth; who, by Belarius stol'n,
> For many years thought dead, are now reviv'd,
> To the majestic cedar join'd, whose issue
> Promises Britain peace and plenty.
> (V, v, 453–458)

Shakespeare's use of the tree as a royal house in the garden of commonwealth may be cited as a further parallel. In *1 Henry VI* (II, v, 41), Richard Plantagenet is a "sweet stem from York's great stock," and before dying the Earl of Warwick compares himself to the "cedar" (V, iii, 11). Richard of Gloucester, in his hypocritical reluctance to accept the throne, exclaims:

> The royal tree hath left us royal fruit
> Which, mellow'd by the stealing hours of time,
> Will well become the seat of majesty,
> And make, no doubt, us happy by his reign.
> (III, vii, 167–170)

Throughout the play, the tyrant is seen as the storm or blast which shakes "the unblown flowers," "small herbs," "sweet flowers," or "a tall tree" (Edward IV; I, iii, 259).[43] The "sea-walled garden" as a symbol of the commonwealth of England and the art of gardening to that of statecraft are well illustrated in the famous garden scene in *Richard II*. At the direction of the gardener, to prune and weed the garden, the servant asks:

---

42. Caroline F. E. Spurgeon, *Shakespeare's Imagery and What It Tells Us* (Cambridge, 1952), pp. 292–294 for the tree imagery in the play; the Arden edition by J. M. Nosworthy (London, 1955), pp. lxxxi–lxxxiv.

43. Spurgeon, pp. 214–222, for the tree imagery in the histories.

> Why should we in the compass of a pale
> Keep law and form and due proportion,
> Showing, as in a model, our firm estate,
> When our sea-walled garden, the whole land,
> Is full of weeds, her fairest flowers chok'd up,
> Her fruit-trees all unprun'd, her hedges ruin'd,
> Her knots disorder'd and her wholesome herbs
> Swarming with caterpillars?
> 　　　　(III, iv, 40–47)

The king's favorites, the gardener explains, were responsible for
the rank weeds, cankered flowers, unpruned trees, and ruined
hedges, and they were justly punished by Bolingbroke (later
Henry IV). The king, who was himself pictured as a tree ("Hath
now himself met with the fall of leaf," III, iv, 49), too was negli-
gent:

> O what pity is it
> That he had not so trimm'd and dress'd his land
> As we this garden!
> 　　　　(III, iv, 55–57)

Hamlet. who sees and feels the sickness around his court and the
world, declares in Scene II of Act I (135–137):

> Fie on't! oh fie, fie! 'Tis an unweeded garden,
> That grows to seed; things rank and gross in nature
> Possess it merely.

As has been pointed out, the image of weed is related to sickness
and corruption, contributing greatly to the unity of the play's
atmosphere and tonality.[44]

In Western epic poetry, the tree images are frequently employed
for warriors underscoring their steadfastness, tenacity, strength,
and tragic death.[45] The use of this epic simile in the account of
war, especially of wounded warriors as they topple to the ground,
is a commonplace. The simile of the oaks upon the mountain
singles out two Greek heroes as they await the attack of "tall"
Asios upon the wall (*Iliad*, XII, 131–134). In the Theomachy,
Achilles is compared first to a lion, then to a fire that "sweeps on

---

44. Wolfgang Clemen, *The Development of Shakespeare's Imagery* (London, 1951),
pp. 117–118.

45. For the imagery in the *Odyssey*, see G. R. Levy, *The Sword from the Rock* (London, 1953), p. 156, and Robert Graves, *The White Goddess*, p. 171.

in fury through the deep angles/ Of a drywood mountain and sets ablaze the depth of the timber" (XX, 490–491).[46] In the *Aeneid*, the simile of a great mountain ash brutally felled stands for the destruction of Troy (II, 626–631). Aeneas, unmoved by the tearful pleadings of Anna and Dido, is likened to a "stalwart oak-tree," a "veteran of the Alps" (IV, 441), and two giants, Pandarus and Bitias, to twin pines (IX, 674) and oaks (IX, 680).

As the simile of tree highlights heroic ideal and behavior, so the tree imagery, at least in Korean poetry, highlights the Confucian pattern and ideal behavior. We have already shown the thematic introduction of scenes from Nature in the *Book of Songs* as earlier examples of the technique known as *hsing*.[47] But it is in the poetry of withdrawal, repose, and contemplation, in accordance with the Confucian moral principles and Taoist contempt for engagement, that the imagery maintains verbal resonance. The Confucian trees of integrity are already alluded to by the master, when he declared, "Only when the year grows cold do we see that the pine and cypress are the last to fade" (*Analects*, IX, 27).[48] In T'ao Ch'ien's poetry of happy rural retirement, which sings his homecoming as a return to himself, the pine takes on a new dimension as a recurrent symbol of an isolated poet who weathers adversity, yet remains untarnished and unyielding. It often signals the acceptance of solitude as the only dramatic resolution of the perennial conflict between society and individual, civic obligations and self-fulfillment, as well as a fit metaphor of the landscape of the poet's regenerated mind. The "Ode to Knight Kilbo" (ca. 742–765), one of the extant Old Korean poems, for example, ends with an encomium:

> Knight, you are the towering pine,
> That scorns frost, ignores snow.

The repudiation of a worldly career wrought with vicissitudes and hypocrisy and the final affirmation of retired leisure as the discovery of the mind's dimensions, is often the keynote of such poetry, especially during the Yi dynasty's period of factional

---

46. Lattimore, p. 417.

47. On the *hsing* technique see Shih-hsiang Chen, "The *Shih-ching*: Its Generic Significance in Chinese Literary History and Poetics," *Bulletin of the Institute of History and Philology of Academia Sinica*, XXXIX (1969), 377 ff.

48. Waley, p. 144; for the symbolism of the pine, especially its magical quality, see *BMFEA*, III (1931), 93.

struggles which inaugurated the brutal pattern of murder for vengeance. In a short poetical form known as *sijo*, comprising some forty syllables, Sŏng Sam-mun (1418–1456), one of the compilers of the *Songs* and later one of the six martyred ministers of King Tanjong, expresses his undying loyalty and determination in the following testament:

> Were you to ask me what I'd wish to be
> In the world beyond this world,
> I would answer, a pine tree, tall and hardy
> On the highest peaks of Mount Pongnae,
> And to be green, alone, green
> When snow fills heaven and earth.[49]

The function of the pine is familiar enough, as is that of oak, cypress, cedar, or simply a tree. A poem by Kim In-hu (1510–1560) explores the possibility of reverberation of the central metaphor, the pine:

> The great pine we felled yesterday
> With its high long branches—
> Had we left it longer, it would
> Have yielded beams, lesser and greater.
> When the Royal Hall declines, alas,
> What tree will serve to uphold the state?

The Royal Hall, a metonymy for the reigning dynasty, is built and sustained by a number of beams; but once a great minister is senselessly felled on the simple account of his outspoken loyalty, where, the poet asks, can we find a tree that "will serve to uphold the state?" The imminent fall of the Royal Hall, instead of proclaiming majesty and provoking loyalty, mirrors the moral decadence of its dweller. The outrage of innocence is a breach of moral and cosmic order, a refusal to accept the metaphysical sanctions inherited from the tradition. The first two lines recall the chorus at the end of *Doctor Faustus*:

> Cut is the branch that might have grown full straight,
> And burned is Apollo's laurel bough,

---

49. Compare the poet's testament with Belarius' description of himself as he explains to Guiderius and Arvigarus how he has incurred the royal displeasure of Cymbeline and was banished (III, iii, 60–64).

That sometime grew within this learned man.
(V, ii, 136–138)[50]

Unlike the Marlovian metaphor, however, the Korean pine is reserved only for the integrity of upright man, never for the damnation elicited by the ambitious soul.

A poem by Chŏng Ch'ŏl (1537–1595), an exercise in veiled vituperation, provides a further elaboration of the same theme in vivid language:

> How could you leave it to rot,
> The lumber fit for beams and rafters?
> Small men indulge in hot debate
> In the torn and tumble-down house.
> O carpenters with ink cup and measure,
> You rush about to no purpose.

"Small men" in the third line are qualified in the fifth as "carpenters" who ought to strengthen the royal edifice. Instead, these fawning flatterers and crafty calumniators disrupt the orderly process of affairs, turning the structure into a "torn and tumbledown house." Hence good and worthy people (line 2) are left abandoned, with no opportunity to put their talents to good use. The imagery of carpentry traces its pedigree to the Confucian paedeutic tradition where the acceptance of honest admonition is a *sine qua non* of a good ruler on his way to becoming a sage. As wood is made straight by the use of the plumb line, so a ruler must accept the rules of the former kings as his norms. Broad learning and daily examination of his conduct are therefore often likened to the application of the plumb line, measure, square, and compass.[51] Hence the poem's oblique censure of royal folly, and the misuse of royal authority which flowed downward to his ministers, culminating in the disastrous disunity in the realm. Thus the poet has arranged his material to ensure that it is the king, the custodian of the dynastic tree, who has deliberately neglected his proper roles, untuning that string and fomenting factiousness at court. The tree is denied the miracle of spring and

50. Gordon W. O'Brien, *Renaissance Poetics and the Problem of Power* (Chicago, 1956), p. 106. Marvell, in "A Poem on the Death of O.C." (lines 269–270), avers: "The tree ere while foreshortened to our view,/When fall'n shows taller yet than as it grew." As far as I know, however, such a sentiment is rare in Korean poetry.

51. *Mencius*, 6A, 20 (Legge, II, 421); 4A, 2 (Legge, II, 292); *Great Learning*, 10 (Chan, p. 92).

the promise of life, turning the royal garden into a bleak, desolate place fit only for the weeds and caterpillars.

The metonymical or synecdochical tree in the Confucian tradition, therefore, sprang from man's acceptance of his place in Nature, his belief in the oneness of man and Nature. Its ancientness, as shown in our discussion, has never been questioned, as the old Chinese or Koreans gathered around the altars of soil and grain, strengthening the bond among themselves and that between man and Nature and the faith in the recurrent miracle of life. The fresh green boughs of Birnam Wood and leafy screens in *Macbeth*, one recent critic asserts, mark "a direct presentation in English literary drama for the first time of man's ancient faith in the recurrent miracle of spring,"[52] representing "the marriage of the figures of natural magic with the accumulated values of the Christian ethos."[53] The Christian themes dominant in the play are those of mercy and grace, "the invisible world of good triumphing over the world of evil,"[54] life over death, and mercy over justice. By citing this and other plays of Shakespeare as possible points of comparison, however, we are not intimating that the *Songs* reflect the same religious and metaphysical elements. Rather, our elucidation of the metaphysical and poetical overtones of the archetype which were the compilers' cultural inheritance, attempts to assess certain similarities as well as differences in the attitudes, conventions, allusions, in short, the richness of the referential world.

We have seen how the Confucian classics emphasized through analogy the place and function of a ruler, Heaven's deputy on earth. He is a pole star around which lesser stars in orbit pay homage (*Analects*, II, 1).[55] His brilliance is akin to that of the sun and the moon, and his order, to that of the four seasons.[56] His virtue's transforming power is a wind, bringing a metaphorical rain, or rain and dew quickening the maturity of man. Hence one satiated with virtue (humanity and righteousness) does not wish

---

52. Honor Matthews, *Character and Symbol in Shakespeare's Plays* (Cambridge, 1962), p. 165; Harold C. Goddard, *The Meaning of Shakespeare* (Chicago, 1966), pp. 520–521, offers the same view ("The legend Shakespeare makes use of is a myth of the coming of spring. War is winter, peace is spring.").

53. Matthews, pp. 190–191; Northrop Frye, *A Natural Perspective* (New York, 1965), p. 62.

54. George R. Elliott, *Dramatic Providence in Macbeth*, pp. 201–202.

55. Waley, p. 88.

56. Chan, p. 264.

for the flavor of fat meat (*Mencius*, 6A, 17).[57] A rich stock of astrological, astronomical, and natural images, invested with the values and ideals of the tradition, demonstrate not only the metaphorical mode of thought characteristic of the tradition but also the belief in the correspondence between all realms in the universe. *The Great Learning* says: "From the Son of Heaven down to the common people, all must regard cultivation of the personal life as the root of foundation. There is never a case when the root is in disorder and yet the branches are in order."[58] *The Mean*, which makes magnificent use of natural analogies, asserts that divine donation of the mandate to the possessor of great virtue is analogous to the nourishment of a "tree that is well taken care of" (17).[59] Later, the same text (20) states the comparison more explicitly: "When the right principles of man operate, the growth of good government is rapid, and when the right principles of soil operate, the growth of vegetables is rapid. Indeed, government is comparable to a fast-growing plant."[60] Therefore, when the compilers declare that the state is metaphorically a tree, they are merely reaffirming and recreating the myth charged with universal relevance and significance. As royal greatness is amplified by analogy with the greatness of past emperors and kings, mythological and historical, so the future greatness of the new dynasty, the vision of a Yi millennium, calls for the use of established analogy.

The use of the polysemous imagery of tree and river is an eloquent reaffirmation of the bond between man and Nature. The Confucian ethical and political system was based on the correspondence of microcosm and macrocosm, society to Nature. The function of the institutions was therefore to bring man into harmony with Nature, whose pattern man must heed in order to be true to himself. The requirements for kingship, the concept of the mandate, and the moral virtues inculcated were all part of ethical politics and political ethics. The ruler who is at the apex of the social pyramid and occupies a vital link in the great chain of Man-Earth-Heaven is the earthly guardian of universal harmony, and the state, in itself a reflection of that harmony at least in its structure, is a moral and paedeutic institution to safeguard the

57. Legge, II, 420.
58. Chan, p. 87.
59. Chan, p. 102.
60. Chan, p. 105.

continuity of society. Man's role in that scheme is to conform to the orderly pattern by discharging his obligations corresponding to his station, determined by the natural bond. Contemplation of the eternal pattern, the source of human mores, will lead man to discover his place as well as to perform his proper roles, as defined by the concept of the five relations. Contrariwise, rebellion against the pattern is at once a rebellion against his nature, a rupture of natural relations unleashing division and chaos. "Weird occurrences arise from men," says the *Tso Commentary*. "If men have no offense, then weird things will not occur of their own. It is when men abandon their constant ways that weird things occur."[61] It is man who causes Nature to reflect his hubristic act..

The vision of history presented in the tradition and especially in the *Songs* is a comic vision in the Dantesque sense. It demonstrates, like Shakespeare's histories and tragedies, that disorder will never succeed and that order will be restored in the end. A transgressor against the norms of Nature will be punished by the embodiment of order who can enlist the assistance of Nature. As a deputy of Heaven and officiator of ceremony required periodically to renew the bond, the ruler has magical and mysterious powers, linked to the elements of Nature. The legitimate but weak king like Richard II can still believe that

> This earth shall have a feeling, and these stones
> Prove armed soldiers, ere her native king
> Shall falter under foul rebellion's arms.
> (III, ii, 24–26)

The murder of the Son of Heaven or the lawful anointed king is a murder of Nature. Nature, which has provided the norms of human society, demands that society continue, and the optimistic vision of history demands the triumphant attainment of order. History is therefore viewed as a record of man's strivings toward that goal, of a perpetual longing for perfect order and harmony. Ups and downs notwithstanding, history will continue; it is in fact endless, like Nature itself, and the cycles of dynasties seem to follow the cycles of Nature. The view of history espoused by the Confucian tradition seems to be akin to that of Plato, Aristotle, Herodotus, Thucydides, Polybius, and Machiavelli, to name only

---

61. *Tso chuan*, Duke Chuang 14 (Legge, V, 92b). I have used the translation of Burton Watson, *Ssu-ma Ch'ien: Grand Historian of China* (New York, 1958), p. 15.

a few. The endless succession of the five elements, the intricate sets of correspondences between these elemental forces and associated virtues, the rise and fall of dynasties, or the cyclical and non-cyclical factors in the rise and fall of a single dynasty—all seem to point to an iterative pattern.

A river having a deep source and coursing on through time to a timeless sea—is this another symbol of a fruitless cyclical history, or of progression and purpose with a clear beginning and end, in brief, of "temporal history tumbling into the vast ocean of eternity?"[62] In *De civitate Dei* (413–426), St. Augustine (354–430) condemns "the wicked [who] walk in a circle" for their circuitous path in which their false doctrine runs (XII. 13)[63] and expounds the lineal nature of history. The timeless sea into which a dynastic river tumbles cannot be said to stand for the ultimate end (*telos*) of history, for strictly speaking, a cyclical view of history, be it Greco-Roman, Renaissance, post-Renaissance, or East Asian, cannot entertain eschatology. What approximates in the context "the myth of the impossible"[64] (*adynata*) is probably the following anonymous Middle Korean song, a popular version of political rhetoric surviving as "Song of the Gong":

> The king reigns; ring the gong.
> In this age, calm and lucky,
> Let us, let us live and love.
>
> In a sand dune, fine and plain,
> Let us plant roasted chestnuts, five pints.
> When the chestnuts shoot and sprout,
> Then we'll part from the virtuous lord.
>
> Let us carve a lotus out of jade,
> And graft the lotus in the stone.
> When it blossoms in the coldest day,
> Then we'll part from the virtuous lord.

62. C. A. Patrides, *The Phoenix and the Ladder* (Berkeley, 1964), p. 6.

63. *Basic Writings of Saint Augustine*, ed. Whitney J. Oates, II (New York, 1948), 193; also XII, 17 (II, 198). For a comparison of Hellenic and Judeo-Christian views of time and history, see Oscar Cullmann, *Christ and Time* (Philadelphia, 1950), *passim*, esp. pp. 51–60, and Tom F. Driver, *The Sense of History in Greek and Shakespearean Drama* (New York, 1960), pp. 19–66.

64. Gerardus van der Leeuw, "Primordial Time and Final Time," in *Man and Time*, papers from the Eranos Yearbooks, 3 (New York, 1957), 339. Cf. Joseph Needham, "Time and Knowledge in China and the West," in *The Voices of Time*, ed. J. T. Fraser (London, 1968), pp. 92–135.

Let us make an iron suit of armor,
Stitch the plates with iron thread.
When it has been worn and is spoilt,
Then we'll part from the virtuous lord.

Let us make an iron ox, and put him
To graze among the iron trees.
When he has grazed all the iron grass,
Then we'll part from the virtuous lord.

Were the pearls to fall on the rock,
Would the thread be broken?
If I parted from you for a thousand years,
Would my heart be changed?

Such pious hope is often visible in national anthems, as in the Republic of Korea's anthem which rightly invokes the pine on South Mountain as an emblem of the country's stability and continuity.

But who hews the tree of dynasty with axes and hatchets? Who peels the bark and shears the leafy boughs that shoot to Heaven? Who wrenches himself away from the tree, poisoning himself and the tree? It is man himself, and only man is capable of breaking the privileges of Nature and suffocating the miracle of growth. Only a vigorous, virtuous rule—and at times, alas, blood—can animate the tree. If a man is glorified and held up as a paradigm, it is not because of his strong sense of pride, honor, or fame, but because of his commitment to a cause, his dedication to a future. He derives his strength from his role in the reassertion of order, a dynasty that safeguards social and moral values, vital to the continuity of civilization. In this kind of work, therefore, it is the dynasty that is the subject, the true protagonist. The unnamed hero, then, is Korea, *res publica*, the first word of the cycle. Should man assume the role of an antagonist? This seems to be the question the *Songs* ask us to contemplate.

Songs of Flying Dragons

Preface

Your Majesty's subject ventures to observe that the Way of Heaven and Earth is extensive and deep, high and brilliant; therefore Heaven that overshadows us and Earth that sustains us are infinite and lasting; many are the virtues of your royal ancestors, accumulated and deep, and their work of foundation is, therefore, infinite and lasting.[1] Now the people merely see the expanse of mountains and seas, the growth of animals and plants, the change of winds, rain and thunder, the course of sun and moon, and the alternation of cold and heat. They do not see that all these are due to the Way of Heaven and Earth, extensive and deep, high and brilliant, [1b] that never ceases to operate. They see only the admirable beauty[2] of royal ancestral halls and palaces, the wealth of prefectures and districts, and culture[3] brought about by rites and music, by laws and government,[4] and the abundance of benevo-

---

1. The text of the following passages is provided by the vocabulary in *The Mean*, 26 (Legge, I, 419–421).

2. For 懿美 see *Erh ya* (*SPPY*), 1, 7, and *BMFEA*, XIV (1942), 232, gloss 368.

3. 文明 has several meanings: in *Chou i* (*SPTK*) 1, 4a (Wilhelm, I, 13) it means "beauty and clarity" or "adorned and brightened"; in *Shang shu* (*SPTK*), 1, 5b (Legge, III, 29), "accomplished and intelligent"; again in *Chou i*, 3, 2a (Wilhelm, II, 135), "form" or "pattern." Here, however, it is used in the sense of "culture," i.e., advancement of knowledge, progress of society, and development of civilization.

4. 刑政: in the Great Preface to the *Book of Songs* (Legge, IV, 36), it means "severity of punishments." But here it is used to mean "laws and government" as in the *K'ung-tzu chia-ya* (*SPPY*), 7, 5a.

lence, and the far-reaching effect of education. They do not see that all these are due to the firm foundation laid by the accumulated and deep virtues of your royal ancestors.

Your Majesty's subject reflects that after your progenitor had assisted the kingdom of Silla as the Master of Works (*sagong*), his heirs, generation after generation,[5] completed excellent works[6] and continued for several hundred years. [2a] It was Mokcho who first laid the foundation in the North. Three sage kings, Ikcho, Tojo, and Hwanjo, successfully made filial piety and brotherly love,[7] loyalty and sincerity,[8] their family code; and the northern people submitted to them in fealty.[9] To this day our elders[10] have told us of their great deeds and admire them. Toward the end of the Koryŏ dynasty, T'aejo, with matchless cultural and military ability,[11] and policies that benefited the age and pacified the people, chastised the south and subjugated the north.[12] His achievements were indeed great. [2b] With the guidance of Heaven, Earth, and spirits,[13] and with the help of those who asked him to arbitrate and those who praised him,[14] he gained the mandate of Heaven[15] and established the state. T'aejong, with his quick apprehension and clear discernment, intelligence and knowledge,[16] and matchless vision, laid the plan, founded the kingdom, restored order, and secured the state.[17] His marvelous achievement[18] and majestic merit became

5. For 緜 〃 see *Book of Songs*, 71 (Karlgren, p. 48), 237 (Karlgren, p. 189); and *BMFEA*, XXIV (1957), 75, gloss 225: "thin and long, drawn out."

6. For 世濟其美 see *Tso chuan*, Duke Wen 18 (Legge, V, 282b): "ages have acknowledged the excellence."

7. 孝弟: *Analects*, I, 2 (Waley, p. 83).

8. 忠信: *Great Learning* 10, 18 (Legge, I, 378) and *Analects*, VII, 24 (Waley, p. 128).

9. See cantos 3, 4, 6, and 18.

10. For 父老 see Moriya Mitsuo, *Tōyōshi kenkyū*, XIV, (1955), 43–60.

11. 神武: *Chou i*, 7, 10a (Wilhelm, I, 340): "unremitting divine power."

12. Refers to his subjugation of the Jürched and Mongols in the North (cantos 35–42, 54, 56) and the Japanese pirates in the South (cantos 49–52, 58–62).

13. For 鬼神 see my *Lives of Eminent Korean Monks* (Cambridge, Mass., 1969), p. 61, n. 275.

14. For 謳歌訴訟之所歸 see *Mencius*, 5A, 5 (Legge, II, 357).

15. 用集大命: *Shang shu*, 4, 8b (Legge, III, 199 and 200b): "caused its great appointment to light on him [T'ang]," literally, "He caused the mandate of Heaven to light on him."

16. 聰明睿智之聖: *Chou i*, 7, 10a (Wilhelm, I, 340): "reason and clear-mindedness; knowledge and wisdom."

17. Refers specifically to the incidents of 1398 and 1400, internecine feuds between Yi Pang-wŏn and his brothers for the throne (cantos 98–99, 102–103, 108–109).

18. 神功: *Chin shu*, 130, 1406c2.

known to all the people. Indeed, before our sovereign had ascended the throne, [3a] with the height of their cultural influence and military achievements, their mandate of Heaven and the submission of the people, and with the advent of auspicious signs, his forbears surpassed the accomplishments of a hundred generations, and we can foretell that their eternal work is coeval with Heaven that overshadows us and Earth that sustains us.

Since Hou Chi[19] was first appointed to rule and the Duke of Liu[20] lived in Pin[21] next to a land of barbarous customs, the Chou made loyalty and honesty their virtues and the care of the people[22] their policy. The Great King[23] and Wang Chi[24] diligently continued works begun, and the people enjoyed the blessings for more than a thousand years. King Wen and King Wu received the mandate of Heaven,[25] held all within the four quarters, and continued the dynasty for eight hundred years. The Duke of Chou established rites and music. [3b] Thereupon the odes *Mien,*[26] *Sheng min,*[27] *Huang yi,*[28] and *Ch'ih yüeh,*[29] based on the kings' achievements, were composed to glorify the royal works. The bells and drums shining luminously and hanging high like the sun and stars resound.[30] O how complete and elegant are these songs!

Your subject bows to observe that Your Majesty lets fall your robes and folds your arms,[31] carries on the succession of our dynasty, and is perfecting rites and music. Now, surely, is the time to compose songs of praise.

Your subject has basked in your favor, and together with the Senior

19.   The clan ancestor of the royal house of Chou. See Legge, III, 43–44, 595, and Maspero, "Légendes mythologiques dans le Chou king," *JA*, CCIV (1924), 1–100, esp. 81–82; *BMFEA*, II (1930), 16: "He who governs the millet."

20.   For 公劉 see Legge, III, 311, and *Book of Songs*, 250 (Karlgren, pp. 206–208).

21.   North of the Ching, near Sanshui. Waley, p. 244, n. 2.

22.   For 養民 see *Shang shu*, 2, 2a (Legge, III, 55–56).

23.   For Tan-fu see canto 3.

24.   Tan-fu's youngest son and father of King Wen. His name was Chi-li. *SC*, 4, 0013b (*MH*, I, 216).

25.   誕庸天命: *Shang shu*, 6, 9a (Legge, III, 311): "*received the great decree of Heaven* to sooth the regions of the great bright land" (italics added).

26.   *Book of Songs*, 237 (Karlgren, pp. 188–191; Waley, pp. 247–249).

27.   *Book of Songs*, 245 (Karlgren, pp. 199–202; Waley, pp. 241–243).

28.   *Book of Songs*, 241 (Karlgren, pp. 193–196; Waley, pp. 255–258).

29.   *Book of Songs*, 154 (Karlgren, pp. 97–99; Waley, pp. 164–167).

30.   鏗鎗: "the mingled sounds of bells and drums." See *Chi yün* (*WYWK*), 4/13, 499, 503, and Pan Ku's "Fu on the Eastern Capital," in *Wen hsüan* (*WYWK*), 1, 20 (Margoulies, *Le "fou" dans le Wen-siuan* [Paris, 1926], p. 66). For 炳燿 see *Tseng-kuang chu-shih yin-pien T'ang Liu hsien-sheng chi* (*SPTK*), 1, 1b.

31.   垂拱: *Suang shu*, 6, 10b (Legge, III, 317a).

Academician of the Hall of Worthies and Fifth State Councillor[32] Kwŏn Che,[33] and the Academician of the Hall of Worthies and Second Minister of Works [4a] An Chi,[34] has been charged with the composition of literary works.[35] It is therefore appropriate to sing of noble virtues in poetry. Vulgar, untutored phrases being no excuse for not performing our task, we respectfully gathered the language of the people's joy and praise and compiled one hundred and twenty-five cantos. We begin with the works of ancient emperors and kings, followed by the works of our ancestors. [4b] We do not praise too much the benevolent government of T'aejo and T'aejong after their enthronement, but emphasize and repeat their virtuous deeds and great accomplishments before they ascended the throne, in order to demonstrate the remoteness in time of the dynastic foundation and the difficulties of the royal task. In order to explain the songs, we composed explanatory verses. [5a] It is our sincerest hope that the songs will echo through the centuries on the wings of the wind and string instruments.[36]

On a certain day of summer, in the fourth month of the tenth year of the era *cheng-t'ung* (1445), *ŭlch'uk, chahŏn taebu*,[37] Seventh State Councillor, Senior Academician of the Hall of Worthies, Second Deputy Director of the Bureau of State Records,[38] and Second Mentor in the Heir Apparent Tutorial Office,[39] your humble subject Chŏng In-ji,[40] bowing his head, respectfully writes this Preface.

32. The *Ŭijŏngbu* (State Council) was an office with general powers of surveillance over all government offices and affairs. It consisted of seven major posts divided into two tiers; three state councillors occupied the top tier, and four the lower tier. The fifth State Councillor occupied the rank 1a (*KT*, 1, 7a-9b; *KTH*, 1, 37; *TYS*, 2, 1a-b). See Suematsu Yasukazu, *Seikyū shisō*, I (1965), 255–294.

33. Son of Kwŏn Kŭn (1352–1409), Kwŏn Che passed the examination in 1414 and rose to be the Fifth State Councillor (1445). He edited the dynastic history of Koryŏ and the *Songs*. His collected works, *Chijae chip*, survive (*CMP*, 247, 14a).

34. After passing the examination in 1414 and 1416, he served as the Minister of Works and Commissioner in the Bureau of Military Affairs. *SjS*, 34, 8a-b.

35. For 文翰 see *Yen-shih chia-hsün* (*SPTK*), 1, 13b-14a.

36. For 管絃 see *Chou li* (*SPTK*), 6, 14b (Biot, II, 52).

37. Corresponds to the rank 2a (*KT*, 1, 5b; *KTH*, 1, 34).

38. *Chi Ch'unch'ugwan sa*. The *Ch'unch'ugwan* (Bureau of State Records) was responsible for the compilation of the veritable records (*KT*, 1, 17a-18b; *KTH*, 1, 54–55; *TYS*, 2, 18a).

39. *Seja ubin'gaek* (*KT*, 1, 27a-29a: *KTH*, 1, 52-53; *TYS*, 2, 28b).

40. He passed the examinations in 1414 and 1427 and served Sejong in the Hall of Worthies and Sejo as Chief State Councillor (1455). He was enfeoffed as Lord of Hadong. His collected works, *Hagijae chip*, survive. *Sŏngjong sillok*, 98, 19a-20b; *HMN*, 4, 157–159; *YK*, 4, 306–307; *CMP*, 244, 6a–b; 247, 14a.

Presentation

Sŭngjŏng taebu,[41] Fifth State Councillor, Senior Academician of the Hall of Worthies, Second Deputy Director of the Bureau of State Records, and Rector of the National Academy, Your Majesty's subject Kwŏn Che; *chahŏn taebu*, Seventh State Councillor,[42] Senior Academician of the Hall of Worthies, Second Deputy Director of the Bureau of State Records, and Second Mentor in the Heir Apparent Tutorial Office, Your Majesty's subject Chŏng In-ji; and *kasŏn taebu*,[43] Second Minister of Works, Academician of the Hall of Worthies, Third Deputy Director of the Bureau of State Records, and Fourth Mentor in the Heir Apparent Tutorial Office, Your Majesty's subject An Chi, report to Your Majesty.

The accomplishments of your royal ancestors—their abundant virtues[44] and goodness, the splendid beginning of the dynasty,[45] together with all merits and the record of achievements[46] and [1b] their vast benefits—ought to be compiled into poetry and made known. Hence, we have composed these simple and imperfect songs,[47] so that they

41   Corresponds to the rank 1b (*KT*, 1, 6b; *KTH*, 1, 34).

42   *Sŏnggyun taesasŏng* (*KT*, 1, 14b-17a; *KTH*, 1, 53-54; *TYS*, 2, 10a).

43.   Corresponds to the rank 2b (*KT*, 1, 6a).

44.   For 積德 see *Shang shu*, 5, 2b (Legge, III, 227).

45.   洪祚 is an elegant term for the throne; see *Feng-su t'ung-i* (*SPPY*). 5, 1b.

46.   For 撰 meaning 算 see *Chi yün*, 7, 1155 and *Shuo-wen chieh-tzu* (*TSCC*), 5A, 14b. Cf. *Chou i*, 8, 6a, 8a (Wilhelm, I, 375).

47.   蕪 in 蕪詞 meaning "luxuriance of weeds" implies a vague, confused style. See *CTS*, 74, 3328a22, where Ts'en Wen-pen (595-645) praises Ma Chou's style.

may, in spite of their demerits, reach Your Majesty's attention. Your subjects venture to think that the deep-rooted tree is luxuriant even to the end of its branches, and that the deep-sourced stream flows longer in its course.[48] The Chou sang the *Mien* and traced its origin; the Shang sang the *Hsüan niao*[49] and searched into its genesis. It is therefore evident that these rulers in their creations relied on the works of their ancestors.

As we look upon our dynasty, [we see that] your royal ancestor started as the Master of Works and his heirs continued for generations,[50] numerous as abundant leaves. Mokcho first rose in the north and [2a] his mandate[51] was revealed in good omens. Ikcho and Tojo were born in Kyŏnghŭng. By the time of August Hwanjo, good fortune came, and with bounty and loyalty the allegiance of the people was no longer a matter of generations. Auspicious omens[52] frequently appeared, and Heaven's mandate[53] lasted many hundred years. T'aejo, Great King Kanghŏn, with the inborn abilities of the sage, responded to the call of the millennium and wielded an august spear to sweep away the northern and southern barbarians with valor and determination. [2b] He then received the mandate of Heaven[54] and spread goodness everywhere which provided peace and harmony for the people.[55] T'aejong, Great King Kongjŏng, with his peerless valor and wisdom,[56] surpassed the ancients, upheld the brightness of the ancestors, established the state,[57] and distinguished himself beyond all times. He also surpassed the virtues of all great rulers, enlarged the [3a] royal works of his ancestors and matched the greatness of ancient sage kings. Why not celebrate these deeds in poetry for those who come after us!

48. The parallel passage occurs in *Yü Tzu-shan chi* (*SPTK*), 7, 14b, and Yi Saek's eulogy in the *Yi Cha-ch'un shindo pi* in Hamhŭng (erected in 1388; *CKS*, I, 710).

49. *Book of Songs*, 303 (Karlgren, pp. 262–263; Waley, pp. 275–276).

50. For 奕葉 see *Ts'ao Tzu-chien chi* (*SPPY*), 9, 23a.

51. 景命: *Book of Songs*, 247, 7 (Karlgren, p. 204): "great appointment."

52. For 禎 meaning 祥 see *Shuo-wen chieh-tzu*, 1A, 2.

53. 眷顧: Yang Hsiung's "Ch'ang-yang fu," in *Wen hsüan*, 9, 105 (Erwin von Zach, *Die Chinesische Anthologie* [Cambridge, Mass., 1958], II, 127).

54. For 籙 see Chang Heng's "Fu on the Eastern Capital," in *Wen hsüan*, 9, 105 (Erwin von Zach, I, 20). Chŏng To-jŏn, on September 3, 1392, presented a eulogy, *Suborok*, consisting of 16 four-word lines (*Sambong chip* [*Han'guk saryo ch'ongsŏ*, XII; 1961], 2; *AHKB*, 2, 28a; 4, 12a-13b; *TS*, 4, 2b; see canto 86).

55. 黎庶: *Book of Songs*, 258, 3 (*BMFEA*, XVI [1944], 39–40); *Shang shu*, 1, 1b, 9b (Legge, III, 17, 43): "the black-haired people."

56. 勇智: *Shang shu*, 4, 2b (Legge, III, 178).

57. 社 (*dia, "spirit pole and altar to the spirit of the soil") and 稷 (*tsiәk, "millet"). See *Shang shu*, 4, 8b (Legge, III, 199); *Chou li*, 3, 112 (Biot, I, 193); *Li chi* (*SPPY*) 3, 11b (Couvreur, *Mémoires sur les Bienséances et les Cérémonies* [Paris, 1950], pp. 225, 233]; *Analects*, XI, 24 (Legge, I, 246); *BMFEA*, II (1930), 10–20.

When your subjects venture to speak, Your Majesty is most discriminating and undivided.[58] You have well preserved and transmitted the royal works. Your ways are in harmony with Heaven, your government is just, and your bounty showers benefit among the people. Rites are perfected; music is harmonious. How dazzling[59] is the perfection of our civilization! In this glorious and peaceful reign, eulogies should be composed.

Your subjects have lavished their meager talent[60] on the fulfillment of their literary task. They have respectfully collected the people's praise and ventured to model them [3b] on the music of the royal ancestral temple. The songs tell of the days of the foundation work of Mokcho to the days when T'aejong was heir apparent. We have sought and gathered all the unique and great happenings, clearly recounted[61] and displayed[62] the hardships of the royal task. We have compiled the events in the vernacular and attached Chinese verses in order to elucidate words. These songs may not be the best description of Heaven and Earth or imitation of sun and moon; but carved in metal and stone and played on wind and string instruments, they may make known the bright and majestic.[63] [4a] If Your Majesty graciously approves and authorizes the publication and distribution of these songs, they will be handed down to sons and grandsons, making them realize the timelessness of the task. In the villages and countries they will be used everywhere and will not be erased from the memory of man. We therefore have respectfully copied the one hundred and twenty-five cantos we have compiled and have bound them,[64] together with the letter of presentation. We now submit them to Your Majesty's inspection.

Unable to suppress the awe and fear[65] that make their untutored

---

58. 惟精惟一: *Shang shu*, 2, 4a (Legge, III, 61): "Be discriminating, be undivided, that you may sincerely hold fast the Mean" (Shun's remarks to Yü).

59. For 煥乎 see *Analects*, VIII, 19 (Legge, I, 244: "How glorious"; Waley, p. 136: "dazzling").

60. 雕篆: Wang Chin's "Dhūta Temple Stele Inscription," in *Wen hsüan*, 12, 29 (*JAOS*, LXXXIII [1963], 354, n. 183): "carved worm-shaped characters and seal-script engraving." Although it is used as a deprecatory term by Wang Chin, here it is used in a more general sense of "literary task" without the overtone of pedantry or rhetoric.

61. For 敷陳 meaning "to state or recount clearly" see *Huai-nan Tzu (SPTK)*, 21, 4a.

62. For 悉備 see *Chou i*, 8, 8b (Wilhelm, I, 377).

63. 光烈: *Shang shu*, 9, 4a (Legge, III, 447): "glorious and meritorious."

64. For 裝璜 see *T'ung ya*, 32, 8a-b.

65. For 戰汗 meaning "to sweat out of fear," see *Tseng-kuang chu-shih yin-pien T'ang Liu hsien-sheng chi*, 35, 2a, and Ernst Robert Curtius, *European Literature and the Latin Middle Ages*, pp. 83–85, for Western modesty topos.

minds tremble,[66] and bowing deeply, [4b] *sŭngjŏng taebu*, Fifth State Councillor, Senior Academician of the Hall of Worthies, Second Deputy Director of the Bureau of State Records, and Rector of the National Academy Kwŏn Che; *chahŏn taebu*, Seventh State Councillor, Senior Academician of the Hall of Worthies, Second Deputy Director of the Bureau of State Records, and Second Mentor in the Heir Apparent Tutorial Office Chŏng In-ji; the *kasŏn taebu*, Second Minister of Works, Academician of the Hall of Worthies, Third Deputy Director of the Bureau of State Records, and Fourth Mentor in the Heir Apparent Tutorial Office An Chi, respecfully submit this presentation letter on a day of the fourth month of the tenth year of the era *cheng-t'ung.*

66. 屛營之至: *HHS*, 85, 0819d12.

[1]

Korea's[1] six dragons[2] flew in the sky.
Their every deed was blessed by Heaven,[3]
Their deeds tallied[4] with those of sage kings.[5]

1.　海東: Interlinear gloss reads: "Korea is called Haedong, because it lies east of Po-hai (Parhae)." Repeated by *Taedong unbu kunok* (1950 ed.), l, 1a.

2.　The six dragons are the four ancestors of Yi Sŏng-gye—Mokcho (d. 1274), Ikcho, Tojo (d, 1342), and Hwanjo (d. 1360)—Yi Sŏng-gye, and his fifth son, Yi Pang-wŏn. *SS*, 1a-11a; *TS*, 1, 1a ff.; *YK*, 1, 3–40, 62–88; 2, 114–132. For the dragon symbolism see *Chou i*, 1, 1b (Wilhelm, I, 8; 390–391) and Chapter V.

3.　天福: The commentary quotes the *Tso chuan*, Duke Hsiang 26 (Legge, V, 526b): "It was thus that T'ang obtained the blessing of Heaven." See also *Book of Songs*, 305, 4 (Karlgren, p. 266; Waley, p. 279).

4.　同符: *Mencius*, 4B, 1 (Legge, II, 316–317): "But when they [Shun and King Wen] got their wish and carried their principles into practice throughout the Middle Kingdom, it was like uniting the two halves of a seal." Compare the Chinese tally with the Greek *skytale*, for which see J. K. Anderson, *Military Theory and Practice in the Age of Xenophon* (Berkeley, 1970), p. 68.

5.　The sage kings are, of course, Yao, Shun, and the founders of the Chou. The ruler can ascend the throne as a Son of Heaven only when he, like Yi Sŏng-gye and his ancestors, receives the mandate of Heaven. Therefore, the achievements of the founders of both Chinese and Korean dynasties tally.

[2]

The tree that strikes deep root
Is firm[1] amidst the winds.
Its flowers are good,
Its fruit abundant.

The stream whose source is deep
Gushes forth even in a drought.
It forms a river
And gains the sea.

1.　Literally, "does not shake or waver." For the interpretation of this canto see Chapter VI.

[3]

The great ruler of Chou
Lived in the valley of Pin
And began
His royal works.

Our founder
Lived in the city of Kyŏnghŭng[1]
And began
His royal works.

Tan-fu is the ninth grandson of the Duke of Liu,[2] who was the great
grandson of Hou Chi,[3] the putative ancestor of Chou. Desirous of
continuing the works of Hou Chi and the Duke of Liu, who established
his country in the valley of Pin,[4] Tan-fu practiced virtue and justice.[5]
The people therefore loved him and made him their king. The wild
Ti attacked the valley of Pin, and Tan-fu appeased them with hides,
silk, dogs, horses, precious stones, and jade. The Ti then behaved
worse, whereupon Tan-fu assembled the elders of Pin and told them:
"What the wild men of Ti want is our land. The soil feeds our people,
but if we are to guard our soil, we shall have to call on the people to
lose their lives. This would be worse than not having a ruler. I shall
therefore leave you." He then left Pin, crossed the Ch'i and Chu[6] and
Mount Liang,[7] and settled at the foot of Mount Ch'i.[8] Claiming the
benevolent and wise duke as their ruler, the young and old of Pin
followed him like people flocking to market. Neighboring countries
also heard of his good government and gave him their allegiance. He
then abolished the customs of the Jung and Ti, built walled cities and
palaces, laid out villages for the people, and changed the name of the
country to Chou. He is the one whom posterity reveres as the Great
King. *SC*, 4, 0013a-b (*MH*, I, 213-215); *Mencius*, 1B, 5; Franke, I,
104 ff.; III, 74-75.

Mokcho ("our founder" in line 5), while living in Chŏnju,[9] had a
dispute with the governor over the official female entertainer (*kisaeng*).
The governor (*allyŏmsa*)[10] was enraged and plotted Mokcho's death.
When Mokcho left Chŏnju for Samch'ŏk[11] in Kangwŏn province, 170
families followed him. Upon arriving in Samch'ŏk, he heard that the
former governor of Chŏnju had been appointed governor of Samch'ŏk.
Disliking the troublemaker, Mokcho took his family, crossed the sea
to the province of Hamgil,[12] and stopped at Tŏgwŏn.[13] The 170
families again followed him. Later he pledged allegiance to the Mongols, moved to Odong,[14] thirty ri east of Kyŏnghŭng, and became a

pentachiliarch there.[15] The people in the northeast returned to his allegiance. This was the beginning of the royal house of Yi. *TS*, 1, 1a-2a; *YK*, 1, 6.

1. Formerly Kongju; in 1437, it became a *kun* and on July 11, 1443, a *tohobu*. (*SnSC*, 100, 31a-b; 155, 16b-18a; *TYS*, 50, 42a f.).

2. *Book of Songs*, 250 (Karlgren, pp. 206–208; Waley, pp. 244 ff.).

3. See n. 19 to the Preface.

4. North of Mount Ch'i in Shensi (*MH*, I, 213, n. 2).

5. *Book of Songs*, 237 (Karlgren, pp. 189–190). See also canto 5.

6. Both the Ch'i and the Chu are in western Shensi (*MH*, I, 212, n. 3); the Chu flows east and enters into the Lo.

7. In Shensi, west of Han-ch'eng hsien (*MH*, I, 214–215, n. 5).

8. Seventy miles west of Sian, northeast of Chi-shan hsien, on the north side of the Wei (*MH*, I, 104, n. 1).

9. In North Chŏlla, called Wansan under Paekche. Kyŏnhwŏn established his capital there. It was destroyed in 936 by Wang Kŏn, the founder of Koryŏ. In 940 it was called Chŏnju; in 1392 again Wansan; and in 1431 again Chŏnju (*KRSC*, 57, 32b-33a); *SGSG*, 36, 3; *SnSC*, 151, 3b-4b; *TYS*, 33, 3a-4a).

10. Also called *anch'alsa* under Koryŏ, in 1389 changed to *kwanch'alsa* or *allyŏmsa* (*KRS*, 77, 34b-35b). See Pyŏn T'ae-sŏp, "Koryŏ anch'alsa ko," *YH*, XL (1968), 1–52.

11. Around 80–112 it became a *chu*; King Kyŏngdŏk changed its name to Samch'ŏk. Under Koryŏ its name was Ch'ŏkchu; in 1393 it became Samch'ŏk pu, and in 1413 a *tohobu* (*KRSC*, 58, 24a-b; *SGSG*, 35, 8; *SnSC*, 153, 9b-10a; *TYS*, 44, 25a-b).

12. Corresponds to modern South and North Hamgyŏng. In 995 it was called Sakpangdo. When northern Hamju was occupied by the East Jürched tribes, Yun Kwan subjugated them (1107–1108) and established the Nine Walled Cities. In 1258, northern Hamju was recaptured and called the Northeast. In 1413, it was named Yŏnggil and, in 1416, finally Hamgil (*KRSC*, 58 15a-16b; *SnSC*, 155, 1a-2b; *TYS*, 48, 1a-3a).

13. Northwest of Wŏnsan in South Hamgyŏng. Originally Ch'ŏngjŏng kun of Koguryŏ; Silla called it Chŏngch'ŏn. Its names under Koryŏ were first Yongju, then Ŭiju. In 1413, it became Ŭiju kun, but in 1437 was called Tŏgwŏn, and finally elevated to be the site of a *tohobu* in 1445 (*SGSG*, 37, 3; *KRSC*, 58, 18b-19a; *SnSC*, 155, 9a-b; *TYS*, 49, 10b-11a).

14. Thirty ri east of Kyŏnghŭng (*TYS*, 50, 44b); the *Puksae kiryak* (CKK, 1911) puts Mokcho's residence in the village of Kŭmdang.

15. Ikeuchi Hiroshi, *Mansenshi kenkyū*, V (1963), 111–117; Naitō Shumpo, *Chōsenshi kenkyū* (Kyoto, 1961), pp. 212–236, 236–239; and *HJAS*, XVI (1953), 237–255.

[4]

He went among the Ti barbarians;
The Ti barbarians rebelled.
That he moved to the Ch'i
Was indeed Heaven's wish.

Ikcho went among the Jürcheds;
The Jürcheds rebelled.
That he moved to Tŏgwŏn
Was indeed Heaven's wish.

For the first stanza see canto 3.

During his stay in Odong, when Mokcho visited the Jürched chiliarchs,[1] they butchered horses and dogs and gave a feast lasting several days. When they, in turn, visited Odong, Mokcho did the same for them. He often met with them and they feasted in this manner. Ikcho continued the practice when he succeeded Mokcho. Later, when Ikcho's influence and moral force were felt everywhere and subjects of the provincial officials all gave their hearts to him, the provincial officials disliked this and plotted against him. Petitioning him, the officials said, "We are going hunting in the north. Let us therefore prolong our next feast for twenty days." Ikcho consented, and when they did not return at the appointed time, he went to Hwŏnjat[2] to search for them. On the roadside, an old woman carrying a jar on her head and a cup in her hand came toward him. He asked her for a cup of water. She rinsed the cup thoroughly and offered it to him, saying, "Do you not know that the people went away to gather soldiers? It would be a pity to lose a man of your stature. I therefore cannot help telling you the truth." Ikcho rushed home and ordered his family to sail down the Tumen[3] and meet him on Chŏk Island.[4] When he climbed the hill, with his wife behind him,[5] and surveyed the field of Odong, he saw it was covered with enemy cavalry and a vanguard of 300 horsemen approaching his village. Ikcho spurred his horse and reached the shore. But Chŏk Island was a good 600 paces away, the water there is generally deep, and without tidal change. The promised ship had not yet arrived with his family; Ikcho was at a loss what to do. At this moment, the sea ebbed and the breadth of the water was not more than a hundred paces. He jumped on his horse and raced across. When all his people had followed him across, the water flowed in again and the enemy was forced to retreat. Even now the people in the north tell of his escape as a heavenly intervention. On the island, Ikcho erected a clay hut, whose site is still preserved. When the people in Odong heard the whereabouts of Ikcho, they all came to the island and lived under his protection. Later, when he moved to Tŏgwŏn, the people followed him like a multitude hastening to market. *TS*, 1, 2b-3a; *YK*, 1, 7-8.

1. For Korean-Jürched relationships see *CMP*, 180, 12a-15a, esp. 14a-b, a series of articles by Ikeuchi in *MCRKH*, II (1916), 203-323; IV (1918), 299-365; V (1918), 299-366; VII (1920), 219-254; *Mansenshi kenkyū*, IV (1944), 119-176, 265-348; and Kim Sang-gi, *KSC*, IV (1959), 65-205. On aspects of trade see Marugame Kinsaku, *Rekishigaku kenkyū*, V (1935), 57-82, and Yi In-yŏng, *Han'guk Manju kwan'gyesa yŏn'gu* (1954), For the employment of the Jürched in early Yi, see Kawachi Yoshihiro, *CG*, XIV (1959), 381-422, and Yi Hyŏn-hŭi, "Chosŏn chŏn'gi yain ŭi yugyŏng yuhoech'aek ko," in *Ilsan Kim Tu-jong paksa hŭisu kinyŏm nonmunjip* (1966), pp. 63-121. For their notice in Chinese records see *MTB*, X (1938), 41 ff., and XVII (1958), 1-25. On their marriage customs see *YC*, 10, 266-268.

2. Seven ri east of the Hunch'un River and five ri west of the Tumen (*YG*, 1, 8a; *TYS*, 50, 22b-23a).

3. Called Tumen from the Jürched word for "ten thousand" because the river is formed of many tributaries. Its source is on Mount Paektu, and it is 324 miles long. The Tumen, together with the Yalu, forms a natural boundary against Manchuria and the maritime province of Siberia (*SnSC*, 155, 1b, 11a, 14b, 16a; *TYS*, 50, 20b).

4. Sixty ri east of Kyŏnghŭng; its circumference is said to be twelve ri (*SnSC*, 155, 17a; *TYS*, 50, 44b-45a).

5. His first wife, who bore him two sons (*TS*, 1, 3a). For her tomb see *TYS*, 49, 17a, and *CKS*, II, 1349-50.

[5]

The Duke of Chou[1] sang
Of the mud shelter by the Ch'i and Chu.
O sorrow and toil of great enterprise,
It was Tan-fu's sorrow, Tan-fu's work.

Today one can still see
The clay hut on Chŏk Island.
O distress and toil of great enterprise,
It was Ikcho's distress, Ikcho's toil.

The Duke of Chou,[2] the younger brother of King Wu, acted as regent for King Ch'eng. He is said to have composed a poem to admonish Ch'eng, in which he praised Tan-fu for leading the people away from Pin to Mount Ch'i and for living there in a clay hut. The *Book of Songs*, 237 (Waley, pp. 247–249) says, "The young gourds spread and spread./ The people after they were first brought into being/ from the river Tu went to the Ch'i./ Of old Tan-fu the duke/ Scraped shelters, scraped holes;/ as yet they had no houses." *SC*, 4, 0013a (*MH*, I, 244 ff.).

The second stanza also points out the difficulty of royal work, expecially the hardship suffered by Ikcho (canto 4), and admonishes royal descendants to continue and preserve the dynasty. *TS*, 1, 3a; *YK*, 1, 8.

1. In the original: "a sage of posterity."
2. *Shang shu*, 7, 8a-10b; 8, 12a-16b; 9, 8b-11b (Karlgren, *The Book of Documents* [1950], pp. 35–36, 48–51, 56–59). He is also praised in the *Book of Songs*, e.g., 157, 259, 262, 300.

[6]

The majesty of Shang lost vigor:
He was about to take charge of the country.[1]
At the time the shores of the West River[2]
Were as crowded as on a market day.

Fortune deserted the Koryŏ House:
He was about to take charge of the country.
At the time the shores of the Eastern Sea
Were as crowded as on a market day.

For the first stanza, see canto 3.

The second stanza also implies that the crowding by the people (cantos 3–4) was an auspicious sign that the Yi family would receive the mandate of Heaven. *TS*, 1, 3a; *YK*, 1, 8.

1. The second line of the first verse in Chinese has 九圍, for which see the *Book of Songs*, 304, 3 (Waley, p. 378: "all the lands") and *BMFEA*, XVIII (1946), 190: "nine circumscriptions."
2. The Ch'i River.

[7]

The red bird with a message in its beak
Perched on his bedroom door.
This revealed the blessing of Heaven,
The rise[1] of the august one was at hand.

The snake held the magpies in its mouth
And hung them on the bough of a tree.[2]
This was the lucky sign,[3]
The rise of the august scion was at hand.

When King Wen received the mandate of Heaven a red bird came
with a message written in cinnabar[4] and perched on the door of his
house in Feng.[5] The message varies according to the text. *SC*, 4, 0013b
(*MH*, I, 216).

When Tojo was in camp, two magpies came and perched on a tall
tree. He wanted to shoot them from a distance of several hundred
paces; his men thought it impossible. His single arrow, however,
brought them down. At that time a snake appeared and carried off
the dead birds and hung them on the bough of a tree. The people
wondered about the strange happenings which foretold the rise of Yi
Sŏng-gye ("the august scion" in line 8). *TS*, 1, 3b-4a.

1.   *Chou i*, 5, 9a (Wilhelm, II, 285).
2.   In the original, *chŭmge*, the name of a large tree of a kind about which
nothing seems to have been known. See Pang Chong-hyŏn, *Ilsa kugŏhak nonmunjip* (1963), p. 188, and Kim Yun-gyŏng, *Han'gyŏl kugŏhak nonjip* (1964),
p. 60.
3.   嘉祥: *HS*, 8, 0310d (Dubs, II, 238): "favorable omen."
4.   Also occurs in *Mo Tzu* (*SPPY*), 5, 9a (Watson, *Mo Tzu: Basic Writings*
[New York, 1963], p. 58) and *Ch'un-ch'iu fan-lu*, 57 (Chan, p. 284).
5.   West of Sianfu, Shensi (*MH*, I, 221, n. 1).

[8]

Heaven chose the heir apparent;
The elder brother's wish was fulfilled.
So Heaven produced
The august scion.

Heaven chose the heir apparent;
The imperial decree favored him.

So Heaven produced
The august son.

Tan-fu had three sons: T'ai-po, Chung-yung, and Chi-li ("heir apparent" in line 1). In the time of Tan-fu, Shang gradually decayed, and Chou increased in prosperity. Chi-li had a virtuous son, Ch'ang. When Tan-fu wanted to punish Shang, T'ai-po disliked the idea. Tan-fu therefore wished to abdicate in favor of Chi-li. T'ai-po detected his father's wish and, together with his brother Chung-yung, fled to the south. Thereupon, Tan-fu had Chi-li ascend the throne and bequeath the kingdom to Ch'ang, who is known as King Wen. He was succeeded by his son Fa (King Wu, "the august scion" in line 4). *SC*, 4, 0013b-c (*MH*, I, 215–216); Franke I, 105–107.

Ikcho succeeded Mokcho; Tojo succeeded Ikcho. On the death of Ikcho, his eldest son, Cha-hŭng,[1] succeeded him but died soon. Therefore Hwanjo ("heir apparent" in line 5) succeeded Cha-hŭng. Hwanjo's son ("the august son" in line 8) became the founder of the Yi dynasty. *TS*, 1, 1a–4a.

1. Tojo's first son, born of Queen Kyŏngsun, née Pak; he was called Prince Wanch'ang. His Mongol name was Tas-puqa (*SS*, 3a; *TS*, 1, 3b).

[9]

Wu served Heaven and punished Chou's crime,[1]
Princes gathered from the four quarters.
Long-standing was his influence,
The western barbarians,[2] too, came in homage.

Yi upheld right and marched back,
People gathered from a thousand leagues.
Deep was his influence,
The northern barbarians, too, came in homage.

Chou Hsin or Chou, the last ruler of the Shang, indulged in women and wine. He had no virtue, used Heaven's gifts recklessly, injured the people, and became the foremost of villains and thieves. When King Wu went east to survey the troops and came to the Meng Ford, princes gathered there and asked him to punish Chou, but Wu bade them to draw back their army, telling them that the mandate of Heaven had not yet come. Two years later, Chou became even crueler and killed his own son and imprisoned Chi Tzu.[3] Thereupon King Wu told the princes that the Shang should be punished for their crimes. Wu marshaled his army and invaded Chou from the east. He led his armies across the Meng and penetrated north of the river. More princes came with their forces and wished him success. After surveying his armies and making his plan known in a clear declaration to all his officers, Wu camped near the Shang city and waited for the Shang army to come out. On the second morning, when he reached the Mu Field (north Honan), he made another declaration. Having heard the news, Chou came out with a large army. Chou's army was enormous, but it lacked war spirit and stood waiting for Wu's troops to attack. The vanguard attacked Chou's men and made them flee, and mutiny among them resulted in a sea of blood. Chou then fled to his palace. He climbed to the Lu terrace, hid treasures under his robe, leapt into the flames he had set, and burned to death. When Wu and the princes approached the Shang city, the people had assembled outside to receive him. Wu had his officials announce that they had come with the mandate of Heaven, and the people bowed and made obeisance. Wu, then, went to the place where Chou had died, cut off Chou's head, impaled it on his white banner, and withdrew with his troops. On the following day he reentered the Shang city wearing the royal robe. *SC*, 3, 0012a-c; 4, 0013c f. (*MH*, I, 199 ff., 205, 222–238); *Shang shu*, 6, 1a ff. (Legge, III, 281 ff.; Karlgren, *The Book of Documents*, p. 29); Franke, I, 107–108.

When Shin U planned an expedition to Liaotung with General Ch'oe Yŏng (d. 1389),[4] Yi Sŏng-gye stated four objections to a mobilization of troops. Shin U did not listen, and ordered the invasion of Liaotung. Yi, therefore, ordered his troops to recross the Yalu when he had reached Wihwa Island, and marched back to the capital.[5] At the time, the northeastern people and Jürched ("northern barbarians" in line 8), who had hitherto not joined in the campaign, followed Yi. *KRS*, 137, 9a, 14b-15a; *KRSCY*, 33, 9a, 13a-14b; *TS*, 1, 21a-24b; *TT*, 53, 454, 458–459; *YK*, 1, 25–28.

1. *Shang shu*, 6, 3b (Legge, III, 290).
2. *Shang shu*, 4, 3b (Legge, III, 181).
3. The uncle of the last monarch of Shang, who fled to Korea in 1122 B.C., when the Shang was deposed by the Chou, and built a capital at P'yongyang. Traditionally, his dynasty is said to have lasted until 194 B.C., but recent scholarship has proved that Chi Tzu never came to Korea (*HGS*, I [1959], 92–114).
4. His dates are 1315 (or 1317)–1389. In 1354, as Second Deputy Commander he went to Yüan to participate in a campaign against Chang Shih-ch'eng; in 1362, he repulsed the Red Turbans; in 1364, crushed the army of

Ch'oe Yu, and in 1378, together with Yi Sŏng-gye, annihilated the Japanese pirates at Sŭngch'ŏnbu. In 1388, when Shin U planned a march to Liaotung, Ch'oe became supreme commander; but upon the return of Yi Sŏng-gye's army from Wihwa Island, he was banished to Koyang and then to Happ'o, where he was killed (*KRS*, 113, 23a-55a; *TYS*, 19, 2b; *YC*, 3, 64–65).

5. According to *MSL*, T'ai-tsu, 193, 2896 [eighth month of 1388], the principal reason for the withdrawal was shortage of provisions.

[10]

A mere fellow injured[1] the people;
They therefore awaited the coming of Wu.
With silk in baskets, square and round,[2]
They looked for him along the roadside.

A mad fellow was reckless and oppressive;[3]
They therefore awaited his banner of justice.
With rice in baskets, wine in bottles,
They welcomed him along the roadside.[4]

When King Wu punished Chou, the people who had suffered under Chou's tyranny came to receive King Wu with black and yellow silk in their square and round baskets. Chou is here called "a mere fellow," as in the *Mencius*, 1B, 8 (Legge, II, 167). See canto 9 and *MH*, 1, 234.

When Yi Sŏng-gye returned from Wihwa Island and marched on the Koryŏ capital, its population rushed out to welcome him with food and drink; children and women pulled away the vehicles which blocked the streets, and the old and sick climbed to the top of the fortress and cheered with joy. The third line of the second verse is reminiscent of the *Mencius*, 1B, 10 (Legge, II, 170): "baskets of rice and vessels of congee." See canto 9.

1. 流毒: *Shang shu*, 6, 3b (Legge, III, 290): "poisonous injuries."
2. 玄黃筐篚: For 玄黃 see *Shang shu*, 6, 9b (Legge, III, 314) and *Book of Songs*, 154, 3 (Karlgren, p. 98). For 筐 see *Book of Songs*, 3 (Karlgren, p. 3): "slanting basket" and for 篚 see *Shang shu*, 6, 9a (Legge, III, 314): "round bamboo basket."
3. 肆虐: *Shang shu*, 6, 3a (Legge, III, 290): "reckless and oppressive."
4. Cf. Claudian, *Panegyric on the Third Consulship of the Emperor Honorius*, 126–130, tr. Maurice Platnauer (LCL, 1922), I, 278–281: "How many youths, how many matrons set modesty aside in eagerness to behold thee!"

[11]

When Yü and Jui appealed to Wen,[1]
Princes gathered from the four quarters.
Because his virtue was so bright,
He served the "paltry fellow" Chou.

When Yi returned from Wihwa Island,[2]
People set their hearts on him.
Because he was thoroughly loyal,
He put up a restored king.[3]

In the time of King Wen the sovereigns of Yü and Jui, who were feuding with each other over their territories, came to the Chou court. When they entered the Chou territory, they saw beautiful manners and customs among the people. They were ashamed of their quarrel even before seeing King Wen and said, "Since our dispute is nothing but a shame to the Chou people, to bring our small problem for solution is disgraceful." They split their differences and made the territory in question a neutral zone. Upon hearing the story, more than forty states gave their hearts to Wen, and the princes acclaimed him as one who would receive the mandate of Heaven. The princes revolted against the wicked Chou, but Wen, who led them, continued to serve the tyrant. *SC*, 4, 0013b-c (*MH*, I, 219–220). The commentary quotes the *Analects*, VIII, 20 (Waley, pp. 136–137).

Shin U was a son of the strange monk Shin Ton (d. 1371)[4] and was born of his servant wife, Panya. King Kongmin had no heir and therefore adopted him. After Ton was executed, U was reared in the palace, and Yi In-im[5] made him successor to the king.

During his retreat from Wihwa Island (canto 9), Yi Sŏng-gye discussed with Cho Min-su (d. 1391)[6] the possibility of placing the descendant of the Wang House on the throne. Cho agreed. But after Shin U was transported to Kanghwa Island,[7] Cho wished to thank Yi In-im for the role he had played in his promotion and proposed to have Ch'ang,[8] son of U's wife, who was a niece of Yi In-im, wear the crown. Because he feared that other generals would insist that a descendant of the house of Wang should be heir, he secretly consulted a famous scholar of the day, Yi Saek.[9] Yi Saek insisted that the son of the former king should ascend the throne. When Yi Sŏng-gye asked Cho Min-su why he changed his mind, Cho answered that there was little else for him to do, as Yi Saek had already chosen Ch'ang (1380–1389) as heir. Ch'ang therefore ascended the throne. *KRS*, 137, 20b-21a; *KRSCY*, 33, 19a-b; *TT*, 53, 464.

Thereupon, Yi Sŏng-gye, together with Sim Tŏk-pu[10] and others, consulted the queen of King Kongmin and had Yo, the sixth grandson of the Duke of Yangyang, who was the second son of King Sinjong (1144–1198–1204),[11] ascend the throne. He was King Kongyang (1354–1389–1392–1394),[12] the last Koryŏ monarch. *KRS*, 45, 1a-3a; *KRSCY*, 34, 18a-19b; *TS*, 1, 26a, 27a-29a; *TT*, 54, 511–512; *YK*, 1, 29–30.

1. For Yü and Jui in western Shensi, see *Book of Songs*, 237, 9 (Karlgren, p. 190; Waley, p. 249); *MH*, I, 219, n. 2. For 質成 see Legge, IV, 441–442 ("decide their strife and made peace"); *SC*, 4, 0013b-c (*MH*, I, 219), and *BMFEA*, XVIII (1946), 29.

2. 振旅: *Shang shu*, 2, 6a (Legge, III, 66): *Book of Songs*, 178 (Karlgren, p. 123). *Lu* is a term for 500 men, and *shih* for 2,500 men (*Shang shu*, 6, 6b; Legge, III, 302); *Book of Songs*, 263, 2 (Karlgren, p. 235): "cohorts." Also in the *Analects*, XI, 25 (Legge, I, 248; Waley, p. 159).

3. Literally, "lord of restoration," for which see Lien-sheng Yang, *Studies in Chinese Institutional History* (Cambridge, Mass., 1961), pp. 3-4.

4. Favorite monk of King Kongmin, he deceived the king and court with his versions of geomancy and advocated the transfer of the capital to P'yong-yang (1369). When he attempted a coup d'état, he was captured and banished to Suwŏn; he was executed on September 30, 1371. *KRS*, 133, *1a*; *YG*, 2, 2a; *YC*, 3, 62; Min Hyŏn-gu, *YH*, XXXVIII (1968), 46–88; XL (1968), 53–119.

5. After the assassination of King Kongmin, he enthroned Shin Ch'ang, adopted a pro-Mongol policy, and engaged in factional strife. *KRS*, 126, 1a-19b.

6. *KRS*, 126, 29a-32b.

7. *TYS*, 12, 16a-28a.

8. *KRS*, 137, 21b-45b.

9. *KRS*, 115, 1a-28a; *TS*, 9, 6b-8a; *YK*, 1, 44-47; *Mogŭn sŏnsaeng yŏnbo*, 1a-7b, in the *Yŏgye myŏnghyŏn chip* (1959). See cantos 77 and 82.

10. *KRS*, 116, 1a-8a; *TnS*, 1, 2b-3a; *HMN*, 3, 112–113; *KIC*, 1, 5.

11. *KRS*, 21, 1a-18a; *KRSCY*, 14, 1a-16b.

12. *KRS*, 45, 1a-46, 47a; *KRSCY*, 35, 1a-60a; *TP*, XLV (1957), 212–218.

[12]

For five years Chou did not mend his ways;[1]
His tyranny worsened every day.
When Chou's army mutinied,[2]
Wu could not fulfill his father's wishes.

From the first day he succumbed to slander;
His wickedness raged every day.

When people entreated Yi to be king,
He could not fulfill his lifelong desire.

Although all claimed that the mandate of Heaven had come to Wen, he was still loyal to the wicked Chou. As time passed, Chou became crueler, indulged in lascivious pleasures, committed atrocities, extended punishment to the most distant relatives of the accused, bestowed government posts only through heredity, and took delight in palaces and towers, artificial ponds, and luxurious garments. He had burned to death the good and loyal and had cut open the wombs of pregnant women. King Wu, therefore, had to fulfill Heaven's bidding by punishing Chou. But by doing so, Wu could not emulate his father, Wen (canto 9).

Even though Yi Sŏng-gye's reputation and power increased after his return from Wihwa Island, in order to continue the legitimate line of the House of Wang, he had King Kongyang ascend the throne. But the king disliked Yi's great achievements and growing reputation and the powerful old families harbored grudges against Yi for his land reform. Aware of the king's dislike, these families made groundless accusations against Yi. The groups around Shin U and Shin Ch'ang, relying on their kinship with the Wang family, defamed Yi day and night. The king believed their slander and planned to do away with Yi. *TS*, 1, 33a, 33b-34a.

When Yi returned from Wihwa Island, several of his men were secretly planning to make him king. In the sixth month of 1392, Yi Pang-wŏn with Chŏng To-jŏn[3] and others planned to enthrone his father, but they feared his anger and did not speak of their decision. Yi Pang-wŏn asked his mother to intervene but she too dared not say anything. Pang-wŏn then told his followers, "Because we cannot tell him of our plan, we must provide a guard of honor and urge him to wear the crown." On August 4, 1392, when the officials, elders, and veterans went to Yi Sŏng-gye's mansion with the royal seal, Yi firmly declined, saying, "Since old times one must have a mandate of Heaven in order to be able to become a sovereign; how could I, who have so little virtue, fulfill this heavy charge?" But the officials and elders remained, stood guard, and pressed him to accept. The next day Yi went to the Such'ang Palace[4] and ascended the throne.[5] *TS*, 1, 36b-37b; *KRS*, 46, 45b-46b; *KRSCY*, 35, 59b; *TT*, 56, 602.

1. *Shang shu*, 10, 9a-b (Legge, III, 500): "Heaven for five years waited kindly and forebore with the descendants of T'ang, to see if he would indeed prove himself the true ruler of the people, but there was nothing in him deserving to be regarded."

2. *Shang shu*, 6, 10a (Legge, III, 315): "inverted their spears and attacked those behind them." Also in *SC*, 4, 0014a (*MH*, I, 234).

3. *KRS*, 119, 1a-30a; *CMP*, 244, 5b-6a; 247, 9b; *YK*, 2, 92–93; *Lieh-ch'ao shih-chi*, 56, 21a-b; *Ming shih-ts'ung*, 95, 6a-b. For a single important study of Chŏng see Yi Sang-baek, *Han'guk munhwasa yŏn'gu non'go* (1954), pp. 251–339. For his collected works, *Sambong chip*, see Suematsu Yasukazu, *Seikyū shisō*, II (1966), 125–139.

4. Constructed in 1384 by Shin U (*SnSC*, 148, 3a; *TYS*, 5, 5a; *CG*, XXVI [1963], 38–39).

5. The commentary lists no fewer than seven episodes: (1) Chŏng To-jŏn once accompanied Yi Sŏng-gye on the northeastern campaign to sound him out on the possibility of a revolution; (2) Kyŏng Pok-hŭng entrusts his children to the care of Yi Sŏng-gye because he thinks Yi will found a new dynasty; (3) upon seeing Yi Sŏng-gye's marksmanship, members of the royal family whispered to one another in admiration. The powerful minister Yi In-im whispered to his clansmen; (4) King Kongyang dislikes the general's growing reputation; and because of his land reform, powerful families harbor a grudge and make groundless accusations against Yi. The general plans to leave for the northeast, but his men stop him; (5) the general goes to Hwangju to meet the heir apparent returning from the Ming. During the hunting trip Yi falls from his horse. Chŏng Mong-ju stirs up the Censorate to impeach Yi for his carelessness and tries to banish Yi's supporters. At the news, Yi Pang-wŏn rushes to his father's side and presses him to return to the capital. He asks his father's permission to kill Chŏng Mong-ju. The general disapproves, but Yi Pang-wŏn goes ahead with the plan. The general reprimands his son and informs the king about the assassination. The king, harassed by the Yi party's maneuvers and fearful for his life, wishes to pledge an oath of allegiance with the general; (6) Yi Sŏng-gye treats U Hyŏn-bo and Yi Saek leniently (canto 77); (7) the memorial of Pae Kŭng-nyŏm finally convinces Yi Sŏng-gye to accept the throne.

[13]

Many could offer advice:
But Wu doubted Heaven's bidding.
With a dream,
Heaven urged him to fulfill its charge.

Many could sing his good works:
But he did not know Heaven's bidding.
With a dream,
Heaven announced its intent.

In his declaration to the assembly at the Meng Ford, King Wu said, "The Shang King, Chou, murdered loyal subjects cruelly and maltreated whoever protested. Contending that he possessed Heaven's mandate, he preached that reverence is superfluous, sacrifices useless, and praised tyranny instead. Unawares, he repeated the crimes of Chieh. Heaven bids me to punish his armies and my dreams coincide with my divinations. Auspicious omen is double. We must perforce subjugate Shang and succeed." *Shang shu*, 6, 3b (Legge, III, 291); *MH*, I 227 ff.

For some time, a prophetic song foretold the return of General Yi Sŏng-gye from Wihwa Island: "The fire rages beyond P'yongyang,[1]/ The smoke rises over the Anju fortress.[2]/ General Yi passes through this turbulence—/ May he save the young and old." Another song also circulated among the people that prophesied the rise of a man with the surname Yi (cantos 69, 83).[3] Soldiers sang it when they marched back from the island. *KRS*, 137, 14b-15a; *TS*, 1, 24a; *TT*, 53, 458–459; *Tonggak chapki* (CKK, 1909), 1, 341.

Before Yi's accession, in a dream, a god-like being descended from Heaven and gave him a gold ruler, saying, "Sir, you combine both military talent and culture and the people have confidence in you. With this measure bring order to the country. Who else is there but you to do the work?"[4] *TS*, 1, 38b; *YK*, 1, 11.

1.　The capital of Tangun, Kija, as well as Wiman Chosŏn. In 427, King Changsu of Koguryŏ transferred his capital from Kungnaesŏng to P'yongyang. In 668, the allied army of Silla and T'ang destroyed the city, and T'ang established there the An-tung tu-fu-hu. In 960, King Kwangjong (923–946–949) established the Western Capital there. In 1270, the Yüan established the Tongnyŏngbu but returned it to Koryŏ in 1290. See *KRSC*, 58, 29b-31a; *SnSC*, 154, 2b-6b; *TYS*, 51, 3a-4b.

2.　In South P'yŏngan (*KRSC*, 58, 32a-b; *SnSC*, 154, 9a-b; *TYS*, 52, 15b-16a).

3.　The song prophesied the rise of a man surnamed Yi (the logograph *Yi* consisting of two elements, "tree" and "son") for which see *KRS*, 137, 15a; *KRSCY*, 33, 14a; *YG*, 1, 42b-43a. Yi Pyŏng-do, in the *Koryŏ sidae ŭi yŏn'gu* (1954), pp. 386-389, has pointed out that a similar prophecy existed in China since the sixth century (e.g., *TCTC*, 165, 5097; 182, 5965; *Sui shu*, 37, 2548c).

4.　On July 26, 1383, Chŏng To-jŏn composed a eulogy to praise the event. The text is preserved in the *Sambong chip*, 2, 61; *AHKB*, 4, 10a-11b; *TS*, 4, 2b. See also *CMP*, 92, 7b-8b; 93, 11b-12a; 107, 10a-b; cf. 101, 6a; and *CKS*, II, 733. According to the *Tonggyŏng chapki* (CKK, 1910), 3, 589, the founder of Silla received from a god a similar gold ruler. When he awoke, he held the object in his hand. The second poem in canto 83 repeats the subject.

[14]

The august grandson blazed in anger;
The capital that ruled for six hundred years[1]
Was moved
To Lo-yang.[2]

The august son declined office thrice;[3]
The capital that ruled for five hundred years[4]
Was moved
To Hanyang.[5]

The commentary quotes the *Mencius*, 1B, 3 (Legge, II, 157): "He [King Wen or Wu] by one display of his anger, gave response to all the people of the kingdom."

Yi Sŏng-gye disliked his responsible position of *Munha sijung* and presented three memorials (early 1391; April 21 and July 29, 1391) requesting permission to resign. But the king did not allow him to leave despite the fact that Yi was ill. *KRS*, 45, 37a-39a; 46, 4a-6b, 16a-17b, 17b-19a, 34b, 39a-b; *KRSCY*, 35, 29a; *TS*, 1, 30a-b, 31a-b, 32a; *TT*, 56, 579, 597.

Less than a month after his enthronement, Yi Sŏng-gye contemplated the transfer of the capital to Hanyang, the former southern capital of Koryŏ, but soon abandoned the idea (*TS*, 1, 52a). On March 2, 1393, Yi, accompanied by his advisers, went to Mount Kyeryong, his second choice for a capital (3, 2a). They reached the mountain on March 20, and Yi inspected the area (3, 2a-b). Construction was already under way when, on January 13, 1394, it was stopped (4, 13b-14a). Ha Yun, then, was asked to choose another site (4, 14a). On March 20 of the same year, Cho Chun inspected the site of Muak, southwest of modern Ansan near Seoul (5, 5b-6a), and on September 6, Yi inspected the chosen area (6, 10b-11a). The next day, however, Chŏng To-jŏn and others admonished the throne, pointing out the unsuitability of the place (6, 11a-13a). Not until the National Preceptor Chach'o (Muhak; d. 1405) was consulted did Yi, finally, decide on Hanyang (6, 13a). Yi reached the new capital on November 21, 1394 (6, 16a). On June 6, 1395, the name Hanyang was changed to Hansŏng (7, 13b), and on February 7, 1396, Yi moved to the new palace in Hansŏng (8, 17b). In 1399, only five years after its establishment, Chŏngjong, intending to forget the aftermath of the internecine feud for the throne, decided to return to the former capital. However, Yi Sŏng-gye disapproved of the move, but the court, nevertheless, moved to Kaesŏng (*Chŏngjong sillok*, 1, 7a). When fire wrecked the Such'ang Palace on January 6,

1400, Yi Pang-wŏn, suspecting it to be an evil omen, discussed the possibility of returning to Hansŏng (*TnS*, 4, 3b-4a). In 1404, construction of palaces and official buildings began (*TnS*, 8, 9b). On September 4, 1405, Yi Pang-wŏn reported to his father his decision to return to Hansŏng (*TnS*, 10, 6a). The royal party, which left Kaesŏng on October 30, reached the new capital on November 2, and Yi Pang-wŏn entered the new Ch'angdŏk Palace on November 11, 1405 (*TnS*, 10, 21b-21b). On November 29, Yi Sŏng-gye arrived from Kaesŏng (*TnS*, 10, 24b). So Hansŏng finally became the seat of government during the Yi dynasty.

1. The interlinear commentary says (*YG*, 3, 12b), Shang ruled a total of 629 years according to the *Ch'un-ch'iu wei-shu* and 644 years according to the *Ching-shih shu*. For the term *wei-shu* (apocryphal books) see *BMFEA*, II, (1930), 54 and XVIII (1946), 232, n. 1, and Tjan Tjoe Som, *Po Hu T'ung*, I (Leiden, 1949), 100, 193. The chronology of the Shang-Yin dynasty varies: (1) the orthodox chronology is 1766 B.C. (or 1765)–1123, or 644 years (Mathias Tchang, *Synchronismes chinois* [1905]); (2) *Chu-shu chi-nien* gives 1558–1051 B.C., or 508 years; (3) Tung Tso-pin, *Chronological Tables of Chinese History* (Hong Kong, 1960), pp. 58–116, gives 1751–1112, or 640 years (also in *Chinese Culture*, I [1957], 1–5); (4) *BMFEA*, XVII (1945), 114–121, gives 1523–1028 (see also *TP*, XL (1951), 322–335); and (5) W. P. Yetts, in A. C. Moule's *The Rulers of China* (1957), p. xiv, gives c. 1600–1050, or 550 years. For this information I am indebted to Professor L. Carrington Goodrich of Columbia University.

2. For King Wu's transfer of the capital, see *SC*, 4, 0014c (*MH*, I, 243, n. 1). For the city under the Northern Wei see Hattori Katsuhiko, *Hoku-Gi Rakuyō no shakai to bunka* (Tokyo, 1965–1968). Also see Ping-ti Ho, "Loyang, A.D. 495–534: A Study of Physical and Socio-economic Planning of a Metropolitan Area," *HJAS*, XXVI (1966), 52–101.

3. For 三讓 see *SC*, 8, 0036b (*MH*, II, 380), where Liu Pang declined the title of emperor for the customary three times before accepting. In the *Analects*, VIII, 1 (Waley, p. 132) Confucius praises T'ai-po: "No less than three times he renounced the sovereignty of all things under Heaven."

4. According to the commentary (*YG*, 3, 12b), Koryŏ ruled a total of 475 years (actually 474 years); hence the round number 500.

5. Originally Namp'yŏngyangsŏng of Koguryŏ, King Kŭnch'ogo (346–375) stayed there, but King Munju (475–477) transferred the Paekche capital to Ungjin to escape the Koguryŏ pressure. Called Yangju in the beginning of Koryŏ, King Ch'ungnyŏl (1236–1275–1308) changed its name to Hanyang (*TYS*, 1, 1a-3, 53a, esp. 3, 1a-2b). See Kim Yong-guk, *Hyangt'o Seoul*, I (1957), 50–99; IV (1958), 82–147; Yi Pyŏng-do, *Koryŏ sidae ŭi yŏn'gu* (1954), pp. 328–337, 390–444; *HGS*, III, 65–69. The Seoul City History Compilation Committee has begun to publish a series of source materials for the study of the city (e.g., *Han'gyŏng singnyak* [1965]; *Kunggwŏl chi* [1957]; *Tongguk yŏji pigo* [1957]) and the periodical, *Hyangt'o Seoul*.

[15]

He loathed the south of the river
And sent envoys.
But who could stop
The rise of the seven dynasties there?

He feared the south of the Kongjwi
And warned his heirs of its danger.
Could the book of oracle[1]
Have been a man's artifice?

In the time of the First Emperor, a diviner, who looked at the mist for portents, said that the air of a "Son of Heaven"[2] hung over Chin-ling. The emperor, consequently, sent prisoners to cut a tunnel through the mountain and to dig a river in order to suppress the threat to his power. He then changed the city's name from Chin-ling to Mo-ling. Nevertheless Wu, Sung, Ch'i, Liang, Ch'en, and Ming had Chin-ling as their capital. *SC*, 8, 0034a (*MH*, II, 332; Watson, I, 81); *HS*, 1A, 0292b (Dubs, I, 36).

Wang Kŏn (877–918–943) left the Ten Injunctions (943)[3] to his successors. The eighth article read, "The orographical features of the south of Ch'ahyŏn[4] and outside the Kongjwi[5] River are geomantically inauspicious. If a man from the region, either at court or through marriage into the royal family, comes to assume the reins of government, he will revolt, and feeling resentment at the unification of the three kingdoms, he will violate the royal carriage and create a disturbance. I warn you, therefore, not to promote him, though he be a good person." Despite this warning, Koryŏ was overthrown by the Yi family whose putative ancestral site was in Chŏnju, in the South. *KRS*, 2, 16a; *KRSCY*, 1, 43a-b.

1. 九變之局: *YG*, 3, 14a reads: "The term refers to the oracle written by Sinji, a contemporary of Tan'gun." This diagram and the *Pisa* may have been the same thing, according to Yi Pyŏng-do, *Koryŏ sidae ŭi yŏn'gu* (1954), pp. 385 ff. For variant readings see *CKS*, II, 733 and *TYS*, 11, 10b.

2. *Chin shu*, 12, 1106b.

3. *KRS*, 2, 14b-17a; *KRSCY*, 1, 41b-44b. See Imanishi Ryū's article in *TG*, VIII (1918), 419–427 and Yi Pyŏng-do's rebuttal, *Koryŏ*, pp. 28–61.

4. Fifty-seven ri northwest of Kongju, South Ch'ungch'ŏng (*TYS*, 17, 3a)

5. In 475, King Munju transferred the Paekche capital to Ungjin (modern Kongju). See *KRSC*, 56, 26b-27a; *SnSC*, 149, 13a-14b; *TYS*, 17, 1a-b. For the reading Kongjwi, see *AY*, V (1962), 104–105.

[16]

While fleeing he believed in the mandate,
In the ballad he believed in his name.
In front of the illustrious lord,
How much must he have been ashamed all along?

Intending to transfer the capital the king came,
A magistrate with a different surname arrived.
Today
Is all their fuss not ludicrous?

Li Mi (582–618)[1] of Sui exiled himself and went to the generals, preaching how one could win the world. At first no one listened, but gradually they paid attention, telling one another, "This man is a descendant of a court noble and he shows spirit. Now everyone says that the Yang family will go to ruin and the Li family will rise. We hear that one chosen to be a sovereign does not die unexpectedly. Li Mi has narrowly escaped death several times; is he not the one the people are talking about?" Soon they respected Li. When Li Hsüan-ying fled from Lo-yang and came to search for Li Mi, he said, "He is sure to replace the Sui dynasty." When they asked him for the reason, he quoted the popular ballad of the time: "Peach-plum Li,/ The emperor and empress go round about Yang-chou,/ And turn about within the flower garden./ Be reserved in speech,/ Who says one may?"[2] This ballad alludes, he explained, to the story which tells that Emperor Yang of Sui will not return from the flower garden in Yang-chou but will fall into a ditch. Instead, the escaped son of the Li family, Li Mi, will become emperor. However, Li Mi lost a battle against Wang Shih-ch'ung (d. 621)[3] and surrendered to Li Yüan (T'ang Kao-tsu). When Li Yüan sent Li Mi to welcome Shih-min[4] at Pin-chou, Li Mi, relying on his resources, had been arrogant toward Li Yüan; but after meeting Shih-min, admired and praised him and told Yin K'ai-shan:[5] "He is indeed an illustrious lord. Were he not so, how could he have crushed the disturbances?" *Sui shu*, 4, 2354b-c; *CTS*, 2, 3066d; 53, 3283c-3285c; *TCTC*, 183, 5706 ff.

In 1096, Kim Wi-je[6] memorialized the throne, recommending the transfer of the capital to Hanyang. This move was according to Sinji[7] and the prophetic diagram by Toson (827–898).[8] King Sukchong (1054–1096–1105),[9] therefore, established the southern capital,[10] constructed palaces, and in 1104 made a royal visit to the new city. But soon he returned to the old capital. Also, swayed by geomancy, the Koryŏ court chose a man with the surname Yi to be the mayor of

Hanyang. Sukchong therefore interpreted the prophecy as relating to himself and to his dynasty, whereas the omens foretold the rise of the Yi family. *KRS*, 11, 31b; 12, 9b-10b; *KRSCY*, 6, 29a-b.

    1. *Sui shu*, 22, 2415a; 70, 2511d-2513a; *CTS*, 53, 3283c-3285c; *HTS*, 84, 3886d-3887d; *PS*, 60, 2939d-2940c; Woodbridge Bingham, *The Founding of the T'ang Dynasty* (Baltimore, 1941), pp. 67–69; *BD*, 1176.

    2. Bingham, "The Rise of Li in a Ballad Prophecy," *JAOS*, LXI (1941), 276.

    3. *Sui shu*, 85, 2539d-2540b; *PS*, 79, 2990a-c; *CTS*, 54, 3285d-3286c; *HTS*, 85, 3888a-d; *BD*, 2222.

    4. *CTS*, 2, 3066c-3070d; *HTS*, 2, 3636b-3638b; *BD*, 1196; C. P. Fitzgerald, *Son of Heaven: A Biography of Li Shih-min, Founder of the T'ang Dynasty* (Cambridge, 1933).

    5. *HTS*, 90, 3896b; *TCTC*, 186, 5822.

    6. *KRS*, 122, 1a-3b; *TYS*, 3, 2b.

    7. Or Sinji Sŏnin, a fictitious figure of the time of Tan'gun, is first quoted by Kim Wi-je in his memorial as the author of the *Pisa*. See *YG*, 3, 18a; Yi Pyŏng-do, *Koryŏ sidae ŭi yŏn'gu*, pp. 149–150; *KRS*, 122, 2b; *KRSCY*, 6, 29a-b.

    8. National Preceptor Sŏn'gak, whose secular name was Kim. At the age of fifteen, he shaved his head, went to the Avataṁsaka monastery on Mount Wŏryu, and studied there. He specialized in Ch'an and is said to have enlightened King Hŏn'gang (875–886). He died on April 4, 898, at the Jade Dragon monastery (*YC*, 18, 255; *TG*, II [1912], 247–263). See also *CKS*, II, 892–897, for a monument erected in 1653.

    9. *KRS*, 11, 1a-12, 14b; *KRSCY*, 6, 26a-7, 9b; *TP*, XLVII (1959), 30–41.

    10. The eleventh king, Munjong (1019–1047–1082–1083), was the first to have ordered construction of new palaces at what is now modern Seoul in 1056 (*KRS*, 7, 41b) and called his new city the southern capital (1068). When his third son, Sukchong, usurped the throne from his young cousin Hŏnjong (1084–1095–1095), Kim Wi-je again proposed the establishment of the southern capital. The discussion of Kim's proposal was, however, not until 1099; in the ninth intercalary month of the same year, the king, together with his family and subjects, inspected the terrain in Yangju for a new capital (*KRS*, 11, 19b-20a). The construction began south of Mount Samgak in the tenth month of 1101 (11, 31b) and ended in the fifth month of 1104 (12, 9b); and in the seventh month of 1104 the king visited the city (12, 10b). In 1234, Kojong (1192–1214–1259) had a dragon robe enshrined in a temporary palace there, hoping to prolong the span of the Wang house (23, 38a-b). In 1357, at the suggestion of the monk Pou, King Kongmin seriously contemplated the transfer of the capital (39, 15b-16a). For a detailed study of the influence of geomancy during Koryŏ and early Yi, see Yi Pyŏng-do, *Koryŏ sidae ŭi yŏn'gu*, pp. 119–154, 272–294, 297–316; *HGS*, II, 248–270; and *KRSC*, 56, 9a-10a. See also *Chōsen no semboku to yogen* (1933), pp. 630–633, and *Chōsen no fūsui* (1931), pp. 671–711.

[17]

He was startled by the incident with the palace girls,
But it was the fault of a palace guard.
Will he put off
The chastisement of Chiang-tu?

He was angry with the incident of the kisaeng,
But it was the fault of an official.
Heaven pressed him
To go north and begin royal works.

When Li Yüan (later T'ang Kao-tsu)[1] was the governor of T'ai-yüan,[2] the Turks attacked Ma-i.[3] Li Yüan sent troops to check the enemy but lost the battle and feared that the court would blame him. At the time, Li Shih-min sent a man with this message: "Now that the emperor is reckless, the people suffer, and the environs of the Chin-yang[4] have become a battlefield. If my father intends to stick to formalities, bandits will increase below and severe punishment will fall from above, and our household and its members will perish. It would be better to follow the people's wishes and raise a loyal army now. By doing so we can turn calamity into blessing. It is really the best opportunity that Heaven has granted us." *CTS*, 1, 3064c; *TCTC*, 183, 5730.

P'ei Chi (560–619)[5] held the office of superintendent of the Chin-yang Palace. He secretly presented imperial concubines, attached to the palace, to Li Yüan. At the time, Li drank with P'ei Chi, who calmly addressed the guest: "Your second son is secretly raising troops and planning a great undertaking. If it comes to light, because I offered the concubines, we may be jointly punished. I therefore inform you of the urgency of the matter. The people's hearts all go to you, what is your intention?" The vacillating Li Yüan finally answered, "If my son has truly planned such a thing and if this is the situation, what else should one do but what is best?" *CTS*, 57, 3292c; *TCTC*, 183, 5731.

At the time, Emperor Yang (569–604–617–618)[6] indulged in the construction of the canals linking Yellow and Yangtze rivers and collected an army to subjugate Koguryŏ.[7] In the third month of 612, the emperor's army, said to be a million men, reached the Liao River[8] and encircled Liaotung Fortress.[9] In the sixth month of that year, his army reached south of the fortress but was defeated by General Ŭlchi Mundŏk[10] who, in the seventh month, crushed the retreating enemy at the Sal River.[11] The second invasion took place in the third month of 613, but in the sixth month the news of the revolt of Yang Hsüankan (d. 613)[12] reached the emperor, who became afraid and withdrew the troops. The third invasion took place in the seventh month of 614. At the time Koguryŏ, which was also exhausted, returned the Sui refugee Hu-ssu Cheng,[13] and proposed truce. In the eighth month the Sui army withdrew. In 617, the emperor planned the fourth invasion but had to call it off. When the emperor visited Chiang-tu (Yang-chou) and indulged in luxury and debauchery, the captains of his palace guard[14] revolted, marched towards the palace, and strangled him. The first stanza's intent is that Li Yüan was not responsible for the loss of the battle against the Turks, or for the incident with palace concubines. Li Yüan resolved to punish the Sui emperor not because he was afraid of possible blame for the incidents, but because Heaven bade him to do so. *Sui shu*, 4, 2353a-2354d; Franke, II, 338–342, 343.

Mokcho left Chŏnju for the north because Heaven urged him to do so in order to lay the foundation of the Yi dynasty. See canto 3; *YK*, 1, 6.

1. *CTS*, 1, 3064c-3066b; *HTS*, 1, 3634a-3636b; *BD*, 1239.

2. In T'ai-yüan hsien in Shansi. Yang-ti changed the name from T'ai-yüan to Ping-chou (*CKT*, 143b).

3. East of So hsien in Shansi, on the east coast of the Ma-i River. See Liu, I, 65, 83 for the Turkish invasion. For *t'u-chüeh* see E. G. Pulleyblank, "The Chinese Name for the Turks," *JAOS*, LXXXV (1965), 121–125, where he asserts that *t'u-chüeh* is "a quite normal transcription of Turk," rather than Pelliot's *türküt* (*TP*, XVI [1915], 687–689). See *MS*, XIX (1960), 463–466, for a summary of Japanese studies on the subject.

4. In T'ai-yüan, Shansi (*CKT*, 704d-705a).

5. *CTS*, 57, 3292c-3293a; *HTS*, 88, 3893a-c.

6. *Sui shu*, 3, 2351a-2355a; *PS*, 12, 2781c-2785c; *BD*, 2393; Peter A. Boodberg, "Marginalia to the Histories of the Northern Dynasties," *HJAS*, IV (1939), 253–270, 282–283, and Arthur F. Wright, "Sui Yang-ti: Personality and Stereotype," in *The Confucian Persuasion* (Stanford, 1960), pp. 47–76.

7. *SGSG*, 20, 2 ff., and Liu, II, 86 (*LG*, pp. 402–417).

8. Also called Siramouren (*LG*, 541–542, 785).

9. In the vicinity of modern Liao-yang (*LG*, 547–548, 548–554).

10. *SGSG*, 44, 1-2; *SnSC*, 154, 9a. For his composite biography in *SGSG*, see Yi Hong-jik, *Sach'ong*, IV (1959), 1–18, esp. 3-7.

11. It begins at Mount Myohyang and it is 123 miles long. It corresponds to modern Ch'ŏngch'ŏn. See *KRSC*, 58, 32b; *SnSC*, 154, 1b, 9a-b; *TYS*, 52, 17a-b; *HGS*, I (1959), see index under "P'aesu."

12. *Sui shu*, 70, 2510d-2511b; *PS*, 41, 2883b-c; *BD*, 2381.

13. *Chung-kuo jen-ming ta-tz'u-tien*, p. 983b.

14. They were Ssu-ma Te-k'an (*Sui shu*, 85, 2539d; *PS*, 79, 2989d) and Yü-wen Hua-chi, the first son of Yü-wen Shu (d. 616), who was killed on March 22, 619, at a battle against the army of Tou Chien-te (*Sui shu*, 85, 2539a-d; *PS*, 79, 2989b; *BD*, 2535).

[18]

On the way to Mount Li he lost his men
And returned home alone.
Heaven, then, moved
The hearts of ten men.

He shunned the official
And sailed northward.
Two hundred families followed him
Of their own accord.[1]

When Liu Pang as village head escorted a group of forced laborers from P'ei to Mount Li, many of them escaped on the way. He thought perhaps all would escape before he reached his destination. When the party reached west of Feng, Liu Pang stopped to drink. That night he freed all forced laborers saying, "Go, all of you, for I, too, will defect." Ten-odd strong men among them were willing to follow him. *SC*, 8, 0033c (*MH*, II, 330; Watson, I, 80); *HS*, 1A, 0292a-b (Dubs, I, 34).

When Mokcho moved from Kangwŏn to Hamgyŏng province (canto 3), one hundred seventy (two hundred in the poem) families, who had formerly followed him from Chŏnju, followed him again (cantos 3, 6).

1.   In the original a rhetorical question: "Who could ask them to move?"

[19]

He lost his way,
Not knowing where the fortress was.[1]
Heaven, then, dispatched
An old man.

Unaware of the crafty bandits,
He waited to see them.
Heaven, then, dispatched
An old woman.

In 24 A.D., when Liu Hsiu (Kuang-wu; "he" in line 1) was chased by Wang Lang,[2] he and his followers fled south, day and night, and had to camp out in the open. When they reached the western section of

Hsia-po,[3] they did not know which way to go. An old man dressed in white standing by the roadside pointed the way, saying, "Exert yourself! The Hsin-tu chün, which lies eighty li from here, is still administered on behalf of Ch'ang-an [still on your side]."[4] Thereupon Liu Hsiu hastened in that direction. The old man was a divine being. *HHS*, 1, 0648a; *TCTC*, 39, 1259–1261; Hans Bielenstein, "The Restoration of the Han Dynasty, with the Prolegomena on the Historiography of the Hou Han Shu," *BMFEA*, XXVI (1954), 70.

For the old woman who warned Ikcho of danger, see canto 4.

1. Nam Kwang-u, in *Kugŏhak nonmunjip* (1962), pp. 381–391, 406, reads; "The road was far, far away."
2. *SKC, Wei chih,* 13, 0958a-0959a.
3. Thirty li southeast of the present Shen hsien in Hopei (see map 1 at the end of Bielenstein's article, in *BMFEA*, XXVI [1954], and 70, n. 5).
4. *BMFEA*, XXVI (1954), 70, n. 8 (*CKT*, 579a).

[20]

Would the four seas be lost?[1]
There was no boat by the river:
But Heaven froze the river,
Melted the river.

Would the Three Han be lost?
There was no boat by the river:
But Heaven drained the sea,
Filled the sea.

When Liu Hsiu, chased by Wang Lang, reached the Hu-t'o River[2] with his men, his advance guide reported that the river was not frozen and could not be forded without a boat. Liu Hsiu dispatched Wang Po[3] to inspect the river. Wang, afraid of disappointing his men, made a false report saying the ice was strong enough. Thereupon Liu's followers rejoiced. Liu Hsiu, however, remarked, laughing, "Our guide has lied well." When they reached the river, they found it was frozen. Liu Hsiu ordered Wang Po to watch for his men, as they crossed. Just before the last man crossed, the ice started to melt again. Heaven, unwilling to give the empire to Wang Lang, protected Liu in this way. See canto 19; *HHS*, 1, 0648a; Bielenstein, *BMFEA*, XXVI, 71–72.

Ikcho was chased by the Jürcheds and had to escape to Chŏk Island,

500 paces from the shores of the Tumen. But there was no boat and he did not know what to do. That moment, the river ebbed to a hundred paces in width. After he and his family had crossed the water flowed in again. The enemy was forced to retreat. It was Heaven's device to entrust the kingdom of the Three Han (Korea) to the Yi family (canto 4).

1.   Literally, "Could . . . be yielded to others?" which makes little sense in English.
2.   *BMFEA*, XXVI (1954), 70, n. 3.
3.   *HHS*, 50, 0739b-d; 113, 0892c.

[21]

Heaven had it planned:
Were it not for the barefooted fairy,
Would Heaven forget
Their country and people?[1]

Heaven had chosen:
Were it not for the robed monk,
Would Heaven forget
Our country and people?

Chao Heng, the third Sung emperor (Chen-tsung, 968–997–1022),[2] had no heir and prayed to the Lord-on-High for a son. The Lord-on-High assembled the fairies and discussed the matter, but no one was willing to go. At the time, only the barefooted fairy laughed, and the Lord-on-High ordered him to go down to the earth as Chao Heng's son. He was Chao Chen (Jen-tsung, 1010–1022–1063).[3] The first song says that because Heaven had entrusted the empire to the Sung House, even if the barefooted fairy had not been sent, the Sung dynasty would have continued. Chao Chin, *Yang-o man-pi* (*Shuo fu*, 47), 5b; Wang Ming-ch'ing, *Hui-chu lu* (*Shuo fu*, 39), 6b.

Ikcho, together with his wife Chŏngsuk,[4] née Ch'oe, prayed for a son at the cave of Avalokiteśvara on Mount Nak[5] in Kangwŏn. In a dream, a monk foretold the birth of a son, and asked Ikcho to name the child Sŏllae.[6] The childhood name of Ikcho's son, Tojo, was Sŏllae. *TS*, 1, 3a; *YK*, 1, 8.

1.   Literally, "His [Chao Heng's] country and people?" For 蒼生 see *Shang shu*, 2, 11a (Legge, III, 83): "the most worthy of the people."

2. *Sung shih*, 6, 4506c-8, 4513c.

3. *Sung shih*, 9, 4513c-12, 4520b.

4. *SS*, 2b.

5. Fifteen ri northeast of Yangyang (*TYS*, 44, 25a); for the grotto see *TYS*, 44, 40a. See also my *Lives of Eminent Korean Monks*, p. 48, n. 204.

6. Namely, *Svāgata* (welcome, well come), the name of an attendant of Buddha and one of 12,000 monks present at the Vulture Peak (*Gṛdhrakūta*) where the Buddha preached. For various transcriptions of the name see *HJAS*, IX (1947), 223–224.

[22]

The Red Emperor, when he rose to power,
Cut down the White Emperor with one blow.
The divine woman proclaimed:
Fire devours gold, red slays white.[1]

He shot the Black Dragon with a single arrow
And saved[2] the White Dragon.
The divine animal foretold
The fortune of his children.

When Liu Pang with ten-odd stout men returned from Mount Li, a man in front turned to report that there was a serpent ahead. "Where a brave man marches, what is there to fear?" Liu Pang replied, and, advancing, drew his sword and cut the serpent in two. When one of his followers at the rear reached the place where the serpent had been slain, he saw an old woman weeping in the night: "A man killed my son. My son is the son of the White God. He changed himself into a serpent and blocked the way. Just now the son of the Red God has cut him in two." The man who heard the story told it to Liu Pang, who quietly rejoiced and gained self-confidence. *SC*, 8, 0033c-0034a (*MH*, II, 330–332; Watson, I, 80); *HS*, 1, 0292a-b (Dubs, I, 34–36).

A man appeared to Tojo in a dream, saying, "I am the white dragon and dwell at a certain place.[3] But the black dragon intends to dispossess me of my abode. Please help me." When Tojo did not take the dream seriously, the man appeared again in a dream and begged for help. Tojo went to the place with a bow and saw the white and black dragon fighting each other in the lake. He shot and killed the black dragon. Later the white dragon appeared in a dream, thanked Tojo, and prophesied that an auspicious event would come to his descendants. *TS*, 1, 3b; *YK*, 1, 8–9.

1. 火德之王: *SC*, 6, 0024b (*MH*, II, 128–129); *HS*, 1B, 0298b (Dubs, I, 150). *YG*, 4, 3b-4a quotes a commentary by Ying Shao (c. 140–206) and a part of the *ts'an* by Pan Ku. According to the first, the Red God is a descendant of Yao. The killing symbolizes that the Han must destroy the Ch'in which reigned by virtue of metal, but was overcome by fire, the virtue of Han. So the Han succeeded to the fortunes of Yao (Dubs, I, 35–36, 150).

2. Literally: caused it to live (*AY*, V, 109–110).

3. Ten ri south of Kyŏnghŭng, called Red Lake (*TYS*, 50, 52a). Many unofficial histories during the Yi period referred to the lake, e.g., *Osan sŏllim ch'ogo* (CKK, 1909), pp. 634–635.

[23]

He shot two eagles with a single arrow.
The Tartars
Knelt and revered
His peerless genius.

He shot two magpies with a single arrow.
The northern people
Admired and praised
His startling skill.[1]

Once Li K'o-yung (T'ai-tsu of the Later T'ang, 856–888–908),[2] a Sha-t'o Turk,[3] had a contest with a Tartar. The Tartar asked him to shoot down two flying eagles; Li K'o-yung shot them with one arrow. *CWTS*, 1, 4230b.

For how Tojo shot two magpies with a single arrow, see canto 7.

1. 曠世奇事: unparalleled marvelous event. The term occurs, for example, in Tsao Chi's "Lo-shen fu" (*AM*, IX [1954], 54): "no equals in the world."

2. Third son of Chu-hsieh (yeh) Kuo-ch'ang. See *CWTS*, 25, 4230a-26, 4233d; *HWTS*, 4, 4397 ff.; *BD*, 1155; Wang Gung-wu, *The Structure of Power in North China during the Five Dynasties* (Kuala Lumpur, 1963), pp. 29–46 *passim*, 57.

3. Chavannes, *Documents sur les Tou-kiue Occidentaux* (Paris, n.d.), pp. 96–99, which is a translation of *HTS*, 218, on the Sha-t'o Turks. Karl A. Wittfogel and Feng Chia-sheng, *History of Chinese Society, Liao* (907–1125), (New York, 1949), p. 107; Wolfram Eberhard, "Some Cultural Traits of the Sha-t'o Turks," *Oriental Art*, I (1948), 50–55.

[24]

Others had different motives:
He saved the ruler.
Also at Liu-ho
He wiped out picked men.

His younger brother had different plans:
He returned to the alliance.
At Ssangsŏng
He put down the rebels.

When Kuo Wei (the founder of the Later Chou, 904–951–954)[1] died and was succeeded by Kuo Jung (Shih-tsung, 921–954–959),[2] Liu Kao (the founder of the Northern Han, 895–947–948)[3] received from the Khitan reinforcement to attack the Later Chou. At the time, Chao K'uang-yin (927–960–976; "he" in line 2), as the *su-wei-chiang*,[4] served the Later Chou. While some generals ran away and surrendered to the enemy, Chao alone fought desperately and saved Kuo Jung (954). Later when Kuo Jung attacked the Southern T'ang, Chao defeated the enemy at Liu-ho (956).[5] *CWTS*, 114, 4345d; *Sung shih*, 1, 4497a-b; *TCTC*, 291, 9501–3, 9504–6; 292, 9534, 9536–7, 9538–9; 293, 9545, 9552–4; Franke, IV, 66, 70.

Qubilai (1215–1260–1294) assembled troops and ships in Korea for the planned invasion of Japan. Ikcho, by command of the Mongol court, came to see King Ch'ungnyŏl several times. Tojo did the same, and Hwanjo, as chiliarch of Ssangsŏng[6] and other places, in 1355, came to the Koryŏ court to pay homage to the king, but not Hwanjo's younger brother Cha-sŏn.[7] *KRS*, 38, 30a-b; *TS*, 1, 3b, 4b; *TT*, 46, 210.

At the time, Ki Ch'ŏl,[8] elder brother of the empress, née Ki, of Togon Tämur (1320–1333–1370), secretly communicated with the rebels in Ssangsŏng and plotted a revolt, and King Kongmin ordered Assistant Commissioner of Military Affairs (*Milchik pusa*)[9] Yu In-u[10] and others to recover Ssangsŏng. But Yu was unable to march beyond Tŭngju.[11] Thereupon the king asked Hwanjo secretly to join the Koryŏ troops. In the seventh month of 1356, Hwanjo captured eight towns and five fortresses. *TT*, 46, 215.

The king granted a rank and mansion to Hwanjo and had him reside in the capital. *KRS*, 39, 10b; *TS*, 1, 4b-5a; *TT*, 46, 218.

1. *CWTS*, 110, 4339c; *HWTS*, 11, 4403d.
2. *CWTS*, 114, 4345c-119, 4353b; *HWTS*, 12, 4404c-4405b.
3. *CWTS*, 99, 4327b-100, 4329c; *HWTS*, 10, 4403a-c.

4. The practice of leaving a part of a governor's army to supervise the emperor and the court was introduced in 901 by the governor of Ch'i at the request of the Chief Minister Ts'ui Yin. See Wang Gung-wu, *The Structure of Power*, pp. 82–83, n. 66.

5. *CKT*, 125b.

6. Modern Yŏnghŭng in South Hamgyŏng. In 1258, the Mongols established the Ssangsŏng ch'onggambu. It was recaptured in 1356. In 1369, it was called Hwaryŏng; in 1393, Yŏnghŭng; and in 1426, Yŏnghŭng taedohobu. *KRSC*, 58, 18a-b; *SnSC*, 155, 4b-5a; *TYS*, 48, 16b-17b; *HGS*, II, 686–687.

7. Third son of Tojo, known as Prince Wanwŏn (*SS*, 1, 3a).

8. Empress Ki, a daughter of Ki Cha-o, first entered the harem of Shun-ti, but was elevated to be his second wife and gave birth to Chao-tsung of the Northern Yüan. Thereupon her father was enfeoffed as Prince of Yongan, and her brothers, Ch'ŏl, Wŏn, Chu, and Yun also received rank. These four, relying on their sister's power, tyrannized the people and did not respect King Kongmin. In 1356, Ch'ŏl was killed and the Ki family destroyed (*KRS*, 131, 14b-21b; *HYS*, 249, 7071c).

9. Under Kongmin it was a senior third rank office. *Milchiksa*, similar in function to the Sung *Shu-mi yüan* (Bureau of Military Affairs; according to Edward A. Kracke, *Civil Service in Early Sung China* [Cambridge, Mass., 1953], p. 38), it was called variously in Koryŏ times: *Milchiksa*, *Chungch'uwŏn*, and *Kwangjongwŏn* (*KRS*, 76, 10b-12b).

10. In 1356, he became *Milchik pusa* and *Tongbungmyŏn pyŏngmasa* and recaptured Ssangsŏng from the Mongols. But he was reckless and devoured wealth. *KRS*, Index, 251a.

11. Modern Anbyŏn in South Hamgyŏng. See *SGSG*, 35, 6; *KRSC*, 58, 16b-17a; *SnSC*, 155, 7a-9a; *TYS*, 49, 1a-b.

[25]

Bright was his fame and influence—
Hence the soldiers who had returned
Clothed him[1]
With the yellow robe.

So great was his loyalty and devotion—
That the people who had survived tyranny[2]
Clothed his son
With the dragon robe.[3]

When, in the time of the third ruler of the Later Chou (Kung-ti, 953-959-960-973), the Northern Han and the Khitan invaded Later Chou, Chao K'uang-yin defended the country. Because Kung-ti was young and weak and Chao's reputation rose daily, Chao's men decided to make him emperor and made him wear the imperial yellow robe. *Sung shih*, 1, 4497b.

Because Hwanjo rendered devoted service to Koryŏ (canto 24), the people who groaned under tyranny at the end of Koryŏ made Yi Sŏng-gye, son of Hwanjo, wear the dragon robe.

1. In the original, "to him," in the honorific form (*AY*, V, 110–111).
2. Literally, "the people who revived from dying," for which the inter-linear commentary on the Chinese verse quotes *Shang shu*, 4, 3b (Legge, III, 181): "Our prince is come, and we revive," which praises the regenerative power of T'ang the Completer's punitive campaign against the Hsia (see *Mencius*, 1B, 11 [Legge, II, 171]).
3. 袞服 for which see *YG*, 4, 22b and n. 1 to canto 112.

[26]

He wished to send him to Lo-yang:
His brothers slandered and stopped him.
Whether he stayed here or went there,
Would it have changed the course of tomorrow?

He wanted to send him to the north:
The memorial of the Censorate stopped him.
Whether he went there or stayed here,
Would that have changed the course of today?

Li Yüan's raising of troops in Chin-yang was entirely due to the stratagem of his second son, Li Shih-min (canto 17). Li Yüan therefore wished to make Li Shih-min heir apparent, but he declined. Mean-while, the name and fame of Shih-min rose daily and his elder brother, Chien-ch'eng (589–626),[1] who was made heir apparent, became en-vious and plotted with his younger brother, Yüan-chi (603–626),[2] to kill Shih-min. Li Yüan ("he" in line 1) detected the scheme and had Shih-min ("him" in line 1 and "he" in line 3) move to Lo-yang, 850 li east of Ch'ang-an. But Chien-ch'eng was afraid of the extension of Shih-min's influence there and plotted with others to prevent him from going to Lo-yang (626). Chien-ch'eng tried to destroy Shih-min's influence, though he could not change the course of history. Shih-min did not go to Lo-yang. Nevertheless, he became the second ruler of T'ang (September 4, 626). *CTS*, 64, 3306b-d, 3306d-3307b; *HTS*, 79, 3873d-3874c; *TCTC*, 190, 5957–5960; 191, 5985–90, 6004–12, 6013–4, 6019; Fitzgerald, pp. 114–115; Woodbridge Bingham, "Li Shih-min's

Coup in A.D. 626. I: The Climax of Princely Rivalry," *JAOS*, LXX (1950), 91.

When King Kongmin appointed Hwanjo as the Commander of the Northern Region (*Sakpangdo pyŏngmasa*), the Censorate presented a memorial to the throne to the effect that Hwanjo, being a northerner, could not be sent to the north (1361). But the king did not concur. Even if Hwanjo had been prevented from going, Yi Sŏng-gye would have founded the Yi dynasty all the same. *KRS*, 39, 36a-b; *KRSCY*, 27, 12a; *TS*, 1, 5a.

1. *CTS*, 64, 3306b-d; *HTS*, 79, 3873d-3874b.
2. *CTS*, 64, 3306d-3307b; *HTS*, 79, 3874b-c.

[27]

His bow was huge beyond compare—
Turks picked it up and treasured it.
Posterity can glimpse
The man who was to save the world.

His arrow was huge beyond compare—
His father saw it and abandoned it.
On the same day he rejoiced
In him whose genius astounded the day.[1]

Li Shih-min's bow was twice the size of an ordinary bow. When he fought against Liu Hei-ta (d. 623)[2] he shot one of the approaching Turks with his arrow. The arrow was picked up by the Turks and circulated among them; they were amazed at its size and said that its owner must be a godlike man. Later, they obtained one bow and five arrows of Li Shih-min's and treasured them in their armory. *HTS*, 86, 3891b (Fitzgerald, pp. 97 ff.); *TFYK*, 44, 12a.

Yi Sŏng-gye's bow was unusually large and his arrows were proportionately heavy and long. He liked arrows that made noise as they flew through the air, preferring wood of the *hu* (redthorn)[3] tree to bamboo; the arrows were decorated with feathers of the crane. When he was still young, he accompanied his father on a hunt. Upon seeing his son's arrow, Hwanjo remarked, "This can't be used by man." When Yi Sŏng-gye shot seven roebucks with seven arrows, Hwanjo was pleased by his son's skill. *TS*, 1, 6a-b; *YK*, 1, 12.

1. In the original 命世才.
2. *CTS*, 55, 3289b-c; *HTS*, 86, 3890d-3891b; Liu, I, 291.
3. The *hu* is already mentioned in the *Book of Songs*, 239 (Karlgren, p. 191; Waley, p. 213), and *SC*, 47, 0162a (*MH*, V, 341–342). For Ikeuchi's study of the tree see *MTB*, V (1950), 97–103; and Yi Chung-hwa, ed., *Chosŏn ŭi kungsul* (1929), pp. 84b-97b.

[28]

He went to the magistrate's house
In order to escape a foe and spoke:
What do you think about it
In the light of the history of both Han?

He stood behind his father—
An envoy leaving for the capital spoke:
What do you think about his word
In the light of Three Han today?

A man of Shan-fu, Lü,[1] ("he" in line 1) was a good friend of the magistrate of P'ei. In order to escape a feud, he came to the magistrate as guest and consequently settled there. When Liu Pang visited the magistrate, the old man Lü said, "I have physiognomized many people, but none had as auspicious a physiognomy as you have. You should take care of yourself. There is a daughter born to your servant whom I would like to make your handmaiden." Despite his wife's protest, Lü gave his daughter to Liu Pang. *SC*, 8, 0033c-d (*MH*, II, 327–329; Watson, I, 78–79); *HS*, 1, 0291d-0292a (Dubs, I, 30–32); *TCTC*, 7, 260.

While Hwanjo was still in the northeast, he said good-bye to Yi Tal-ch'ung (d. 1385),[2] who had visited him. When Hwanjo offered the guest a cup, Yi took it standing, but when Yi Sŏng-gye, who stood behind his father, offered a cup, Yi Tal-ch'ung took it on his knees. Hwanjo thought it strange and asked the guest for the reason. Yi Tal-ch'ung replied, "Your son is indeed an extraordinary man and he is sure to make your family great." As expected, Yi Sŏng-gye founded the Yi dynasty. *TS*, 1, 5b-6a; *YK*, 1, 13.

1. *SC*, 8, 0033c-d (*MH*, II, 327–329; Watson, I, 78–79); *HS*, 1, 0291d-0292a; *HHS*, 92, 0592b; *TCTC*, 7, 260.
2. In 1360, he became Minister of Taxation and in 1366, *Milchik chehak*

(3a). After the death of Shin Ton, he was enfeoffed as Great Lord of Kyerim. His writings are praised by Yi Che-hyŏn. He died between September 5 and October 4, 1385 (*KRS*, 112, 21b-23b).

[29]

Though Han lost its vigor,
Its heir was about to rise.
Hence the Sleeping Dragon assisted
The big-eared Man.

He was born to save the world—
His mien was noble and mighty.
Hence the Ming envoy praised
The big-eared Minister.

Liu Pei (161–221–223),[1] a descendant of Emperor Kuang-wu, was over seven feet tall. His ears were so large, he could see them from the corner of his eyes. Chu-ko Liang (Sleeping Dragon) assisted him in founding the Shu Han. *SKC, Shu chih*, 2, 1008a; 5, 1012a-b (cf. *HHS*, 105, 0896a; *TCTC*, 62, 2006-7).

When Chu Ti's (Ming Ch'eng-tsu) envoys, Yü Shih-chi (d. 1435),[2] Wang T'ai,[3] and others came, Yi Sŏng-gye received them at Mount Ch'ŏnbo.[4] At the banquet, both Yü and Wang are said to have admired Yi Sŏng-gye's large ears.

Yi Sŏng-gye used to close his eyes when he sat, and his presence was awe-inspiring. But he became mild and warmhearted when he came in contact with others. *TS*, 1, 17a; *YK*, 1, 10.

1.   *SKC, Shu chih*, 2, 1008a-1010b; *BD*, 1338.
2.   He held the title of the *Tu-ch'a-yüan ch'ien-tu yü-shih* (Assistant Censor-in-Chief of the Censorate) for which see Charles O. Hucker, "Governmental Organization of the Ming Dynasty," *HJAS*, XXI [1958], 49, and Mano Senryū, "Kōbuchō no Tosatsuin ni tsuite," *Ōtani daigaku kenkyū nempō*, XIII (1960), 209-236. For Yü see *MS*, 149, 7440b.
3.   He held the office of *Hung-lu-ssu shao-ch'ing* (*HJAS*, XXI, 34):
4.   Fifteen ri east of Yangju (*YG*, 5, 9a), 21 ri west of P'ŏch'ŏn. Also called Mount Hoeam. See *SnSC*, 148, 10a; *TYS*, 11, 2b, 37a (25 ri east of Yangju).

[30]

Behind him the treacherous rebels,
Before him a sombre road.
Suddenly lightning flashed;
Heaven lighted the sky.

Behind him a fierce animal,
Before him a fathomless water.
Suddenly a coat of ice hardened;
Heaven froze the pond.

On the night of June 11, 884, Chu Ch'üan-chung (852–907–912)[1] planned to kill Li K'o-yung by stratagem. Chu had invited Li to a drinking bout and toward dusk when Li became drunk and fell asleep, Chu blocked the roads with vehicles and ordered his men to murder Li. Suddenly, lightning flashed, thunder filled the air, and heaven and earth were wrapped in darkness. Taking advantage of the moment, Li K'o-yung and his men jumped over the wall and escaped.[2] *HTS*, 218, 4144c; *CWTS*, 1, 4a-b; *HWTS*, 4, 4397d-8a; *TCTC*, 255, 8306; *TFYK*, 187, 3a; Franke, II, 516–517; Wang Gung-wu, *The Structure of Power in North China during the Five Dynasties* (Kuala Lumpur, 1963), pp. 30–31, 57.

In his boyhood, on a hunt, a leopard jumped Yi Sŏng-gye from a bush. He had no time to shoot. Before him was a deep pond, its surface covered with a thin coat of ice. He crossed it on horseback. Although the ice gave at every hoofmark, horse and rider escaped. *TS*, 1, 6b.

1. His former name was Wen. Ch'üan-chung was granted to him in 883 by Hsi-tsung. He killed Chao-tsung (867–888–904) and Ai Ti (892–904–907–908) and ascended the throne on June 1, 907 (*TCTC*, 266, 8673). He was murdered by his illegitimate son, Yu-kuei, who was in turn murdered by the supporters of another son, Yu-chen (*HWTS*, 13, 4406b; *TCTC*, 268, 8759). For Chu see *CWTS*, 1, 4199a-7, 4208d; *HWTS*, 1, 4395b-7a; Wang Gung-wu, *The Structure of Power*, pp. 26–29, 30–31, 47 ff., 83–84, 125; and Miyakawa Hisayuki, *Rikuchōshi kenkyū* (Tokyo, 1956), pp. 163–168.

2. Wang (pp. 30–31, 57) thinks Chu's unsuccessful treachery not only weakened the imperial power in north China by splitting Ho-nan and Ho-tung into two rivaling powers but was the turning point for Chu's rise to power.

[31]

The crippled horse stumbled and stumbled:
He was to reign thirty years.[1]
Could such an evil scheme
See its day?

Just a foot away from a precipice:
He was to reign a country of myriad leagues.
How could he fall over
A precipice a hundred fathoms deep?[2]

Li Shih-min's brothers, Chien-ch'eng and Yüan-chi, envied him and planned to kill him if the occasion arose. When Li Yüan went on a hunt (624), Chien-ch'eng gave Shih-min ("he" in line 2) a crippled horse. Shih-min chased a deer; when the horse fell, he ran several steps ahead and then mounted again. After he was thrown three times, Shih-min said to his friend, Yü-wen Shih-chi,[3] "He [Chien-ch'eng] intends to kill me with this horse. But life and death are ordained by providence; how can he hurt me?" *TCTC*, 191, 5990; Fitzgerald, p. 113.

In his boyhood, Yi Sŏng-gye ("he" in line 6) went hunting at the foot of a mountain. While he chased a boar, he suddenly found himself before a precipice. He jumped off the horse, but horse and boar plunged over the precipice. *TS*, 1, 5b.

On another occasion, as Yi passed by a precipice, two roebucks broke cover (1385). He urged on his horse, shot one of them, steered the horse back, and stopped it a few steps before the precipice. *TS*, 1, 19b.

1. Actually, he ruled for twenty-three years. Enthroned September 4, 626, he died July 10, 649.
2. Literally, "an empty space of a hundred fathoms deep." *Jen*, a measure of about eight feet, occurs in the *Hsün Tzu* (*SPTK*), 1, 8b. Dubs gives "an eighty foot" (p. 33) and Watson, "a hundred fathoms" (p. 16).
3. *CTS*, 63, 3305d-3306a; *HTS*, 100, 3913c-d.

[32]

Heaven sent its charge to him
In order to found the empire.

Hence his arrows alighted three times
In the placard of the pavilion.

Heaven sent the genius
In order to save the people.[1]
Hence he shot with twenty arrows
Twenty sables in the bush.

In 1127, the Chin army captured the Sung capital, K'ai-feng, and two emperors (Hui-tsung and Ch'in-tsung) were taken to the north. Chao Kou (Kao-tsung 1101–1127–1162–1187; "him" in line 1),[2] son of Chao Chi (Hui-tsung), raised a loyal army and made his men happy by hitting three logographs on a placard bearing the name of the Fei-hsien pavilion.[3] However, Sung rule was limited to the central and southern parts of China (Southern Sung, 1127–1279). *San-ch'ao pei-meng hui-pien* (1878 ed.), 90, 6a; *Chung-hsing hsiao-chi* (*TSCC*), 1, 2.

While Yi Sŏng-gye sat by the river after a bath on a hot summer day, a sable broke cover from a nearby bush. He shot it with an arrow and then another with a second arrow, until he had shot twenty sables with twenty arrows. *TS*, 1, 5b.

1. 拯民: *Mencius*, 1B, 11 (Legge, II, 171).
2. *Sung shih*, 24, 4537c-32, 4556a.
3. According to the *Chung-hsing hsiao-chi*, this took place on the *mou-shen* day of the eleventh intercalary month of the first year of *ching-k'ang* (January 1, 1127).

[33]

Bandits besieged the temporary palace;
The Son of Heaven wept.
When he went to give help and deceived the foe,
The bandits ran away.

Bandits looted the capital;
The king took refuge.
He led the van and won,[1]
And the king returned.

In the eighth month of 615 (or 616), Emperor Yang of Sui inspected the northern frontier (fifth day). The T'u-chüeh Turks ("bandits" in line 1) under Shih-pi Khan[2] made a surprise attack with several hundred thousand cavalry. The emperor hurried to Yen-men (twelfth day),[3] but thirty-nine of forty-one fortresses in the district had already fallen to the enemy. The invaders surrounded Yen-men (thirteenth day), and their arrows alighted before the emperor, who was frightened, hugged his youngest son, Kao (607–618), and wept till his eyes were swollen. The emperor then issued an edict and collected an army. Li Shih-min ("he" in line 3), then sixteen years old, enlisted in a rescue party and joined Yün Ting-hsing.[4] Shih-min persuaded his commander that the best scheme was to deceive the enemy by exaggerating the size of their army. Yün followed Shih-min's suggestion, and the Turks raised the siege and retreated (fifteenth day of the ninth month). *Sui shu*, 4, 2354a; 84, 2538a; *CTS*, 2, 3066a; *TCTC*, 132, 5697–8, 5699; Bingham, *The Founding of the T'ang Dynasty* (Baltimore, 1941), p. 49; Fitzgerald, pp. 15–17; Liu, I, 65, 71, 73, 88; Franke, II, 337–338.

In 1361, the Red Turbans[5] crossed the frozen Yalu with 200,000 men and captured the Koryŏ capital. King Kongmin fled to Pokchu (Andong).[6] The Korean army, under the command of General Chŏng Se-un (d. 1362),[7] drove back the enemy. At the time, Yi Sŏng-gye led 2,000 men and is said to have slain 100,000 rebels. *KRS*, 39, 30a and 40b; *KRSCY*, 27, 15b; *TS*, 1, 4b; *TT*, 47, 227 and 235.

1. 獻捷: *Tso chuan*, Duke Ch'eng 2 (Legge, V, 349).

2. Liu, II, 545–546, n. 403, for the date. For Shih-pi Khan see *Sui shu*, 84, 2536b ff.; *CTS*, 194A, 3596b.

3. Northwest of Tai hsien in Shansi (*CTK*, 964d).

4. *Sui shu*, 61, 2495a-b; *PS*, 79, 2989a-d.

5. Variously written as Honggun (Hung-chün), Hongjŏk, Hongdujŏk, or Hyanggun (*KRS*, Index, 916a-917b), the Koryŏ court knew something of their movements in China through envoys sent by Chang Shih-ch'eng and Fang Kuo-chen during 1358–1359 (*KRS*, 39, 23a, 23a-b, 25b-26a, 28a-b, 29a). On December 19, 1359, 3,000 rebels under Mao Chü-ching crossed the Yalu and seized four northwestern cities. They were defeated by General Yi Pang-sil and his army in the second month of 1360 (*KRS*, 39, 29b ff.; *KRSCY*, 27, 5a ff.; *TT*, 47, 227). The leaders of the second invasion of 1361 included such names as Sha-liu, Kuan-hsien-sheng, and P'an-ch'eng; the first two were killed during the war at the Korean capital. During the second invasion, the capital was in their hands for more than fifty days (December 21, 1361-February 13, 1362). F. W. Mote, *The Poet Kao Ch'i, 1336–1374* (Princeton, 1962), pp. 11–15 *passim*. For Chang Shih-ch'eng see *HYS*, 225, 7030a-d; *MS*, 123, 7389d-7390b. For other leaders see *HYS*, 225–227, and *MS*, 122–123. *HGS*, II, 658–659; *Seikyū shisō*, I, 297–309.

6. Modern Andong in North Kyŏngsang. See *SnSC*, 150, 12b-13b; *TYS*, 24 1a-2a.

7. Originally of Kwangju, he escorted King Kongmin to the Yüan capital

and was named Second Deputy Commander. After subjugation of the Red Turbans, he became Second Privy Councillor (*Ch'amji chŏngsa*). He was murdered by his rival, General An U, in 1362. *KRS*, 113, 13b-18s.

[34]

The water was deep and the ships were away.
But as Heaven bade him,
He forded the river
On horseback.

Walls were high with no scaling ladder.
But as Heaven helped him,
He flew across the wall
On horseback.

In 1115, when Aguda (the founder of the Chin, 1068–1113–1123)[1] attacked Huang-lung fu[2] of the Liao, and he and his men reached the Amur, there was not a single boat. Aguda ordered one man to go ahead and told others to follow, as he pointed with his whip. The water reached the horses' bellies, but his men successfully crossed the river. Later, when a boatman measured the depth of the area across which Aguda had led his army, he found it immeasurably deep. Without Heaven's assistance, so the first poem says, he and his men could not have forded the Amur. *Chin shih*, 2, 5860c.

While Yi Sŏng-gye fought against the Red Turbans in the Koryŏ capital (canto 33), the enemy attempted to flee at night. General Yi hastened to the gate where there was a fierce struggle between his soldiers and the enemy. Taking advantage of the confusion, a rebel struck the general from the rear with his spear and wounded Yi's right ear. The situation was urgent; Yi beheaded seven or eight enemies and fled across the fortress wall on horseback. The horse did not stumble and the people thought it a miracle. *KRS*, 40, 1a-b; *KRSCY*, 27, 19a-b; *TS*, 1, 4b; *TT*, 47, 239.

1. *Chin shih*, 2, 5859c-5862b.
2. Modern Nung-an, also known as Lung-man (*LG*, 39, 306–308).

[35]

They heard of the change at court;
He rode singly
And repulsed
The wicked enemy.

When he was winning in the plains,[1]
He was pursued and he feigned to flee.
Thus he snared
The ferocious enemy.

After Li Shih-min had killed (July 2, 626) his brothers, Chien-ch'eng and Yüan-chi, the Turks under Hsie-li Khan (d. 634) assumed that the T'ang court was weak and raided Shensi in the seventh month of 626. Shih-min ("he" in line 2) marshaled his troops for battle, rode forward attended only by six officers to display his influence. The Turks then asked for peace. On the thirtieth day of the eighth month,[2] Shih-min met Hsie-li Khan at the Pien Bridge[3] and they concluded a peace treaty by sacrificing a white horse. *CTS*, 2, 3067c; 194, 3596d; *HTS*, 2, 3636c; Fitzgerald, pp. 138–140; Liu, I, 139–140, 190–191.

The Mongol minister, Naɣačư[4] raided the Hongwŏn area.[5] King Kongmin named Yi Sŏng-gye as Commander of the Northeast. Yi fought a close fight several times. After days of rest, Yi prepared for an ambush at strategic points, divided the army into three columns, and, leading the central column himself, encountered the enemy on the plain of Hamhŭng.[6] Yi rode alone toward the enemy's ranks; three enemy generals came forward. Yi feigned flight and they pursued him. When Yi drew rein and turned his horse to the right, the three could not stop their horses. Yi then shot them from behind. In this manner he drew out the enemy, and with his left and right columns annihilated the Mongols. Naɣačư realized that he was powerless against Yi Sŏng-gye and fled (1362). *KRS*, 40, 2a, 6a-9b; *KRSCY*, 27, 21a, 24a-27b; *TS*, 1, 4b-5a; *TT*, 47, 240–241, 245–249.

1. In the original "country" as opposed to "capital" (in the first poem rendered as "at court").

2. Liu, II, 576, n. 722 (September 25, 626). For Hsie-li Khan see *CTS*, 194A, 3596c-3597c.

3. Liu, II, 577, n. 735.

4. For an account of Naɣačư, who died on August 31, 1388, aboard ship near Wu-ch'ang, see Henry Serruys, "Mongols Ennobled during the Early Ming," *HJAS*, XXII (1959), 211–213, and *The Mongols in China during the Hung-wu Period (1356–1398)*, (*MCB*, XI [1959]), 74–75, 82–83, 114–115.

5. Also known as Honggŭng or Honghŏn. In 1398, it was attached to Ham-hŭng pu (*SnSC*, 155, 2b; *TYS*, 49, 31a).

6. Formerly of Koguryŏ; in the beginning of the twelfth century, the East Jürched settled there. In 1107, Yun Kwan (d. 1111) repulsed them and established the Hamju taedohobu. In 1109, the region was again in the hands of the Jürched. In 1356, King Kongmin had Hwanjo pacify the area, and the regained territory was placed under Koryŏ control. In 1369, it became a *mok* and in 1416, a *pu* (*KRSC*, 58, 15b ff.; *SnSC*, 155, 2a-3a; *TYS*, 48, 4a-5a).

[36]

His elder brother fell from the horse;
Enemies chased him.
Swiftly, he went downhill and attacked
Until two sword blades were nicked.

He raced his horse,
Three enemies raced after him.
He swerved sharply and struck
The three men with three arrows.

In 617, Li Yüan and his two sons attacked Sui Kung-ti (Yang Yu, 605–617–618–619).[1] Sung Lao-sheng, a Sui general, sent troops against Li Yüan. The Sui army attacked first the eastern position held by Li Yüan and Chien-ch'eng. Chien-ch'eng fell from his horse; his soldiers fell into disorder; Li Yüan had to withdraw. Shih-min ("he" in line 3) came to his aid from the southern camp, broke through the enemy ranks, and appeared at their flank and rear. He killed dozens of the enemy until the blades of his two swords were nicked and his sleeves were running with blood. Li Yüan's soldiers, finally, regained their position. *CTS*, 1, 3064d; 2, 3066c; *HTS*, 1, 3634c; 2, 3636b; *TCTC*, 184, 5748; Fitzgerald, pp. 39 ff.

For the story of how Yi Sŏng-gye killed three Mongol generals see canto 35.

1. *Sui shu*, 5, 2355a-b.

[37]

In the capital there was a rebel:
Only one man had Heaven's mandate.

So Heaven rescued
The drowning horse.

The country was devoid of loyal hearts:
He alone burned with true heart.
So Heaven hardened
The swampy ground.

Ts'ao Ts'ao (155–220)[1] removed the last Han emperor, Hsien-ti (181–189–220–234),[2] and the empire came under his control. When Liu Pei of the Shu Han stationed his troops in Fan-ch'eng,[3] the governor of Ching-chou, Liu Piao (d. 208),[4] dreading Liu Pei's extraordinary character, gave a feast during which he planned to kill him. Liu Pei detected this, feigned to go to the toilet, and fled on horseback. The horse fell in the waters of T'an-ch'i[5] and struggled. Pressed by imminent danger, Liu Pei addressed his horse, "Ti-lu, exert yourself in this adverse situation." The horse jumped thirty feet and out of the water. *SKC, Shu chih*, 2, 1008c.

Because the elder brother of the Mongol Empress, née Ki (of Koryŏ origin), wielded power, the Ki family was massacred by the Koryŏ court (1356). The empress, wanting to avenge her family, sent troops to Koryŏ. The Koryŏ army was divided into three columns, the left wing under the command of An U-gyŏng (d. 1372),[6] the middle wing under Ch'oe Yŏng, and the right wing under Yi Sŏng-gye. Yi led a thousand picked cavalry and pounded the invaders unmercifully. During the campaign, Yi's horse fell into the mud but quickly freed itself. Many saw and thought it a miracle. That day, Yi, together with two old generals, routed the enemy. Only seventeen enemy cavalrymen escaped (1364). *KRS*, 40, 34a-b, 35a-b; *KRSCY*, 28, 1b, 2a-3b; *TS*, 1, 9a-b; *TT*, 48, 262, 263–264; *YK*, 1, 19.

1.   Wu-ti of Wei (*SKC, Wei chih*, 1, 0916d-0922a; *BD*, 2013).
2.   *HHS*, 9, 0669b-0670d.
3.   North of Hsiang-yang hsien, Hupeh (*CKT*, 1170c-d).
4.   *HHS*, 104B, 0866c-0867b; *SKC, Wei chih*, 6, 0937c-0938a.
5.   Southwest of Hsiang-yang hsien (*CKT*, 1278d-1279a).
6.   In 1360, An U-gyŏng, under An U, repulsed the Red Turbans and regained the capital. He distinguished himself when the Mongol Ch'oe Yu invaded and the Japanese pirates plundered the southern coasts. He planned with others to remove the powerful evil monk Shin Ton but was banished to Namwŏn, only to be recalled after Shin Ton's death (1371). In 1371, he joined in a campaign against the Northern Yüan. He died on May 27, 1372 (*KRS*, 43, 15a; 113, 18a-23a).

[38]

Matchless, he punished the four quarters,
Only his arrival could relieve the people.
Hence when he went to the East,
The West-I waited for his arrival.

Skillfully, he manipulated his troops,
Only his advance could win the war.
Hence when he went to the West,
People in the East waited for his arrival.[1]

Ch'eng T'ang or King T'ang the Completer ("he" in line 1) punished eleven corrupt states. The people wanted T'ang to subjugate their state first so that peace would reign. *SC*, 3, 0011b-c (*MH*, I, 176–187); *Shang shu*, 4, 1a ff. (Legge, III, 173–190 *passim*).

Taking advantage of Yi Sŏng-gye's absence when he went to defend the country against the Mongol invaders (canto 37), Yi's cousins, Samsŏn and Samgye[2] conspired with the Jürched who then invaded the northern borders. The odds were against the government troops. They, therefore, waited for Yi Sŏng-gye ("he" in lines 5 and 7) who defeated the invaders (1364). Samsŏn and Samgye fled to the Jürched and never returned to Korea. *KRS*, 40, 34b-35a, 35b; *KRSCY*, 28, 3b; *TS*, 1, 9b-10a; *TT*, 40, 262–263; *YK*, 1, 19.

1. The interlinear gloss (*YG*, 5, 46b) quotes *Mencius* 1B, 11 (Legge, II, 171): "Thus the people looked to him, as we look in a time of great drought to the clouds and rainbows" (cf. *Shang shu*, 4, 3b [Legge, III, 180–181]).

2. According to *YG*, 5, 46a, Kim Pang-gwe married Tojo's daughter, who bore him Samsŏn and Samgye. They were brought up among the Jürched and excelled in equestrian archery. They occupied the region north of Hamju (Yŏnghŭng) until Yi Sŏng-gye returned from the northwestern campaign to repulse them.

[39]

He wanted to prevent by visit
The emanation of the Son of Heaven in Ch'u.
How absurd was
His silly mind?

The king said it was for him,
The general's emanation over the Yalu.
Was it not right,
His royal remark?

The First Emperor of Ch'in used to say, "In the southeast is the emanation of a Son of Heaven" (canto 15). He then traveled to the east in order to check and obstruct his rival. When Liu Pang was hiding in the mountains and marshes of Mang and Tang, Lady Lü sought him and easily found him. When Liu Pang asked how, she replied, "Above the place where you are, there is always a misty emanation, so we follow it and always find you." *SC*, 8, 0034a (*MH*, II, 322–323; Watson, I, 81); *HS*, 1A, 0292b (Dubs, I, 36–37).

King Kongmin dispatched Yi Sŏng-gye as Commander of the Northeast (*Tongbungmyŏn wŏnsu*) to destroy Tongnyŏngbu[1] in order to sever relations with the Northern Yüan.[2] Yi crossed the Yalu with 5,000 cavalry and 10,000 infantry (1370). In the evening (on or about February 10), from the northeast a purple mist emanated stretching to the south. The astronomer divined that it was the emanation of a "general." The king heard it and rejoiced. *KRS*, 42, 1a; *KRSCY*, 29, 1a; *TS*, 1, 10a-b; *TT*, 49, 304; *YK*, 1, 15.

1. In 1269, Ch'oe T'an and others revolted at the Western Capital (P'yong-yang) and escaped to Peking. Qubilai praised Ch'oe's submission and ordered Meng-ko-tu to pacify the capital with 3,000 men. The Yüan, then, changed its name to Tongnyŏngbu (1270), and drew a line of demarcation along Chabi Pass. In 1290, however, the Yüan returned the territory north of the demarcation line to Koryŏ. In 1369, King Kongmin established a myriarch site there. Later, its name was changed to the present P'yongyang. See *YS*, 59, 6273d, and *TYS*, 51, 4b. For Ch'oe see *KRS*, 130, 33b-37b. *HGS*, III, 28–32.

2. Wada Sei, *Tōashi kenkyū: Mōko hen* (Tokyo, 1959), pp. 835–843. See Wolfgang Franke, "Addenda and Corrigenda to Pokotilov's History of the Eastern Mongols during the Ming Dynasty," *Studia Serica*, VIII (Chengtu, 1949), 64, for a genealogical table of the Mongol khans from Toγon to Lindan and for a useful bibliography for the study of Sino-Mongolian relations during the Ming (pp. 65–72).

[40]

He shot seventy arrows from the base of the fortress
And hit seventy men.
Then he made
A mound of the slain rebels.[1]

He shot seventy arrows over the wall,
And hit the faces of seventy men.
Then he returned
Singing in triumph.

When Li Yüan reached Lung-men hsien, near the mouth of the Fen River, the enemy general Wu Tuan-erh, with several thousand men, suddenly rushed to the foot of the fortress. No defense preparations had been made within the fortress and the enemy thought it could easily be taken. However, Li Yüan, personally leading about ten mounted men, rushed out, and engaged the enemy. Whenever he shot an arrow, an enemy soldier fell, and the dead bodies were strewn along the road. Li Yüan had shot seventy arrows. The following day a mound was built of the slain rebels and Li's seventy arrows were recovered. So great was his skill. *CTS*, 1, 3064c; *HTS*, 1, 3634b; Bingham, *The Founding of the T'ang Dynasty* (Baltimore, 1941), p. 77.

In 1370, when Yi Sŏng-gye subjugated the Northern Yüan, 300 families in the Yat'un village[2] surrendered; but their chief, occupying a position on the mountain, resisted. Yi had not brought his bow with him; he therefore borrowed a sleeve bow[3] amd shot about seventy enemy soldiers with an equal number of arrows (canto 39).

---

1. 京觀: *Tso chuan*, Duke Hsüan 12 (Legge, V, 320b).

2. West of Wiwŏn, known as Yat'undong. *YG*, 5, 48a pronounces it as *yat'un* and comments: "After crossing the Yalu, thirty ri west of Wiwŏn, there is a village. It is on a smooth, level land, named Yat'un. Its distance from Wu-la-ch'eng is one day's journey." *KRS*, 42, 1b; *TYS*, 55, 23a; *MTB*, X (1938), 10–13. This is the famous Wu-la shan-ch'eng, 270 ri from Isan kun (*TYS*, 55, 24b-25a; *YG*, 5, 48a). "If one goes from Angt'origuja (Angt'oguja in *TYS*, 55, 26a) and crosses the Yalu and P'o-chu (*TYS*, 55, 26a), one reaches it in the center of a vast plain. The fortress has insurmountable walls of immense height. It can be approached only from the western side." It is variously transcribed in Korean sources: Wu-la 兀剌 (*TYS*, 55, 26a); Yü-lo 亏羅 (*KRS*, 42, 1b); and Wu-lao 五老 (*KRS*, 43, 6b). The site of the fortress is generally agreed to be Wu-nü shan-ch'eng on the right bank of the T'ung-chia River (*HGS*, II, 662–663). See also Pak Si-hyŏng, *Kwanggaet'owang nŭngbi* (P'yongyang, 1966), pp. 12–24, for the importance of the *YG* gloss about the monument of King Kwang-gaet'o.

3. *YG*, 5, 48b (6, 45a, 46a) describes the sleeve bow: "A tube (or gun) over a foot long, from which an arrow is shot forth. A bamboo is cut in half to a length sufficient to take arrows like those in use with the common bow, and the arrow fits inside it. The notch of the arrow is placed on the spring, and at the side of the tube there is a hole through which a string is put and attached to the wrist. When the bow is cocked and ready to be fired, the arrow comes out past

the back of the hand. It has such force that it can penetrate right through an enemy." I owe this translation to Professor Joseph Needham, Caius and Gonville College, Cambridge.

[41]

He had no success in the eastern campaign
But he set free the captured men.
Their rapturous cry
Shook the roads.

He returned victoriously from the western campaign
And returned the spoils to the people.
The people in Liaotung rejoiced[1]
In the army of humanity and justice.[2]

In 644, Li Shih-min ("he" in line 2) declared war against Koguryŏ and marched to Liaotung at the head of his army. In the fourth month of 645, Kaemusŏng[3] fell; in the fifth month Liaotung and Paegam[4] fell; and in the sixth month the T'ang army besieged the walled city of Ansi.[5] The walled city was stubbornly defended and the invaders suffered heavy losses. In the ninth month, as the winter was approaching in Liaotung, Li was forced to withdraw after a siege of some sixty days. At the time, the commander of Ansi fortress appeared on the rampart and bade farewell to the retreating army. Li praised his heroism and granted him a hundred rolls of silk.[6] During the campaign, whenever he captured Koguryŏ soldiers and people, Li Shih-min is said to have set them free. *CTS*, 3, 3070a-b; 199, 3615b ff.; *SGSG*, 21, 1–9;[7] *TCTC*, 197, 2606 ff.; 198, 6230, 6231; Fitzgerald, pp. 187–198; Franke, II, 380–382.

During his campaign against the Northern Yüan (cantos 39–40), especially against their chief Ko An-wi, Yi Sŏng-gye captured 10,000 families, 2,000 oxen, and more than a hundred horses. The oxen and horses were returned to their owners, and the people in Liaotung praised his humanity. *KRS*, 42, 2b; *KRSCY*, 29, 1b; *TS*, 1, 10b.

1. For the expression *Liao-tso* see *JAOS*, LXXXII (1962), 376–383.
2. The commentary (*YG*, 6, 1a-b) quotes section 15, "Debating Military Affairs," *Hsün Tzu*, 10, 7b, 13b-14b; Watson, *Hsün Tzu: Basic Writings* (New York, 1963), pp. 69–70; Dubs, *The Works of Hsüntze* (London, 1928), pp. 167–169.

3. Modern K'ai-p'ing, 240 li south of Liaotung fortress, 530 li east of the Yalu. Yi Pyŏng-do argues that the place corresponds to southeast of modern Mukden (*HGS*, I, 491; *LG*, 389; *YG*, 6, 12b).

4. Or Yen-chou, southeast of modern Liao-yang (*HGS*, I, 492; *LG*, 981).

5. Corresponds to southeast of Hai-ch'eng, Ying-ch'eng-tzu. In *CTS*, 83, 3345a, it is entered as An-ti ch'eng; in *HTS*, 220, 4148c7-8, its population was reckoned at 100,000. See *TYS*, 52, 4b-5a; *LG*, 89-90 (seventy li northeast of Kai-p'ing hsien); *HS*, 28B, 0426c; *HHS*, 33, 0710a; *CTS*, 39, 3219d; *HTS*, 43B, 3734b; *Tu-shih fang-yü chi-yao* (*WYWK*), 37, 1580. For T'ang invasions of Koguryŏ, see Ikeuchi, *Mansenshi kenkyū*, II (1960), 267-418; Suematsu Yasukazu, *Seikyū shisō*, I, 87-101.

6. For this episode, see *TCTC*, 198, 6230; *T'ang hui-yao* (*TSCC*), 95, 1706; *TFYK*, 117, 25b; 138, 16b-17a.

7. Kim Pu-sik (*SGSG*, 22, 3; *YG*, 6, 26b-27a) cites a certain story of Liu Kung-ch'üan: "Upon seeing the lines of the allied army of Koguryŏ and Malgal stretching to forty li, Li Shih-min betrayed fear. When a scout reported the siege of Li Shih-chi's troops, Li Shih-min likewise lost heart." This episode was omitted in the T'ang history, both Old and New, as well as the *Tzu-chih t'ung-chien*. Kim also laments that history does not preserve the name of the commander who so stoutly defended the Ansi fortress. The official biographies in *CTS*, 165, and *HTS*, 165, do not list Liu's works. The *Shou fu*, 44, however, cites a work containing only three items, two of a supernatural character. Subsequent compilations of *hsiao-shuo* and *pi-chi* also include the three items by Liu, under the same title, but none contains the anecdote referred to by Kim Pu-sik. I am indebted for this information to Professor C. T. Hsia of Columbia University.

[42]

Long was he in the Western campaign,
A magic animal[1] spoke.
He followed
The diviner's advice.

He had seized Tongnyŏng.
A red light[2] shone.
He followed
The astronomer's advice.

During Cinggis Qan's campaign in the southwest, when he reached Iron Gate Pass,[3] a green animal in the shape of a deer, with the tail of a horse and a single horn, appeared to one of his bodyguards and addressed him in human speech, "Your army should return as soon as possible." The Qan thought it strange and consulted Yeh-lü Ch'u-ts'ai (1189–1243).[4] Yeh-lü answered, "This auspicious animal is called *chüeh-tuan*. It can travel 18,000 li a day and understands the languages of the four barbarians. Because our army has been in the western campaign for four years, Heaven, disapproving of reckless killing, has dispatched the animal to you. If you are indulgent to the people of these regions, you will secure eternal happiness." The Qan instantly withdrew the army. *YS*, 146, 6774a; Igor de Rachewiltz, "Yeh-lü Ch'u-ts'ai (1189–1243): Buddhist Idealist and Confucian Statesman," in *Confucian Personalities* (Stanford, 1962), p. 194; Chun-chiang Yen, "The *chüeh-tuan* as Word, Art Motif and Legend," *JAOS*, LXXXIX (1969), 590–591.

During his campaign against the Ki family (cantos 37–38), Yi Sŏng-gye encamped ten ri west of Liao-yang. On the night of November 23, 1370, a red mist as bright as fire, spread in the sky and reached Yi's camps, as if to pierce them.[5] The astronomer divined that it would be best to transfer the camps. Yi therefore moved the troops the following day. *KRS*, 42, 24a; *KRSCY*, 29, 8a-9a; *TS*, 1, 11a-12a; *TT*, 49, 311–313.

1.   Rachewiltz identifies it with a rhinoceros (*Confucian Personalities*, pp. 194–195, 363, n. 36). He also thinks that the incident might have happened during the raid into the Punjab in the summer of 1222 (p. 195). *MS*, 332, 7939c-d refers to the incident. See also *Sŏngho sasŏl*, 2, 175.

2.   In the original: "the clouds shone" or "the clouds were shining with [red light]."

3.   The present Buzgala Pass in Uzbekistan (*MS*, 332, 7939c-d).

4.   *YS*, 146, 6474a-6465a; *HYS*, 127, 6873a-6874a; *BD*, 2446. For a bibliography on Yeh-lü, see Rachewiltz, p. 361, n. 4.

5.   Not in *KRS*, 42, 24a but in *KRSCY*, 29, 9a: 赤氣射營熾如火.

[43]

At the Hsüan-wu Gate he shot two boars
With a single arrow.
An artist drew the rare happening
To show it to the people.

On Mount Chorae he struck two roebucks
With a single arrow.
Must we paint
This natural genius?[1]

During a hunting trip, Li Lung-chi (Hsüan-tsung, 685–712–756–762; "he" in line 1) shot two wild boars with a single arrow at the Hsüan-wu Gate and had Wei Wu-t'ien² paint the scene. *T'ang yü-lin* (Wu-ying-tien chu-chen-pan ch'üan-shu ed.), 4, 1b-2a.

During a hunting trip on Mount Chorae³ in 1372, Yi Sŏng-gye shot a roebuck with an arrow. Two roebucks then started to escape, and he felled them with a single arrow, which, after having killed the animals, embedded itself in the trunk of a tree. *TS*, 1, 12a-b; *YK*, 1, 12.

1. 天縱之才: *Analects*, IX, 6 (Waley, p. 139).

2. *Li-tai ming-hua chi* (Chi-ku-ko ed.), 9, 15a; *T'ai-p'ing kuang-chi*, 212, 1625; *T'ang-Sung hua-chia jen-ming tz'u-tien* (Peking, 1958), pp. 148b-149b; *T'ang-ch'ao ming-hua lu* (Mei-shu ts'ung-shu, 2), 6a-b (Alexander Soper, *Artibus Asiae*, XXI [1958], 217); *HTS*, 59, 3770b.

3. Twelve ri east of Hongwŏn in South Hamgyŏng (*TYS*, 49, 33a-b).

[44]

It was a game of polo¹—
He struck the ball on horseback.
Only the players in the two parties
Rejoiced in his skill.

It was a polo match played by royal order—
He hit the ball by "sideway block."
People on nine state roads²
Admired his skill.

Li Shen, the eighteenth T'ang ruler (Hsüan-tsung, 810–846–859; "he" in line 2),³ was an expert in archery and polo. *T'ang yü-lin*, 7, 13a.

In Koryŏ, young military officials and sons of the nobility were trained for the polo contest which was held on the fifth day of the fifth month. On that day, tents lined the streets before the palace, and the king and the court watched the game. Yi Sŏng-gye was chosen as a champion and revealed his skill which astounded the spectators (1356). *TS*, 1, 6b-7a; *YK*, 1, 13. See also Chapter III for details.

1. For polo in China see Bertold Laufer, "The Early History of Polo," *Polo: The Magazine for Horsemen*, VII (April 1932), 13-14, 43-44, and L. C. Goodrich, "Polo in Ancient China," *Horse and Horseman*, XIX, 5 (April 1938), 27, 38-39; Lo Hsiang-lin, "T'ang-tai po-lo ch'iu-hsi k'ao," *Shih-hsüeh chüan-*

k'an, I, 1 (Canton, 1935), 87–100; Yang Yin-shen, "T'ang-tai te yu-i," *Hsüeh-lin*, IV (February 1941), 129–142, esp. 131–132. For a study of the subject in Koryŏ and Yi periods, see Imamura Tomo, *Ōgi, Hidarinawa, Dakyū, Hisago* (1937), pp. 275–397 (281–308 for the subject in Koryŏ, and 302–307 for illustrations).

2. 九達: *Chiao-cheng San-fu huag-t'u* (Shanghai, 1958), 1, 11.

3. *CTS*, 18B, 3129d-3133d; *HTS*, 8, 3654a-d.

[45]

There was one who wished to go:
But he chose a generous man.[1]
Since he was a generous man,
He made the people of Ch'in happy.

Many could shoot an arrow:
But he was aware of his heroic virtue.[2]
With his heroic virtue
He saved many.

When King Huai of the Ch'u ("he" in line 2) was about to punish the Ch'in, Hsiang Yü ("one" in line 1) wanted to go west and enter through the pass with Liu Pang (Lord of P'ei). But King Huai's older generals suggested that Hsiang Yü was violent and destructive and that he should not be allowed to go. Instead, they proposed to send Liu Pang ("he" in line 3), who was generous and righteous. Liu therefore went to the west and won every battle, but ordered his men not to pillage; and the people of the Ch'in were delighted. When the King of Ch'in, Tzu-ying, surrendered, some generals proposed his execution. But Liu Pang replied, "When at first King Huai sent me, it was certainly because I am able to be generous and indulgent. Moreover, once a man has surrendered, it would be inauspicious to kill him." So he charged his officials with the safety of Tzu-ying. When he finally entered Hsien-yang (207 B.C.), he made it known that the purpose of his coming was to deliver them from tyranny. When the Ch'in people brought cattle, sheep, wine, and food for his troops, Liu did not accept them. The people were glad and their only fear was that Liu Pang might not become King of Ch'in. *SC*, 8, 0034c-0035a (*MH*, II, 324 ff.; Watson, I, 85–90); *HS*, 1A, 0292d-0293c (Dubs, I, 47–59).

King Kongmin greatly admired Yi Sŏng-gye's divine skill in archery. One day, the king held a contest at Tŏkpahŭi,[3] east of the capital, and asked the contestants to hit the target fifteen paces away. Yi hit the target every time he shot. Later, a famous archer Hwang Sang[4] arrived, but after hitting the target fifty times, he fell short of the mark. Yi, however, never missed the mark and the king praised him highly (1372). With this military prowess he saved the people. *TS*, 1, 12b; *YK*, 1, 13.

1. 長者: *SC*, 7, 0029c, an epithet for Ch'en Ying. *MH*, II, 253 renders it "chef," but Watson, I, 39, "a man of exceptional worth."

2. In *Tso chuan*, Duke Hsüan 12 (Legge, V, 320), seven virtues are enumerated, and in *Sun Tzu*, 1, 1, five (wisdom, sincerity, benevolence, courage, and strictness) as those for which the commander stands. Also, Liu Pang inaugurated a dance of heroic virtues in 203 B.C. (*HS*, 22, 0381c). Li Shih-min, in 633, ordered the choreographic diagram to be drawn for the *Ch'in-wang p'o-chen yüeh* (*TCTC*, 194, 6101) and instructed Lü Ts'ai to teach 120 musicians how to perform the dance. Later it was called the "Dance of Seven Virtues."

3. Eastern Peak of Paeyamkol, nine *ri* east of Kaesŏng (*TYS*, 4, 7b).

4. In the time of King Kongmin, he was *milchik pusa*. At the time of the subjugation of the Ki family, he rendered conspicuous service and was rewarded. During the invasion of the Red Turbans he escorted the king to the south. Later he became the Great Lord of Hoesan (*KRS*, 114, 8b-9b).

[46]

Wishing to send out the wise king,[1]
Heaven induced the father-in-law
And caused him to paint
Two peacocks.

Wishing to display his august power,[2]
Heaven induced him to have a game
And caused him to place
Ten silver mirrors.

Tou I,[3] the Duke of Shen-wu, was married to an elder sister of Yü-wen Yung (Wu-ti of the Later Chou, 543–560–578),[4] and she gave birth to a girl. At the time of her birth, the child's hair was long; when she reached the age of three, it was as long as her height. In order to choose a wise man for her, Tou I painted two peacocks on the gate and promised her to the one who could hit the eyes of the birds. Scores of people came but all missed the mark. Later Li Yüan arrived and sent two arrows straight to the mark. Tou I, greatly pleased, made him his son-in-law. *CS*, 30. 2307d-2308a; *PS*, 61, 2944b; *CTS*, 51, 3278c-d; *TCTC*, 183, 5728.

King Kongmin asked the contestants to shoot ten small silver mirrors from eighty paces away. Yi Sŏng-gye hit them with ten arrows (1372). Heaven caused the king to hold such a contest in order to display Yi's divine skill. *TS*, 1, 12b-13a.

1. 賢君 refers to Li Shih-min (*YG*, 6, 43b).
2. 聖武: *Shang shu*, 4, 6b (Legge, III, 194): "sacred prowess," and *Chou i*, 7, 10a (Wilhelm, I, 340): "unremitting divine power." The term was commonly used with emperors (and kings in Korea) for their accomplishments, e.g., Han Wu-ti, Wei Wu-ti, and Yüan T'ai-tsu.
3. *CS*, 30, 2307d-2308a; *PS*, 61, 2933b-d; *BD*, 1957; *TCTC*, 183, 5728.
4. *CS*, 5, 2271c-6, 2275d; *PS*, 10, 2773b-2775d. For the chronology of his family, see *HJAS*, IV (1939), 280.

[47]

By his single arrow
The Turks were frightened.
No place was far enough—
His influence was felt everywhere.

By his single arrow from the sleeve bow
Island savages were awed.
No place was strong enough—
He crushed the foe everywhere.

For the arrow of Li Shih-min see canto 27.

In 1377, the Japanese pirates sailed from Tsushima and infested the southern coast. Yi Sŏng-gye engaged them on Mount Chii.[1] A pirate, standing about 200 paces away, slapped his hips to show his insolence. General Yi used the sleeve bow and shot him down. The enemy climbed a cliff and looked down on Yi's men with swords and spears in their hands. Yi ordered his colonel to scale the cliff, but he returned and said his horse could not do it. General Yi sent his son, Pang-wŏn, but he came back with the same report. Thereupon, Yi personally led the cavalry, climbed the cliff and cut the despoilers to pieces.[2] This took place in the fifth month of 1377. *KRS*, 114, 39b-40a; *KRSCY*, 30, 29b-30b; *TS*, 1, 12a-b; *YK*, 1, 16.

1. Also called Chiri, Pangjang, or Turyu; 6,283 feet high. *KRSC*, 57, 36a; *SnSC*, 150, 1a; *TYS*, 30, 3a-5b; *Oju yŏnmun changjŏn san'go* (KKH, 1959), 47, 507a-512b.

2. For the subject see Shin Ki-sŏk, "Koryŏ malgi ŭi tae-Il kwan'gye," *Sahoe Kwahak*, I (1957), 3-31; Shin Sŏk-ho, "Yŏmal Sŏnch'o ŭi woegu wa kŭ taech'aek," *KSC*, III (1959), 103-164; Tamura Hiroyuki, "Sensho wakō no keifu ni tsuite," *CG*, XXIII (1962), 37-72; Mori Katsumi, "Nis-Sō-Rai kōshō to wakō no hassei," in *Ishida Hakushi shōju kinen Tōyōshi ronsō* (Tokyo, 1965), pp. 483-497. Cf. Claudian, *On Stilico's Consulship*, I, 127, where Stilico is pictured as climbing the snowy peak of Athos (LCL, 1922; I, 372-373).

[48]

He had his horse jump across the gully,
Enemies turned back.
Only a few feet deep it was:
But who could have crossed it?

Swiftly he had his horse scale a cliff
And seized all the pirates.
Many would dare and try:
But who could have scaled it?

Aguda ("he" in line 1), on his return from a battle, was pursued by the enemy and lost his way in a narrow lane. Before him lay a muddy pit and a steep bank. Aguda's horse, however, galloped over the abyss without touching ground. *Chin shih*, 2, 5859d.

For the second stanza see canto 47.

[49]

Looters entered the capital,
And the Son of Heaven escaped.
Many generals gained fame,
But the One-Eyed Dragon stood above them.

Pirates entered the capital,
The king wished to leave.
Singly he achieved
The merits of two generals.

In the time of the T'ang emperor Hui-tsung (Li Huan, 862–873–888), Huang Ch'ao[1] revolted and captured Ch'ang-an (881); the emperor fled to Ch'eng-tu. Li K'o-yung distinguished himself by extraordinary exploits in the recovery of the capital (881, 883). One of Li's eyes was smaller than the other; hence, he was known as "One-Eyed Dragon." *TCTC*, 255, 8295; Franke, II, 515–516.

In 1378, the Japanese pirates plundered Kanghwa Island and killed innocent women and children. The Koryŏ army under the command of Ch'oe Yŏng and Yang Paeng-nyŏn (d. 1379)[2] encountered the pirates at Haep'ung,[3] but Ch'oe Yŏng was unsuccessful. Thereupon, Yi Sŏng-gye led the picked cavalry and together with Yang Paeng-nyŏn beat off the despoilers. The court planned to evacuate the capital when Ch'oe Yŏng withdrew. But when the news of Yi's victory reached the court, the officials congratulated Yi. *KRS*, 133, 24a ff.; *KRSCY*, 30, 36b-37a; *TS*, 1, 14b; *TT*, 51, 374-375.

1. *CTS*, 200B, 3622d-3623d; *HTS*, 225C, 4175d-4177c; Howard S. Levy, *Biography of Huang Ch'ao* (Berkeley, 1955); *BD*, 847; Hori Toshikazu, "Kō Sō no hanran," *Tōyō bunka kenkyūjo kiyō*, XIII (1957), 1–108.

2. He repulsed the Japanese pirates at Sŏnju and subjugated, together with Yi Sŏng-gye, the Tongnyŏngbu. But he was arrogant, and Yi In-im banished him to Sŏpchu. Later he was killed by Ch'oe Yŏng (*KRS*, 114, 32a-35a).

3. Chŏngju of Koguryŏ; in 1018, it belonged to Kaesŏng. In 1108, it was called Sŭngch'ŏnbu. In 1442, it merged with Tŏksu hyŏn and was given the present name of P'ungdŏk (*KRSC*, 56, 5b-6a; *TYS*, 13, 1a-b; 48, 4a; *SnSC*, 148, 4a).

[50]

Longing for the sovereign,
He raided the harem.
At the time stars in the sky
Fell like snow.

Pitying his own people,
He passed by Changdan.
At the time a white rainbow
Cut across the sun.

Empress (née) Wei[1] of T'ang Chung-tsung (656–684–705–710)[2] poisoned the emperor (710), took over the helm of the state, and gave all important posts to members of her family. When Hsüan-tsung ("he" in line 2), on the night of July 21, 710, led the soldiers and was about to enter the palace to kill the empress and her family, stars fell like snow. His followers remarked, "As it is Heaven's wish, we must not lose this chance." They rushed in, killed the empress, and massacred the members of the Wei family. Princess An-lo,[3] the youngest and favorite daughter of the empress, was slain while drawing her eyebrows before a mirror. *CTS*, 8, 3080d; *TCTC*, 209, 6641–6; Franke, II, 425–426.

In 1380, the Japanese pirates with 500 ships landed in Chinp'o[4] and ravaged three southern provinces. Koryŏ generals, Na Se (d. 1397),[5] Sim Tŏk-pu,[6] and Ch'oe Mu-sŏn (d. 1395)[7] used the gunpowder first invented by Ch'oe and destroyed enemy ships. The bandits fled to Sangju[8] and Sŏnju[9] in the eighth month, plundered the two towns, and killed innocent women and children. Dead bodies covered the hills and plains. Thereupon, Yi Sŏng-gye led his picked army to crush the bandits; when they reached Changdan,[10] a white rainbow appeared across the sun. The astronomer divined that it was the sign of victory. *KRS*, 126, 34b; *KRSCY*, 31, 19a; *TS*, 1, 15a; *TT*, 51, 392 (*Sŏngho sasŏl*, 1, 72).

Yi engaged the bandits on Unbong[11] and annihilated them in the ninth month. This is the famous victory of Mount Hwang,[12] east of Unbong. *KRS*, 126, 35a-38b; 134, 22a; *KRSCY*, 31, 19b-23a; *TS*, 1, 15a-16a; *TT*, 51, 392–396.

The court rejoiced over the signal victory, and Ch'oe Yŏng welcomed Yi's army in front of the Ch'ŏnsu monastery.[13] Holding Yi's hand, Ch'oe said, "Were it not for you, on whom could our country depend?" Yi Saek, the Lord of Hansan, and others composed eulogies to celebrate Yi's success. *KRS*, 126, 39a; *KRSCY*, 31, 24a-b; *TS*, 1, 16b-17a; *TT*, 51, 397–398; *YK*, 1, 17–18.

1. *CTS*, 51, 3279c-3280a: *HTS*, 76, 3868b-d; Howard S. Levy, *Harem Favorites of an Illustrious Celestial* (Taichung, 1958), pp. 4–5.
2. *CTS*, 7, 3077b-3079a; *HTS*, 4, 3642d-3643c.
3. *CTS*, 51, 3279c-3280a; *HTS*, 83, 3884d-3885a; *BD*, 10.
4. Twenty-six ri south of Sŏch'ŏn, South Ch'ungch'ŏng (*SnSC*, 149, 14b; *TYS*, 19, 8a).
5. A Mongol who joined the Koryŏ army and helped repulse the invasion of the Red Turbans (1361–1362). He was enfeoffed as the Lord of Yŏnan and became *Haedo wŏnsu*. In 1380, he destroyed the Japanese fleet at Chinp'o (*KRS*, 114, 14a-15b; *TnS*, 12, 5b).
6. See n. 10 to canto 11.
7. He learned the method of making gunpowder from a certain Li Yüan, a supplier of saltpeter for the Mongol army (*KRS*, 133, 31b) and convinced the court of its importance in defense. In the tenth month of 1377, the office in

Charge of Barrel Guns was established (*KRS*, 77, 29a; 81, 27b; 113, 31b). In 1380, the Koryŏ army used gunpowder and destroyed the Japanese fleet off Chinp'o (*KRS*, 114, 15a-b; 134, 19a-b). Ch'oe Mu-sŏn died May 8, 1395 (*TS*, 7, 8b-9a). For the invention and use of gunpowder and firearms in China, see *Isis*, CIV (1946), 114-123, 250-251; CIX-CX (1947), 160-178. For the development of firearms in late Koryŏ and early Yi, see Hŏ Sŏn-do, "Yŏmal Sŏnch'o hwagi ŭi chŏllae wa paltal," *YH*, XXIV (1964), 1-60; XXV (1964), 39-98; XXVI (1965), 141-165.

8.   Originally Sabŏlguk, the twelfth Silla king, Ch'ŏmhae (247-261), made it a *kun*. King Hyegong (765-780) changed its name to Sabŏlchu. In the beginning of Koryŏ, it was the site of Andong tohobu; Hyŏnjong (1010-1031) made it the site of Andong taedohobu (*KRSC*, 57, 19a-b; *SnSC*, 150, 20b-22a; *TYS*, 28, 1a-b).

9.   Ilsŏn kun of Silla; in 1018, it was attached to Sangju and in 1143 it became a *hyŏn*. Under Yi Pang-wŏn, it became Sŏnsan kun, and later was elevated to be the site of a *tohobu* (*KRSC*, 57, 23b; *SnSC*, 150, 23a-b; *TYS*, 29 29, 1a-b).

10.   Changch'ŏnsŏng hyŏn of Koguryŏ, King Kyŏngdŏk gave it its present name. In 1419, it became a *hyŏn* and in 1469 was elevated to be the site of a *tohobu* (*SGSG*, 37, 3; *KRSC*, 56, 6b; *SnSC*, 148, 18a-b; *TYS*, 12, 1a-2a).

11.   Musan hyŏn of Silla, it was made a *hyŏn* in 1392 (*SGSG*, 34, 7; *KRSC*, 57, 37a-b; *SnSC*, 151, 18b-19a; *TYS*, 39, 41a).

12.   Sixteen ri east of Unbong (*TYS*, 39, 41b). For a monument erected in 1577 to celebrate Yi Sŏng-gye's victory, see *CKS*, II, 784-786 (*TYS*, 39, 42a-43b).

13.   East of Kaesŏng, located near modern Changdan. For various transcriptions see *TYS*, 4, 17a-18b, *KRSC*, 31, 24a, and *YG*, 7, 11a.

[51]

His battle array was different,
They noticed it and retreated.
Had they advanced,
Would they have survived after all?

He marshaled troops unlike others,
They noticed it but came forward.
Had they retreated,
Would they have survived after all?

Cinggis Qan punished the chief of the Naiman,[1] Tayang Qan.[2] When Tayang Qan's lieutenant Jamuqa[3] surveyed the battle array of the qan, he realized the superiority of the Mongol army and ran away. *YS*, 1, 6134b.

When Yi Sŏng-gye assailed the Japanese bandits on Unbong (1380), the bravest enemy captain, Agi-batur,[4] galloped forward with a spear in his hand. He wished to spare him and ordered his men to capture him alive. His men pointed out that Agi-batur would be a danger to Koryŏ if he stayed alive. Yi Sŏng-gye therefore first shot down his helmet, and his men shot at his face and killed him. Later, Koryŏ soldiers who had been prisoners of the Japanese, returned and said, "Agi-batur warned his men when he saw that General Yi Sŏng-gye's battle array was different from the others." *KRS*, 126, 37a ff.; *KRSCY*, 31, 21a-b; *TS*, 1, 15b-16a; *YK*, 1, 17-18.

1. Paul Pelliot and Louis Hambis, *Histoire des Campagnes de Gengis Khan, Cheng-wou ts'in-tcheng lou*, I (Leiden, 1951), 215-221.
2. Son of Inanca-bilge Qan; defeated in 1204 by Cinggis Qan (*MCB*, XI [1959], 263; Pelliot and Hambis, pp. 307-311; René Grousset, *L'Empire des Steppes*(Paris, 1939), pp. 269-271; *Yüan-ch'ao pi-shih* (*TSCC*), 8, 199-214 (Erich Haenisch, *Die geheime Geschichte der Mongolen* [Leipzig, 1948], pp. 76-84).
3. Pelliot and Hambis, 27-28, n. 3.
4. *Agi* in Korean means "boy," and *batur* (*ba'atur, bayatur*) in Mongolian, "general," "hero," etc. On the usage of *agi* in the Yi dynasty see Yi Kyu-gyŏng, *Oju yŏnmun changjŏn san'go*, 33, 273a; and *Tongsa kangmok* (CKK, 1915), 4, 200.

[52]

He went hunting with bribed Tartars.
Had his shot missed the needles,
Would he and his father
Have survived?

He fought against the bribed Japanese.[1]
Had he not unmasked his helmet,
Would he have saved
The people of his country?

Li Wen, Hsien-tsu of the Later T'ang, lost a battle against Ho-lien To,[2] chief of the T'u-yü-hun,[3] and together with his son, Li K'o-yung, fled to the Tartars. Ho-lien bribed the Tartars into killing Li Wen and his son. Li K'o-yung ("he" in line 1) detected the plan and, in order to overawe them, hung a needle on a bough—or planted a whip—and shot it from a hundred paces away. The Tartars feared his prowess and dared not harm him and his father. Later Li K'o-yung crushed the rebellion of Huang Ch'ao. *HTS*, 218, 4144b; *HWTS*, 4, 4937d.

For Yi Sŏng-gye's exploit see cantos 50–51.

1. Agi-batur, a young Japanese commander (*YG*, 7, 11a).
2. *HTS*, 218, 4144b ff.; *HWTS*, 74, 4479b-c.
3. Thomas D. Carroll, *Account of the T'u-yü-hun in the History of the Chin Dynasty* (Berkeley, 1953) and Wada Hironori, "Tokokkon to Namboku ryōchō tono kankei ni tsuite," *Shigaku*, XXV (1951), 80–104; Franke III, 250–254.

[53]

He pacified the four seas,
Travelers need not take packed rice.
Even the northern barbarians outside the borders,
How could they not come to him?

He opened the four borders,
Men on islands had no more fear of pirates.
Southern barbarians beyond our waters,[1]
How could they not come to him?

When Li Shih-min ("he" in line 1) established peace in the country, prosperous years followed, and travelers could go without taking packed rice. Peace reigned, and the Turks came to pay tribute. *TCTC*, 193, 6084–5.

Yi Sŏng-gye ("he" in line 5) finally subjugated the Jürched in the north and the Japanese pirates in the south, and the inhabitants of even the remotest island in the south enjoyed peace. After Yi's enthronement, the king of Liu-ch'iu sent an envoy to pay his respects (1392, 1394, 1397)[2] and the Siam sent an envoy with tributes (1393).[3] *TS*, 1, 2a; 3, 12a; 12, 4a.

1. For 徼 see *Shuo-wen chieh-tzu*, 2B, 56; *Chi yün*, 3, 374; *SC*, 30, 0120c (Watson, II, 100): "patrol posts."
2. On August 26, 1392, the king of the Liu-ch'iu, Satsudo (1321–1350–1395), sent back the Koreans captured by the Japanese pirates (*TS*, 1, 52a; 2, 21b), and his envoys arrived on September 27, 1392 (*TS*, 2, 1a), on October 4, 1394 (*TS*, 6, 14b), and on September 27, 1397 (*TS*, 12, 4a). For Liu-ch'iu see *Wen-hsien t'ung-k'ao* (Chiu-t'ung ch'üan-shu ed.), 327, 4a ff.; *Hsü T'ung-tien* (in *Chiu-t'ung*), 147, 12b-13b; Majikina Ankō and Shimakura Ryūji, *Okinawa is-*

sennen shi (Tokyo, 1952), pp. 72–80, 117–124. For Korean-Okinawan relations, see *CMP*, 180, 1a-4b; Charles Haguenauer. "Relations du Royaume des Ryukyu avec les Pays des Mers du Sud et la Corée," *Bulletin de la Maison Franco-Japonaise*, III (Tokyo, 1931), 4–16; and Kobata Jun, "Ryūkyū Chōsen no kankei ni tsuite," *Tayama Hōnan kakō kinen rombunshū* (Tokyo, 1963), pp. 235–255. For Chinese-Ryukyuan relations see Robert K. Sakai, "The Ryukyu (Liu-ch'iu) Islands as a Fief of Satsuma," in *The Chinese World Order: Traditional China's Foreign Relations*, ed. John K. Fairbank (Cambridge, Mass., 1968), pp. 112–134; and Ta-tuan Ch'en, "Investiture of Liu-ch'iu Kings in the Ch'ing Period," *ibid.*, pp. 135–164.

3. The Siam mission, consisting of twenty, arrived in the Korean capital on July 25, 1393 (*TS*, 3, 12a). For Korean-Siamese relations at the end of Koryŏ and in the early Yi, see Min Pyŏng-ha, "Yŏmal Sŏnch'o ŭi Sŏmna kuk kwaŭi kwan'gye," *Kukche munhwa*, II (March 1965), 3–17.

[54]

Valuing their rites and justice,
He stopped his men.
Even southern barbarians beyond the borders,
How could they not come to him?

Prizing his skill and valor,
He threw away his iron arrowhead.
Even northern barbarians outside the borders,
How could they not come to him?

The army of Liu Pang (Han Kao-tsu) killed Hsiang Yü (202 B.C.) and chastised Ch'u: Lu alone did not submit. Liu Pang ("he" in line 2) therefore led the troops to Lu intending to massacre its inhabitants. Because the state of Lu had guarded itself well and was known for its decorum and righteousness, Liu Pang had the head of Hsiang Yü held up and shown to the elders of Lu. Lu, then, surrendered. *SC*, 8, 0036c (*MH*, II, 378–380; Watson, I, 105–106); *HS*, 1B, 0295d (Dubs, I, 97).

The commandant of Nan-hai, Chao T'o,[1] taking advantage of the Ch'in's weakness, declared himself King Wu of Nan-yüeh. Because he was a good governor, Liu Pang established him as King of Nan-yüeh and commissioned Lu Chia[2] to transmit his kingly seal and cord. Chao T'o made obeisance to Liu Pang's edict and acknowledged himself as his subject (196 B.C.). *HS*, 1B, 0297c (Dubs, I, 133–134).

The Mongol general Chao Wu[3] deserted the declining Mongols and occupied a position in Kongju (Kyŏngwŏn). Yi Sŏng-gye was then in

208

the northeast, and, in anticipation of Chao Wu's attack, forestalled him. Chao was dauntless, and Yi Sŏng-gye wished to spare him. He therefore used wooden arrowheads (*paktu*; *YG*, 7, 28a; 9, 41b, 42a), but shot at him many times. Chao then dismounted and surrendered (1364). Henceforth Chao served Yi Sŏng-gye faithfully. *TS*, 1, 10a; *YK*, 2, 107.

1. *HS*, 95, 0603d-0604a; *BD*, 187.
2. *SC*, 97, 0228d-0229c (Watson, I, 275–280, esp. 280); *HS*, 43, 0465b-d.
3. See *YK*, 2, 107.

[55]

He chased a deer and groped after its leg.[1]
The Yen people adored him,
And sent him a host of bold horsemen
To help him in the battlefield.

While he was still a sleeping dragon,
The northern people obeyed him.
With bows and swords
They followed him left and right.

When Liu Pang encamped at Kuang-wu and was about to attack Hsiang Yü, people of the northern Mo and of Yen sent intrepid cavalry to assist him (203 B.C.). *HS*, 1A, 0295b (Dubs, I, 92–93).

Yi Sŏng-gye ("him" in lines 6 and 8) civilized the wild Jürched in the northeast and enjoyed the esteem of their chiefs.[2] They were obedient to him and followed him in his campaigns.

1. Here the conquest of the empire is compared to the chase of a deer. See the biography of the Marquis of Huai-yin in *SC*, 92, 0222d29-30 (*HJAS*, X [1947], 214). The same phrase occurs again in *HS*, 45, 0469c. The *Yen-fan-lu hsü-chi* (Hsüeh-chin t'ao-yüan ed.), 5, 9a, quotes from *Tso chuan*, Duke Hsiang 14 (Legge, V, 464a) that the phrase existed already in the Spring and Autumn period (722–481 B.C.). Cf. *TCTC*, 189, 5921.
2. *YG*, 7, 21b-24a lists Jürched chiefs of various places who submitted to Yi Sŏng-gye. The most famous was Yi Tu-ran (later changed his name to Yi Chi-ran) for whose Jürched name see *YG*, 7, 22a. Henry Serruys, *Sino-Jürced Relations during the Yung-lo Period* (Wiesbaden, 1955), pp. 1–2, 32, 39, 41 ff. *passim*; and Hwang Ch'ŏl-san, *Yŏksa nonmunjip*, I (P'yongyang, 1957), 77–138; cf. canto 4, n. 1.

[56]

His fame and influence spread,
Even the barren lands[1] were brought into the realm.
After he had secured the mandate,
Men thanked him for his favors.

His power and bounty pervaded,
Even the wild tribes wore caps and gowns.
Even today
They shed grateful tears.

In 648, "the blue-eyed, red-haired, and tall" Chieh-ku (Kirghiz)[2] and T'ieh-lu (West Turks)[3] came to the T'ang court to pay homage to Li Shih-min ("his" in line 1). On New Year's Day envoys from neighboring kingdoms thronged Ch'ang-an. *CTS*, 3, 3070c; *TCTC*, 198, 6252–3; Fitzgerald, p. 200; Liu, II, 491–492, n. 24.

Yi Sŏng-gye granted ranks to the Jürched chiefs who submitted to him. They consequently abandoned their barbarous customs and observed decorum (canto 55).

1. *TCTC*, 198, 6253, dates the event in 648. For the term 窮髮, see, for example, *Nan-hua chen-ching* (*SPTK*), 1, 6b (Watson, p. 25): "bald and barren."

2. Also transcribed as Hsia-chia-ssu 黠戛斯 (*HTS*, 217B, 4143b-c) or chü-wu 居勿; see Chavannes, *Documents sur les Tou-kiue* (*Turcs*) *Occidentaux* (Paris, n.d.), p. 29, n. 5; *TP*, VII (1906), 68; XVII (1916), 370, n. 4; and *Tu-shih fang-yü chi-yao* (*WYWK*), 45, 1892.

3. West Turkish tribes north of the Eastern T'ien-shan, later part of the Uigur nation. See *Sui shu*, 84, 2538b-c; *PS*, 99, 3050b-c; Liu, I, 127–131; II, 491–492.

[57]

With three arrows he shot three sparrows.
The Liao envoy in the office[1]
Praised
His remarkable skill.

With a single arrow he shot two larks.
Two farmers on the roadside
Gained
Fame and name.

The Liao envoy to the Jürched asked Aguda to shoot a flying bird. Aguda, then fifteen, shot three birds with three arrows. The Liao envoy admired his skill. *Chin shih*, 2, 5859c.

On his return from a successful campaign against the Jürched (1382) Yi Sŏng-gye, in Anbyŏn,[2] killed two larks perched on a mulberry bush with one shot. Han Ch'ung[3] and Kim In-ch'an (d. 1392),[4] who were weeding rice fields, witnessed Yi's feat, followed him, and later became "meritorious subjects."[5] *TS*, 1, 17a-18b; *YK*, 1, 19.

1. 府中: *SC*, 96, 0227c (Watson, I, 266): "office."
2. See n. 11 to canto 24.
3. *KRS*, 111, 20b.
4. A chiliarch of Pukch'ŏng, he followed Yi Sŏng-gye when the latter returned from Wihwa Island; in 1392, he became a meritorious subject and later was enfeoffed as the Lord of Ikhwa. His death was entered in *TS*, 1, 50b. See *KRS*, 45, 14b, 23b; 46, 39a; 120, 13a; 133, 20a.
5. For *kongshin* (meritorious subject) see *Kosa ch'waryo*, 1, 85b-88a, esp. 85b.

[58]

They stopped him but he went
And laid an ambush by the roadside.
Then, with four horsemen
He gathered up his reins.

He came forward
And laid an ambush below the mountain.
Then, with a hundred horsemen
He unsaddled before them.

In Lo-yang, Wang Shih-ch'ung (573–621) proclaimed himself emperor of Cheng, and Li Shih-min ("he" in lines 1, 4) laid seige to Lo-yang. The emperor of Hsia, Tou Chien-te (d. 621),[1] came to Wang's aid, passed the Yellow River with a huge army, and moved westward along the road to Lo-yang. Li Shih-min therefore devised a stratagem by which his army could both halt the advance of Tou and hold Wang in Lo-yang. Ignoring the opposition of his generals, Li left the blockade of Lo-yang to Ch'u-t'u T'ung (557–628)[2] while he himself rode east to Ssu-shui.[3] When Li Shih-min entered Wu-lao, he posted his forces in ambush along the road, and rode on with only four horsemen until he was within three li of the Hsia camp. When they encountered a party of enemy scouts, Li Shih-min shouted, "I am the Prince of Ch'in," and shot an enemy officer. This roused the enemy camp from which five or six thousand horsemen came dashing out. Two of Li Shih-min's followers changed color, but the Prince of Ch'in remarked, "You go first; Yü-ch'ih Ching-te (585–658)[4] and I will act as rearguard." Li Shih-min rode slowly and whenever the pursuers were within range, he shot one. While the enemy hesitated to come within range of his arrows, he and Yü-ch'ih Ching-te retreated farther, luring them to where his ambush party was concealed. *CTS*,2, 3067a ff.; *TCTC*, 188, 5886–5905 *passim*; 189, 5908–16 *passim*; Fitzgerald, pp. 70–81; Franke, II, 351.

In 1385, the Japanese pirates invaded Hamgyŏng province with 150 ships; the Koryŏ generals could not stop their advance. Thereupon, Yi Sŏng-gye volunteered, went to Hamju, and made preparations. As usual, Yi had the conch blown at the head of the army. Its sound made the invaders tremble with fear. Having laid an ambush, Yi rode on with a hundred horsemen until he was within a short distance of the enemy camp and ordered his men to unsaddle their horses. The bewildered pirates dared not make a sortie. Yi, then, by a new stratagem led them to where his ambush lay. Yi's soldiers closed in on the frightened enemy and cut them to pieces. This happened in the ninth month of the same year. During the campaign, armed Jürched adventurers recklessly killed captured pirates. Yi admonished them, "Don't kill the hungry bandits, capture them alive!" *KRS*, 116, 24a; 135, 43b-44a; *KRSCY*, 32, 31a-33a; *TS*, 1, 20a-b; *TT*, 52, 434–435.

1. *CTS*, 54, 3286c-3287d; *HTS*, 85, 3888d-3889c; *BD*, 1954; Liu, I, 316–317.

2. *CTS*, 59, 3296a-b; *HTS*, 89, 3894b-c.

3. On the western border of Ssu-shui hsien, Honan (*CKT*, 322c). *YG*, 7, 46b has Wu-lao for Hu-lao, for the logograph *hu* was taboo during the T'ang.

4. *CTS*, 68, 3314d-3315b; *HTS*, 89, 3894c-3895a; *BD*, 2267.

[59]

Rebels in the eastern capital
Knew well[1] his majesty and power.
When they saw two columns of black cavalry,
They trembled with fear.

Rebels in the Eastern Sea
Knew well his wisdom and valor.
When they heard the shrill of a conch,
They trembled with horror.

During his campaign against Wang Shih-ch'ung (see canto 58), Li Shih-min chose a thousand picked horsemen, and had them wear black armor and helmet (621). Himself wearing black armor, he charged the enemy at the head of the cavalry. *TCTC*, 188, 5901.

For the conch of Yi Sŏng-gye, see canto 58.

1. Or "accustomed to."

[60]

Endlessly mapping out clever schemes,
He passed the enemy by.
Ignorant of his true intent,
Rebels could not dash out.

Forever mapping out clever tactics,
He passed right through the enemy.
Ignorant of his true intent,
They huddled together in fear.

Li Shih-min ("he" in line 2), with only 3,500 picked troops, went east from Lo-yang to check the advance of Tou Chien-te. At high noon, his army passed by Wang Shih-ch'ung's camp.[1] Wang saw the movement from the top of the fortress but was unable to fathom the intention of Li's move and dared not make a sortie. *TCTC*, 189, 5910; Fitzgerald, pp. 80–81.

When Yi Sŏng-gye ("he" in line 6), with a hundred cavalry, passed slowly between the enemy camps, the Japanese pirates, puzzled by the daring deed, would not come out (1385). See canto 58.

1. *YG*, 7, 48b gives the route of Li Shih-min's movement. His army encamped northwest of Lo-yang, passed Pei-mang, Ho-yang, and went to Kung in order to reach Hu (Wu)-lao.

[61]

They were afraid of his name—
Alone he stood behind
And shot down several scouts,
Conquering five thousand rebels.

They trembled at his name—
Alone he came forward from behind
And slew pirates beyond count,
Catching the thieves of a hundred ships.

When Li Shih-min met enemy scouts, he shouted out, "I am the Prince of Ch'in" and shot the commander of the enemy party (621). *TCTC*, 189, 5910. See canto 58.

During his campaign against the Japanese pirates in Hamju (1385), Yi Sŏng-gye sent a message to the pirates in Japanese. "This time General Yi Sŏng-gye commands, so surrender at once." See cantos 58–60.

[62]

Riding ahead he surveyed the enemy
And announced his name.
A man of august power,[1]
They would not dare dash out.

Pirates asked where he was,
They dreaded his name.
A Heaven-sent,[2]
They would not dare come near.

In the eighth month of 624, Li Shih-min ("he" in line 1) met the Turkish khans, Hsie-li and T'u-li, at Pin-chou, on the border of Shensi and Kansu. Li Shih-min, with a hundred cavalry, rode forward to the enemy camp and addressed Hsie-li, "We have made truce with the khan. But you have not abided by our promise and have invaded my kingdom. I am the Prince of Ch'in, so let's have a single combat if you will. If you come out with your troops, I will fight you with a hundred horsemen." The khan smiled and refused to accept the challenge. Then, Li Shih-min rode forward alone and started to cross the water which divided his army from T'u-li's. Hsie-li, noting this seeming confidence in T'u-li's friendship, suspected that there was a secret understanding between T'u-li and Li Shih-min. That night, under continuous rain, Li Shih-min made a surprise attack upon Hsie-li.[3] *HTS*, 215A, 4130c-d; *TCTC*, 191, 5992–3; Fitzgerald, pp. 137–138.

Whenever the Japanese pirates caught a Korean soldier, they asked him the whereabouts of Yi Sŏng-gye and dared not approach him. *TS*, 1, 14a.

1. For the term 聖武 *YG*, 8, 2b quotes *Li Wei-kung wen-tui* (*Wu-ching ch'i-shu*; Taipei, 1965), 1, 1b5. See n. 2 to canto 46.
2. For 天威 see *Shang shu*, 6, 1b (Legge, III, 285); *Book of Songs*, 272, 3 (Karlgren, p. 241); *Mencius*, 1B, 3 (Legge, II, 155).
3. Liu, I, 137–138, 186–188, 235; *CTS*, 194A, 3596c-d. See n. 2 to canto 35.

[63]

He hit a whip from a hundred paces away,
Displaying his prowess to the chiefs.
Their intrigue
Did not see its day.

He shot pears from a hundred paces away,
Displaying his prowess to the guests.
They therefore
Drank a toast.

For the anecdote of how Li K'o-yung overawed the Tartars, see canto 52.

Before his accession, Yi Sŏng-gye held an archery match. The target was a pear tree laden with ripe fruit. Yi loosed an arrow from a hundred paces away and all pears fell to the ground. Thereupon the guests offered him a congratulatory cup. *TS*, 1, 12b.

[64]

His magnanimity contained
All the heroes[1] under the sun.
Hence he set free
A traitor.

All the heroes under the sun
Could not outstrip his scope and norm.[2]
Hence he purposely ended the game
In a tie.[3]

Upon learning that Yü To[4] and others were conspiring, Aguda ("he" in line 3) called Yü To and calmly said, "I hear that you are about to plot treason against me. If you need saddles and horses, armor and arms, I'll give them to you. If you fall into my hands again, however, I'll not spare your life. But if you remain here and serve me, I'll not suspect you any longer." Yü To trembled with fear but was forgiven. *Chin shih*, 2, 5861d–5862a.

Yi Sŏng-gye was always humble and never liked to stand out. In an archery match he would never score more points than his rivals; only when urged would he loose another arrow, for "a superior man does not wish to be always showing superiority over others" (*Tso chuan*, Duke Huan 5 [Legge, V, 46a]). *TS*, 1, 13a; *YK*, 1, 13.

1. For 英雄 the commentary quotes *Jen-wu chih* (Peking, 1958), 8, 10 (John K. Shryock, *The Study of Human Abilities* [New Haven, 1937], pp. 127–128).
2. For 範圍 see *Chou i*, 7, 3b (Wilhelm, I, 318).
3. The third and fourth lines of the second Chinese verse has: 勝耦之籌廼故 齊之: "Even the game where he could have scored against the opposing team [of two],/ He deliberately ended in a tie."
4. *Chin shih*, 133, 6121d; *Ch'i-tan kuo-chih* (Sao-yeh shan-fang ed.), 19, 3b–4a.

[65]

He slew a boar in the park
And addressed the minister.
What do you say about
The gallant word of this great man?

He went downhill and shot a roebuck
And addressed his captains.
What do you say about
The gallant word of this great man?

When Li Shih-min went on a hunting trip in the park of Lo-yang (637), a herd of boar dashed from the forest. Li loosed four arrows and shot four boar. But then a fifth rushed out and charged the horse's stirrup. At that moment, the Minister of Finance (*Hu-pu shang-shu*) T'ang Ch'ien[1] dismounted and struck the animal with his hand. Li unsheathed his sword, killed the animal, and, looking back at the confused minister, said, "Have you not seen the general destroying the rebels? Why are you so scared?" T'ang replied, "Although the founder of the Han obtained the empire on horseback, he did not govern it from his saddle. Your Majesty conquered the four quarters with your divine military skill. But how could you satisfy your impulse at a simple beast?" Li Shih-min thought it a good answer and stopped the hunt. *TCTC*, 195, 6134; *T'ang yü-lin*, 1, 15b-16a.

One day, Yi Sŏng-gye went hunting with his officials. But they could not chase a roebuck which ran down a steep hill. Yi Sŏng-gye chased and shot it. *TS*, 1, 19b.

1. *CTS*, 58, 3294c-d; *HTS*, 89, 3895b-c. For his title. *Min* (or *Hu*)-*pu shang shu*, see Robert des Rotours, I, 71, 75, n. 3 where it is explained that the name Min-pu was changed in 656 to Hu-pu to avoid the taboo logograph *Min* appearing in the given name of the second emperor of T'ang, Li Shih-min.

[66]

> He upheld the cause of justice,
> The princes rushed toward him.
> But because he despised and reviled them,[1]
> Some rose against him.
>
> About to fulfill royal works,[2]
> He won the hearts of the people.
> Polite with his men, kind in words,
> He stabilized their feelings.

Hsiang Yü banished and caused the Emperor Yi of Ch'u to be murdered by Ch'ing Pu's general (206 B.C.). Liu Pang ("he" in line 1) proclaimed a state of mourning for the dead emperor (205 B.C.). *SC*, 8, 0035c (*MH*, II, 364; Watson, I, 96-97); *HS*, 1A, 0294a-b (Dubs, I, 72, 76).

When Liu Pang was about to punish Hsiang Yü, nobles gathered around him. But because he belittled and abused the knights, the King of Wei, Wei Pao (d. 204 B.C.)[3] rebelled. *SC*, 8, 0035c-d (*MH*, II, 367; Watson, I, 98-100); *HS*, 1A, 0294c (Dubs, I, 81-82).

Upon his return from P'ing-ch'eng, Liu Pang passed through Chao, but did not treat the King of Chao, Chang Ao,[4] courteously. This act aroused the Chancellor of Chao, Kuan Kao,[5] and others to avenge the shame suffered by their lord. Passing through Po-jen, Liu Pang barely escaped the assassins set by Kuan Kao (200 B.C.). *SC*, 8, 0036d (*MH*, I, 291-292; Watson, I, 111); 89, 0218d (Watson, I, 184-185); *HS*, 1B, 0297a (Dubs, I, 117, 119, n. 3).

Toward the end of Koryŏ, the government did not register the names of soldiers; instead, they belonged to the generals. Some generals

treated their men contemptuously, even beat them. General Yi Sŏng-
gye alone loved his subordinates and many longed to serve him. *TS*, 1,
17a; *YK*, 1, 13.

1. 善罵: *Book of Songs*, 257 (Karlgren, p. 223).
2. 大勳: *Shang shu*, 6, 1b (Legge, III, 285).
3. *SC*, 40, 0291b-c (Watson, II, 189–191); *HS*, 33, 0443c-d. For how he
died, see *SC*, 8, 0035d (*MH*, II, 369; Watson, I, 100).
4. Dubs, I, 117, n. 1.
5. Biography in *HS*, 32, 0443a-b.

[67]

He pitched a camp by the river,
The tide was low for three days.
Only after his departure
Was the bank submerged.

He pitched a camp on the island,
A torrential rain poured three days.
Only after he left
Was the island submerged.

The Mongol prince Bayan (1237–1295; "he" in line 1)[1] camped by
the Ch'ien-t'ang River in order to attack Hangchow. The inhabitants
of Hangchow hoped that the tide (bore) would rush in and drown the
Mongols; but for three days the tide was low. *HYS*, 159, 6926a; Yüan
Ming-shan, *Ch'eng-hsiang Huai-an chung-wu wang pei* in *Kuo-ch'ao wen-lei*
(*SPTK*), 24, 14b5–6;; F. W. Cleaves, "The Biography of Bayan of the
Bārin in the *Yüan shih*," *HJAS*, XIX (1956), 280.

Yi Sŏng-gye decided to march back from Wihwa Island, instead of
attacking the Ming garrisons in Liaotung. Astride a white horse on the
beach and shouldering a vermilion-lacquered bow and white-feathered
arrows, he watched his troops until the last man had been successfully
evacuated. His men saw him and praised him as the greatest general in
history. Though it was the rainy season, the rain did not cause the Yalu
to overflow. Only after the soldiers had crossed the water did the river
swell rapidly and the island was surrounded by rushing torrents. The
people thought it a miracle. See canto 9; *YK*, 1, 27.

1. His title at the time was *Chung-shu yu-ch'eng hsiang*, for which see *HJAS*,
XIX, 206, n. 24 and 233. For his biography see *YS*, 127, 6436d-6438d; *HYS*,
159, 6924d-6926c; *BD*, 1663; and *HJAS*, XIX, 185–303.

[68]

Heaven did not ban the river bank,
But kept the tide away from him.
Blue Heaven[1]
Showed its wishes on purpose.[2]

Heaven did not stop a copious rain,
But kept the tide away from him.
Blue Heaven
Showed its wishes on purpose.

Repetition of the content of canto 67.

1. The third line of the first and second Chinese verses, 彼蒼者天, is from the
Book of Songs, 131, 1 (Karlgren, p. 84).
2. The fourth line of the first Chinese verse, 示人孔昭, is from the *Book of
Songs*, 161, 2 (Karlgren, p. 104: "very brilliant") and 256, 11 (Karlgren, p.
218: "very bright").

[69]

"Dragons shall contend in the field—
Four times seven men will be of avail."
Even if he were ordered to come,
Would he come to him?

A flame blazed outside the walled city,
Only "Ten-eight-son" could save the people.
Even if he were ordered to advance,
Would he to the north?

Liu Hsiu (Kuang-wu, 5 B.C.–25–27) of Later Han, while still a
subordinate of Emperor Keng-shih (?–23–25–26), took Han-tan by
storm and defeated Wang Lang (d. 24).[1] The emperor ordered Liu
Hsiu ("he" in line 3) to withdraw troops and come to his temporary
headquarters. But Liu Hsiu refused to obey his order and consequently
ascended the throne.[2] At the time Ch'iang Hua brought the Ch'ih-fu
oracle.[3] *HHS*, 1A, 0648b-d.
Before Yi Sŏng-gye's accession, a prophecy told that a family of the
surname Yi (logographs *ten*, *eight*, and *son* make the one for *Yi*) would
become King of Korea.[4] *TS*, 1, 38b (cantos 13, 86).

1. *HHS*, 1A, 0684b; Hans Bielenstein, "The Restoration of the Han Dynasty. II: The Civil War," *BMFEA*, XXXI (1959), 74–76, 78.

2. On August 5, 25, at Ch'ien-ch'u, seven li west of Ho (*BMFEA*, XXXI, 104).

3. Bielenstein's version reads: "Liu Siu will mobilize troops and arrest the impious./The barbarians of the four directions will gather like clouds./ Dragons will fight in the open country./At the junction of four and seven, fire will be the ruler" (*BMFEA*, XXXI, 240–241, 244). Tjan Tjoe Some's version goes: "Liu Hsiu shall send out armies and apprehend the unprincipled; the Four Barbarian Tribes shall gather like clouds; the dragons shall fight in the plains; fire shall rule at the junction of four and seven" (*Po Hu T'ung. The Comprehensive Discussions in the White Tiger Hall*, I [Leiden, 1949], 127, n. 428). See also Chang Heng's "Fu on the Eastern Capital," in *Wen hsüan*, 3, 51 (E. R. Hughes, *Two Chinese Poets: Vignettes of Han Life and Thoughts* [Princeton, 1960], p. 63): "He gave battle-axes to twenty-eight generals, and the usurper was destroyed."

4. *YG*, 8, 22a has 十八子正三韓. Compare the versions in *CKS*, II, 733 木子更正三韓 and in *TYS*, 30, 18a-b 木子乘豬復正三韓, a text of which is said to have been discovered in a cave on Mount Chii (cf. canto 13).

[70]

Heaven elected him
Who was to bring peace to the people.
Hence six steeds
Appeared at the proper time.

Heaven gave him courage and wisdom[1]
Who was to bring order to the country.
Hence eight steeds[2]
Appeared at the proper time.

Li Shih-min ("him" in line 1) had six horses:[3] T'e-lo-piao (ridden in the campaign against Sung Chin-kang); Sa-lu-tzu (ridden in the siege of Lo-yang); Ch'ing-chiu (ridden in the campaign against Tou Chien-te); Ch'uan-mao-kua (ridden in the campaign against Liu Hei-ta); Shih-fa-ch'ih (ridden in the battles against Wang Shih-ch'ung and Tou Chien-te); and Pai-t'i-wu (ridden in the battle against Hsüeh Jen-kuo).

Yi Sŏng-gye had eight famous steeds:[4] Hoengun'gol (ridden in the campaign against Naɣaču and the Red Turbans); Yuinch'ŏng (ridden in the battle against the Japanese pirates at Unbong); Ch'up'ungŏ (a black Jürched horse ridden on various occasions); Palchŏnja (ridden in a hunting expedition at Changdan); Yongdŭngja (ridden in the battle against the Japanese pirates at Haeju); Ungsangbaek (ridden in the march from Wihwa Island); Sajahwang (ridden in the battle against the Japanese pirates at Mount Chii); and Hyŏnp'yo (ridden in the campaign against the Japanese pirates).

1. 天錫勇智: *Shang shu*, 4, 2b (Legge, III, 178): "Heaven hereupon gifted our king with valor and wisdom."

2. In the Chinese verses, the adjectives used are 騤騤 for the first stanza, and 蹻蹻 for the second. For the first see the *Book of Songs*, 167, 5 (Karlgren, p. 112: "strong"), and for the latter, the poems 159, 4, and 299, 2 (Karlgren, pp. 227 and 256: "robust" and "vigorous").

3. John C. Ferguson, "The Six Horses at the Tomb of the Emperor T'ai-tsung of the T'ang Dynasty," *Eastern Art*, III (Philadelphia, 1931), 61–71, esp. 65–68, and Helen E. Fernald's rebuttal, "In Defense of the Horses of T'ang T'ai-tsung," *The University Museum Bulletin* (Philadelphia, 1942), pp. 18–28; and Arthur Waley, "T'ai-tsung's Six Chargers," *Burlington Magazine*, XLIII, 246 (September 1923), 117–118. For the map of the tomb and other informa-tion on the horses, see *Li-ch'üan hsien-chih* (1783 ed.), 1b-2a; 3b; 3, 1a-b; 11, 1b-2b, 35a, 37a-b. See also *CTS*, 3, 3069a; 38, 3208a; *HTS*, 2, 3637b; 37, 3719d. For Li Shih-min's love of horses, see *HJAS*, IV (1939), 275, n. 200.

4. An Kyŏn, a famous artist under Sejong, painted Yi Sŏng-gye's eight horses in 1446 or 1447. See *Pohanjae chip*, 16, 10a-b; *Tongmun sŏn* (1966–1967 ed.), 44, 22a-23b; 50, 12b-16a (Sŏng Sam-mun's eulogies); 51, 28a-30a (Yi Kye-jŏn's eulogy); *Tonggak chapki*, 1, 345–346; *YC*, 1, 5. For An Kyŏn, see Kim Al-lo, *Yongch'ŏn tamjŏk ki* (CKK, 1910), 287; *Pohanjae chip*, 14, 5a-b; and Kim Yŏng-yun, *Han'guk sŏhwa inmyŏng sasŏ* (1959), p. 71.

[71]

Plotting to remove the heir apparent,[1]
She made a comet[2] an excuse for a slander.
He was common and unable:
But his nature was bright.[3]

Scheming to consolidate the puppet's rule,
He requested an audience.
But wise was the Son of Heaven:
He discerned the mandate of Heaven.

While T'ang Hsüan-tsung (Li Lung-chi) was still heir apparent, Princess T'ai-p'ing (d. 713; "she" in line 2)[4] disliked his surpassing valor and intended to wield her own power by placing a weak and incapable man on the throne. She therefore often slandered Hsüan-tsung to Jui-tsung. When a comet appeared in the summer of 711, the princess spoke to Jui-tsung, "The appearance of the comet is a sign that the heir apparent will ascend the throne." Jui-tsung ("he" in line 3) did not listen to her and abdicated in favor of his third son (Hsüan-tsung) who ascended the throne on September 14, 711. *HTS*, 83, 3884b-c; Franke, II, 428.

When Shin Ch'ang acceded to the throne, Yi Saek ("he" in line 6), in an attempt to strengthen his royal authority, went to Ming and requested an audience for Ch'ang. *KRS*, 115, 15a-b; *KRSCY*, 33, 45a-b.

In 1396, when Yi Sŏng-gye sent Sŏl Chang-su (1341–1399)[5] to Ming, the emperor summoned Sŏl and other members of the embassy and remarked, "Your king became a ruler of Korea because Heaven gave him the mandate. It was indeed not due to human power." *TS*, 10, 8b; 11, 11a.

1. 元良: *Shang shu*, 4, 11b (Legge, III, 211); *Li chi* (*SPPY*), 6, 19a (Couvreur, *Mémoires sur les Bienséances et les Cérémonies*, I, 479).

2. 垂象: *Chou i*, 7, 11a (Wilhelm, I, 344).

3. 天性: *Hsiao ching* (*SPTK*), 10, 9b-10a.

4. Daughter of Kao-tsung and Empress Wu, she married Hsüeh Shao in the summer of 681; but when he and his younger brother were involved in rebellion and were executed, she married Wu Yu-chi (690). In 710, she assisted Hsüan-tsung to restore Jui-tsung. But when she planned a rebellion herself, she and her clique were annihilated by Hsüan-tsung. Levy, *Harem Favorites of an Illustrious Celestial* (Taichung, 1958), pp. 11–17; *HTS*, 83, 3884b-c; *BD*, 1863.

5. A naturalized Uigur, "whose ancestors had come from Qara-qoco" (*MCB*, XI [1959], 290, n. 372). According to *SnS*, 27, 10a, he came to Korea at the age of nineteen, and passed the civil service examination in 1362. When Kongyang ascended the throne, he became, on the strength of his service, one of the meritorious subjects. When Chŏng Mong-ju was assassinated, Sŏl was considered a member of the Chŏng party and was banished to Yŏngil in North Kyŏngsang. On February 12, 1393, he was recalled, and on August 30, 1396, was named the *P'an samsa sa*. Later, he was enfeoffed as the Great Lord of Yŏnsan. He went to China as envoy at least five times (1387, 1388, 1391–1392, December 23, 1396–May 14, 1397, and February 8–July 30, 1399). During the 1396–1397 mission, he was personally interviewed by Ming T'ai-tsu and the conversations held between the two are recorded in colloquial Chinese in *TS*, 11, 10b-11a. On January 21, 1399, he was enrolled in the list of Chŏngnan kongshin. Sŏl died between October 29 and November 27, 1399, at the age of fifty-nine. His commentaries on the *Lesser Learning* are said to have been popular in his day. See *KRS*, 112, 24a-28a; *Chŏngjong sillok*, 2, 14b-15a; *YK*, 2, 107; *Yangch'on chip* (1937 ed.), 23, 9b-10a; Kang Sin-hang, "Yijo ch'ogi yŏkhakcha e kwanhan yŏn'gu," *CH*, XXIX-XXX (1966), 325–338, esp. 332–333.

[72]

Heaven deserted a mere fellow.
Even our people praised his merits.
How much more so did
The people of Han?

Heaven abandoned a mere fellow.
Even the Han people praised his merits.
How much more so did
Our people?

"A mere fellow" (*Mencius*, IB, 8) is Sui Yang-ti and "his" in the second line refers to Li Shih-min. See cantos 10, 17, and 41.

"A mere fellow" refers to Shin Ch'ang and "his" in the second line, to Yi Sŏng-gye. See cantos 10 and 71.

[73]

Because the people were exhausted,[1]
He fixed the rent for land.
After a war among seven princes,
He labored for a good government.

Because robbers[2] poisoned[3] the people,
He initiated a land reform.
First he drove away the usurper,
He then labored to restore the state.

During the Five Dynasties (907–960), princes with seven different surnames[4] contended against one another and the people were reduced to poverty. Realizing that the well-field system was the root of good government, Kuo Jung (Shih-tsung of the Later Chou) distributed in the seventh month of 958 a *chün-tien* chart to military governors and magistrates, and in the tenth month an edict on the same matter. He ordered a survey of the fields of the people, and local authorities joined to carry out the project over the entire area of Honan and part of Hopei. *TFYK*, 495, 35a-36a; *TCTC*, 294, 9585, 9587–8; *CWTS*, 118, 4352a; 146, 4384a; *Wu-tai hui-yao* (*WYWK*), 25, 307; *HWTS*, 12, 4405a and b; Sudō Yoshiyuki, *Chūgoku dochi seidoshi kenkyū* (Tokyo, 1954), pp. 416–426.

Yi Sŏng-gye dethroned Shin Ch'ang, restored the Wang House to
the throne (Kongyang), and set the Koryŏ dynasty in order (canto 11).
He also confiscated the estates monopolized by powerful families and
burnt the public and private land registers in the ninth month of 1390.
In 1391, he made a new distribution of the land.[5] *KRS*, 78, 38a; 38a-
42b; *KRSCY*, 34, 64a-b; *TS*, 1, 13b; *TT*, 55, 552.

1. 生靈凋喪: according to the *Hsü Tzu-chih t'ung-chien* (Peking, 1957), 17,
398, as quoted by *YG*, 8, 31a, at the banquet celebrating the first full moon of
the year 994, Chao Kuei (Sung T'ai-tsung) spoke to Lü Meng-cheng (*Sung
shih*, 265) about how during the Five Dynasties people were driven into poverty.
2. 寇攘: *Shang shu*, 8, 4a (Legge, III, 392); *Book of Songs*, 255 (Karlgren, p.
215: "robbers and thieves").
3. 毒痛: *Shang shu*, 6, 5a (Legge, III, 295): "poisoned and sickened."
4. They were:
    Chu: T'ai-tsu (852-907-912) of the Later Liang (907-923). *CWTS*, 1,
4199a; *HWTS*, 1, 4395b.
    Chu-hsieh: Chuang-tsung (885-908-926) of the Later T'ang (923-936).
CWTS, 27, 4233d; *HWTS*, 4, 4397c.
    ————: Ming-tsung (Mo-chi-lieh) of the Later T'ang, an adopted son
of Li K'o-yung, had no surname. *CWTS*, 35, 4245c-44, 4258d; *HWTS*, 6,
4399c-4400d; *BD*, 1205.
    Wang: King Lu (Ts'ung-k'o; 885-934-937) of the Later T'ang. *CWTS*,
46, 4260a-48, 4264d; *HWTS*, 7, 4401a.
    Shih: Kao-tsu (892-936-942) of the Later Chin (936-947). *CWTS*, 75,
4293a; *HWTS*, 8, 4401c.
    Liu: Kao-tsu (895-947-948) of the Later Han (947-950). *CWTS*, 99,
4327b; *HWTS*, 10, 4403a.
    Kuo: T'ai-tu (904-951-954) of the Later Chou (951-960). *CWTS*, 110,
4339c; *HWTS*, 11, 4403d.
5. For the land reform, see Yi Sang-baek, *Yijo kŏn'guk ŭi yŏn'gu* (1954), pp.
117 ff. and *HGS*, II, 691-697 and III, 40-52.

[74]

Traitors abused the norm of nature,
Slandered him for having won the people's hearts.
But how could he forget
His wise brother?

Small men defied Heaven's wishes,
Begged for the invasion of their own land.
But how could he ignore
His loyal subject?

When Qubilai (Shih-tsu, 1215–1260–1294) was pacifying central China, some slandered him in the eyes of his elder brother Möngke (Hsien-tsung, 1209–1251–1259) reporting that he was aspiring to be the khan. Möngke relieved Qubilai of his office; but when Qubilai came to see his brother, he wept and they were reconciled (1257). *YS*, 158, 6499c; Franke, IV, 321.

In 1390, Yun I[1] and Yi Ch'o, in an attempt to restore Shin U to the throne, went to Ming, asked that troops be sent for the subjugation of their own country, and told the Ming that General Yi had revolted against China. But the Ming emperor ("he" in line 7) knew Yi Sŏng-gye's loyalty and did not believe their slander.[2] *KRS*, 45, 26b ff.; 104, 49b–54b; 115, 24a–25b; *KRSCY*, 34, 59a ff.; *TT*, 55, 547–549.

When Yi Sŏng-gye sent An Ik to Ming in 1396,[3] the emperor remarked, "Your aged sovereign is an extraordinary man. He has both culture and courage, virtue and talents. A peerless general, he once came as far as the Yalu, but turned immediately (1388) and rendered great service to our country." *TS*, 11, 5a; *YK*, 1, 3b; *Kosa ch'waryo*, 1, 6b–7a.

1. He called himself Lord of P'ap'yŏng from 1389 and slandered Yi Sŏng-gye. He was banished by the Ming (*KRS*, Index, 34a-b).
2. The Ming Board of Rites summoned Wang Pang and Cho Pan, who were then at the Ming capital on a diplomatic mission (1389–1390) and informed them that Yun I and Yi Ch'o had slandered Yi Sŏng-gye and that they had entreated the Ming emperor to subjugate Korea. At the same time, the board produced a list of names, submitted by Yun I and Yi Ch'o, of nineteen Koreans, who were allegedly imprisoned by Yi Sŏng-gye as a consequence of their opposition to his planned invasion of China. In 1390, upon their return to Korea, Cho and Wang promptly reported the urgency of the matter, and U Hyŏn-bo and others whose names appeared on the list were either imprisoned or banished. The Ming court, knowing the calumny of Yun I and Yi Ch'o, banished them and the matter was settled. On July 27, 1390, Yi Sŏng-gye sent Chŏng To-jŏn and Han Sang-jil to Ming to clarify the situation. See *KRS*, 45, 29a; *KRSCY*, 34, 61a; *TT*, 55, 549; *Kosa ch'waryo*, 1, 5a.
3. An Ik's party left the capital on November 3, 1396, and returned on April 6, 1397 (*TS*, 10, 6a; 11, 4b ff.).

[75]

The Turks invaded
But feared his glorious name.
Hence they did not follow up
The challenge for a battle.

His majestic person[1] was held in awe far and wide,
Jürched came to bring homage.
First they disputed over their status,
But one refused to wrangle.

For the invasion of the Turks see canto 62.

In the time of King Kongyang, two Jürched[2] chiefs visited the Koryŏ court. First they quarreled with each other over who had more status, but one of them remarked, "We have not come here to decide who the chief is but rather to express our admiration for General Yi's authority and dignity" (March 30, 1392). Yi Sŏng-gye invited them to feast at his residence. *TS*, 1, 33b; *KRS*, 46, 34b; *KRSCY*, 35, 47b; *TT*, 56, 589.

1. 威靈: *Ch'u Tz'u* (*SPTK*), 2, 30a (David Hawkes, *Ch'u Tzu: The Songs of the South* [Oxford, 1959], p. 44).

2. Their names are transcribed as 兀良哈 and 斡朶里 in *YG*, 8, 41b, which are in all likelihood not their names, but the tribes to which they belong. For the former, see *MCB*, XI, 68–69, n. 3, 282–283, and Henry Serruys, *Sino-Jürčed Relations during the Yung-lo Period* (Wiesbaden, 1955), pp. 5–7, n. 8 and p. 32; Hellmut Wilhelm, "A Note on the Migration of the Uriangkhai," in *Festschrift für Nikolaus Poppe zum 60. Geburtstag am 8. August 1957*, ed. Julius von Farkas and Omeljan Pritsak (Wiesbaden, 1957), pp. 172–176; Sonoda Kazuki, *Mindai Kenshū Jochokushi kenkyū* (2 vols.; Tokyo, 1948–1953).

[76]

He granted favor to his kin,
Ignoring his look of a rebel.
After a thousand years
A poet praised his bright virtue.

Kind and selfless to his brothers,
He covered their past misdeeds.
Thus today we enjoy
Humane manners and customs.

Seeing that the cause of the Ch'in's fall was its isolation, Liu Pang granted fiefs to his brothers and relatives in order to consolidate the empire. His cousin Liu Chia was made King of Ching; his younger brother Liu Chiao, King of Ch'u; his elder brother Liu Hsi, King of Tai; his son Liu Fei, King of Ch'i. Liu Chia had no son, so his nephew

Liu P'i[1] was made King of Wu. After he had been installed as king, Liu Pang summoned Liu P'i and said to him, "You have the appearance of a rebel. . . . The world is one house and we are one family. You must be careful not to rebel." Liu P'i bowed his head and replied, "I would not dare." *HS*, 1B, 0296c-d, 0297d (Dubs, I, 112 and 139). Su Shih (1036–1101; "poet" in line 4)[2] praised Liu Pang for not killing Liu P'i. *Tung-p'o hsü-chi* (*SPPY*), 8, 16a-b.

Munificent by birth, Yi Sŏng-gye loved his stepbrothers. Upon the death of Hwanjo, his stepbrother, Ch'ŏn-gye, plotted a revolt in 1371 but failed (*TS*, 1, 12a; *YG*, 8, 44a-45a). When Ch'ŏn-gye was involved in a murder case and sentenced to death, Yi Sŏng-gye did everything to help him but could not save his life (1375). After Yi's accession Ch'ŏn-gye's son enjoyed high rank. *TS*, 1, 13a.

1. Liu P'i was the son of Liu Pang's elder brother, Liu Chung (*SC*, 9, 0038a [*MH*, II, 468; Watson, I, 322]). Liu P'i led a revolt against the Han in 154 B.C. (*SC*, 11, 0042a-b [*MH*, II, 498–499; Watson, I, 368]; *HS*, 5, 0303a [Dubs, I, 313]), and was executed by the people of Yüeh at Tan-t'u (*SC*, 57, 0174d [Watson, I, 436]; *HS*, 5, 0303a [Dubs, I, 314]). See *SC*, 106, 0238d-0240b (Watson, I, 465–486, esp. 466); *HS*, 35, 0448b–0449d.

2. *Sung shih*, 388, 5382c-5384c; *BD*, 1785.

[77]

Others branded him as an enemy:
As he was wise like the sun and moon,
He recalled his enemy and employed him,
Enriching his country and people.

Others proposed to slay them:
As his mind was large as heaven and earth,
He let his enemies live,
Bestowing upon them tally and salary.

Wei Cheng[1] (581–643) once advised Li Chien-ch'eng to kill his brother Li Shih-min. After the punishment of Chien-ch'eng and Yüan-chi, Shih-min summoned Wei and asked him why he had served Chien-ch'eng in his plots. The latter remarked, "Chien-ch'eng was foolish. Had he taken my advice the events of today would have been otherwise." Shih-min knew his talents, admired his frankness, spared him, and made him his adviser. Wei subsequently enjoyed the confidence of Shih-min. *HTS*, 97, 3906c; Fitzgerald, p. 123.

After Yi Sŏng-gye's enthronement, Chŏng To-jŏn proposed that Yi Saek and others should be killed.[2] But Yi Sŏng-gye spared them and gave them their former rank.[3] *KRS*, 119, 16b; *TS*, 1, 45a; 8, 13b-15a.

1. *PS*, 56, 2932b; *CTS*, 71, 3320a-3322b; *HTS*, 97, 3906c-3908c; *BD*, 2264.

2. According to *YG*, 2, 30a-b and the sources cited above, Chŏng To-jŏn hated U Hyŏn-bo and was ready to do everything to ruin U's family. Upon Yi Sŏng-gye's accession, Chŏng, in a decree which he himself wrote and presented to Yi Sŏng-gye on August 16, 1392 (*KRS*, 119, 16b; *TS*, 1, 45a), demanded that U Hyŏn-bo, Yi Saek, and others be punished with death. Yi Sŏng-gye replied, "They have committed no great crime. Why should I kill them?" Chŏng To-jŏn reduced their crime by one degree and demanded justice, but Yi Sŏng-gye took no action.

3. Yi Sŏng-gye summoned Yi Saek from his retreat on Mount Tae in Kangwŏn and greeted him as an old friend (January 5, 1396). He offered the guest a cup, granted him 120 *kyŏl* of land, 300 *kok* of rice and beans, five *kok* of salt, and wine and meat, saying that he should nourish himself with them in his later years. It was Yi Sŏng-gye's order because Yi Saek was then a Buddhist and abstained from wine and meat. Yi Sŏng-gye also gave him wood and tiles for the construction of a house, enfeoffed him again as the Lord of Hansan, and named him tho *Ogo tojejo* of Ŭisŏng and Tŏkch'ŏn (January 8, 1396). He also reissued the same tablet to U Hyŏn-bo. For Yi Saek's Buddhism see An Kyehyŏn, "Yi Saek ŭi pulgyogwan," in *Cho Myŏng-gi paksa hoegap kinyŏm pulgyosahak nonch'ong* (1965), pp. 99-127.

[78]

At first he awed his guest,
But later granted him a great favor.
Who would not
Like to follow him?

From the start he treated them with true heart,
To the end his heart was true.
Who would not
Adore him?

When Ch'ing Pu,[1] having been defeated by Hsiang Yü's army, came to Liu Pang with his men, Liu received him sprawled upon a couch having his feet washed. Ch'ing Pu was angry and regretted his coming. But when he noticed that Liu Pang ate the same food his soldiers did, Ch'ing Pu changed his mind and stayed. *SC*, 91, 0220c (Watson, I, 201).

After his enthronement, Yi Sŏng-gye honored meritorious subjects who assisted in the foundation of the dynasty. During the night of the *kyŏngsin*[2] day of the tenth month of 1395 (December 12, 1395), Yi Sŏng-gye gave a banquet and entertained Chŏng To-jŏn and other meritorious subjects. Yi Sŏng-gye ordered the *Mundŏk kok*[3] to be sung and asked its author, Chŏng, to dance. *TS*, 8, 12a-b.

On his way to P'yŏngju[4] hotspring, Yi Sŏng-gye stopped at Sŏl-metkol[5] (March 1, 1398); and together with Kim Sa-hyŏng (d. 1407)[6] and Nam Ŭn (d. 1398)[7] he reminisced while exchanging cups.[8] *TS*, 13, 7b.

1. *SC*, 91, 0220a-d (Watson, I, 196–207); *HS*, 34, 0446c-0447b.
2. According to the San-shih theory, one must observe all-night vigil on the *keng-shen* (cyclic day of the Metal and the Monkey) in order to prolong life by preventing the three noxious insects residing within the body from ascending to Heaven and reporting on the individual's misdeeds to the God of Life. For an account of how the Koreans observed the night of the *kyŏngsin*, see *YG*, 9, 25a. For the origin of the celebration and the Japanese observance, see Kubo Noritada, *Kōshin shinkō* (Tokyo, 1956) and *Kōshin shinkō no kenkyū* (Tokyo, 1961).
3. On September 2, 1393, Chŏng To-jŏn presented to the throne the texts of four eulogies, known as the *Mundŏk kok* (*TS*, 4, 2b-3a). They were first performed on December 1, 1393 (*TS*, 4, 12a). The poems are written in the seven-word *chüeh-chü* form. See *Sambong chip*, 2, 60–61.
4. Fifty-five ri south of P'yŏngsan, Hwanghae (*SnSC*, 152, 9b-10a; *TYS*, 41, 15b).
5. About five ri south of Chŏksŏng, Kyŏnggi (*TYS*, 11, 40b).
6. Died September 1, 1407 (*KRS*, 104, 32b-35a; *TnS*, 14, 14a-b).
7. Involved in the internecine feud of 1398, he was killed by Yi Pang-wŏn. In 1421, he was granted the posthumous epithet of Kangmu (*KRS*, 116, 24a-30b; *YK*, 2, 100).
8. The commentary cites twelve episodes; here only the relevant information is given.

[79]

Because he was inconsistent,
Meritorious subjects harbored suspicion.
A few years after the foundation[1]
His royal works were disrupted.

He was consistent from beginning to end,
Meritorious subjects were truly loyal to him.

He secured the throne for myriad years.
Would his royal works ever discontinue?

When Liu Pang killed the meritorious subjects Han Hsin[2] and P'eng
Yüeh,[3] Ch'ing Pu was forced to revolt. *HS*, 34, 0444d ff.

On October 12, 1392, Pae Kŭng-nyŏm (d. 1392)[4] and others asked
Yi Sŏng-gye to grant more land to princes; but Yi replied that it would
be right to grant land first to meritorious subjects. *TS*, 2, 6b.

On another occasion, Censor-General Nam Chae (d. 1419)[5] com-
plained that the distribution of rewards to meritorious subjects was too
generous. *TS*, 2, 21.

On still another occasion, Pyŏn Chung-nyang (d. 1398)[6] and Yi
Hoe[7] slandered Cho Chun, Chŏng To-jŏn, and Nam Ŭn, saying that
they abused their authority. Yi Sŏng-gye, however, banished the
slanderers and divested them of their ranks; so high was his esteem of
meritorious subjects. *TS*, 6, 16b. Cf. canto 78.

1. 定鼎: *Tso chuan*, Duke Hsüan 3 (Legge, V, 393).
2. *SC*, 93, 0223a-b (*HJAS*, X [1947], 179–215); *HS*, 34, 0444d-0446b.
3. *SC*, 90, 0219c-d; *HS*, 34, 0446b-c.
4. One of Yi Sŏng-gye's closest supporters, Pae was most active in enthron-
ing Yi. Later he was enfeoffed as the Lord of Songsan; he died December 10,
1392 (*TS*, 2, 15a; *YK*, 2, 90).
5. Nam Ŭn's elder brother, Chae was enfeoffed as the Lord of Ŭisŏng and
later became a tutor of Sejong. He went to China twice, in 1393 and 1394.
He excelled in mathematics and died on December 30, 1419 (*SnS*, 6, 15a; *YK*,
2, 137).

6. Elder brother of Pyŏn Kye-ryang, son-in-law of Yi Sŏng-gye's elder
brother (Wŏn-gye), he wrote verse; he was killed during the 1398 princely
feud (*TS*, 14, 20a, 25a).
7. In 1392, he served in the Board of War and in 1402 presented a map of
Korea to the throne.

[80]

He not only valued military merit
But knew the way of the scholar.[1]
The three states stood like a tripod,[2]
He saw them firmly rooted.

Though he was busy with war,
He loved the way of the scholar.

His work of achieving peace
Shone brilliantly.

Liu Pei (121–221–223; "he" in line 1) of the Shu Han once remarked,
"When I studied under Ch'en Chi[3] and Cheng Hsüan (127–200),[4] at
each instruction they taught me how to govern, but they never mentioned amnesties." *Hua-yang kuo-chih* (*SPTK*), 7, 10b-11a.

Yi Sŏng-gye loved learning, discussed the classics with scholars
between battles, and read books far into the night. *TS*, 1, 21a; *YK*, 2,
117.

1. *YG*, 9, 30b, quotes *Hua-yang kuo-chih* (same in *TCTC*, 75, 2366–7): in the
sixth month of 246 (Yen-hsi 9), an amnesty was granted. The *Ssu-nung* Meng
Kuang (*HHS*, 113, 0892d; *SKC, Shu chih*, 12, 1023d-1024a) reprimanded Fei
I for the inadvisability of the move. The source then cites the remarks of Chu-ko
Liang (181–234), who believed the empire should be governed by great virtue,
not petty favor. Quoting the precedents of K'uang Heng in 42 B.C. (*SC*, 96,
0228d; *HS*, 81, 0561a-0562b; *TCTC*, 28, 918–919) and Wu Han in 44 A.D.
(*HHS*, 48, 0734d-; 735d; *TCTC*, 35, 1398), Chu-ko Liang cites Liu Pei's
remark. *The Chronicle of the Three Kingdoms*, tr. Achilles Fang, II (Cambridge,
Mass., 1965), 2–3.
2. For 峕 in 鼎峕之業 see *Chi yün*, 5, 682.
3. *HHS*, 92, 0839c-d.
4. *HHS*, 65, 0774c-0775a; *BD*, 274.

[81]

Unsparing of thousands of gold pieces,
He sought for rare books.
His magnificent statesmanship
Was indeed great.

He did not boast of his natural gift,
His learning was equally deep.
The vast scope of royal works[1]
Was indeed great.

Chao K'uang-yin loved books. He was seldom seen without a book
in his hand and he bought rare books at an enormous expense. *Hsü
Tzu-chih t'ung-chien ch'ang-pien* (Chekiang shu-chü ed.), 7, 6a.

Yi Sŏng-gye was born with magnanimity and benevolence and
never boasted of his brilliant exploits. Regretting that his family had

hitherto not produced any scholar, he urged his son, Pang-wŏn, to study the classics. Pang-wŏn became a *chinsa* in 1382,[2] passed the final civil service examination in 1383,[3] and became *Milchik chehak*[4] in 1392. At a state banquet, Yi Sŏng-gye used to ask Pang-wŏn to improvise linked verse with the guests. *TS*, 1, 18b-19a; *YK*, 2, 117.

1. For 規模(摹) see *HS*, 1B, 0298b (Dubs, I, 146): "designs and plans."
2. *SS*, 9a.
3. He passed the examination as a seventh in the *pyŏngkwa* between May 3 and June, 1, 1383 (*KRS*, 135, 4a; *SS*, 9a).
4. This is the rank given by *YG*, 9, 33a. In *SS*, 9a and *YK*, 2, 114, however, his highest rank is given as *Milchiksa taeŏn*. Both titles correspond to rank 3a (*KRS*, 46, 39a).

[82]

Upon facing a small scholar
He stood up from his seat.
What do you say about
His reverence for the learned man?

Upon receiving an old scholar
He knelt down with due politeness.
What do you say about
His respect for scholarship?[1]

In 1290, Chŏng Ka-sin (d. 1298)[2] and Min Chi (1248–1326)[3] accompanied the heir apparent to the Mongol court. Qubilai received the heir apparent (who was a grandchild by his daughter and the future King Ch'ungsŏn) leaning on a low table. But when he interviewed Chŏng and Min, Qubilai put on his cap and honored them with due politeness.[4] When Qubilai discussed the subjugation of Chiao-chih (Tongking in Indochina), he instructed his ministers to consult with the two Koryŏ scholars. *KRS*, 105, 25a-b.

When Yi Saek returned from his banishment in the eleventh month of 1391, Yi Sŏng-gye received him in the upper seat, and, kneeling down, offered him a cup. *KRS*, 30, 23b; 115, 26b; *TS*, 1, 33b.

1. In the original 右文之德 for which the commentary (*YG*, 9, 33b) quotes *Mencius* 5B, 8 (Legge, II, 392). Cf. Horace's fourth Roman ode (III, 4, 37–69), which praises Augustus for admitting literary men to his court and comments on the power of literature to civilize the world.

2. He passed the civil service examination during the time of King Kojong and in 1277 rose to be the Academician-in-Waiting of the Pomun Hall (*Pomungak taeje*; *KRS*, 105, 24a) and *Chŏngdang munhak* (*KRS*, 30, 28a). In 1290, he accompanied the heir apparent to the Mongol capital (*KRS*, 30, 23b). He died between July 10 and August 7, 1298 (*KRS*, 33, 12a). See *KRS*, 105, 23b-28a.

3. He was Auxiliary Han-lin Academician at the Mongol court and in 1321 was enfeoffed as the Lord of Yŏhŭng. He died between July 30 and August 27, 1326. He was a compiler of several books which are no longer extant (*KRS*, 107, 27b-32a).

4. Qubilai must have used an interpreter when he received Chŏng and Min. Chŏng and Min probably spoke little Mongolian, and Qubilai spoke little Chinese. Herbert Franke, in "Could the Mongol Emperors Read and Write Chinese?" *AM*, III (1952), 29-30, remarks: "Qubilai's knowledge of Chinese was rather poor, as was already pointed out by Fuchs. He had to use interpreters while receiving Chinese scholars."

[83]

He knew the crown was a precious jewel:[1]
Heaven wished to tell him its plan.
Hence the gold tower soared
In the middle of the sea.

He was to map the norms with a ruler:
So wishing to charge him with a good government,[2]
Heaven sent down
A gold ruler.

Before accession, in his dream, the founder of Koryŏ, Wang Kŏn (877-918-943),[3] climbed atop the nine-storied gold pagoda in the middle of the sea. This was interpreted as an omen of his future success. *KRS*, 1, 6a.

For the gold ruler, see canto 13.

1. 大寶: *Chou i*, 8, 1b (Wilhelm, I, 352).
2. *Mencius*, 2A, 1 (Legge, II, 184).
3. The legends connected with his origin and clan show not only the influence of native Shamanism, but also the fact that his was a powerful seafaring clan which controlled maritime trade with T'ang. The sphere of their influence extended from Hwanghae to Kanghwa Island, centering around the lower reaches of the Han. See *KRS*, 1, 1a-2, 19b; *KRSCY*, 1, 1a-46b; Ikeuchi Hiroshi, *Mansenshi kenkyū*, IV (1944), 1-90; Kim Sang-gi, "Koryŏ T'aejo ŭi kŏn'guk kwa kyŏngnyun," *KSC*, I (1959), 69-91; II, 45-83. For his clan, see *KRS*,

Koryŏ segye, 1a-8b, and Kim Ch'ŏl-chun, "Husamguk sidae ŭi chibae seryŏk ŭi sŏngkyŏk e taehayŏ," in *Yi Sang-baek paksa hoegap kinyŏm nonch'ong* (1964), pp. 261–267. For the Wang clan's maritime activities, see Pak Han-sŏl, "Wang Kŏn segye ŭi muyŏk hwaltoṅ e taehayŏ," *Sach'ong*, X (1965), 255–287. Yi Yong-jung proposes several hypotheses concerning the founder of Koryŏ and his ancestors: the sphere of the clan's (maritime) activities centered around Kaesŏng and Changdan, the fertile plain along the Yellow Sea; the clan ancestors had no surname; Wang Kŏn probably adopted his after accession. This fact, together with the fantastic stories about the marriage of some clan ancestors, mainly to strengthen the myth of pedigree, attests to their relatively low social status; Chakchegŏn's (Wang Kŏn's grandfather) defeat of the Dragon King's adversary may allude to his victory over the pirates on the Yellow Sea; the fact that Kangch'ung and Chakchegŏn could transport or mobilize local people for corvée seems to indicate their independence from the central authority; and naming of the sacred mountain of Koguryŏ, Mount Paektu, as the sacred place of the clan's origin, together with Wang Kŏn's effort, upon accession, to regain the former territory of Koguryŏ in the north, may suggest that clan ancestors were Koguryŏ nationals. See *Husamguk ŭi ch'urhyŏn kwa Koryŏ e ŭihan kŭ̈i t'ongil* (P'yongyang, 1963), pp. 121-131.

[84]

The emperor was wise,
But his heir was not yet born.
Then the dead willow
Grew again.

The country had a long history,
But it was about to lose Heaven's charge.
Then a withered tree
Put forth green leaves.

During the reign of the seventh Han emperor Chao-ti (Liu Fu-ling, 95–87–74 B.C.)[1] a large stone in T'ai-shan stood up (79 B.C.) and in Shang-lin park a dead willow grew again. The stone and the willow alluded to the people, so Kuei Hung interpreted, and they were omens to the effect that a commoner would ascend the throne. As was expected, because Chao-ti had no heir, Hsüan-ti[2] (Liu Ping-yi, 91–74–48 B.C.), a commoner, succeeded him. *HS*, 7, 0308c (Dubs, II, 167–168).

A tall tree in Tŏgwŏn which had been dead for several years grew again a year before the enthronement of Yi Sŏng-gye. The people thought the event foretold the foundation of a new dynasty. *KRSCY*, 35, 46a; *TS*, 1, 38b-39a; *YK*, 1, 11. For the discussion of the tree symbolism, see Chapter VI.

1. *HS*, 7, 0307d-0309a (Dubs, II, 151–175). The commentary quotes Li Te-yü *Li Wei-kung hui-ch'ang i-p'in chi* (*TSCC*), *wai-chi*, I, 253–254.

2. *HS*, 8, 0309a-0311d (Dubs, II, 199–265, esp. 183–184).

[85]

Not noticing his square face
He elevated him in rank.
This was Heaven's will,
Who would change it?

We were unable to divine a prophecy,
But he changed our country's name.
The thought of the Son of Heaven,
Who could induce it?[1]

Kuo Jung, on his way from a campaign against the Khitan (959), examined piles of documents and found among them a three-foot-long wooden tablet inscribed with the prophetic word, *Tien-chien tso T'ien-tzu* (*Tien-chien*[2] will become a Son of Heaven). Chang Ying-te[3] was then tien-chien, but Kuo Jung ordered Chao K'uang-yin to substitute for him. Whenever he found a square-faced and large-eared man among his followers, Kuo would kill him, bearing in mind the folk prophecy that a square-faced and long-eared individual would be destined for great power. Even though Chao had a square face and large ears and held the office of the tien-chien (959), Kuo Jung overlooked him. Chao went on to found the House of Sung. *Sung shih*, 1, 4497b; *CWTS*, 119, 4352d.

A prophetic diagram, "Early Brilliance," was considered a puzzle in Korea. But the first Ming emperor ("he" in line 6) thought Chosŏn ("the brightness of the morning sun") to be the fittest name for Korea. It is said that the new name of Korea, Chosŏn, coincided with the yet unknown meaning of the prophecy. *TS*, 1, 38b; *YG*, 9, 37b; *YK*, 1, 62.

1. For the fourth line in the second Chinese verse, see *Tso chuan*, Duke Hsiang 25 (Legge, V, 516b); Duke Ch'eng 13 (Legge, V, 382b); and Duke Ting 4 (Legge, V, 757a).

2. For this office, see *Chin shih*, 56, 5968d, and *Wen-hsien t'ung-k'ao*, 58, 34a.

3. *Sung shih*, 255, 5188b-5189a.

[86]

He shot six roebucks,
He shot six crows,
He flew across
The slanting tree.

Were it not for the old oracle
Hidden in the stone cave,
Who would not notice
Heaven's will?

While still young, Yi Sŏng-gye shot six roebucks and five crows perched on top of a wall with a single arrow. *TS*, 1, 5b.

One day, while he hunted with Yi Tu-ran (d. 1402),[1] a deer escaped below a slanting tree. Yi Sŏng-gye jumped over the tree, while the horse ran under it, landed in the saddle on the other side of the tree, and shot the fleeing deer. *TS*, 1, 12b.

Before Yi Sŏng-gye became king, a monk presented prophecy discovered among the stones on Mount Chii which prognosticated that "a tree son rides on the pig and will bring order to the Three Han." A combination of "tree" and "son" makes the logograph *Yi*, and he rides on the pig because the year he was born was *ŭrhae*, the year of the Pig according to the Chinese zodiac (cf. canto 69). *TS*,1, 38b; *YK*, 1, 11; *TYS*, 30, 18a-b; *CKS*, II, 733.

1. A Jürched chiliarch who surrendered to the Koryŏ side on March 7, 1371 (*KRS*, 43, 1b; *KRSCY*, 29, 10b; *TT*, 49, 314), he served Yi Sŏng-gye faithfully. He died May 10, 1402 (*TnS*, 3, 20b). See *KRS*, 116, 22a-24a; *YK*, 2, 99; and canto 55. For his *shindo pi* in Pukch'ŏng see *CKS*, II, 1206-10: on the reverse side of the monument to Yi Sŏng-gye, drafted by Kwŏn Kŭn, Yi Tu-ran appears three times as meritorious subject (*CKS*, II, 737-738). See n. 2 to canto 55.

[87]

With a bare hand he attacked
A tiger that sprang upon his horse.
With both hands he caught
The raging, large bulls.

He drew rein and helped
The horse about to fall from the bridge.

How could we relate all
The divine power of this inspired man?

While Yi Sŏng-gye was still in Hamgyŏng province, he went to hunt tigers. A tiger broke cover from a nearby bush, jumped on his horse, and attacked him. Yi struck the raging animal with his right hand and then shot it.[1] *TS*, 1, 5b.

When Yi was in Hamju, two bulls fought each other. Many had failed to part them. Yi came, caught them by the horns, and unlocked them (1389). *TS*, 1, 26a-b.

Once Yi went to view Ch'ongsŏkchŏng.[2] He was dozing on his horse while he crossed the Hakp'o Bridge[3] in Anbyŏn and his horse slipped. Yi quickly jumped off and caught the horse's mane; the animal was suspended in the air. He then cut off the saddle to free the horse. The animal sank at first but managed to emerge from the water. *TS*, 1, 26b.

1.   Between October 25 and November 23, 1375, Yi Sŏng-gye presented a tiger to Shin U (*KRS*, 133, 8a). Again, between August 24 and September 21, 1378, he shot a tiger which raged through the streets of the capital (*KRS*, 133, 37a).

2.   Eighteen ri north of T'ongch'ŏn, one of the eight views of Kwandong (*SnSC*, 153, 14a; *TYS*, 45, 21a-23b).

3.   In Anbyŏn, South Hamgyŏng (*SnSC*, 155, 8a; *TYS*, 49, 8b-9a).

[88]

He hit the back of forty tailed deer,
He shot the mouths and eyes of the rebels,
He shot down three mice from the eaves,
Were there any like him in the past?

He was sure to flush out
The pheasants lying in the field.
What do you say about
The peerless gallantry of this inspired man?

In 1385, Yi Sŏng-gye accompanied Shin U on a hunting trip to Haeju.[1] Yi shot forty deer, his arrows always hitting the animals' backs. *KRS*, 135, 34b; *TS*, 1, 19a.

During his campaign against the Mongol minister in 1362 (canto 35), Yi shot the rebels through their mouths. *KRS*, 40, 8b-9a; *KRSCY*, 27, 26b; *TS*, 1, 8b; *TT*, 47, 248.

When he fought against the Japanese pirates in the eighth month of 1377, he shot at their left eyes. *KRS*, 133, 30a; *KRSCY*, 30, 34a; *TS*, 1, 14a; *TT*, 50, 372.

On yet another occasion, he saw pheasants on the outskirts of the capital. First, he had his attendant flush the birds into flight before he shot them with wooden arrowheads. *TS*, 1, 9b-20a.

In 1377, Yi used wooden arrowheads and dislodged from the eaves of his house three mice without having hurt them. *TS*, 1, 14a.

1. *SnSC*, 152, 6a-b; *TYS*, 43, 1a-b.

[89]

> Seven pine cones,
> The trunk of a dead tree,
> Three arrows piercing the helmet—
> None like him in the past.
>
> Outside the East Gate
> He felled a young pine tree.
> What do you say about
> The eminent deeds of this inspired man?

When Yi Sŏng-gye reached Hamju to subjugate the Japanese pirates (1385; see canto 58), he found an old pine in the camping ground. From seventy paces away he shot down seven pine cones with seven arrows. *TS*, 1, 20a; *KRSCY*, 32, 31b. On another occasion, his arrows hit the trunk of a dead tree three times. *TS*, 1, 20b.

On yet another occasion (eighth month of 1377), before charging the pirates, Yi Sŏng-gye placed a helmet 140 or 150 paces away and divined the outcome of the campaign by hitting the target three times (canto 88). *KRS*, 133, 29b; *KRSCY*, 30, 34a; *TS*, 1, 14a; *YK*, 1, 16–17.

On his return from Wihwa Island in 1388 (canto 9), in order to win the confidence of his men, he shot at a pine tree from a hundred paces away. The tree fell from the impact of one arrow. *KRS*, 137, 18a; *KRSCY*, 33, 16b; *TS*, 1, 23b; *YK*, 1, 27.

[90]

Two brothers had many plots;
But their poison could not win Heaven.
What do you say about
The name his father gave him?

Two ships turned turtle on the sea;
But the winds could not win Heaven.
What do you say about
The word his mother had heard?

Li Shih-min's two brothers, Chien-ch'eng and Yüan-chi, envious of
his name and rising fame, plotted to kill him (626). To celebrate Shih-
min's return from the frontier, Chien-ch'eng gave a feast and offered
him poisoned wine. Shih-min vomited blood but was saved through
the care of his uncle, the Prince of Huai-an. *CTS*, 64, 3306c; *HTS*, 79,
3874a; *TCTC*, 191, 6004; Fitzgerald, pp. 113–114.

Li Yüan named his second son Shih-min, because a bibliomancer
came to see the four-year-old boy and prophesied that the child would
"benefit the age and soothe the people" (*chi-shih an-min*). *CTS*, 2, 3066c;
HTS, 2, 3636b; *T'ai-p'ing kuang-chi*, 135, 7a.

On his way home from Nanking, Yi Pang-wŏn and his party encountered a tempest on the Yellow Sea. Two passenger boats were
wrecked; but Yi's ship escaped danger (1389). *KRS*, 113, 16a-b; *TS*,
1, 25a-b; *YK*, 2, 118.

When Yi Pang-wŏn was still young, the fortune teller Mun Sŏng-
yun came to his mother, Queen Sinŭi (1337–1391),[1] and revealed that
the child had the mandate of Heaven and urged her to keep the
knowledge to herself. *TnS*, 1, 1a.

1. Yi Sŏng-gye's first wife and Yi Pang-wŏn's mother, she died on October
21, 1391. For the "Inscription on the Avenue to the Grave" (*shindo pi*) in
P'ungdŏk in Kyŏnggi, erected in 1401 and repaired in 1744, see *CKS*, II,
1162-6. For the stone mark of the tomb, erected in 1900, see *CKS*, II, 1348; for
the monument erected at her birthplace in Anbyŏn, South Hamgyŏng, see
CKS, II, 1279–1280 (*SS*, 5b; *TYS*, 13, 4a-7a).

[91]

When he was serving his father,
He shed tears over the dead mother.

Women on the right and left slandered him;
His father was stirred to anger.

When he came to see his father,
He shed tears over the dead mother.
The whole court sorrowed over his loss;
His father praised his love.

At a state banquet, Li Shih-min, thinking of his mother,[1] shed secret tears and remained silent. Chang Chieh-yü,[2] his stepmother, and the women in the harem, slandered him. His father believed their account and was stirred to anger. *TCTC*, 190, 5989; Fitzgerald, pp. 109–110. For the story *YG* refers to canto 26 (4, 27a-b).

Whenever he left the hut beside his mother's grave in order to visit his father, Yi Pang-wŏn used to shed secret tears on the way. Yi Sŏng-gye's attendants all sympathized with his sorrow; Yi Sŏng-gye, too, praised his filial piety. *TnS*, 1, 1a-b.

1. *CTS*, 51, 3278c-d; *HTS*, 65, 3866b-c.
2. *CTS*, 63, 3306b-d; *HTS*, 79, 3873c-3874b; Fitzgerald, pp. 108 ff.

[92]

He was a dutiful son;
While others feasted the day,
He did not feast,
Quoting the *Book of Songs*.

He was a dutiful son;
While others took off mourning,
He alone wore it,
Following the *Book of Rites*.

On his birthday,[1] Li Shih-min told Chang-sun Wu-chi,[2] "How sad it is not to be able to live under the parental roof any longer. The 'Lu ngo'[3] of the *Book of Songs* says, 'Thick grows [the] tarragon/ . . . alas for my father and mother,/ Alas for all their trouble in bringing [me] up!' How can I enjoy myself today when my parents toiled to rear me!" *TCTC*, 198, 6242-3.

After the Three Kingdoms, it was no longer the custom for an heir apparent to observe mourning for three years. Upon the death of Yi

Sŏng-gye, Yi Pang-wŏn, despite opposition from his ministers, mourned for three full years.[4]

1. See A. C. Moule, *The Rulers of China, 221 B.C. to A.D. 1949* (London, 1957), p. 54, n. 2 (cf. *TCTC*, 198, 6242-3).
2. *CTS*, 65, 3309c-3310d; *HTS*, 105, 3922b-d.
3. *Book of Songs*, 202 (Karlgren, pp. 152-153; Waley, pp. 316-317).
4. *TnS*, 16, 1a; *CMP*, 67, 1a; *YKP* (CKK, 1913), 2, 65. See the *Hsiao ching*, chaps. 15 and 18.

[93]

Had he not gone to Kao-p'ing
Yearning after his father's coffin,
How could he have secured
The works that match Heaven?[1]

Had he returned to the Village of Millet
Yearning for his deceased mother,
Could he have achieved
The merits of the foundation?

Before departing for the battle front to meet the forces of the Northern Han (947–950), Kuo Jung ordered Feng Tao (822–954),[2] to entomb the royal coffin. He then went to Kao-p'ing and solidified the groundwork for a new kingdom (954). *CWTS*, 126, 4369a-b; *HWTS*, 54, 4450b. Franke, IV, 67. (See commentary to canto 24, *YG*, 4, 10b-15b.)

On the way to Hwangju[3] to receive heir apparent Sŏk,[4] General Yi Sŏng-gye held a hunt at Haeju. While he pursued a deer his horse slipped and fell into the mud. Yi fell from the horse and was hurt. At the time, his fifth son, Yi Pang-wŏn, dwelt in a hut by his mother's grave at the Village of Millet[5] but upon hearing of his father's injury, he hastened to the capital. He heard that Chŏng Mong-ju was about to raise a rebellion on the day of the general's arrival in the capital. Yi Pang-wŏn spurred his horse to Pyŏngnando,[6] revealed Chŏng's plot to his father, and added that Chŏng was about to ruin the Yi family. He then pressed his father to enter the capital as soon as possible without losing time. Indeed, Chŏng was intriguing among the Censorate, demanding that the king kill Cho Chun (d. 1405)[7] and Chŏng To-jŏn, Yi Sŏng-gye's staunch supporters. Yi Pang-wŏn therefore came alone to his father and asked him for permission to kill Chŏng Mong-ju; but the general did not allow him to. Yi Pang-wŏn urged his father several times, but the general remained adamant and ordered his son to return to his mother's grave to complete his mourning. Yi Pang-wŏn thereupon retreated to his old house but returned to his father's mansion, gathered his men, and killed Chŏng Mong-ju on April 26, 1392. *KRS*, 46, 35a ff.; *KRSCY*, 36, 48a ff.; *TS*, 1, 34a-36b; *TT*, 56, 589, 592-595; *YK*, 1, 37-39.

1. 配天: *Chou i*, 7, 4b (Wilhelm, I, 324); *Tao te ching*, 68 (Duyvendak, p. 144; Waley, p. 227); *The Mean*, 31 (Legge, I, 429).

2. *CWTS*, 126, 4359a-4360b; *HWTS*, 54, 4450a-b; Wang Gung-wu, "Feng Tao: An Essay on Confucian Loyalty," in *Confucian Personalities* (Stanford, 1962), pp. 123-145, 230-231.

3. *SnSC*, 152, 2b-3a; *TYS*, 41, 2a-b.

4. *KRS*, 91, 19a-b.

5. Fifteen ri north of P'ungdŏk in Kyŏnggi. Yi Pang-wŏn's mother was buried in Chenŭng (*TYS*, 13, 4a-7a).

6. Thirty-six ri west of Kaesŏng, generally called Hindari (*SnSC*, 148, 3b; *TYS*, 4, 8b).

7. After Yi Sŏng-gye's return from Wihwa Island, Cho was most active in strengthening the prestige and power of the Yi party. After Yi Sŏng-gye's enthronement, he was enfeoffed as the Marquis of P'yongyang and enrolled in "class one dynasty foundation meritorious subjects." He served the first three kings of the new dynasty and died on July 23, 1405. *KRS*, 118, 1a-34a; *TnS*, 9, 24a-27a; *YK*, 2, 91.

[94]

Others stopped him, wanted to go instead.
But he went to secure the state.
The Jürched were unable to fathom
The charge of Emperor Kao-tsung.[1]

He asked him to go,[2]
So he went to secure the state.
The Son of Heaven realized
The true heart of his loyalty.

The Jürched destroyed the Khitan Liao (1125) and according to the terms of their treaty returned six prefectures around Peking to Sung. When the dissatisfied Sung laid claim to more territories, the Chin army marched south. Hui-tsung abdicated in favor of his son Ch'in-tsung (1100–1126–1127–1161), who attempted to buy off the Chin.

The Chin demanded the heir apparent as hostage. Li Kang[3] offered himself in the prince's stead, but Ch'in-tsung did not consent. The Prince of K'ang (later Kao-tsung) finally went in person. But he was a good archer and manifested his skill to the Jürched, who did not believe he was heir apparent and released him (1126). *Sung shih*, 23, 4536a; 24, 4537d; *Chin shih*, 3, 4863a; *San-ch'ao pei-meng hui-pien*, 30, 1b; 31, 2a-b; *Hsü Tzu-chih t'ung-chien*, 96, 2505 ff.; Franke, IV, 210–211. Cf. canto 32.

During the reign of Yi Sŏng-gye, the Ming court reprimanded Korea for having communicated with the Jürched and asked Korea to send one of the royal sons to Nanking. Yi Pang-wŏn, together with Cho Pan (d. 1401)[4] and Nam Chae, went to Ming and dispelled the emperor's suspicion (1394).[5] *TS*, 6, 17a; *MSL*, 234, 3222–3.

1. In the original 紹興之命. *Shao-hsing* is the reign-title used between January 31, 1131 and July 24, 1162.

2. Or " 'You must go,' his father said."

3. For this episode see *Sung shih*, 358, 5246c and *Ta-Chin kuo-chih* (Kuo-hsüeh chi-pen ts'ung-shu ed.), 7, 67–69. For Li's biography see *Sung shih*, 358, 5426b-359, 5430a.

4. At the age of twelve, he went with his father to Peking and studied Chinese and Mongolian. Toqto thought highly of him and had him work in the translation bureau of the secretariat. In 1389–1390 he went to Ming and cleared the false charge made by Yun I and Yi Ch'o against Yi Sŏng-gye (*KRS*, 45, 5a, 26b). His missions to Ming include those in 1382–1383, 1385, 1389–1390, July 18–October 22, 1392, and the one with Yi Pang-wŏn (1394, see *MCB*, XI [1959], 68–70). *TnS*, 2, 16b–17a; *YK*, 2, 103–104; *KIC*, 1, 22–23.

5. Yi Pang-wŏn's party left the capital on July 5 and returned on December 12, 1394 (*TS*, 6, 1b ff. and 17a).

[95]

When he first came, he was haughty:
When he met him,
The lord who was to save the world,
He was struck with awe.

Wherever he went he was insolent:
But, at the feast,
He bowed before him,
The illustrious and majestic lord.

For the first stanza, see canto 16.

The Ming envoy to Korea, Niu Niu,[1] was insolent and offended the officials. Upon meeting Yi Pang-wŏn at the banquet, however, he changed his manners and kowtowed (1396).[2] *TS*, 9, 10a.

After the enthronement of Yi Pang-wŏn, the Ming emperor Ch'eng-tsu (Yung-lo; 1360–1402–1424) sent a eunuch, Huang Yen,[3] to Korea. On his way home, Huang told an interpreter, "In Korea there have been many benevolent kings, but no one is more so than your reigning monarch. Our sovereign therefore favors him greatly."

1. In *YG*, 9, 49a-b, his title is *Shang-pao ssu-ch'eng* (6a), an officer in the Seal Office (*HJAS*, XXI [1958], 25).
2. This took place on July 31, 1396.
3. He told the Korean interpreter Kim Si-u when he reached the Moraeo-gae (*YG*, 9, 49b-50a).

[96]

He read with pity
The petition of a devoted daughter.
He perpetuated
The humane customs of the Han house.

He heard with pity
The tearful voice of a devoted son.
He helped perpetuate
The humane state begun by his father.

In the time of the fourth Han emperor Wen-ti (Liu Heng, 202/1–180–157 B.C.), Ch'un-yü I[1] committed an offense and was about to be punished. His daughter, T'i-jung,[2] implored the emperor to pardon him and offered herself as a slave in order to atone for her father's offense. The emperor pardoned her father and abolished the law requiring mutilating punishment (167 B.C.). *SC*, 10, 0040d-0041a (*MH*, II, 474–476), 105, 0236c; *HS*, 4, 0301d (Dubs, I, 255), 23, 0385c-d; *TCTC*, 15, 495–496.

In 1397, Pak Cha-an (d. 1408)[3] unwittingly divulged a military secret to the Japanese pirates and was sentenced to death. His son, Pak Shil (d. 1432),[4] came to the mansion of Yi Pang-wŏn and wailed loudly entreating him to pardon his father. Yi Pang-wŏn begged Yi Sŏng-gye to save the condemned and Pak escaped punishment. For his filial piety, Yi made Shil a palace guard. *TS*, 11, 15a-b; *Chŏngjong sillok*, 4, 17b-18a.

1. *SC*, 105, 0236c-d; *HS*, 23, 0385c-d; *BD*, 512.
2. *BD*, 1912.
3. He fought against the Japanese pirates in 1377 (*KRS*, 135, 48a) and in 1379 (*KRS*, 137, 37a, 44b). In 1389, together with Pak Wi (*KRS*, 116, 19b-22a), he attacked the Japanese strongholds in Tsushima, burnt 300 enemy ships, and brought back the Koreans held by the Japanese (*KRS*, 116, 20b). He died on November 24, 1408 (*TnS*, 16, 36a). See *Haedong chamnok* (CKK, 1910), 3, 582–583.
4. Died January 4, 1432 (*SnS*, 54, 29b; *TYS*, 31, 7a; *YK*, 2, 144).

[97]

Many were generals,
But he alone was lofty and resourceful.[1]
"A mad man" heard his name
And came to see him through a villager.

Many were kin,
But he alone had a prominent nose and dragon face.[2]
A scholar read his mien
And came to see him through a friend.[3]

A man of Kao-yang, Li I-chi,[4] was nicknamed "a madman." When Liu Pang (Han Kao-tsu) went west past Kao-yang, Li asked to see Liu Pang. Liu Pang was just then squatting on a bed, two maids were washing his feet. Li reproached Liu Pang, who finally arose, begged his pardon, and conducted him to the seat of honor. Li then advised Liu Pang to make a surprise attack upon Ch'en-liu. For that Liu Pang made Li the Lord of Kuang-yeh. *SC*, 8, 0034c (*MH*, II, 345–346; Watson, I, 86–87); *HS*, 1A, 0293a (Dubs, I, 51).

Yi Sŏng-gye had a prominent nose and majestic face, and among his sons only Yi Pang-wŏn bore a striking resemblance to his father. Ha Yun[5] and Min Che[6] were friends; one day Ha Yun told Min Che "I have physiognomised many, but no one has a more striking face than your son-in-law [Yi Pang-wŏn was married to the second daughter of Min Che]. Please arrange a meeting for me." Later, Ha Yun assisted Yi Pang-wŏn and became a meritorious subject. *TS*, 1, 5b and *TnS*, 1, 1a.

1.   大略: *SC*, 97, 0228b (Watson, I, 269): "great plans."

2.   隆準龍顏: *SC*, 8, 0033c (*MH*, II, 325; Watson, I, 77): "a prominent nose and a dragonlike face." *HS*, 1A, 0291d (Dubs, I, 29): "a prominent nose and a dragon forehead."

3.   For the fourth line of the second Chinese verse, *YG*, 9, 54a quotes *Yang Tzu* (*SPPY*), 11, 1a (Bruno Belpaire, *Le Catéchisme philosophique de Yang-Hiong-Tse* [Bruxelles, 1960], p. 88).

4.   *SC*, 97, 0228b-d (Watson, I, 269–275); *HS*, 1A, 0293a (Dubs, I, 51), 43 0464d-0465b.

5.   He passed the civil service examination in 1365. He opposed the northern march planned by Ch'oe Yŏng (d. 1389) and was banished to Yangju. After the coup, in 1392, he served as Governor of Kyŏnggi. In 1398, he sided with Yi Pang-wŏn. He was one of the compilers of *TS*. He died on November 24, 1416 (*TnS*, 32, 25b-27b). For his collected works, *Hojŏng chip*, see *CMP*, 247, 10a.

6.   He passed the civil service examination at nineteen. In 1392, he was mayor of Kaesŏng (*KRS*, 46, 38b). After the foundation of the Yi dynasty, he was enfeoffed as the Marquis of Yŏhŭng; he died on October 4, 1408 (*KRS*, 108, 4a-5a; *TnS*, 16, 14a-b; *HMN*, 3, 115–116; *YK*, 2, 113–114).

[98]

Aspiring to dynastic legitimacy,[1]
He opposed the advice of his men.
Hence the trees and grass of the mountain
Turned into a host of horsemen.

They opposed the royal order,
Rudely insulting the royal heir.
Hence the empty streets of the capital
Were filled with[2] a host of horsemen.

The ruler of the Former Ch'in, Fu Chien (338–357–385),[3] despite stout opposition of his ministers, attacked the emperor Hsiao-wu of the Eastern Chin (Ssu-ma Yao, 362–372–396)[4] and suffered a crushing defeat (383). The retreating army feared ambush in every tree and tuft of grass[5] and was scared by the sound of the wind and the whoop of the cranes. *Chin shu*, 9, 1098a; 114, 1376c; *TCTC*, 104, 3301–105, 3313; Franke, II, 95–97.

Chŏng To-jŏn and Nam Ŭn plotted with heir apparent Pang-sŏk[6] to kill other princes; they falsely reported that Yi Sŏng-gye was gravely ill, and assembled the princes in the palace. But their plot was leaked; Yi Pang-wŏn rose to the emergency and crushed the rebels. At the time, the rebels saw a line of cavalrymen stretching from South Mountain[7] to Kwanghwa Gate.[8] The people thought it a heavenly intervention. *TS*, 14, 19b-26a; *TnS*, 1, 2b.

1. For the term 正統 see *TCTC*, 69, 2185–8; *The Chronicle of the Three Kingdoms (220–265)*, tr. Achilles Fang, I (Cambridge, Mass., 1952), 45–48; *Ou-yang wen-chung-kung ch'üan-chi (SPPY)*, 16, 2a-6b. Herschel Webb, *The Japanese Imperial Institution in the Tokugawa Period* (New York, 1968), pp. 154 ff.

2. *Poeningida* means "to fill" or "be covered with," not "to see" (*AY*, V, 112–113).

3. *Chin shu*, 113, 1372c-114, 1378c; *BD*, 579; Michael C. Rogers, *The Chronicle of Fu Chien: A Case of Exemplary History* (Berkeley, 1968).

4. *Chin shu*, 9, 1097b-1099a.

5. Literally, the trees on Mount Pa-kung looked like the Chin soldiers. This is the version in *TCTC*, 105, 3311–2; *Chin shu, Tsai-chi* version differs slightly (114, 1376c). See Michael C. Rogers, pp. 169–170. The similar topos is also in Claudian, *Against Eutropius*, II, 452–455, where Eutropius' lieutenant Leo, in a battle against Tribigild, mistook a breeze in the foliage for the whistle of an arrow and dropped dead from fright.

6. Born of Yi Sŏng-gye's second wife, Queen Sindŏk (née Kang), he was the eighth and youngest son, known as Prince Ŭian (*SS*, 6b). He was made heir apparent on September 7, 1392 (*TS*, 1, 52b).

7. Also known as Mount Mongmyŏk or In'gyŏng (*SnSC*, 148, 2a; *TYS*, 3, 4b).

8. The South Gate of the Kyŏngbok Palace in Seoul (*TYS*, 1, 15a; *SnSC*, 148, 2a). The miracle occurred on October 6, 1398.

[99]

Fearing his aunt,
He wished to yield the crown to his brother.
But to whom would he hand over
The merits of his subjugation?

Resisting the entreaty of ministers,
He saw his brother become an heir.
Who would not come to this man,
Whose genius firmly secured the state?

Before accession, T'ang Hsüan-tsung (Li Lung-chi) feared the slander of his aunt, Princess T'ai-p'ing, and wanted his elder brother, King of Sung, to be heir apparent. But Jui-tsung (622–684–690–716)[1] knew that he owed the throne to the assistance of his third son (Hsüan-tsung) and abdicated in his favor. *TCTC*, 210, 6656–65. See canto 71.

After Yi Pang-wŏn had crushed the rebellion of Chŏng To-jŏn, the court wanted to make him heir apparent. But the prince declined firmly. Because Yi Pang-gwa (Chŏngjong, 1357–1399–1400–1419) had no heir, he made his younger brother Yi Pang-wŏn his successor on February 25, 1400. *Chŏngjong sillok*, 3, 4a, 9b-10b; *TnS*, 1, 1b; *YK*, 2, 110.

1. *CTS*, 7, 3079a-3080b; *HTS*, 5, 3643c-3644a.

[100]

A dragon in the river
Swam toward his pavilion in the water.
Indeed this was a lucky sign[1]
That he would soon restore peace.

A dragon on the roof
Came toward his bedroom.
Indeed this was a lucky sign
That he would soon ascend the throne.

While Chao K'uang-yin, as a general of the Later Chou, was in a campaign at Chiang-ting south of the Huai, a dragon leapt toward him. The people guessed that Chao would soon be emperor. *Sung shih*, 62, 4634a.

In the ninth month of 1399, before he ascended the throne, one day, at dawn, a white dragon appeared on the roof of Yi Pang-wŏn's bedroom in Karaeol[2] in Songdo. The dragon was as large as a beam and its scales shown brilliantly in the sun. A lady in waiting, née Kim, saw it under the eaves and called a cook who also dashed out and glimpsed the auspicious animal. But before long, clouds and mist obscured their view. The advent of the dragon foretold Yi's elevation to the throne. *TnS*, 1, 1b; *YK*, 2, 118.

1. For the meaning of the word, *nŭt*, see Yi Sung-nyŏng, *Kugŏhak nonch'ong* (1966), 78–97, esp. 97.
2. In the Namgye ward, center of the capital. After his enthronement, the mansion was enlarged and named the Kyŏngdŏk Palace (*TYS*, 4, 14a; *YG*, 10, 19b).

[101]

Great were his merits under Heaven,
But another became heir apparent.
Hence Venus
Shone at high noon.[1]

Great were his merits for the state.
When the heir apparent was not yet chosen,
A red halo
Shone at night.

The foundation and consolidation of the T'ang was the work of Li
Shih-min; but Chien-ch'eng, not Shih-min, became heir apparent.
When Li Shih-min was about to punish his wicked brothers (July 2,
626), the star Venus appeared in the daytime. Grand Astrologer Fu I
(555–639)[2] reported the event to the throne and remarked that the
appearance of Venus was a sign that the Prince of Ch'in (Li Shih-min)
would become a Son of Heaven. *CTS*, 79, 3338d; *HTS*, 107, 3926d;
TCTC, 191, 6009; Franke, II, 366–367.
The foundation of the Yi dynasty was chiefly the work of Yi Pang-
wŏn. Before he became heir apparent, in the northwestern sky above
the capital, a red halo shone at night (February 24, 1400).[3] *Chŏngjong
sillok*, 3, 7b.

1. The third line of the first Chinese verse has 煌煌太白, for which see
Book of Songs, 140, 1 (Karlgren, p. 89: "shining" and Waley, p. 56: "bright").
2. *CTS*, 79, 3338a-c; *HTS*, 107, 3926c-d; Arthur F. Wright, "Fu I and the
Rejection of Buddhism," *JHI*, XII (1951), 33–47. He came to the T'ang court
about 618 and was appointed Grand Astrologer and submitted two anti-
Buddhist memorials in 621 and 624.
3. This halo appeared eight days before the rebellion of Yi Pang-gan. For
祲 see *Shuo-wen chieh-tzu* (*TSCC*), 1A, 4; *Tso chuan*, Duke Chao 15 (Legge, V,
659a); and *Chou li* (*SPTK*), 6, 46a.

[102]

He had no fears,
But instead of passing the night at this house,
Heaven
Intervened and moved his heart.

> He had not been ill,
> But when he was about to go to that house,
> Heaven
> Intervened and made him ill.

On his return from the subjugation of Han Hsin's men at Tung-yüan, Liu Pang ("he" in line 1) passed Chao (200 B.C.). The chancellor of Chao, Kuan Kao, and others plotted to assassinate him. When Liu Pang was about to pass the night at Po-jen, he thought it meant "a harassed person," and went away, thus escaping death. *SC*, 8, 0036d (*MH*, II, 391–392; Watson, I, 111); *HS*, 1B, 0297a (Dubs, I, 119, n. 3). Cf. canto 66.

On February 24, 1400, Yi Pang-gan,[1] elder brother of Pang-wŏn, intending to assassinate him, invited him to his mansion. But Pang-wŏn suddenly fell ill and could not go. *Chŏngjong sillok*, 3, 4b; *YK*, 1, 74–76.

1. The fourth son of Yi Sŏng-gye (*SS*, 6a), he died in Hongju on April 10, 1421 (*SnS*, 11, 13b).

[103]

> His younger brothers were wicked:
> But he never did them evil.[1]
> He laid the foundation for royal works
> Which were to last two hundred years.
>
> His elder brother was wicked:
> But he never harbored enmity against him.[2]
> He inspired beautiful customs
> Which were to endure myriad years.

The founder of the Liao, A-pao-chi's (872–907–926) brothers, La-ko (d. 923), Tieh-la (-ko), Yin-ti-shih, and An-tuan,[3] often revolted. But the emperor always forgave them. *Liao shih*, 1, 5738c-5739a.

Although Yi Pang-gan plotted to kill his younger brother Pang-wŏn (canto 102), the latter treated him as a brother even after his enthronement. *YG*, 10, 17a-18b.

1. 無相猶矣: *Book of Songs*, 189, 1 (Karlgren, p. 130; Waley, p. 282).
2. 不宿怨焉: *Mencius*, 5A, 3 (Legge, II, 349), quoted in *YG*, 10, 21b.

3. Their revolts occurred in 911, 912, 913, 914, 917, and 918. For translation of the relevant passages in the *Liao shih*, see Wittfogel and Feng, *History of Chinese Society: Liao (907–1125)* (New York, 1949), pp. 400–402, 411–414, 574–575. In *YG*, 10, 21b, Su is given as A-pao-chi's fifth brother.

[104]

She slandered the founding minister:
He intervened but could not save him.
Because he fell under suspicion,
His love could not make him live.

They slandered the founding minister:
He intervened and saved him.
Thus he rewarded his deeds for the state,
His benevolence made him live.

Liu Wen-ching (568–619)[1] rendered meritorious services in the foundation of the T'ang, but his rank was lower than that of P'ei Chi. The two therefore did not get on well with each other. At the time, Liu fell victim to his former concubine's slanderous tongue and was imprisoned by the T'ang emperor. Li Shih-min intervened in Liu's favor, but P'ei Chi insisted on Liu's death. Liu was beheaded and his property confiscated. *TCTC*, 187, 5861–2.

In 1400, in the eighth month, a meritorious subject, Cho Chun, was imprisoned on a false charge. Yi Pang-wŏn did his utmost to save the innocent man and Cho was able to clear his name. *Chŏngjong sillok*, 5, 9a-10a.

1. *CTS*, 57, 3293a-c; *HTS*, 88, 3892c-3893a; Liu, I, 83–84.

[105]

By betraying his lord,
He had once saved the other lord's life,
Who did not reward the personal favor
But taught posterity a lesson.

Loyal to his lord,
He disobeyed a royal call.

Unforgetful of justice,
He told his son of this man.

Hsiang Yü's general, Lord Ting,[1] pursued Liu Pang's army to the west of P'eng-ch'eng. The situation was urgent, and Liu Pang addressed his opponent, "Why should we be at odds?" Lord Ting then withdrew his troops, and Liu Pang escaped calamity. After Hsiang Yü's army had been destroyed, Lord Ting came to visit Liu Pang. Liu Pang ordered his men to behead him, saying, "Lord Ting as a subject was disloyal to his master and caused Hsiang Yü to lose the battle. You should in no case follow his example." *HS*, 37, 0454c; *SC*, 100, 0231c-d (Watson, I, 303).

While Yi Pang-wŏn was heir apparnet, he invited Kil Chae (1353–1419)[2] from Sŏnsan.[3] Kil came to the capital but, because he had held an office under Koryŏ, refused to serve two dynasties. Yi Pang-wŏn told his son (Sejong) about Kil Chae and had Kil's son, Kil Sa-sun[4] summoned to the court as a high officer. Sejong also conferred upon Kil Chae a posthumous title. *Chŏngjong sillok*, 5, 7b-8a; *YK*, 1, 47–50.

1. *HS*, 37, 0454c; *BD*, 1936.

2. Native of Sŏnsan, he first studied Confucius and Mencius before going to the capital where he frequented such writers as Yi Saek and Chŏng Mong-ju. In 1386, he took a *chinsa* and became professor in the National Academy. His reputation was so high that the students in the academy and the sons of officials flocked to him. In 1389, he declined an offer and retired to Sŏnsan to attend to his ailing mother. Yi Pang-wŏn was a classmate of Kil Chae. When Pang-wŏn became heir apparent, he named his friend Professor of Royal Sacrifice (*T'aesang paksa*). But Kil declined, arguing that he could not serve two dynasties. King Chŏngjong honored him and allowed him to retire to his village. There Kil devoted himself to the education of qualified pupils. He died on May 6, 1419 (*SnS*, 3, 31a-32a). King Sejong bestowed upon him the posthumous title of *Chwa sagan* in 1419 (*Taedong unbu kunok*, 18, 51b-52a) and again in 1426 (*SnS*, 34, 13b). In 1570, an academy was erected in his honor, and in 1575 it became a chartered academy (*saaek sŏwŏn*) when King Sŏnjo named it Kŭmo sŏwŏn (*CMP*, 213, 10a). His writings are collected in the *Yaŭn chip* (*CMP*, 247, 8b). See *HMN*, 1, *TYS*, 29, 2a, 10b-11a; *YC*, 3, 65–66; *YK*, 1, 47–50; and his *yŏnbo*, 2a-4b, in the *Yaŭn sŏnsaeng sokchip* (in the *Yŏgye myŏnghyŏn chip*). There is a modern translation of his works under the title of *Kugyŏk Yaŭn Kil sŏnsaeng munjip* (1965).

3. *TYS*, 29, 1a ff., esp. 10b-11a.

4. Yi Pang-wŏn appointed him *Chongmyo pusŭng* (8a) (*CMP*, 223, 11a; *YG*, 10, 31b; *TYS*, 29, 11a). On July 15, 1440, Sejong granted him an office in the fifth rank (*SnS*, 89, 30a).

[106]

He wrongly slew a loyal general,
And he hated this evil deed.
Hence he never gave him
A staff and axe.[1]

He praised the loyal retainers
And respected the learned men.
Hence he never spared
Office and rank.

Chao K'uang-yin and his men marched to Pien-chou (K'ai-feng) for the enthronement (canto 25). Vice-general of the Later Chou army, Han T'ung,[2] rushed out with his men to check Chao's army. Wang Yen-sheng[3] ("he" in line 1) chased them and killed Han T'ung and his family. Thereupon, Chao ("he" in line 2) conferred upon Han the posthumous title of *Chung-shu ling*[4] and commended his loyalty. He censured Wang for his reckless deed and never made him a general. *Sung shih*, 1, 4497b; 250, 5180a; *Hsü Tzu-chih t'ung-chien ch'ang-pien* (Chekiang shu-chü ed.), 1, 3a-b, 5a.

After the rebellion of Chŏng To-jŏn in 1398 (canto 98), all members of Yi Pang-sŏk's party fled except Kim Kye-ran.[5] As for Nam Ŭn, one of his servants, Ch'oe Un[6] gave him shelter. Yi Pang-wŏn ("he" in line 5), praising their sense of loyalty, summoned both Kim and Ch'oe and enrolled them in the royal guards. Yi Pang-wŏn granted a posthumous title and epithet to Chŏng Mong-ju (canto 93).[7] Members of Yi Pang-gan's party enjoyed ranks after the enthronement of Yi Pang-wŏn (cantos 102–103).

1. For 節鉞 see *K'ung-ts'ung-tzu* (in *Chi-hai*), 6, 11a-b.
2. *Sung shih*, 484, 5703b-d.
3. *Sung shih*, 250, 5180a.
4. Secretary-General of the Secretariat (Kracke, *Civil Service in Early Sung China, 960–1067* [Cambridge, Mass., 1953], p. 229).
5. Said to have reached the third rank (*YG*, 10, 33a).
6. Said to have reached the second rank (*YG*, 10, 33a).
7. On January 28, 1401, Kwŏn Kŭn memorialized the throne, urging Yi Pang-wŏn to honor Chŏng Mong-ju posthumously (*TnS*, 1, 7a-8a; *P'oŭn munjip*, 4, 50a-b). See *P'oŭn munjip*, 4, 17b and *P'oŭn sŏnsaeng chip songnok*, 2, 1a.

[107]

The whole court acclaimed Buddhism:
He upheld the stand of the right man.
Hence at a stroke he defrocked
Hundreds of thousands of monks.

Widely the country enjoyed Buddhism:
He alone detected its fallacies.[1]
Hence in a day he reformed
Hundreds of thousands of temples.

Under the reign of Li Yüan, Fu I[2] advocated the rejection of Buddhism. Li Yüan, therefore, despite the opposition of the court, reduced the number of monks and monasteries. *CTS*, 79, 3338a-b; Franke, II, 390.

Buddhism was the state religion during the Koryŏ dynasty. Yi Pang-wŏn, who abhorred Buddhism, secularized Buddhist monks and nuns, and closed monasteries (1402).[3] *TnS*, 3, 23a-24a.

1. For the second line of the second Chinese verse, the commentary quotes *Yang Tzu* (*SPPY*), 2, 4b (Bruno Belpaire, *Le Catéchisme*, p. 27; *Sources of Chinese Tradition*, ed. W. T. de Bary *et al.* [New York, 1960], p. 250).

2. For Fu I see canto 101. It was not Liu Yüan, but Li Shih-min in 626 (*CTS*, 1, 3066a; *HTS*, 1, 3636a) who reduced monks and monasteries. See Kenneth K. S. Ch'en, *Buddhism in China* (Princeton, 1964), pp. 215 ff.

3. For the suppression of Buddhism in the beginning of Yi, see Han U-gŭn, "Yŏmal Sŏnch'o ŭi pulgyo chŏngch'aek," *STN*, VI (1957), 3–80; Yi Sang-baek, *Han'guk munhwasa yŏn'gu non'go* (1954), pp. 76 ff.

[108]

She overheard the talk,
To fulfill the people's wishes,
She brought out the royal armor
And had him wear it.

To fulfill Heaven's wishes,
She feigned illness and sent for him.
She got weapons ready
And helped him.

Kung Ye,[1] King of T'aebong (901–918), became more tyrannous every day and the people suffered from his misgovernment. At the time, Generals Hong Yu (d. 936),[2] Pae Hyŏn-gyŏng (d. 936),[3] Shin Sung-gyŏm (d. 927),[4] Pok Chi-gyŏm,[5] and others came to Wang Kŏn's home and disclosed that they intended to proclaim him king. Wang Kŏn firmly declined. His wife, née Yu (later Queen Sinhye; "she" in line 1),[6] after overhearing their conversation, came forward and said, "It is only meet and just to punish tyranny with righteousness." With these words, Lady Yu brought out the armor, and the generals with Wang Kŏn left the house and helped him to mount his horse. The following day (July 25, 918), Wang ascended the throne at P'ojŏng Hall and called his country Koryŏ. *KRS*, 1, 7b-8a; 88, 1b-2b; 92, 1a-3b; *KRSCY*, 1, 1a-b, 5a ff.

Chŏng To-jŏn invited all the princes to the palace where he planned to massacre them (canto 98). At the time Queen Wŏn'gyŏng (1365–1420), née Min,[7] feigned illness and sent for Yi Pang-wŏn. The queen and Yi then devised a counterplan and punished the rebels (1398).[8] *TS*, 14, 19b ff.

1. *SGSG*, 50, 1–5. See Yi Yong-jung, *Husamguk ŭi ch'urhyŏn kwa Koryŏ e ŭihan kŭŭi t'ongil* (P'yongyang, 1963), Part I.

2. His earlier name was Sul. In 994, his tablet was placed in the royal temple of Wang Kŏn (*KRS*, 92, 2a-b).

3. *KRS*, 92, 2b-3a.

4. When Kyŏnhwŏn (892–935) of the Later Paekche ravaged the Silla capital in the tenth month of 927, Wang Kŏn was angry, gathered troops and with them attacked Kyŏnhwŏn at Mount Kong, northeast of Taegu. When Wang was surrounded by the enemy, Shin and others made a last minute resistance and saved Wang. Later, Wang built the Chimyo monastery for Shin and prayed for his soul. King Yejong composed the "Dirge" (1120) to honor Shin and Kim Nak, another general who fell in the battle (*KRS*, 14, 35b). Shin was granted the posthumous epithet of *Kaeguk changjŏl kong* (*KRS*, 60, 34a). See *KRS*, 92, 3a; *TYS*, 39, 36a. For King Yejong's poem, "Dirge," see my *Anthology of Korean Poetry* (New York, 1964), p. 51.

5. Became Grand Preceptor (*T'aesa*) posthumously in 994 (*KRS*, 3, 27a). His posthumous epithet is Mugong (*KRS*, 60, 34a; 92, 3b).

6. *KRS*, 88, 1b-2b.

7. Daughter of Min Che, she was born July 28, 1365, and died August 18, 1420 (*SnS*, 8, 17b). She was buried in Hyŏnnŭng, thirty ri west of Kwangju, on October 23, 1420 (*SS*, 9b; *TYS*, 6, 14b ff.; *YK*, 2, 115).

8. Cf. Claudian, *In Praise of Serena*, 225–236 (LCL, II, 254–257), for ho Serena, wife of Stilico, watched over his interests while he was away on the battlefield and how she followed the political machinations of Rufinus, keeping Stilico informed of the latest plots.

[109]

Her horse got sick
And could not scale the rocky ridge.
Pouring wine into a gold cup,
She yearned after her beloved king.

Struck by an arrow,
His horse returned to the stable.
She resolved to follow her lord
To the nether world.

The consort of King Wen, thinking of her beloved, wrote the following poem: "I am climbing that high ridge,/ My horses are sick and spent,/ And I stop for a little while to drink from that horn cup/ To still my heart's pain," *Book of Songs*, 3 (Waley, p. 45; Karlgren, p. 3); *YG*, 10, 42b–43a.

During the rebellion of Yi Pang-gan (1400), Mok In-hae's horse which belonged to Yi Pang-wŏn's stable, returned with an arrow in its flank. Upon seeing the exhausted animal, Queen Wŏn' gyŏng ("she" in line 7) feared that Yi Pang-wŏn had lost a battle and resolved to follow him in death. While five servants were restraining her and a sixth was blocking the road, news of victory arrived, and the queen returned home. *Chŏngjong sillok*, 3, 7a.

[110]

Your four ancestors never enjoyed peace—
How often did they move around?
How did they live,
In how large an abode?

When you live in a deep sumptuous palace,[1]
When you enjoy golden days of peace,
Remember, my Lord,
Their hardships and sorrow.

The four ancestors are Mokcho, Ikcho, Tojo, and Hwanjo. See cantos 1, 3–6, 17–20.

1. 九重: *Ch'u tz'u* (*SPTK*), 8, 8a (Hawkes, p. 95): "But *ninefold* are the gates of my Lord" (italics mine).

[111]

Because the wolves[1] wrought havoc,
Because not even a grass roof remained,
They bore hardships
In a clay hut.

When you are in a great carpeted room,[2]
When you sit on the richly woven throne,
Remember, my Lord,
Their hardships and sorrow.

For how the Jürched chiefs ("wolves" in line 1) conspired against the life of Ikcho, Yi Sŏng-gye's great-grandfather, see cantos 4–5.

1. 豺狼: *Tso chuan*, Duke Min 1 (Legge, V, 124): *Mencius*, 4A, 17 (Legge, II, 307).
2. 廣厦: *Han-shih wai-chuan* (*SPTK*), 5, 9b (James R. Hightower, *Han Shih Wai Chuan* [Cambridge, Mass., 1952], p. 174): "great room."

[112]

Anxious only to fulfill the royal cause,
He led his men from camp to camp.
How many days did he run
Without doffing his armor?

When you are wrapped in a dragon robe,[1]
When you wear the belt of precious gems,
Remember, my Lord,
His fortitude and tenacity.

While Yi Sŏng-gye was subjugating the north and the south, he never had time to doff his armor.

In 1430, the fifth Ming emperor Hsüan-tsung (1399–1425–1435) granted King Sejong a royal robe and a belt of precious gems. This event was entered in *SnS*, 49, 4b, under the seventeenth day of the seventh month (August 5, 1430). However, in the *MS*, 320, 7902c, it was in the third year of *Hsüan-te* (1428). *CMP*, 174, 6a; *Kosa ch'waryo*, 1, 12b; *YG*, 10, 45a; *YKP*, 5, 288–289.

In 1444, the sixth Ming emperor Ying-tsung (1427–1435–1449–1464) granted King Sejong a dragon robe and a jade belt. In *SnS* this event was entered under the twenty-fourth day of the third month (April 12, 1444). *CMP*, 174, 6b, 7a; *Kosa ch'waryo*, 1, 14b; *YG*, 10, 45a; *YKP*, 5, 250; *Ta-Ming hui-tien* (1587 ed.), 111, 113b.

1.   *YG*, 10, 45a comments: "Hsüan-tsung bestowed upon our majesty [Sejong] a four-clawed dragon robe with a hoop belt set with precious ornaments. The four-clawed dragon robe was woven with golden dragons, three *ts'un* in size. The main dragon's head and right foreleg were on the breast, the left foreleg on the left shoulder, the right rear leg on the back, and the tail and left rear leg on the right shoulder. The narrow band stretching across the skirt below the knees (*hsi-lan*) was woven with small, walking dragons in gold, four in front and four in back. The belt was faced with purple silk and the jewel settings were of gold. The belt was ornamented with sapphires, rubies, and bright pearls." Professor Schuyler Cammann points out that the Korean compilers' description of the robe was inaccurate. Cammann's corrections are: (1) It was customary in the Ming to place two large dragons on the upper half of the robe: one with its head on the chest of the robe, its body arching backward over the left shoulder; the other with its head on the back of the robe, its body arching forward over the right shoulder. Thus, the front and back of the robe had exactly the same basic pattern, an important requirement in all Chinese robes. Those who never saw an actual Ming robe but knew about it from portraits might get the impression that there was only one dragon, whose form began on the chest of the robe with the head. (2) The description of the band of decoration across the skirt below the knees is faulty. The Ming robes never had more than four small dragons on the front band, and four on the back, a total of eight. Hence by "eight dragons at front and back" (as in *YG*, 10, 45a, which I have corrected in translation), the compilers probably meant eight in all. (3) The Ming-style hoop belt was made of a stiff substance like wood or bamboo, covered with silk, and set with ornamental stones. The settings that held the stones were commonly called 環. For the description of the robe, see also *Shang shu*, 2, 10a-b (Legge, III, 80–81); *Chou li* (*SPTK*), 5, 40a–41a (E. Biot, *Le Tcheou-li ou Rites des Tcheou* [Peking, 1930], II, 6); and Schuyler Cammann, *China's Dragon Robes* (New York, 1952), esp. pp. 159–163, which contains a number of factual errors.

[113]

Zealous to deliver the suffering people,[1]
He fought on the mountains and plains.[2]
O how many times did he go
Without food and drink?

When you sup northern viands and southern dainties,[3]
When you have superb wine[4] and precious grain,[5]
Remember, my Lord,
His fortitude and fervor.

Yi Sŏng-gye, during his campaign against the Jürched and Japanese pirates, went without food for many days.

1. For 拯民 see canto 32, n. 1.
2. 攻戰: *Chan-kuo ts'e* (*SPPY*), 12, 4b.
3. Chang Heng's "Fu on the Southern Capital," in *Wen hsüan* (*WYWK*), 4, 5 (Von Zach, I, 41): "prächtige Delikatessen." Also in Li Po's poem, "Hsing-lu nan," in *Ch'üan T'ang shih*, 162, 1684 (Waley, *The Poetry and Career of Li Po* [London, 1950], p. 41): "choice meat."
4. 流霞: *Lun heng* (*SPPY*), 7, 5b (Forke, I, 340); *Li Yi-shan shih-chi* (*SPTK*), 6, 22a; *Pao-p'u Tzu* (*SPPY*), 20, 4b; sometimes translated as "streaming cloud."
5. 玉食: *Shang shu*, 7, 4b (Legge, III, 334): "precious grain."

[114]

Wishing to entrust him with a great task,
Heaven flexed his bones and sinews,[1]
And let his body suffer
Wounds and scars.

While the stately guards stand row after row,
While you reign in peace[2] and give audience,
Remember, my Lord,
His piety and constancy.

While Yi Sŏng-gye was fighting against the Red Turbans, he suffered a wound below the right ear (1362). See canto 33.

During a campaign against the Japanese pirates at Unbong (1380), an enemy arrow hit Yi Sŏng-gye's left knee. *KRS*, 126, 36a-b; *KRSCY*, 31, 21a; *TS*, 1, 15b; *TT*, 51, 394. See also cantos 50–51.

1. 先勞筋骨: *Mencius*, 6B, 15 has 勞其筋骨 (Legge, II, 447).
2. The term 垂拱 refers, in *Shang shu*, 6, 10b (Legge, III, 316; 317a), to King Wu, who "had only to let his robes fall, and fold his hands, and the empire was orderly ruled." Here, the compilers, in an attempt to sing of an era of peace, extol the king that he, like all sage rulers, governs the kingdom effortlessly with dangling robes and folded hands.

[115]

Because he loved men and sought their welfare,
He overawed
The fierce rebels
And caught them alive.

When you have men at your beck and call,[1]
When you punish men and sentence men,
Remember, my Lord,
His mercy and temperance.

For the stories, see cantos 41, 54 and 58.

1. 頤指: *HS*, 48, 0476d.

[116]

Seeing the bodies lying in heaps,
He abandoned food and sleep.
Moved by love for his people,[1]
He labored assiduously.

If you are unaware of people's sorrow,
Heaven will abandon you.
Remember, my Lord,
His labor and love.

In 1380, Japanese pirates ravaged three southern provinces (canto 50). On his way to a decisive battle which annihilated the bandits, Yi Sŏng-gye saw dead bodies piled up on the plains and hills. Overwhelmed with pity, he could neither eat nor sleep. *KRS*, 126, 35a; *TS*, 1, 15a.

1. 旻天之心: for 旻天 see *Shang shu*, 2, 5b (Legge, III, 66: "compassionate Heaven"); *Book of Songs*, 195 (Karlgren, p. 142: "the severe Heaven"); and *Mencius*, 5A, 1 (Legge, II, 342: "pitying Heaven").

[117]

He battled against the king's enemy,[1]
And his fame was unrivaled.
But he never boasted of his deeds.
Such was his virtue of modesty.[2]

If a deceitful minister flatters you,[3]
If you are roused to pride,
Remember, my Lord,
His prowess and modesty.

The first stanza celebrates the victories won by Yi Sŏng-gye over the Japanese pirates in 1377 (canto 47), 1378 (canto 49), 1380 (canto 50), and 1385 (cantos 58 and 60).

1. 敵王所愾: *Tso chuan*, Duke Wen 4 (Legge, V, 239): "When they had battled with any against whom the king was angry."
2. 勞謙: *Chou i*, 2, 6a (Wilhelm, I, 68).
3. 善諛: *Lü-shih ch'un-ch'iu* (*SPPY*), 16, 2b.

[118]

He had many to help him;[1]
Even the Jürched served him with constancy.
Can we tell in words
How our people gave their hearts to him?

If a king loses his inward power,
Even his kin will rebel.
Remember, my Lord,
His fame and virtue.

For the first stanza, see cantos 55 (n. 2), 56, 75, and 86 (n. 1).

1. 多助之至: *Mencius*, 2B, 1 (Legge, II, 210): "When the being assisted by many reaches its highest point, the whole kingdom becomes obedient to the prince."

[119]

The brothers rebelled against one another:
But in their heart they were friendly.[1]
Despite their crimes
Their ties remained firm.

If brothers are split,
A villain will enter and sow discord.
Remember, my Lord,
His sagacity and love.

The first poem alludes to the rebellion of Yi Sŏng-gye's brother, Ch'ŏn-gye, in 1371 (canto 76) and that of Yi Pang-wŏn's elder brother, Yi Pang-gan, in 1400 (canto 103).

1. Literally: his heart was friendly to them. For 因心則友 see *Book of Songs*, 241 (Waley, p. 256): "Now this Wang Chi/ Was of heart accommodating and friendly,/ Friendly to his elder brother,/ So that his luck was strong" (cf. Karlgren, p. 194). The commentary also quotes another poem, no. 223 (Karlgren, p. 177): "These good brothers are generous and indulgent; but the bad brothers mutually do harm to each other."

[120]

Because the government burdened the people,
The people who are Heaven to a ruler,[1]
He defied a multitude of opinions
And reformed the system of private lands.

If a ruler taxes[2] his people without measure,[3]
The basis of the state[4] will crumble.
Remember, my Lord,
His justice and humanity.

1. 民者王所天: *SC*, 97, 0228c (Watson, I, 271): "Li I-chi said, 'He who knows the "heaven" of Heaven may make himself a king, but he who lacked this knowledge may not. To a king the people are "heaven," and to the people food is "heaven." ' "
2. For 征 in 征斂 see *Tso chuan*, Duke Hsi 15 (Legge, V, 169) and *Mencius*, 1B, 5 (Legge, II, 162).

3. 無藝: *Tso chuan*, Duke Chao 20 (Legge, V, 683).

4. 邦本: *Shang shu*, 3, 11b (Legge, III, 158): "The people are the root of a country; if the root is firm, the country is tranquil." For the land reform carried out by the Yi Sŏng-gye party see canto 73.

[121]

Even though they were rebellious,
They were loyal to their lord.
Hence he forgave them
And employed them again.

If your advisers wrangle before you[1]
Only to assist and secure the Throne,[2]
Remember, my Lord,
His goodness and justice.

As illustrations of the first stanza, the interlinear commentary (10, 49b) quotes two stories, one from Han China and another from Yi Korea. The first is a story of Chi Pu who as a commander of Hsiang Yü's army several times made serious trouble for Liu Pang. After Hsiang Yü was destroyed, Liu ordered a search made for Chi Pu, offering a reward of a thousand pieces of gold for his capture. He also threatened extermination of the entire family to the third degree of anyone who dared to quarter or hide him. Chi Pu hid at the home of a certain Chou of P'u-yang who shaved his head, put a collar around his neck, and took him to the home of Chu Chia in Lu to sell. Chu Chia, guessing that it was Chi Pu, bought him and set him to work in the fields. He then journeyed to Lo-yang to visit Lord T'eng, the Marquis of Ju-yin. Chu addressed the host, "What great crime is Chi Pu guilty of? Every subject serves his own lord. When Chi Pu served Hsiang Yü, he was merely doing his duty. The emperor has only recently won control of the world. Now if he is to search all over for one man simply because of some private resentment he bears, what an example of pettiness he will be showing to the world." Later Lord T'eng spoke to the emperor about Chi Pu. The emperor pardoned Chi Pu and honored him with the post of palace attendant. *SC*, 100, 0231b-d (Watson, I, 299–301). The second stanza refers to canto 106 which tells how Yi Pang-wŏn forgave and employed the members of Yi Pang-sŏk's party after the princely feud for the throne in 1398.

1.　面折: *SC*, 9, 0038b (*MH*, II, 415); 120, 0262d2–3 (Watson, II, 344): "denounce people to their faces." The term occurs, for example, in *TCTC*, 192 6040 in a conversation between Li Shih-min and Wei Cheng; *Tu-shih kuan-chien*, 3, 29a where the minister Han Hsien defines the function of the minister to be that of "denouncing people to their faces at court." Han committed suicide because Emperor Kuang-wu dismissed him for his admonition; *KRS*, 118, 20a where Cho Chun and Yi Sŏng-gye, in a memorial submitted to King Kong-yang, point out that the wise king must accept such denunciation and honest advice.

2.　For 袞職 the commentary quotes the *Book of Songs*, 260 (Waley, p. 142): "I find none but Chung Shang Fu that could raise it;/ For alas! none helped him./ When the *robe of state* was in holes/ It was he alone mended it" (italics mine). Cf. *Tso chuan*, Duke Hsüan 2 (Legge, V, 290a).

[122]

His nature being one with Heaven,[1]
He knew learning surpassed mere thinking.[2]
Hence he made friends
With learned men.

If a small man wishes to curry favor
And preaches "No leisure for culture,"[3]
Remember, my Lord,
His effort and erudition.

For the first stanza, see canto 80.

1.　性與天合: *The Mean*, 20, 18 (Legge, I, 413; Chan, p. 107).
1.　思不如學: *Analects*, XV, 30 (Waley, p. 199): "The Master said, 'I once spent a whole day without food and a whole night without sleep, in order to meditate. It was no use. It is better to learn.' "
3.　不可令閑: Ch'iu Shih-liang who held the office of commander of the palace guards (*nei-shih chien*; des Rotours, I, 122, 242) advised members of his group how to obtain imperial favor and said, "The Son of Heaven should not be allowed to have leisure; you should always regale his eyes and ears with luxurious pageantry." *HTS*, 207, 4113b-d and *TCTC*, 247, 7985 (843, the sixth month).

[123]

Many slandered him;[1]
An innocent man was about to perish.

He narrowly saved
The man of merit from death.

When slanderers craftily make mischief,[2]
When they grossly exaggerate small mistakes.[3]
Remember, my Lord,
His wisdom and justice.

For how Yi Pang-wŏn ("he" in line 3) saved Cho Chun ("an innocent man" in line 2 and "man of merit" in line 4), see canto 104.

1.   Literally: "slanderous mouths are many," for which see *Book of Songs*, 193 (Karlgren, p. 139): "the slanderous mouths are clamorous."
2.   Literally: "When the artful slanders are excessive," for which see *Book of Songs*, 198 (Karlgren, p. 148): "Pretentious are the great words, they come from the mouths; the artful words are like a reed organ; that shows the thickness of their face."
3.   貝錦: *Book of Songs*, 200 (Karlgren, p. 151): "Rich and ornate is truly this shell-brocade; those slanderers, they are verily too excessive."

[124]

Because his bright nature
Was versed in the teachings of the sage,[1]
He proscribed
Heresy.

If perverse theories[2] of the Western barbarians[3]
Threaten you with sin and allure with bliss,[4]
Remember, my Lord,
His judgment and orthodoxy.

For how Yi Pang-wŏn upheld Confucian orthodoxy and suppressed Buddhism, see canto 107.

1.   In the original, "the orthodox teachings of the Chu and Ssu," names of the two rivers in whose region Confucius taught. *Shang shu*, 3, 8b (Legge, III, 139–140); *SC*, 47, 0163c-d (*MH*, V, 426–427, n.4).
2.   *Mencius*, 3B, 9 (Legge, II, 281).
3.   For 裔 as referring to the *i* and *ti* barbarians see *Fang yen* (*TSCC*), 12, 114. Anti-Buddhists in China and Korea often used the same argument, for which see, for example, Mou Tzu's fourteenth question, in *Taishō Tripiṭaka*, 52, 3c

(*TP*, XIX [1918–1919], 303–304); Fu I's argument, in *JHI*, XII (1951), 42–43, where he labels Buddhism "the barbarian miasma," "the teachings of a crafty wizard of the Western Barbarians," or "of the seductive barbarians," and Han Yü's anti-Buddhist memorial (819). See also Kenneth K. S. Ch'en, "Anti-Buddhist Propaganda during the Nan-ch'ao," *HJAS*, XV (1952), 169–171, 185, and Stefan Balazs, "Der Philosophe Fan Dschen und sein Traktat gegen den Buddhismus," *Sinica*, VII (1932), 220–234.

4. For the same argument during the Nan-ch'ao, see *HJAS*, XV (1952), 181 (*Liang shu*, 48, 1828c).

[125]

A millennium ago,
Heaven chose the north of the Han.
There they accumulated goodness and founded the state.
Oracles foretold: myriad years;[1]
May your sons and grandsons reign unbroken.
But you can secure the dynasty only
When you worship heaven[2] and benefit the people.[3]
Ah, you who will wear the crown, beware,
Could you depend upon your ancestors
When you go hunting by the waters of Lo?

T'ai K'ang 太康[4] of Hsia gave himself up to pleasure, and the people lamented his misgovernment. Moreover, he was excessively fond of hunting, went to the south of the Lo River, and did not return after a hundred days. I 羿,[5] Prince of Ch'iung and a famous archer, had prevented T'ai K'ang from returning to the capital, and seized the throne. *Shang shu*, 3, 11a-b (Legge, III, 156 ff.); *Tso chuan*, Duke Hsiang 4 (Legge, V, 424); *SC*, 2, 0010b (*MH*, I, 166–167); *Chu-shu chi-nien* (*SPPY*), 1, 5a.

1. For 卜年 see *Tso chuan*, Duke Hsüan 3 (Legge, V, 293b).

2. For 敬天 see *Book of Songs*, 254 (Legge, IV, 503; Karlgren, p. 214).

3. Here 勤民 means "to toil for the affairs of people." In *Tso chuan*, Duke Hsi 33 (Legge, V, 225a), however, a quite opposite meaning, "impose toil on the people."

4. *The Rulers of China, 221 B.C.-A.D. 1949* (London, 1957), p. xiii, and Karlgren, "Legends and Cults in Ancient China," *BMFEA*, XVIII (1946), 313, 316, 323, 325.

5. *BMFEA*, XVIII (1946), 267–270, 311, 319; *BD*, 668; Mori Mikisaburō, "Kōgei densetsu kō," *Tōhō gakuhō*, XII (Kyoto, 1941), 71–98; *MH*, I, 167,n.1.

Postscript

The *Sung*[1] in the *Book of Songs* are used to narrate the virtues and accomplishments of former kings in order to register the feelings of commemoration and admiration and thereby to demonstrate the way future generations should take. As we survey the past, [we see] more than one dynasty was established. But none can equal our ancestors who rose royally and succeeded gloriously, who were invested by Heaven,[2] and welcomed by the people. None can equal them in the height of their virtues, in the magnificence of their merits, and in the miraculous wonder of their deeds. How could we not help praising them in songs?

In the year *ŭlch'uk*, Your Majesty's subjects, Fifth State Councillor Kwŏn Che, Seventh State Councillor Chŏng In-ji, and Second Minister of Works An Chi compiled one hundred twenty-five cantos of songs and presented them to Your Majesty. The compilation was based on facts, (1b) and we collected the past events and drew upon contemporary happenings, recounted them, and ended with admonitions to your royal heirs. Your Majesty inspected these songs with approval and granted them the title of *Yongbi ŏch'ŏn ka*. Although the narrated events are recorded in the annals, Your Majesty graciously showed concern for the difficulty the people would encounter in reading and therefore ordered addition of annotations to your subjects, Ch'oe Hang;[3] Collator of the Hall of Worthies (*su Chiphyŏnchŏn kyori*) Pak P'aeng-nyŏn;[4] Auditor of the Bureau of the Royal Household Administration (*su*

Tollyŏngbu p'an'gwan)[5] Kang Hūi-an;[6] Assistant Auditor of the Hall of
Worthies (*Chiphyŏnchŏn pugyori*) Shin Suk-chu;[7] Junior Assistant Auditor
of the Hall of Worthies (*su pugyori*) Yi Hyŏl-lo;[8] Compilers (*such'an*)
Sŏng Sam-mun[9] and Yi Kae;[10] and Assistant Section Chief of the Board
of Personnel (*Yijo chwarang*) Shin Yŏng-son.[11] In ten books we have,
therefore, discussed the cause and effect of the contents in simple terms
(2a), added the pronunciation and meaning of difficult words to make
them easily comprehensible. Sage kings of old times made poetry a
part of education, set it up in rhymes,[12] and used it throughout the
country in order to enlighten the world. These poems still move and
arouse[13] us after thousands of years; how much more will the events of
the present reign move us!

When your heirs read these songs, they will inquire into the origin
of current prosperity, strive to continue unfailingly the glorious line of
our dynasty, and dare not change the norms of preserving the past.
When your subjects read them, they will trace in them the cause of
current peace, will resolve to perpetuate it to posterity, and the irresistible sense of loyalty and admiration will never be ended. The composition of these songs, like the Shang odes of *T'ien tso* and *Hsüan
niao*,[14] should therefore be transmitted (2b) unfailingly to posterity.
Indeed that would be great!

On a certain day in the second month of the twelfth year of the era
cheng-t'ung (1447), *chobong taebu*,[15] Drafter of the Hall of Worthies
(*chiphyŏnchŏn ünggyo*), Drafter in the Office of Royal Decrees (*Yemungwan
ünggyo*),[16] *chi chegyo*,[17] Junior Second Tutor in the Heir Apparent
Office Tutorial (*up'ilsŏn*),[18] and *chwajungho*,[19] Your Majesty's subject
Ch'oe Hang, respectfully writes this postscript.

---

1. The *sung* (hymns), the last section of the *Book of Songs*, comprises forty
poems (nos. 266–305); divided into three groups, thirty-one are attributed to
Chou, four to Lu, and five to Shang.

2. 天授: *SC*, 92, 0222d7 (*HJAS*, X [1947], 211; Watson, I, 230).

3. He passed the examination in 1434. He was one of the compilers of
SjS, Yejong sillok (1470–2), and *KT* (1469). See *Sŏngjong sillok*, 41, 14b–15b;
HMN, 4, 168–169; *YK*, 5, 380–381. For his collected works, *T'aehŏjŏng chip*,
compiled first in 1486, see *CMP*, 247, 16a and *YC*, 8, 201.

4. *SjS*, 4, 14b; *HMN*, 3, 155; *YK*, 4, 310–313.

5. The *Tollyŏngbu* (Council of the Royal Kinsmen) was established in 1414.
Auditor of the Bureau corresponds to rank 5b (*KT*, 1, 7a–8b, 9a; *KTH*, 1,
38–39).

6. He passed the final civil service examination in 1441 and in 1455 went
to Ming. He excelled in verse, painting, and calligraphy. He died November
8, 1464 (*SjS*, 34, 32a).

7. In 1438, he joined the Hall of Worthies and the following year took a

third in the final civil service examination. In 1445, he accompanied the Ming-bound Korean envoy and visited the Chinese philologist Huang Ts'an. In 1460, he commanded the subjugation of the Jürched beyond the Tumen, and in 1462, became Chief State Councillor. He died July 23, 1475 (*Sŏngjong sillok*, 56, 10b-12b). One of the compilers of *SnS* and *TT*, his works include the *Chewang myŏnggam* (*CMP*, 245, 17a), *Haedong cheguk ki* (*CMP*, 246, 26b), and *Pohanjae chip* (*CMP*, 247, 16a). See *HMN*, 4, 160–161; *YK*, 5, 368–372; Yi In-yŏng, "Shin suk-chu ŭi pukchŏng," *Han'guk Manju kwangyesa ŭi yŏn'gu* (1954), pp. 88–128.

8. Or Yi Sŏl-lo; under Tanjong, he was a section chief of the Board of War and was killed October 31, 1453 (*Nosan'gun ilgi*, 8, 9b-10b). See Kim Min-su, *Chuhae Hunmin chŏngŭm* (1957), p. 95.

9. The paragon of loyal subjects in Korean history, he passed the final civil service examination in 1438 and in 1447 took a first in another examination. He was killed by Sejo on July 10, 1456 (*SjS*, 4, 10a-11b, 14b). *HMN*, 3, 155; *YK*, 4, 313–315; *CMP*, 247, 15b.

10. Great-grandson of Yi Saek, he passed the examinations in 1436 and 1447. He was killed the same day as Sŏng Sam-mun. The *Yuksŏnsaeng yugo* (*CMP*, 247, 15a) contains his writings. See also *Hyojong sillok*, 9, 43b-46a; *Sukchong sillok*, 23, 31a, 40b; *Yŏngjo sillok*, 92, 18b-19b.

11. In 1464, he was Third Minister of Personnel (*SjS*, 34, 37b).

12. 聲律: *SC*, 24, 0099b (*MH*, III, 231). See *Wen-hsin tiao-lung*, section 33 (Vincent Yu-chung Shih, *The Literary Mind and the Carving of Dragons* [Taipei, 1970], pp. 257–261).

13. 感發: *Wen hsüan*, 51, 84 (Erwin von Zach, II, 949).

14. *Book of Songs*, 270 (Karlgren, p. 241; Waley, p. 228); 303 (Karlgren, pp. 262–263; Waley, pp. 275–276).

15. Corresponds to rank 4b (*KT*, 1, 6b; *KTH*, 1, 34).

16. Corresponds to rank 4a (*KTH*, 1, 52), concurrently held by officials in ranks 3a to 5a in the Office of Special Counselors.

17. Concurrently held by the Second Counselors (3a) to Assistant Compiler (6b) in the Office of Special Counselors (*HGS*, III, 172, n. 3).

18. *KTH*, 1, 53.

19. The function of the office under Sejong's reign is uncertain. See, however, *KRS*, 76, 4a-b, and *Taedong unbu kunok*, 14, 18b.

Bibliography, Chronology, Glossary, and Index

Bibliography

Bibliographical Note

Principal Editions:

I. The Karam edition in the collection of the late Yi Pyŏng-gi. This volume, containing the first two chapters, is believed to be a partial copy of the first woodblock edition, 550 copies of which were distributed on November 23, 1447 (*SnS*, 118, 2b).

II. The unidentified old block edition. Two copies in the Kyujanggak Collection, Seoul National University Library. One copy lacks the volume containing chapters 5 and 6 because of fire damage; in another copy, part of chapter 6 (cantos 41–49) and Korean verses of cantos 42, 46, 48, and 49 have been lost. Lacunae mar the copy throughout, especially in the Chinese commentary, and, owing probably to the imperfect state of the blocks, the tonemic marks are often missing. Another anomaly is that in the preface and postscript the *Songs* are said to comprise 123, instead of 125, cantos. Cantos 107 and 110 are numbered twice, and cantos 109 and 122 are missing. The size of logographs indicating the canto numbers is larger than that of the original, indicating a later addition. Despite the oddities, the edition is generally considered to be the most important extant, probably dating before the Japanese invasion of 1592–1598.

III. The Sejong Annals edition. The *Sejong Annals* (compiled 1452–1454; printed 1466–1472) contain in chapters 140–145 the manuscript of the Korean verses, repeated four times: 140, 9a-50a; 141, 1a-42a; 142, 1a-144, 30b; and 145, 1a-38b. The annals in the *Chosŏn wangjo sillok* edition (1955–1958) are based on the Mount T'aebaek copy, deposited in the Veritable Record Hall in North Kyŏngsang. The copy which used to be preserved in the Mount Chŏngjok depository on Kanghwa Island is preferred for its accuracy. The Korean verses in the latter, however, contain a number of verbal discrepancies.

IV. The 1612 edition. Two copies in the Kyujanggak Collection; one was originally in the Mount T'aebaek depository (IVa), the other was located in the Mount Odae depository (IVb). This is a close block reprint, based on the second and probably also on the first edition, with corrections of the lacunae in the second. Because of a marked difference between the language of early seventeenth and the original mid-fifteenth century, the editors, in an attempt to adjust to certain linguistic changes, introduced new faults, especially in tonemic marks.

V. The 1659 edition. Two copies in the Kyujanggak Collection. Based on IV, this block edition often repeats the errors contained in IV and introduces new ones as well.

VI. The 1765 edition. A new woodblock edition, based on V, with more irregularity in tonemic marks.

On July 19, 1457 (*SjS*, 8, 10b-11a), Yang Sŏng-ji (d. 1482) presented to the throne an album (or scroll) of illustrations accompanying the *Songs*. It is divided into seven parts: remoteness of ancestry; founding of the dynasty; difficulty of preserving the dynasty; magnificence of virtue; greatness of accomplishments; mandate of Heaven; and allegiance of the people. The divisions show the illustrations represented the thematic design of the *Songs*. The album perished subsequently.

Modern Editions:

VII. The photolithographic edition of 1937–1938. Reproduction of the Mount T'aebaek copy of the 1612 edition (IVa). A curious hybrid resulted from the editors' attempt to add tonemic marks, based on II. As for accuracy of the Korean verses, the collation of variants appended to the edition (twelve pages) is of little value. A printed edition of 1911, based on IV, is incomplete and defective in many respects and is not recommended.

I have used the text of VII (1937–1938) because it is available in major libraries; for the Korean verses, however, I have consulted older editions in Seoul as well as contemporary scholarship, notably that of Yi Ki-mun, with collation of variants and suggested emendations. I have also taken into consideration the glosses provided by the late

Pang Chong-hyŏn (*Ilsa kugŏhak nonjip* [1964], 115–191), Hŏ Ung, Kim Yung-gyŏng (*Han'gyŏl kugŏhak nonjip* [1964], 151–189), and Nam Kwang-u (*Kugŏhak nonmunjip* [1962]). The reader may also consult Yu Ch'ang-don's *Yijoŏ sajŏn* (1964) for Middle Korean vocabulary in the *Songs* and elsewhere (for more bibliographical information, see my *Korean Literature: Topics and Themes* [Tucson, 1965], 35).

Various aspects of fifteenth century Korean have been extensively studied by Korean scholars, whose findings have been helpful in understanding the Korean verses. There are still unsettled topics, such as the honorifics, a subject of intense investigation by Yi Sung-nyŏng (*Kugŏhak nonch'ong* [1960]) and Hŏ Ung (*Chungse kugŏ yŏn'gu* [1963], 8–122).

For the interlinear glosses, the editors of the *Songs* provided the transcription in the new alphabet of a total of 173 items including Korean place names and Jürched and Mongol proper names. Father Henry Serruys writes that experience has told him that Korean transcriptions of foreign words in Chinese logographs presented more difficulty than similar transcriptions in the Chinese sources, for the Koreans tried to transcribe foreign words in their pronunciation of Chinese. Personal and place names of foreign peoples are seldom known in their original form; it is difficult, therefore, to make identifications. At times the Jürched names consist of Mongol and native elements, adding further difficulty to the reconstruction. Variant readings of the same person or place, however, can provide valuable hints as to the origin of the word. Yi Ki-mun argues that the transcriptions help in the study of the phonological system of Middle Korean as well as the Jürched and Mongolian languages of the period (*Tonga munhwa*, II, 226–231).

Of the many background studies in Korean and East Asian history, the pre-1945 studies are dated. Some may still prove to be useful, but I have found little of value for the intellectual and literary aspects of the *Songs*. One interesting exception is Ikeuchi Hiroshi's earlier study, "The Legends of the Four Ancestors of the Yi Dynasty and Their Formation," *TG*, V (1915), 229–266, 328–357, a magnificent demolition work, written to destroy the legends and myths connected with the four ancestors of Yi Sŏng-gye. If Ikeuchi cannot accept the legendary nature of the official accounts, although his title seems to indicate that he did, why did he spill so much ink to disprove the stories? What history, including Japanese, is without myth or legend?

In this study, I have cited the latest works, where they, like the *HGS* series, are equipped with critical apparatus, instead of cluttering the pages with superfluous citations. The third volume (3d ed., 1964) of *HGS*, written by the late Yi Sang-baek, furnishes in its introduction and first chapter an excellent consideration of the period and is equipped with critical apparatus as well as nine maps, six charts, and fifty illustrations. The reader desiring a more comprehensive list may consult a number of annual and specialized bibliographies now available in several languages. In Korean, one may cite the *Korean Periodicals Index*, published annually by the National Assembly Library, and the *Korean National Bibliography*, published by the National Central Library. I have found most useful the *Japanese Studies on Asian History* (four volumes), a catalogue of articles on the history of Asia, written 1880–1962, compiled by the Nippon Gakujutsu Shinkōkai (Tokyo, 1964–1967). Available in English are Korea University's *Bibliography of Korean Studies*, I (1961), II (1965); Okamoto Yoshiji, ed. "Japanese Studies on Korean History since World War II," *Monumenta Serica*, XXII (1965), 470–532, and "Studies on the History of Manchuria and Mongolia in Postwar Japan," *Ibid.*, XIX (1960), 437–479, a useful summary of Japanese scholarship on Manchurian and Mongolian history before and after the fourteenth century.

There is no body of literary criticism on the *Songs*. Standard histories of Korean literature usually contain a few descriptive paragraphs without evaluation or criticism. One attempt was made by Kim Sa-yŏp, in his *Studies in Yi Dynasty Poetry* (1956), 126–193; but he is primarily concerned with the forms of the *Songs* based on syllable count. That he failed in the task he set out to perform has been pointed out by Chŏng Pyŏng-uk, *Kungmunhak san'go* (1960), 255–284.

The first symposium on the *Songs*, held on September 29, 1963, was sponsored by the Institute of Asian Studies of Seoul National University. The topics included the date of composition, the philological and literary value, rhythm and syntax, and the musical aspect of the *Songs*. The proceedings were subsequently published in *Tonga munhwa*, II (1964), 220–261. The musical aspect, like the literary, is probably the least investigated and most difficult to investigate, owing chiefly to the specialized nature of the subject. The student with knowledge of classical East Asian music may wish to read Yi Hye-gu's studies (*CH*, XVI, 111–136; *AY*, VIII, 49–75). Here is a summary of his findings: the score of the *Ch'ihwap'yŏng* was modeled on T'ang music, while that of the *Ch'wip'unghyŏng* was patterned on Korean music. In the *Ch'ihwa-p'yŏng*, the Korean verses of cantos 3–124 are used, in the *Ch'wip'unghyŏng*, only cantos 3–8 are used. The score for the Chinese verses is called *Yŏmillak*. Yi proposes that from a musical viewpoint the *Songs* can be divided into three parts: cantos 1–2; cantos 3–124; and canto 125 (for more on this, see *AHKB*, chapters 2–5 *passim*; *Akchang kasa*, 1a-b; *CMP*, chapter 101; and *Kukcho akchang* [1765 ed.], 2a-34b).

A typical canto comprises: Korean verses, interlinear glosses if place or personal names require them; Chinese verses, followed by glosses indicating the pronunciation, using the *fan-ch'ieh* system, and meaning of logographs; and commentary consisting mainly of quotations from Chinese and Korean sources, with the usual glosses on proper nouns of persons, places, titles, as well as on difficult logographs. At times, a gloss takes the form of quotations; these, in turn, are equipped with another set of glosses to explain difficult points in the quotation. Thus the work is meticulously annotated and cross-referenced.

The order in my translation is as follows: the literal version of the Korean verses, a concise account of the background or circumstances necessary for the understanding of the cryptic, asyndetic verses, followed by citation of the sources, available translations, and standard studies in Western languages. Much commentary is lifted directly from the classics, the official histories of China and Korea, or other standard compilations such as *Tzu-chih t'ung-chien*. To reproduce in translation all quoted commentary, at times irrelevant or out of place, would be redundant especially where translations of the works are available in European languages. Indeed, I had translated the commentary for the first four chapters, but I judged it a distraction from my main purpose and discarded it subsequently. For a convenient listing of existing translations the reader may consult the *Catalogue of Translations from the Chinese Dynastic Histories for the Period 220–960*, ed. Hans H. Frankel (Berkeley, 1957), and other annual or specialized bibliographies.

The exact dates of the composition of the Korean and Chinese verses are not known nor which versions came first. But I should like to point out that the two versions are not always the same. A comparison of parallel lines in the two versions reveals a certain number of divergencies, and I have tried to call attention to them at appropriate places in the footnotes. A tentative list is as follows: 6/1: 2 (canto 6, stanza 1, line 2); 9/9: 2; 12/1: 1; 14/1: 1; 31/2: 3–4; 35/2: 2; 42/2: 2; 52/2:3; 58/2: 2; 95/2: 1; 98/2: 3–4; 118/1: 2; 120/1: 3; 125/7. At times the Korean verses seem to be more compact than the Chinese (for example, cantos 3, 13, 19, 34, 40, 42, 46, 52, 57, 60, 63, 67, 70, 72, 101, 108, and the fifth line of canto 125).

This bibliography contains all the works cited in the notes except for certain items listed under "Abbreviations." Unless otherwise noted, all the Korean books are published in Seoul.

East Asian Sources

An Chŏng-bok 安鼎福. *Tongsa kangmok* 東史綱目. 4 vols. CKK, 1915.

An Kye-hyŏn 安啓賢. "Yi Saek ŭi pulgyogwan" 李穡의佛敎觀, *Cho Myŏng-gi paksa hoegap kinyŏm pulgyosahak nonch'ong* 趙明基博士回甲紀念佛敎史學論叢 (1965), pp. 99–127.

Ch'a Ch'ŏl-lo 車天輅. *Osan sŏllim cho'go* 五山說林草藁. CKK, 1909.

Chan-kuo ts'e 戰國策 (*SPPY*).

Chang Tŏk-sun 張德順. "Minjok sŏrhwa ŭi pullyu wa yŏn'gu" 民族說話의分類와研究, *Tonga munhwa* 東亞文化, V (1966), 29–59.

Chang Yen-yüan 張彥遠, ed. *Li-tai ming-hua chi* 歷代名畫記. Chi-ku-ko 汲古閣 ed.

Ch'ang Chü 常璩. *Hua-yang kuo-chih* 華陽國志 (*SPTK*).

Chao Chin 趙溍. *Yang-o man-pi* 養疴漫筆. Wan-wei-shan-t'ang-pen Shuo-fu 宛委山堂本說郛, 47.

Ch'eng Ta-ch'ang 程大昌. *Yen-fan-lu hsü-chi* 演繁露續集. Hsüeh-chin t'ao-yüan 學津討原 ed.

Chiang Ch'i-ch'ang 蔣騏昌 and Sun Hsing-yen 孫星衍. *Li-ch'üan hsien-chih* 醴泉縣志. 1783 ed.

Ch'ien Ch'ien-i 錢謙益, ed. *Lieh-ch'ao shih-chi* 列朝詩記. Shanghai, 1910.

Chindan hakhoe 震檀學會, ed. *Han'guk sa.* 7 vols. 1959–1965.

Ch'oe Chŏng-yŏ 崔正如. "Sejong taewang ŭi munhwa saŏpchung ak chŏngni ko" 世宗大王의文化事業中樂整理考, *Ch'ŏngju taehakkyo nonmunjip* 淸州大學校論文集, II (1958), 1–54; III (1960), 9–73.

Ch'oe Hang 崔恒 et al. *Yongbi ŏch'ŏn ka* 龍飛御天歌. Kyujanggak series 奎章閣叢書 IV-V. 1937–1938.

Ch'oe Hang et al. *Kyŏngguk taejŏn* 經國大典. 1934 ed.

Ch'oe Sŭng-hŭi 崔承熙. "Chiphyŏnchŏn yŏn'gu" 集賢殿研究. *YH*, XXXII (1966), 1–58; XXXIII (1967), 39–80.

Chŏng To-jŏn 鄭道傳. *Sambong chip* 三峯集. 1961.

Chŏng In-ji 鄭麟趾 et al. *Koryŏ sa* 高麗史 in Tongbanghak yŏn'guso 東方學研究所 ed. 1955–1961.

Chōsen sōtokufu 朝鮮總督府, ed. *Chōsen no fūsui* 朝鮮の風水. 1931.

———, ed. *Chōsen no semboku to yogen* 朝鮮の占卜と予言. 1933.

———, ed. *Chōsen kinseki sōran* 朝鮮金石總覽. 2 vols. 1919.

Chou i 周易 (*SPTK*).

Chou li 周禮 (*SPTK*).

Chu Chu-yü 朱鑄禹, ed. *T'ang-Sung hua-chia jen-ming tz'u-tien* 唐宋畫家人名辭典. Peking, 1958.

Chi Huang 嵆璜, ed. *Hsü T'ung-tien* 續通典 in *Chiu-t'ung* 九通.

Chu I-tsun 朱彝尊, comp. *Ming shih-ts'ung* 明詩綜. Preface dated 1705.

Chu-shu chi-nien 竹書紀年 (*SPPY*).

Ch'u Tz'u 楚辭 (*SPTK*).

Erh-shih-wu shih 二十五史. K'ai-ming ed.

Erh-ya 爾雅 (*SPPY*).

Fan Tsu-yü 范祖禹. *T'ang chien* 唐鑑 (*TSCC*).

Fang I-chih 方以智. *T'ung-ya* 通雅. Fou-shan-tz'u-ts'ang-hsien 浮山此藏軒 ed.

Han Fei Tzu 韓非子 (*SPPY*).

Han U-gŭn 韓㳍劤. "Yŏmal Sŏnch'o ŭi pulgyo chŏngch'aek" 麗末鮮初의佛教政策, *STN*, VI (1957), 3–80.

Han Ying 韓嬰. *Han-shih wai-chuan* 韓詩外傳 (*SPTK*).

Han'guk kojŏn kugyŏk wiwŏnhoe 韓國古典國譯委員會, ed. *Kugyŏk Taejŏn hoet'ong* 國譯大典會通. 1960.

Hattori Katsuhiko 服部克彦. *Hoku-Gi Rakuyō no shakai to bunka* 北魏洛陽の社會と文化, Tokyo, 1965–1968.

Hŏ Sŏn-do 許善道. "Yŏmal Sŏnch'o hwagi ŭi chŏllae wa paltal" 麗末鮮初火器의傳來와發達 *YH*, XXIV (1964), 1–60; XXV (1964), 39–98; XXVI (1965), 141–165.

Hŏ Ung 許雄. *Yongbi ŏch'ŏn ka*. 1956.

Hong Yang-ho 洪良浩. *Puksae kiryak* 北塞記略. CKK, 1911.

Hori Toshikazu 堀敏一. "Kō Sō no hanran" 黃巢の叛亂, *Tōyō bunka kenkyūjo kiyō* 東洋文化研究所紀要, XIII (1957), 1–108.

Hsiao ching 孝經 (*SPIK*).

Hsiung K'e 熊克. *Chung-hsing hsiao-chi* 中興小紀 (*TSCC*).

Hsü Meng-hsin 徐夢莘. *San-ch'ao pei-meng hui-pien* 三朝北盟會編. 1878 ed.

Hsü Shen 許慎. *Shuo-wen chieh-tzu* 說文解字 (*TSCC*).

Hsü Shih-kuei 徐式圭. *Chung-kuo ta-she k'ao* 中國大赦考. Shanghai, 1934.

Hsün Ch'ing 荀卿. *Hsün Tzu* 荀子 (*SPTK*).

Hu Yin 胡寅. *Tu-shih kuan-chien* 讀史管見. Preface dated 1635.

Hwang Ch'ŏl-san 黃哲山. "Sipsa segi mal sibo segi chungyŏp ŭi Pukkwan kaech'ŏk kwa kaech'ŏngmin e kwanhan yŏn'gu" 十四世紀末十五世紀中葉의北關開拓과開拓民에干한研究, *Yŏksa nonmunjip* 歷史論文集, I (1957), 77–138.

Ikeuchi Hiroshi 池內宏. "Sensho no tōhokukyō to Joshin tono kankei" 鮮初の東北境と女眞との關係, *MCRKH*, II (1916), 203–323; IV (1918), 299–365; V (1918), 299–366; VII (1920), 219–254.

——— *Mansenshi kenkyū* 滿鮮史研究. 5 vols. Tokyo, 1943–1963.

Imumura Tomo 今村鞆. *Ōgi, Hidarinawa, Dakyū, Hisago* 扇, 左繩, 打毬, 匏. 1937.

Iryŏn 一然. *Samguk yusa* 三國遺史. Ch'oe Nam-sŏn 崔南善 ed. 1954.

Izushi Yoshihiko 出石誠彦. *Shina shinwa densetsu no kenkyū* 支那神話傳說の研究. Tokyo, 1943.

Kang Sin-hang 姜信沆. "Yongbi ŏch'ŏn ka ŭi p'yŏnch'an kyŏngwi e taehayŏ" 龍飛御天歌의編纂經緯에対하여, *Mullidae hakpo* 文理大學報, VI (1958), 147–151.

——— "Yijo ch'ogi yŏkhakcha e kwanhan yŏn'gu" 李朝初期譯學者에關한研究, *CH*, XXIX–XXX (1966), 325–338.

Kawachi Yoshihiro 河內良好. "Richō shoki no Joshinjin jiei" 李朝初期の女眞人侍衞, *CG*, XIV (1959), 381–422.

Kim Al-lo 金安老. *Yongch'ŏn tamjŏk ki* 龍泉談寂記. CKK, 1910.

Kim Ch'ŏl-chun 金哲埈. "Husamguk sidae ŭi chibae seryŏk ŭi sŏngkyŏk e taehayŏ" 後三國時代의 支配勢力의 性格에 對하여, *Yi Sang-baek paksa hoegap kinyŏm nonch'ong* 李相佰博士回甲紀念論叢 (1964), pp. 251-267.

Kim Kŭn-su 金根洙. "Yongbi ŏch'ŏn ka ŭi yŏn'gu sŏsŏl" 龍飛御天歌의 研究 序說 in *Karam Yi Pyŏng-gi paksa songsu nonmunjip* 嘉藍李秉岐博士頌壽論 文集 (1966), pp. 63-89.

Kim Min-su 金敏洙. *Chuhae Hunmin chŏngŭm* 註解訓民正音. 1957.

Kim Pu-sik 金富軾. *Samguk sagi* 三國史記. 1928 ed.

Kim Sang-gi 金庠基. "Koryŏ T'aejo ŭi kŏn'guk kwa kyŏngnyun" 高麗太祖의 建國과 經綸, *KSC*, I (1959), 69-91; II (1959), 45-83.

——— "Yŏjin kwangye ŭi simal kwa Yun Kwan ŭi pukchŏng" 女眞關係의 始末과尹瓘의北征, *KSC*, IV (1959), 65-205.

——— "Yi Ikchae ŭi chae-Wŏn saengae e taehayŏ" 李益齋의 在元生涯에 對 하여, *Taedong munhwa yŏn'gu* 大東文化研究, I (1963), 219-244.

Kim Yong-guk 金龍國. "Seoul chŏndo e tonggi wa chŏnmal" 서울奠都의動機 와顛末 *Hyangt'o Seoul*, I (1957), 50-99.

——— "Seoul kŏnsŏl ŭi kongroja" 서울建設의 功勞者, *Hyangt'o Seoul*, IV (1958), 82-147.

Kim Yŏng-yun 金榮胤, ed. *Han'guk sŏhwa inmyŏng sasŏ* 韓國書畫人名辭書. 1959.

Kim Yuk 金堉. *Haedong myŏngsin nok* 海東名臣錄. CKK, 1914.

Kim Yun-gyŏng 金允經. *Han'gyŏl kugŏhak nonjip* 한결 國語學論集. 1964.

Ko Hung 葛弘. *Pao-p'u Tzu* 抱朴子 (*SPPY*).

Kobata Jun 小葉田淳. "Ryūkyū Chōsen no kankei ni tsuite" 琉球朝鮮の關係 について, *Tayama Hōnan kakō kinen rombunshū* 田山方南華甲紀念論文集 (Tokyo, 1963), pp. 235-255.

Ku Tsu-yü 顧祖禹. *Tu-shih fang-yü chi-yao* 讀史方輿紀要 (*WYWK*).

Kubo Noritada 窪德忠. *Kōshin shinkō* 庚申信仰. Tokyo, 1956.

——— *Kōshin shinkō no kenkyū* 庚申信仰の研究. Tokyo, 1961.

Kuksa p'yŏnch'an wiwŏnhoe 國史編纂委員會, ed. *Chosŏn wangjo sillok* 朝鮮王 朝實錄. 48 vols. 1955-1958.

K'ung Fu 孔鮒. *K'ung-ts'ung Tzu* 孔叢子 in *Chi-hai* 指海.

Kwŏn Kŭn 權近. *Yangch'on chip* 陽村集. 1937 ed.

Kwŏn Mun-hae 權文海. *Taedong unbu kunok* 大東韻府群王 in *Kukko ch'ongsŏ* 國故叢書, I. 1950.

Kwŏn Pyŏl 權鼈. *Haedong chamnok* 海東雜錄 .CKK, 1910.

Li chi 禮記 (*SPPY*).

Li Fang 李昉 *et al. T'ai-p'ing kuang-chi* 太平廣記. Peking, 1959.

Li Shang-yin 李商隱. *Li Yi-shan shih-chi* 李義山詩集 (*SPTK*).

Li Tao 李燾. *Hsü Tzu-chih t'ung-chien ch'ang-pien* 續資治通鑑長編. Chekiang shu-chü 浙江書局 ed., 1881.

Li Te-yü 李德裕. *Li Wei-kung hui-ch'ang i-p'in-chi* 李衞公會昌一品集 (*TSCC*).

Li Tung-yang 李東陽 *et al. Ta-Ming hui-tien* 大明會典. 1587 ed.

Li Wei-kung wen-tui 李衞公問對 in *Wu-ching ch'i-shu* 武經七書. Taipei, 1965.

Liu An 劉安. *Huai-nan Tzu* 淮南子 (*SPTK*).

Liu Shao 劉韶. *Jen-wu chih* 人物志. Peking, 1958.

Liu Tsung-yüan 柳宗元. *Tseng-kuang chu-shih yin-p'ien T'ang Liu hsien-sheng chi* 增廣註釋音辯唐柳先生集 (*SPTK*).

Lo Hsiang-lin 羅香林. "T'ang-tai po-lo ch'iu-hsi k'ao" 唐代波羅毬戲考, *Shih-hsüeh chüan-k'an* 史學專刊, I, 1 (1941), 129-142.

Lü Pu-wei 呂不韋. *Lü-shih ch'un-ch'iu* 呂氏春秋 (*SPPY*).

Ma Tuan-lin 馬端臨. *Wen-hsien t'ung-k'ao* 文獻通考 in *Chiu-t'ung* 九通.

Maema Kyōsaku 前間恭作. "Kaikyō kyūden hu" 開京宮殿簿, *CG*, XXVI (1963), 1-55.

Majikina Ankō 眞境名安興 and Shimakura Ryūji 島倉龍治. *Okinawa issennen shi* 沖繩一千年史. Tokyo, 1952.

Mano Senryū 間野潛龍. "Kōbuchō no Tosatsuin ni tsuite" 洪武朝の都察院について, *Ōtani daigaku kenkyū nempō* 大谷大學研究年報, XIII (1960), 209-236.

Marugame Kinsaku 丸龜金作. "Kōrai to Kittan Joshin tono bōeki kankei" 高麗と契丹女眞との貿易關係, *Rekishigaku kenkyū* 歷史學研究, V (1935), 57-82.

Min Chu-myŏn 閔周冕. *Tonggyŏng chapki* 東京雜記. CKK, 1910.

Min Hyŏn-gu 閔賢九. "Shin Ton ŭi chipkwŏn kwa kŭ chŏngch'ijŏk sŏngkyŏk" 辛旽의 執權과 그 政治的 性格 *YH*, XXXVIII (1968), 46-88; XL (1968), 53-119.

Min Pyŏng-ha 閔丙河. "Yŏmal Sŏnch'o ŭi Sŏmna kuk kwaŭi kwan'gye" 麗末鮮初의 暹羅國과의 關係, *Kukche munje* 國際問題, II (1965), 3-17.

Mishina Shōei 三品彰英. "Kodai Chōsen ni okeru ōja shutsugen no shinwa to girei ni tusite" 古代朝鮮における王者出現の神話と儀禮について, *Shirin* 史林, XVIII (1933), 67-96, 328-372, 453-480.

Miyakawa Hisayuki 宮川尚志. *Rikuchōshi kenkyū* 六朝史研究. Tokyo, 1956.

Mo Ti 墨翟. *Mo Tzu* 墨子 (*SPPY*).

Mori Katsumi 森克己. "Nis-Sō-Rai kōshō to wakō no hassei" 日宋麗交涉と倭寇の發生 in *Ishida hakushi shōju kinen Tōyōshi ronsō* 石田博士頌壽紀念東洋史論叢 (Tokyo, 1965), pp. 483-497.

Mori Mikisaburō 森三樹三郎. "Kōgei densetsu kō" 后羿傳說考, *Tōhō gakuhō* 東方學報, XII (Kyoto, 1941), 71-98.

Moriya Mitsuo 守屋美都雄. "Furō" 父老 *Tōyōshi kenkyū* 東洋史研究, XIV (1955), 43-60.

Naitō Shumpo 內藤雋輔. *Chōsenshi kenkyū* 朝鮮史研究. Kyoto, 1961.

Nam Kwang-u 南廣祐. *Kugŏhak nonmunjip* 國語學論文集. 1962.

Nam Su-mun 南秀文 et al. *Koryŏ sa chŏryo*. KKH, 1960.

Nan-hua chen-ching 南華眞經 (*SPTK*).

No Sa-sin 盧思愼 et al. *Sinjŭng Tongguk yŏji sŭngnam*. KKH, 1958.

Ŏ Suk-kwŏn 魚叔權. *P'aegwan chapki* 稗官雜記. CKK, 1909.

—— *Kosa ch'waryo* 攷事撮要. 1941.

Ou-yang Hsiu 歐陽脩. *Ou-yang wen-chung-kung ch'üan-chi* 歐陽文忠公全集 (*SPPY*).

Pak Han-sŏl 朴漢卨. "Wang Kŏn segye ŭi muyŏk hwaltong ŭi taehayŏ" 王建世系에 貿易活動에 對하여, *Sach'ong* 史叢, X (1965), 255-287.

Pak Si-hyŏng. *Kwanggaet'owang nŭngbi* 廣開土王陵碑. P'yongyang, 1966.

Pak Yong-dae 朴容大 et al. *Chŭngbo munhŏn pigo*. 3 vols. KKH, 1957.

Pang Chong-hyŏn 方鐘鉉. *Ilsa kugŏhak nonmunjip* 一簑國語學論文集. 1963.

Pi Yüan 畢沅, ed. *Hsü Tzu-chih t'ung-chien* 續資治通鑑. Peking, 1957.

—— *Chiao-cheng San-fu huang-t'u* 校正三輔皇圖. Shanghai, 1958.

Pyŏn T'ae-sŏp 邊大燮. "Koryŏ Anch'alsa ko" 高麗按察使考, *YH*, XL (1968), 1–52.

Seoul City History Compilation Committee, ed. *Han'gyŏng singnyak* 漢京識略. 1956.

———, ed. *Kunggwŏl chi* 宮闕志. 1957.

———, ed. *Tongguk yŏji pigo* 東國輿地備攷. 1957.

———, ed. *Sŏul yaksa* 서울略史. 1963.

Shang shu 尙書 (*SPTK*).

Shin Ki-sŏk 申基碩. "Koryŏ malgi ŭi tae-Il kwan'gye" 高麗末期의 對日關係, *Sahoe kwahak* 社會科學, I (1957), 3–31.

Shin Sŏk-ho 申奭鎬. "Yŏmal Sŏnch'o ŭi woegu wa kŭ taech'aek" 麗末鮮初의 倭寇와 그 對策, *KSC*, III (1959), 103–164.

Shin Suk-chu 申叔舟. *Pohanjae chip* 保閑齋集. 1937 ed.

Sŏ Kŏ-jŏng 徐居正. *P'irwŏn chapki* 筆苑雜記. CKK, 1909.

——— *Tongmun sŏn* 東文選. 3 vols. 1966–1967.

Sŏ Kŏ-jŏng *et al. Tongguk t'onggam* 東國通鑑. 3 vols. CKK, 1912.

Sŏng Hyŏn 成俔. *Akhak kwebŏm* 樂學軌範. 1930 ed.

——— *Yongjae ch'onghwa* 慵齋叢話. CKK, 1909.

Sonoda Kazuki 園田一龜. *Mindai Kenshū Jochokushi kenkyū* 明代建州女直史研究. 2 vols. Tokyo, 1948–1953.

Ssu-ma Kuang 司馬光. *Tzu-chih t'ung-chien* 資治通鑑. Peking, 1957.

Su Shih 蘇軾. *Tung-p'o hsü-chi* 東坡續集 (*SPPY*).

Su T'ien-chüeh 蘇天爵. *Kuo-ch'ao wen-lei* 國朝文類 (*SPTK*).

Sudō Yoshiyuki 周藤吉之. *Chūgoku dochi seidoshi kenkyū* 中國土地制度史研究. Tokyo, 1954.

Suematsu Yasukazu 末松保和. *Seikyū shisō* 靑丘史草. 2 vols. Tokyo, 1965–1966.

Sun Wu 孫武. *Sun Tzu* 孫子 (*SPPY*).

Taedong munhwa yŏn'guwŏn 大東文化研究院, ed. *Yŏgye myŏnghyŏn chip* 麗季名賢集. 1959.

Tagawa Kōzō 田川孝三. *Richō kōnōsei no kenkyū* 李朝貢納制の研究. Tokyo, 1964.

Tamura Hiroyuki 田村洋幸. "Sensho wakō no keifu ni tsuite" 鮮初倭寇の系譜について, *CG*, XXIII (1962), 37–72.

Teng Shih 鄧實, comp. *T'ang-ch'ao ming-hua lu* 唐朝名畫錄 in *Mei-shu ts'ung-shu* 美術叢書, 2.

Ting Tu 丁度 *et al. Chi yün* 集韻 (*WYWK*).

Ts'ang Li-ho 臧勵龢 *et al. Chung-kuo ku-chin ti-ming ta-tz'u-tien* 中國古今地名大辭典. Shanghai, 1930.

Ts'ao Chi 曹植. *Ts'ao Tzu-chien chi* 曹子建集 (*SPPY*).

Ts'ao Yin 曹寅 *et al. Ch'üan T'ang shih* 全唐詩. Peking, 1960.

Wada Hironori 和田博德. "Tokokkon to Namboku ryōchō tono kankei ni tsuite" 吐谷渾と南北兩朝との關係について, *Shigaku*, XXV (1951), 80–104.

Wada Sei 和田清. *Tōashi kenkyū: Manshūhen* 東亞史研究. 滿州篇. Tokyo, 1955.

——— *Tōashi kenkyū: Mōko hen* 東亞史研究. 蒙古篇. Tokyo, 1959.

Wang Chin-jo 王欽若 *et al. Ts'e-fu yüan-kuei* 冊府元龜. Chung-hua shu-chü 中華書局 ed. Hong Kong, 1960.

Wang Ming-ch'ing 王明清. *Hui-chu lu* 揮麈錄 in *Shuo fu*, 39.

Wang Ch'ung 王充. *Lun heng* 論衡 (*SPPY*).

Wang P'u 王溥. *T'ang hui-yao* 唐會要 (*TSCC*).

—— *Wu-tai hui-yao* 五代會要 (*WYWK*).

Wang Su 王肅. *K'ung-tzu chia-yü* 孔子家語 (*SPPY*).

Wang Tang 王讜. *T'ang yü-lin* 唐語林. Wu-ying-tien chu-chen-pan ch'üan-shu
武英殿聚珍版全書 ed.

Yang Hsiung 揚雄. *Fang yen* 方言 (*TSCC*).

—— *Yang Tzu* 揚子 (*SPPY*).

Yang Yin-shen 楊蔭深. "T'ang-tai te yu-i" 唐代的游藝, *Hsüeh-lin* 學林, IV
(1941), 129-142.

Yeh Lung-li 葉隆禮. *Ch'i-tan kuo-chih* 契丹國志. Sao-yeh shan-fang 掃葉山房 ed.

Yen Chih-t'ui 顏之推. *Yen-shih chia-hsün* 顏氏家訓 (*SPTK*).

Yi Chung-hwa 李重華. *Chosŏn ŭi kungsul* 朝鮮의 弓術. 1929.

Yi Hong-jik 李弘稙. "Samguk sagi Koguryŏin chŏn ŭi kŏmt'o" 三國史記高句
麗人傳의 檢討, *Sach'ong*, IV (1959), 1-18.

Yi Hyŏn-hŭi 李炫熙. "Chosŏn chŏn'gi yain ŭi yugyŏng yuhoech'aek ko" 朝鮮
前期野人의 誘京綏懷策攷, *Ilsan Kim Tu-jong paksa hŭisu kinyŏm nonmunjip*
一山金斗鍾博士稀壽紀念論文集 (1966), pp. 63-121.

Yi Ik 李瀷. *Sŏngho sasŏl* 星湖僿說. 2 vols. 1967.

Yi In-yŏng 李仁榮. *Han'guk Manju kwan'gyesa ŭi yŏn'gu* 韓國滿洲關係史의 研究.
1954.

Yi Ki-mun 李基文. "Yongbi ŏch'ŏn ka kungmun kasa ŭi chemunje" 龍飛御天
歌國文歌詞의諸問題, *AY*, V (1962), 87-128.

Yi Kŭng-ik 李肯翊. *Yŏllyŏsil kisul* 燃藜室記述. 3 vols. CKK, 1912-1924.

—— *Yŏllyŏsil kisul pyŏlchip* 燃藜室記述別集. 3 vols. CKK, 1913.

Yi Kyu-gyŏng 李圭景. *Oju yŏnmun changjŏn san'go* 五洲衍文長箋散藁. KKH,
1959.

Yi Pyŏng-do 李丙燾. *Koryŏ sidae ŭi yŏn'gu* 高麗時代의 研究. 1954.

—— *HGS*, I (1959), II (1962).

Yi Sang-baek 李相佰. *Han'guk munhwasa yŏn'gu non'go* 韓國文化史研究論攷.
1954.

—— *Yijo kŏn'guk ŭi yŏn'gu* 李朝建國의 研究. 1954.

—— *HGS*, III (1964).

Yi Sung-nyŏng 李崇寧. "Sejong ŭi ŏnŏ chŏngch'aek e kwanhan yŏn'gu" 世宗
의言語政策에關한研究, *AY*, I (1958), 29-81.

—— *Kugŏhak nonch'ong* 國語學論叢. 1966.

Yi Yong-jung. *Husamguk ŭi ch'urhyŏn kwa Koryŏ e ŭihan kŭŭi t'ongil* 後三國의出現
과高麗에依한그의統一. P'yongyang, 1963.

Ying Shao 應劭. *Feng-su t'ung-i* 風俗通義 (*SPPY*).

Yü Hsin 庾信. *Yü Tzu-shan chi* 庾子山集 (*SPTK*).

Yü-wen Mou-chao 宇文懋昭. *Ta-Chin kuo-chih* 大金國志. Kuo-hsüeh chi-pen
ta'ung-shu 國學基本叢書 ed.

Yüan-ch'ao pi-shih 元朝秘史 (*TSCC*).

Western Sources

Anderson, J. K. *Military Theory and Practice in the Age of Xenophon*. Berkeley: University of California Press, 1970.

Apollonius Rhodius. *Argonautica*. Tr. R. C. Seaton. LCL, 1955.

Aristophanes. *The Birds*. Tr. Dudley Fitts. New York: Harcourt, Brace and World, 1957.

Armstrong, W. A. "The Elizabethan Conception of the Tyrant," *The Review of English Studies*, XXII (1946), 161–181.

Ascham, Roger. *The Schoolmaster*. Ed. Lawrence V. Ryan. Ithaca: Cornell University Press, 1967.

Auden, W. H. *The Enchafèd Flood or The Romantic Iconography of the Sea*. New York: Random House, 1950.

Augustine, St. *Basic Writings of Saint Augustine*. Ed. Whitney J. Oates. 2 vols. New York: Random House, 1948.

Aurelius, Antoninus Marcus. *The Communings with Himself of Marcus Aurelius Antoninus*. Tr. C. R. Haines. LCL, 1961.

Bachelard, Gaston. *L'Eau et les Rêves: Essai sur l'Imagination de la Matière*. Paris: J. Corti, 1942.

Balazs, Stefan. "Der Philosophe Fan Dschen und sein Traktat gegen den Buddhismus," *Sinica*, VII (1932), 220–234.

Ball, Albert. "Charles II: Dryden's Christian Hero," *MP*, LIX (1961), 25–35.

Barnard, Mary. *The Mythmakers*. Athens, Ohio: Ohio University Press, 1966.

Bell, Richard. *The Qur'ān*. 2 vols. Edinburgh: T. and T. Clark, 1937.

—— *Introduction to the Qur'ān*. Edinburgh: Edinburgh University Press, 1953.

Belpaire, Bruno. *Le Catéchisme philosophique de Yang-Hiong-Tse*. Bruxelles: Editions de l'Occident, 1960.

Benjamin, Edwin B. "Fame, Poetry, and the Order of History in the Literature of the English Renaissance," *Studies in the Renaissance*, VI (1959), 64–84.

Berman, Ronald, ed. *Twentieth Century Interpretations of Henry V*. Englewood Cliffs: Prentice-Hall, 1968.

Berthoff, Ann E. *The Resolved Soul: A Study of Marvell's Major Poems*. Princeton: Princeton University Press, 1970.

Bevington, David. *Tudor Drama and Politics: A Critical Approach to Topical Meaning*. Cambridge, Mass.: Harvard University Press, 1968.

Bielenstein, Hans. "The Restoration of the Han Dynasty, with the Prolegomena on the Historiography of the Hou Han Shu," *BMFEA*, XXVI (1954), 1–209.

—— "The Restoration of the Han Dynasty: II. The Civil War," *BMFEA*, XXXI (1959), 1–287.

Bingham, Woodbridge. *The Founding of the T'ang Dynasty*. Baltimore: Waverly Press, 1941.

—— "The Rise of Li in a Ballad Prophecy," *JAOS*, LXI (1941), 272–280.

—— "Li Shih-min's Coup in A.D. 626. I: The Climax of Princely Rivalry," *JAOS*, LXX (1950), 89–95.

Biot, Edouard. *Le Tcheou-li ou Rites des Tcheou*. Peking: Wentienko, 1930.

Boccaccio. *The Fates of Illustrious Men*. Tr. Louis B. Hall. New York: Frederick Unger, 1965.

Bodde, Derk, and Clarence Morris. *Law in Imperial China*. Cambridge, Mass.: Harvard University Press, 1967.

Bodin, Jean. *The Six Bookes of a Commonweale*. Tr. Richard Knolles. Ed. Kenneth Douglas McRae. Cambridge, Mass.: Harvard University Press, 1962.

Bodkin, Maud. *Studies of Type-images in Poetry, Religion and Philosophy*. Oxford: Oxford University Press, 1951.

Bonaparte, Marie. *Myths of War*. Tr. John Rodker. London: Imago Publishing Company, 1947.

Boodberg, Peter A. "Marginalia to the Histories of the Northern Dynasties," *HJAS*, IV (1939), 230–283.

Born, Lester K. "The Perfect Prince: A Study in the 13th and 14th Century Ideals," *Speculum*, III (1938), 470–504.

Bowra, C. M. *From Virgil to Milton*. London: Macmillan, 1945.

——— *Heroic Poetry*. London: Macmillan, 1952.

——— "The Meaning of a Heroic Age," in *The Language and Background of Homer*. Ed. G. S. Kirk. Cambridge: W. Heffer, 1964. Pp. 34–41.

Bullough, Geoffrey. "The Uses of History," in *Shakespeare's World*. London: Edward Arnold, 1964. Pp. 96–115.

Burne, A. H. "The Battle of Agincourt, October 25, 1415," *History Today*, VI (1956), 598–605.

Bush, Geoffrey. *Shakespeare and the Natural Condition*. Cambridge, Mass.: Harvard University Press, 1956.

Cameron, Alan. *Claudian: Poetry and Propaganda at the Court of Honorius*. Oxford: Clarendon Press, 1970.

Cammann, Schuyler. *China's Dragon Robes*. New York: Ronald Press, 1952.

Campbell, Joseph. *The Hero with a Thousand Faces*. New York: Pantheon Books, 1961.

Campbell, Lily B. *Shakespeare's "Histories": Mirror of Elizabethan Policy*. San Marino: The Huntington Library, 1947.

———, ed. *The Mirror for Magistrates*. Cambridge: Cambridge University Press, 1938.

——— *Shakespeare's Tragic Heroes: Slaves of Passion*. New York: Barnes & Noble, 1961.

Carroll, Thomas D. *Account of the T'u-yü-hun in the History of the Chin Dynasty*. Berkeley: University of California Press, 1953.

Chadwick, Hector M. *The Heroic Age*. Cambridge: Cambridge University Press, 1912.

Chan, Wing-tsit. *A Source Book in Chinese Philosophy*. Princeton: Princeton University Press, 1963.

Charney, Maurice. *Shakespeare's Roman Plays*. Cambridge, Mass.: Harvard University Press, 1961.

Chavannes, Édouard. "Le Cycle turc des douze Animaux," *TP*, VII (1906), 51–122.

——— *Documents sur les Tou-kiue Occidentaux* Paris: Adrien-Maisonneuve, n.d.

——— *Les Mémoires historiques de Se-ma Ts'ien*. 5 vols. Paris: E. Leroux, 1895–1905.

——— "Le Dieu du Sol dans la Chine antique," in *Le T'ai Chan*. Paris: E. Leroux, 1910. Pp. 437–525.

Chen, Shih-Hsiang. "The *Shih-ching*: Its Generic Significance in Cninese Literary History and Poetics," *Bulletin of the Institute of History and Philology of Academia Sinica*, XXXIX (1969), 371–414.

Ch'en, Kenneth K. S. "Anti-Buddhist Propaganda during the Nan-ch'ao," *HJAS*, XV (1952), 166–192.

———— "A Study of the Svāgata Story in the Divyāvadāna in Its Sanskrit, Pali, Tibetan, and Chinese Versions," *HJAS*, IX (1947), 207–314.

———— "Economic Background of the Hui-ch'ang Persecution," *HJAS*, XIX (1956), 67–105.

———— *Buddhism in China: A Historical Survey*. Princeton: Princeton University Press, 1964.

Chernaik, Warren L. *The Poetry of Limitation: A Study of Edmund Waller*. New Haven: Yale University Press, 1968.

Chew, Samuel C. *The Virtues Reconciled: An Iconographic Study*. Toronto: University of Toronto Press, 1947.

Ch'ü, T'ung-tsu. *Law and Society in Traditional China*. Paris: Mouton, 1961.

Claudian. Tr. Maurice Platnauer. 2 vols. LCL, 1922.

Cleaves, F. W. "The Biography of Bayan of The Bārin in the *Yüan shih*," *HJAS*, XIX (1956), 185–303.

Clemen, Wolfgang. *The Development of Shakespeare's Imagery*. London: Methuen, 1951.

Clemens, Robert J. "Pen and Sword in Renaissance Emblem Literature," *MLQ*, V (1944), 131–141.

———— "Princes and Literature: A Theme of Renaissance Emblem Books," *MLQ*, XVI (1955), 114–123.

Clodd, Edward. *Magic in Names*. London: Chapman and Hall, 1920.

Cook, Albert C. *The Classic Line: A Study in Epic Poetry*. Bloomington: Indiana University Press, 1966.

Cormican, L. A. "Medieval Idiom in Shakespeare," *Scrutiny*, XVII (1950), 186–202, 298–317.

Couvreur, Séraphin. *Li Ki ou Mémoires sur les Bienséances et les Cérémonies*. Paris: Cathasia, 1950.

Cullman, Oscar. *Christ and Time*. Philadelphia: Westminster Press, 1950.

Curtius, Ernst Robert. *European Literature and the Latin Middle Ages*. Tr. Willard R. Trask. London: Routledge and Kegan Paul. 1953.

Danby, John F. *Poets on Fortune's Hill*. London: Faber and Faber, 1952.

———— *Shakespeare's Doctrine of Nature: A Study of King Lear*. London: Faber and Faber, 1951.

De Bary, William Theodore *et al.* *Sources of Chinese Tradition*. New York: Columbia University Press, 1960.

De Francis, John. "Biography of the Marquis of Huai-yin," *HJAS*, X (1947), 179–215.

Demiéville, Paul. "Enigmes taoistes," in *Silver Jubilee Volume of the Zinbun Kagaku Kenkyusho*. Kyoto, 1954. Pp. 54–60.

Des Rotours, Robert. *Traité des Fonctionnaires et Traité de l'armée*. 2 vols. Leiden: E. J. Brill, 1947–1948.

Dio Chrysostom. "On Kingship." Tr. J. W. Cohoon. LCL, 1949.

Dodd, Eric R. *The Greeks and the Irrational*. Berkeley: University of California Press, 1951.

Driver, Tom F. *The Sense of History in Greek and Shakespearean Drama*. New York: Columbia University Press, 1960.

Dryden, John. *The Poems of John Dryden*. Ed. James Kinsley.II. Oxford: Clarendon Press, 1958.

────── *The Works of John Dryden*. Ed. E. N. Hooker *et al.* Vol. I. Berkeley: University of California Press, 1961.

Dschi, Hian-lin. "Indian Physiognomical Characteristics in the Official Annals for the Three Kingdoms, the Chin Dynasty and the Southern and Northern Dynasties," *Studia Serica*, VIII (Chengtu, 1949), 96–102.

Dubs, Homer H. *The Works of Hsüntze*. London: Arthur Probsthain, 1928.

────── *The History of the Former Han Dynasty*. 3 vols. Baltimore: Waverly Press, 1938–1955.

────── "The Archaic Royal Jou Religion," *TP*, XLVI (1958), 217–259.

Dudley, Edmund. *The Tree of Commonwealth*. Ed. D. M. Brodie. Cambridge: Cambridge University Press, 1948.

Eberhard, Wolfram. "Some Cultural Traits of the Sha-t'o Turks," *Oriental Art*, I (1948), 50–55.

Eliade, Mircea. *Images and Symbols: Studies in Religious Symbolism*. Tr. Philip Mairet. New York: Sheed and Ward, 1961.

Elliott, George R. *Dramatic Providence in Macbeth: A Study of Shakespeare's Tragic Theme of Humanity and Grace*. Princeton: Princeton University Press, 1958.

Elyot, Thomas. *The Governour*. London: Everyman's Library ed., 1937.

Erasmus. *The Education of a Christian Prince*. Tr. Lester K. Born. New York: Columbia University Press, 1936.

Fairbank, John K., ed. *The Chinese World Order: Traditional China's Foreign Relations*. Cambridge, Mass.: Harvard University Press, 1968.

Fang, Achilles, tr. *The Chronicle of the Three Kingdoms (220–265)*. 2 vols. Cambridge, Mass.: Harvard University Press, 1952–1965.

Farnham, Willard. *The Medieval Heritage of Elizabethan Tragedy*. Berkeley: University of California Press, 1936.

Ferguson, John C. "The Six Horses at the Tomb of the Emperor T'ai-tsung of the T'ang Dynasty," *Eastern Art*, III (1931), 61–71.

Fernald, Helen E. "In Defense of the Horses of T'ang T'ai-tsung," *The University Museum Bulletin* (Philadelphia, 1942), 18–28.

Fisher, Peter F. "The Trials of the Epic Hero in Beowulf," *PMLA*, LXXIII (1958), 171–183.

Fitzgerald, C. P. *Son of Heaven: A Biography of Li Shih-min, Founder of the T'ang Dynasty*. Cambridge: Cambridge University Press, 1933.

Fitzgerald, Robert. "Generation of Leaves," *Perspectives USA*, no. 8 (1954), 68–85.

Fletcher, Angus. *Allegory: The Theory of a Symbolic Mode*. Ithaca: Cornell University Press, 1964.

Franke, Herbert. "Could the Mongol Emperors Read and Write Chinese?" *AM*, III (1952), 28–41.

Franke, Otto. *Geschichte des chinesischen Reiches*. 5 vols. Berlin and Leipzig; Walter de Gruyter, 1930–1952.

Franke, Wolfgang. "Addenda and Corrigenda to Pokotilov's History of the Eastern Mongols during the Ming Dynasty," *Studia Serica*, VII (1949), 1–95.

Frye, Northrop. *The Educated Imagination*. Bloomington: Indiana University Press, 1965.

———— *A Natural Perspective*. New York: Columbia University Press, 1965.

———— *Fools of Time: Studies in Shakespearean Tragedy*. Toronto: University of Toronto Press, 1967.

Frye, Roland M. *Shakespeare and Christian Doctrine*. Princeton: Princeton University Press, 1963.

Gaster, Theodor H. *The Oldest Stories in the World*. New York: Viking Press, 1952.

Geoffrey of Monmouth. *The History of the Kings of Britain*. Tr. Lewis Thorpe. Harmondsworth: Penguin Books, 1966.

Gilbert, Lucien. *Dictionnaire historique et géographique de la Mandchourie*. Hong Kong, 1934.

Giles, Herbert A. *A Chinese Biographical Dictionary*. Shanghai: Kelly & Walsh, 1898.

Goddard, Harold C. *The Meaning of Shakespeare*. Chicago: University of Chicago Press, 1966.

Goodrich, L. Carrington. "Polo in Ancient China," *Horse and Horseman*, XIX (1938), 27, 38–39.

———— and Feng Chia-sheng. "The Early Development of Firearms in China," *Isis*, CIV (1946), 114–123, 250–251.

Graves, Robert. *The White Goddess: A Historical Grammer of Poetic Myth*. New York: Farrar, Straus and Giroux, 1966.

Greene, Thomas M. *The Descent from Heaven*. New Haven: Yale University Press, 1963.

Gregory of Tours. *The History of the Franks*. Tr. O. M. Dalton. 2 vols. Oxford: Clarendon Press, 1927.

Griffith, Samuel B. *Sun Tzu: The Art of War*. Oxford: Clarendon Press, 1963.

Grousset, René. *L'Empire des Steppes*. Paris: Payot, 1939.

Haenisch, Erich. *Die geheime Geschichte der Mongolen*. Leipzig: Otto Harrassowitz, 1948.

Haguenauer, Charles. "Relations du Royaume des Ryukyu avec les Pays des Mers du Sud et la Corée," *Bulletin de la Maison Franco-Japonaise*, III (Tokyo, 1931), 4–16.

Hainsworth, J. B. *The Flexibility of the Homeric Formula*. Oxford: Clarendon Press, 1968.

Hambis, Louis. "Notes sur l'Histoire de Corée à l'Époque Mongole,' *TP*, XLV (1957), 151–218.

Hardison, O. B., Jr. *The Enduring Monument: A Study of the Idea of Praise in Renaissance Literary Theory and Practice*. Chapel Hill: University of North Carolina Press, 1962.

Hastings, James, ed. *Encyclopaedia of Religion and Ethics*. 13 vols. New York: Scribner, 1917–1955.

Havelock, Eric A. *Preface to Plato*. Cambridge, Mass.: Harvard University Press, 1963.

Hawkes, David. *Ch'u Tz'u: The Songs of the South*. Oxford: Clarendon Press, 1959.

Hexter, J. H. "The Education of the Aristocracy in the Renaissance," *The Journal of Modern History*, XXII (1950), 1–20.

Hightower, James R. *Han Shih Wai Chuan*. Cambridge, Mass.: Harvard University Press, 1952.

Ho, Ping-ti. "Loyang, A.D. 495–534: A Study of Physical and Socio-economic Planning of a Metropolitan Area," *HJAS*, XXVI (1966), 52–101.

Hooke, Samuel H., ed. *Myth, Ritual and Kingship*. Oxford: Clarendon Press, 1958.

Hooker, Edward N. "The Purpose of Dryden's *Annus Mirabilis*," *HLQ*, X (1946–1947), 49–67.

Horace. *The Odes and Epodes*. Tr. C. E. Bennett. LCL, 1964.

Hornsby, Roger A. *Patterns of Action in the Aeneid: An Interpretation of Vergil's Epic Similes*. Iowa City: University of Iowa Press, 1970.

Howard, Donald R. *The Three Temptations: Medieval Man in Search of the World*. Princeton: Princeton University Press, 1966.

Howell, James. *Dendrologia, Dodona's Grove, or the Vocall Forrest*. 2d ed. London, 1644.

Hucker, Charles O. "Governmental Organization of the Ming Dynasty," *HJAS*, XXI (1958), 1–66.

——— *The Censorial System in Ming China*. Stanford: Stanford University Press, 1966.

Hughes, E. R. *Two Chinese Poets: Vignettes of Han Life and Thoughts*. Princeton: Princeton University Press, 1960.

Huizinga, Johan. *Homo Ludens: A Study of the Play-Element in Culture*. Boston: Beacon Press, 1964.

Hyman, Stanley. "Myth, Ritual, and Nonsense," *Kenyon Review*, XI (1949), 455–475.

Ikeuchi, Hiroshi. "A Study of the Su-Shen," *MTB*, V (1930), 97–163.

Isocrates. "To Nicocles." Tr. George Norlin. I (LCL, 1961), 57–59.

Jaeger, Werner. *Paideia: The Ideals of Greek Culture*. Tr. Gilbert Highet. Vol. I. New York: Oxford University Press, 1939.

James, Edwin O. *The Tree of Life: An Archaeological Study*. Leiden: E. J. Brill, 1966.

John of Salisbury. *The Statesman's Book of John of Salisbury*. Tr. John Dickinson. New York: A. A. Knopf, 1927.

Jorgensen, Paul A. *Shakespeare's Military World*. Berkeley: University of California Press, 1956.

——— *Lear's Self-Discovery*. Berkeley: University of California Press, 1967.

Kantorowicz, Ernst H. *The King's Two Bodies: A Study in Medieval Political Theory*. Princeton: Princeton University Press, 1957.

Karlgren, Bernhard. "Some Fecundity Symbols in Ancient China," *BMFEA*, II (1930), 1–54.

——— "Some Weapons and Tools of the Yin Dynasty," *BMFEA*, XVII (1946), 101–144.

——— "Glosses on the Kuo feng Odes," *BMFEA*, XIV (1942), 71–247.

——— "Glosses on the Siao ya Odes," *BMFEA*, XVI (1944), 25–169.

———— "Glosses on the Ta ya and Sung Odes," *BMFEA*, XVII (1945), 1–198.

———— "Legends and Cults in Ancient China," *BMFEA*, XVIII (1946), 199–365.

———— "Some Sacrifices in Chou China," *BMFEA*, XL (1968), 1–31.

———— *The Book of Odes*. Stockholm: The Museum of Far Eastern Antiquities, 1950.

———— *The Book of Documents*. Stockholm: The Museum of Far Eastern Antiquities, 1950.

Kirk, Geoffrey S. *Heraclitus: The Cosmic Fragments*. Cambridge: Cambridge University Press, 1954.

———— *The Songs of Homer*. Cambridge: Cambridge University Press, 1960.

Klapp, Orrin E. "The Folk Hero," *Journal of American Folklore*, LXII, no. 243 (1949), 17–25.

Kluckhohn, Clyde. "Myths and Rituals," *Harvard Theological Review*, XXXV (1942), 45–79.

Knight, G. Wilson. *Myth and Miracle*. London: Ed. J. Burrow, n.d.

———— *The Imperial Theme*. London: Oxford University Press, 1931.

Knights, L. C. *Further Explorations*. Stanford: Stanford University Press, 1965.

Knox, Bernard M. W. "The Serpent and the Flame," *American Journal of Philology*, LXXI (1950), 279–300.

Koht, Halvdan. "The Dawn of Nationalism in Europe," *American Historical Review*, LII (1947), 265–280.

Kracke, Edward A. *Civil Service in Early Sung China*. Cambridge, Mass.: Harvard University Press, 1953.

Krappe, A. H. "The Dream of Charlemagne in the Chanson de Roland," *PMLA*, XXXVI (1921), 131–141.

Lattimore, Richmond. *The Iliad of Homer*. Chicago: University of Chicago Press, 1951.

———— *The Odyssey of Homer*. New York: Harper and Row, 1965.

Laufer, Bertold. "Walrus and Narwhal Ivory," *TP*, XVII (1916), 348–389.

———— "The Early History of Polo," *Polo: The Magazine for Horsemen*, VII (1932), 13–14, 43–44.

Lee, Peter H. *Anthology of Korean Poetry*. New York: John Day, 1964.

———— *Korean Literature: Topics and Themes*. Tucson: University of Arizona Press, 1965.

———— *Lives of Eminent Korean Monks*. Cambridge, Mass.: Harvard University Press, 1969.

Leech, Clifford. *Shakespeare's Tragedies*. New York: Oxford University Press, 1950.

Leeuw, Geradus van der. "Primordial Time and Final Time," in *Man and Time*, Papers from the Eranos Yearbooks, III (New York: Pantheon Books, 1957), 324–350.

Legge, James. *Li Ki*, in *Sacred Books of the East*, XXVII-XXVIII. Oxford: Clarendon Press, 1926.

———— *The Chinese Classics*. 5 vols. Hong Kong: Hong Kong University Press, 1960.

Lehmberg, Stanford E. *Sir Thomas Elyot: Tudor Humanist*. Austin: University of Texas Press, 1960.

Levin, Harry. *The Overreacher: A Study of Christopher Marlowe.* Cambridge, Mass.: Harvard University Press, 1952.

—— *Refractions.* New York: Oxford University Press, 1966.

Levenson, Joseph R., and Franz Schurmann. *China: An Interpretive History.* Berkeley: University of California Press, 1969.

Levy, Gertrude R. *The Sword from the Rock.* London: Faber and Faber, 1953.

Levy, Howard S. *Biography of Huang Ch'ao.* Berkeley: University of California Press, 1955.

—— *Harem Favorites of an Illustrious Celestial.* Taichung, 1958.

Liu, Mau-tsai. *Die chinesischen Nachrichten zur Geschichte der Ost-Turken (T'u-küe).* 2 vols. Wiesbaden: Otto Harrassowitz, 1958.

Lord, Albert B. *The Singer of Tales.* Cambridge, Mass.: Harvard University Press, 1960.

Lord, George de F. "The Odyssey and the Western World," *SR,* LXII (1954), 406–427.

Lucan. *Pharsalia.* Tr. Nicholas Rowe, in *The Works of the English Poets.* Ed. Alexander Chalmers. Vol. XX. London, 1810.

Lucian. "Slander." Tr. A. M. Harmon. LCL, 1953.

Margouliès, Georges. *Le "Fou" dans le Wen-siuan.* Paris: P. Geuthner, 1926.

Martin, Samuel E. *et al. A Korean-English Dictionary.* New Haven: Yale University Press, 1967.

Marvell, Andrew. *The Poems and Letters of Andrew Marvell.* Ed. H. M. Margoliouth. 3 vols. Oxford: Clarendon Press, 1927.

Maspero, Henri. "Légendes mythologiques dans le Chou king," *JA,* CCIV (1924), 1–100.

Mather, Richard B. "Wang Chin's 'Dhuta Temple Stele Inscription' as an Example of Buddhist Parallel Prose," *JAOS,* LXXXIII (1963), 338–359.

Matthews, Honor. *Character and Symbol in Shakespeare's Plays.* Cambridge: Cambridge University Press, 1962.

Mazzeo, Joseph A. *Renaissance and Seventeenth-Century Studies.* New York: Columbia University Press, 1964.

Miner, Earl. *Dryden's Poetry.* Bloomington: Indiana University Press, 1967.

—— "Formulas: Japanese and Western Evidence Compared," *Proceedings of the Vth Congress of the International Comparative Literature Association.* Amsterdam: Swets and Zeitlinger, 1969. Pp. 405–417.

Morris, William. Tr. *Volsunga Saga.* New York: Collier, 1962.

Mote, F. W. *The Poet Kao Ch'i, 1336–1374.* Princeton: Princeton University Press, 1962.

Moule, A. C. *The Rulers of China, 221 B.C. to A.D. 1949.* London: Routledge and Kegan Paul, 1957.

Murray, Henry A. "Definitions of Myth," in *The Making of Myth.* Ed. Richard M. Ohmann. New York: Putnam, 1962. Pp. 7–37.

Needham, Joseph. *Science and Civilization in China.* Vol. II. Cambridge: Cambridge University Press, 1956.

—— "Time and Knowledge in China and the West," in *The Voices of Time.* Ed. J. T. Fraser. London: Penguin Press, 1968. Pp. 92–135.

Nivison, David S., and Arthur F. Wright, ed. *Confucianism in Action.* Stanford: Stanford University Press, 1959.

Notopoulos, James A. "Coutinuity and Interconnexion in Homerical Oral Composition," *Transactions and Proceedings of the American Philological Association*, LXXXII (1951), 81–101.

O'Brien, Gordon W. *Renaissance Poetics and the Problem of Power*. Chicago: Institute of Elizabethan Studies, 1956.

OHehir, Brendan. *Expans'd Hieroglyphicks: A Critical Edition of Sir John Denham's Coopers Hill*. Berkeley: University of California Press, 1969.

Olschki, Leonardo. *Machiavelli the Scientist*. Berkeley: The Gillick Press, 1945.

Otis, Brooks. *Virgil: A Study in Civilized Poetry*. Oxford: Clarendon Press, 1963.

Paige, Denys L. *History and the Homeric Iliad*. Berkeley: University of California Press, 1959.

Parry, Milman. "Studies in the Epic Technique of Oral Verse Making. I. Homer and Homeric Style," *Harvard Studies in Classical Philology*, XLI (1930), 73–147.

Patrides, C. A. *The Phoenix and the Ladder: The Rise and Decline of the Christian View of History*. Berkeley: University of California Press, 1964.

Pausanius. *Description of Greece*. Tr. W. H. S. Jones. LCL, 1965.

Pelliot, Paul. "Meou-tseu ou les Doutes levés," *TP*, XIX (1918–1919), 255–433.

——— and Louis Hambis. *Histoire des Campagnes de Genghis Khan, Cheng-wou ts'in-tscheng lou*. Vol. I, Leiden: E. J. Brill, 1951.

Phillips, James E., Jr. *The State in Shakespeare's Greek and Roman Plays*. New York: Columbia University Press, 1940.

Plato. *The Republic of Plato*. Tr. Francis M. Cornford. New York: Oxford University Press, 1959.

——— *The Collected Dialogues of Plato*. Ed. Edith Hamilton and Huntington Cairns. New York: Pantheon Books, 1961.

Plutarch. "Brotherly Love." Tr. W. C. Helmbold, in *Moralia*, VI. LCL, 1957.

——— "To an Uneducated Ruler." Tr. Harold N. Fowler, in *Moralia*, XI. LCL, 1949.

——— "How to Tell a Flatterer from a Friend." Tr. Frank C. Babbitt, in *Moralia*, Vol. I. LCL, 1960.

Poppe, Nicholas. "Der Parallelismus in der epischen Dichtung der Mongolen," *Ural-Altaische Jahrbücher*, XXX (1958), 195–228.

Pöschl, Viktor. *Die Dichtkunst Virgils*. Tr. Gerda Seligson. Ann Arbor: University of Michigan Press, 1962.

Post, Gaines. "Two Notes on Nationalism in the Middle Ages," *Traditio*, IX (1953), 281–320.

Průšek, Jaroslaw. "History and Epics in China and in the West," *Diogenes*, XLII (1963), 20–43.

Pulleyblank, E. G. "The Chinese Names for the Turks," *JAOS*, LXXXV (1965), 121–125.

Putnam, Michael C. J. *The Poetry of the Aeneid*. Cambridge, Mass.: Harvard University Press, 1965.

Quinn, Kenneth. *Virgil's Aeneid*. Ann Arbor: University of Michigan Press, 1968.

Quinn, Michael. "Providence in Shakespeare's Yorkist Plays," *Shakespeare Quarterly*, X (1959), 45–52.

Rachewiltz, Igor de. "Yeh-lü Ch'u-ts'ai (1189–1243): Buddhist Idealist and Confucian Statesman," in *Confucian Personalities*. Ed. Arthur F. Wright and Denis Twitchett. Stanford: Stanford University Press, 1962. Pp. 189–216.

Ransom, John C. "On Shakespeare's Language," *SR*, LV (1947), 181–198.

Redford, Donald B. "The Literary Motif of the Exposed Child," *Numen*, XIV (1967), 209–228.

Reese, Max M. *The Cease of Majesty: A Study of Shakespeare's History Plays*. London: Edward Arnold, 1961.

Ribner, Irving. *The English History Play in the Age of Shakespeare*. Princeton: Princeton University Press, 1957.

────── *Patterns in Shakespearean Tragedy*. London: Methuen, 1960.

Ricks, Christopher. *Milton's Grand Style*. London: Clarendon Press, 1963.

Rodwell, J. M. *The Koran*. London: J. M. Dent, 1950.

Rogers, Michael C. "Studies in Korean History," *TP*, LXVII (1959), 30–62.

────── *The Chronicle of Fu Chien: A Case of Exemplary History*. Berkeley: University of California Press, 1968.

Roper, Alan. *Dryden's Poetic Kingdoms*. New York: Barnes & Noble, 1965.

Ross, Malcolm M. *Poetry and Dogma: The Transfiguration of Eucharistic Symbols in Seventeenth Century English Poetry*. New Brunswick: Rutgers University Press, 1954.

Ryan, Lawrence V. *Roger Ascham*. Stanford: Stanford University Press, 1963.

Sayers, Dorothy L. *The Song of Roland*. Harmondsworth: Penguin Books, 1957.

Schirmer, Walter F. *John Lydgate: A Study in the Culture of the XVth Century*. London: Methuen, 1961.

Seneca. *The Stoic Philosophy of Seneca*. Tr. Moses Hadas. Gloucester, Mass.: P. Smith, 1965.

Serruys, Henry. *Sino-Jürčed Relations during the Yung-lo Period (1403–1424)*. Wiesbaden: Otto Harrassowitz, 1955.

────── "Mongols Ennobled during the Early Ming," *HJAS*, XXII (1959), 209–260.

────── *The Mongols in China during the Hung-wu Period (1356–1398)*, in *MCB*, XI (1959).

Shakespeare, William. *The Complete Plays and Poems*. Ed. William A. Neilson and Charles J. Hill. Boston: Houghton Mifflin, 1942.

────── *Coriolanus* Ed. Harry Levin. Baltimore: Penguin Books, 1956.

────── *Cymbeline* Ed. J. M. Nosworthy. London: Methuen, 1955.

────── *King Henry V*. Ed. J. Dover Wilson. Cambridge: Cambridge University Press, 1955.

Shih, Vincent Yu-chung. *The Literary Mind and the Carving of Dragons*. Taipei: Chung Hua Book Company, 1970.

Shiratori, Kurakichi. "The Legend of King Tung-ming, the Founder of the Fu-yu-kuo," *MTB*, X (1938), 1–39.

Shryock, John K. *The Study of Human Abilities*. New Haven: American Oriental Society, 1937.

Shumaker, Wayne. *Unpremeditated Verse: Feelings and Perception in Paradise Lost*. Princeton: Princeton University Press, 1967.

Smith, D. Howard. "Divine Kingship in Ancient China," *Numen*, IV (1957), 171–203.

———— "Chinese Religion in the Shang Dynasty," *Numen*, VIII (1961), 142–150.

Soper, Alexander C. "T'ang Ch'ao Ming Hua Lu," *Artibus Asiae*, XXI (1958), 204–253.

Spurgeon, Caroline F. E. *Shakespeare's Imagery and What It Tells Us*. Cambridge: Cambridge University Press, 1952.

Stadter, Philip A. *Plutarch's Historical Methods: An Analysis of the Mulierum Virtutes*. Cambridge, Mass.: Harvard University Press, 1965.

Stanford, W. Bedell. *Greek Metaphor: Studies in Theory and Practice*. Oxford: Blackwell, 1936.

Steadman, John M. *Milton and the Renaissance Hero*. Oxford: Clarendon Press, 1967.

Steinmeyer, Karl-Josef. *Untersuchungen zur allegorischen Bedeutung der Träume im altfranzösischen Rolandslied*. Munich: M. Hueber, 1963.

Swedenberg, Hugh, T., Jr. *The Theory of the Epic in England 1650–1800*. Berkeley: University of California Press, 1944.

Tatlock, J. S. P. *The Legendary History of Britain*. Berkeley: University of California Press, 1950.

Taylor, Archer. "The Biographical Pattern in Traditional Narrative," *Journal of Indiana University Folklore Institute*, I (1964), 114–129.

Tchang, Mathias. *Synchronismes chinois*. Variétés Sinologiques, 24. Shanghai, 1905.

Thomas Aquinas, St. *Selected Political Writings*. Tr. J. G. Dawson. Oxford: Blackwell, 1948.

Tillyard, E. M. W. *The Elizabethan World Picture*. New York: Macmillan, 1944.

Tjan, Tjoe Som. *Po Hu T'ung: The Comprehensive Discussions in the White Tiger Hall*. 2 vols. Leiden: E. J. Brill, 1949–1952.

Toliver, Harold E. *Marvell's Ironic Vision*. New Haven: Yale University Press, 1965.

Tolkien, J. R. R. "Beowulf: The Monsters and Critics," in *An Anthology of Beowulf Criticism*. Ed. Lewis E. Nicholson. Notre Dame: University of Notre Dame Press, 1963. Pp. 51–103.

Traversi, D. A. *An Approach to Shakespeare*. Garden City: Doubleday, 1956.

Virgil. *The Aeneid of Virgil*. Tr. C. Day Lewis. New York: Oxford University Press, 1952.

———— *Virgil's Georgics*. Tr. Smith Palmer Bovie. Chicago: University of Chicago Press, 1956.

Von Zach, Erwin. *Die chinesische Anthologie*. 2 vols. Cambridge, Mass.: Harvard University Press, 1958.

Vries, Jan de. *Heroic Song and Heroic Legend*. London: Oxford University Press, 1963.

Wada, Sei. "The Northeast Asian Tribes in the T'ang Period," *MTB*, XII (1958), 1–25.

Waley, Arthur. "T'ai-tsung's Six Chargers," *Burlington Magazine*, XLIII, 246 (1923), 117–118.

———— *Three Ways of Thought in Ancient China*. London: George Allen and Unwin, 1946.

———— *The Analects of Confucius*. London: George Allen and Unwin, 1949.

————— *The Poetry and Career of Li Po.* London: George Allen and Unwin, 1950.

————— *The Book of Songs.* London: George Allen and Unwin, 1954.

Wallace, John M. "Marvell's Horatian Ode," *PMLA*, LXXVII (1962), 33–45.

————— "Andrew Marvell and Cromwell's Kingship: 'The First Anniversary,'" *ELH*, XXX (1963), 209–235.

————— "Dryden and History: A Problem in Allegorical Reading," *ELH*, XXXVI (1969), 265–290.

————— *Destiny His Choice: The Loyalism of Andrew Marvell.* Cambridge: Cambridge University Press, 1968.

Wang, Gung-wu. *The Structure of Power in North China during the Five Dynasties.* Kuala Lumpur: University of Malaya Press, 1963.

————— "Feng Tao: An Essay in Confucian Loyalty," in *Confucian Personalities.* Ed. Arthur F. Wright and Denis Twitchett. Stanford: Stanford University Press, 1962. Pp. 123–145.

Wang, Ling. "On the Invention and Use of Gunpowder and Firearms in China," *Isis*, CIX-CX (1947), 160–178.

Wasserman, Earl R. "Nature Moralized: The Divine Analogy in the 18th Century," *ELH*, XX (1953), 39–76.

————— *The Subtler Language: Critical Readings of Neoclassical and Romantic Poems.* Baltimore: Johns Hopkins University Press, 1959.

Watson, Burton. *Ssu-ma Ch'ien: Grand Historian of China.* New York: Columbia University Press, 1958.

————— *Records of the Grand Historian of China.* 2 vols. New York: Columbia University Press, 1961.

————— *Mo Tzu: Basic Writings.* New York: Columbia University Press, 1963.

————— *Hsün Tzu: Basic Writings.* New York: Columbia University Press, 1963.

————— *Han Fei Tzu: Basic Writings.* New York: Columbia University Press, 1964.

————— *Chuang Tzu: Basic Writings.* New York: Columbia University Press, 1964.

Webb, Herschel. *The Japanese Imperial Institution in the Tokugawa Period.* New York: Columbia University Press, 1968.

Wedgewood, Cicely V. *Poetry and Politics under the Stuarts.* Cambridge: Cambridge University Press, 1961.

Werner, E. T. C. *A Dictionary of Chinese Mythology.* Shanghai: Kelly and Walsh, 1932.

Wheelwright, Philip. *The Burning Fountain: A Study in the Language of Symbolism.* Bloomington: Indiana University Press, 1954.

————— *Heraclitus.* Princeton: Princeton University Press, 1959.

————— *Metaphor and Reality.* Bloomington: Indiana University Press, 1962.

Whitaker, K. P. K. "Tsaur Jyr's 'Luohshern fuh,'" *AM*, IV (1954), 36–56.

Whitman, Cedric H. *Homer and the Heroic Tradition.* Cambridge, Mass.: Harvard University Press, 1958.

Wilhelm, Hellmut. "A Note on the Migration of the Uriangkhai," in *Festschrift für Nikolaus Poppe zum 60. Geburtstag am 8. August 1957.* Ed. Julius von Farkas and Omeljan Pritsak. Wiesbaden, 1957. Pp. 172–176.

————— *Change: Eight Lectures on the I Ching.* New York: Pantheon Books, 1960.

Wilhelm, Richard. *The I Ching or Book of Changes.* 2 vols. New York: Pantheon Books, 1950.

Willis, William H. "Athletic Contests in the Epic," *Transactions and Proceedings of the American Philological Association,* LXXII (1941), 392–417.

Wilson, Elkin C. *England's Eliza.* Cambridge, Mass.: Harvard University Press, 1939.

Wittfogel, Karl A., and Feng Chia-sheng. *History of Chinese Society, Liao (907–1125).* New York: Macmillan, 1949.

Wright, Arthur F. "Fu I and the Rejection of Buddhism," *JHI,* XII (1951), 33–47.

——— "Sui Yang-ti: Personality and Stereotype," in *The Confucian Persuasion.* Ed. Arthur F. Wright. Stanford: Stanford University Press, 1960. Pp. 47–76.

Wright Celeste T. "The Elizabethan Female Worthies," *Studies in Philology,* XLIII (1946), 628–643.

Yang, Lien-sheng. *Studies in Chinese Institutional History.* Cambridge, Mass.: Harvard University Press, 1961.

Yates, Frances A. "Queen Elizabeth as Astraea," *Journal of the Warburg and Courtauld Institutes,* X (1947), 27–82.

Yen, Chun-chiang. "The *Chüeh-tuan* as Word, Art Motif and Legend," *JAOS,* LXXXIX (1969), 578–599.

Chronology

1274	April 18	Yi An-sa (Mokcho) d.
1335	October 27	Yi Sŏng-gye b.
1342	August 25	Yi Ch'un (Tojo) d.
1355		Yi Cha-ch'un (Hwanjo) arrives at the Koryŏ capital.
1356		Chu Yüan-chang seizes Nanking.
1360	June	Yi Cha-ch'un d. (b. 1315).
1361	November	Yi Sŏng-gye becomes Kŭmowi sang-janggun and high myriarch of the North-east and subjugates the rebellion of the myriarch Pak Ŭi.
1362	February	Korean army regains the capital from the Red Turbans.
	July-August	Yi Sŏng-gye defeats the forces of the Mongol general Naɣaču.
1364	February	Koryŏ defector Ch'oe Yu routed by Yi Sŏng-gye.
	March	Yi Sŏng-gye defeats the forces of Samsŏn and Samgye.
1367	June 13	Yi Pang-wŏn (fifth son of Yi Sŏng-gye; T'aejong) b.
1368	January 23	Chu Yüan-chang becomes emperor.
1369	June 8	Use of the Mongol reign-title discontinued.

1370	January	Yi Sŏng-gye becomes General of the Northeast and *chi munhasŏng sa*.
	February-November	Yi Sŏng-gye subjugates Tongnyŏngbu.
	July 31	The Ming reign-title, Hung-wu, adopted.
1371	August	Yi Sŏng-gye repulses the Japanese pirates along the Yesŏng River.
	August 21	Evil monk Shin Ton executed.
1373		Korean envoys sent to China, unable to proceed beyond Liaotung, return; envoys sent earlier return with the emperor's edicts. (*MSL*, 72, 1330; 76, 1397, 1400–1; *KRS*, 44, 4a).
1374	April-July	Korean mission sent to request a land route and one annual tribute mission (*MSL*, 89, 1574–5); the Ming Secretariat suggests a sea route and a triennial mission (*KRS*, 44, 27a ff.).
	October 19	King Kongmin murdered by eunuchs.
	October 30	Shin U ascends the throne.
	December 28	The Ming envoy Ts'ai Pin murdered by the Korean escort.
1375		Imprisonment of Korean envoy sent to report the death of King Kongmin.
1377	June-July	Yi Sŏng-gye crushes the Japanese pirates below Mount Chii.
1378	April-May	Yi Sŏng-gye, together with Ch'oe Yŏng, wipes out Japanese pirates in Sūngch'ŏnbu.
	September	Ming reign-title adopted again (temporarily discontinued since March 1377).
1380		One Korean envoy, upon reaching Liaotung, is transported to Nanking (*MSL*, 131, 2090); another is turned back at Liaotung (140, 2210; see also 145, 2274).
	August-October	Victory at Mount Hwang.
1383	August-September	Yi Sŏng-gye repels the Jürched chief Hupa-tu.
1385	January-February	Yi Sŏng-gye becomes *munha ch'ansŏngsa*.
	October-November	Yi Sŏng-gye destroys the Japanese pirates in the northeast.
	September	Ming envoy brings the posthumous title for King Kongmin (*MSL*, 174, 2645, 2649).

1387	July	Korean envoys rejected at Liaotung border according to Ming emperor's order.
1388	February-March	Yi Sŏng-gye becomes *su munha sijung*.
	May 7	Yi Sŏng-gye advances four objections to the planned invasion of Liaotung.
	May 27	Use of Ming reign-title discontinued; adopted again July 7.
	June 11	Korean army crosses the Yalu and is stationed on Wihwa Island.
	June 26	Yi Sŏng-gye's army refuses to advance and marches back, reaching the Koryŏ capital on July 6.
	July 12	Shin Ch'ang enthroned; Shin U deposed and banished (both U and Ch'ang executed on December 31, 1389).
1389	December 2	Kongyang enthroned.
1390–1391		Yi Sŏng-gye's party enforces land reform.
1392	April 26	Chŏng Mong-ju assassinated.
	July 31	Kongyang deposed and banished.
	August 5	Yi Sŏng-gye ascends the throne as first monarch of the Yi dynasty.
	August 6	Cho Pan sent to the Ming to notify the dynastic change (*MSL*, 221, 3233–5).
	August 26	Yi Pang-wŏn sent to the northeast to report the founding of the Yi dynasty to the spirits of the four royal ancestors.
	September 7	Liu-ch'iu envoys arrive. Yi Pang-sŏk, eighth and youngest son of Yi Sŏng-gye, becomes heir apparent.
	September 27	Liu-ch'iu and Siam envoys arrive.
1393	March 8	Chŏng Ch'ong ordered to draft the inscription on monument to Hwanjo.
	March 27	New name for Korea, Chosŏn, adopted (*MSL*, 223, 3267).
	July 2	Ming envoy arrives with a message accusing Korea of enticing the Jürched.
	July 10	Nam Chae sent to exculpate Korea of false charges.
1394	May 25	Ming envoy Huang Yung-ch'i offers sacrifices to the mountains and rivers of Korea. The prayer contains erroneous information concerning the genealogy of

		Yi Sŏng-gye. Despite repeated requests for correction, the error was not rectified until 1588 (*Sŏnjo sillok*, 22, 11b-12a).
	June 28	Chŏng To-jŏn presents the *Chosŏn kyŏngguk chŏn*.
	July-December	Yi Pang-wŏn goes to Nanking; Ming founder orders the opening of the Liaotung border blocked for more than a year (*MSL*, 234, 3422–3).
	November	Capital transferred to Hanyang (later Hansŏng).
1395		Ming founder finds in diplomatic documents disrespectful phrases and orders the extradition of their writers (*MSL*, 243, 3533–4; 244, 3538).
1396	August	Kwŏn Kŭn and Ha Yun go to Nanking and succeed in convincing the Ming emperor of Korea's sincerity; on October 4 they have an audience with the emperor (*MSL*, 247, 3583, 3585).
1397		Cho Chun compiles the *Kyŏngje yukchŏn*.
1398	October 6	Yi Pang-wŏn initiates a coup, kills Chŏng To-jŏn and Nam Ŭn, and instigates the murder of his half-brothers, Pang-bŏm and Pang-sŏk.
	October 14	Yi Pang-gwa (Chŏngjong) becomes the second ruler.
1400	February 22	Yi Pang-gan and Yi Pang-wŏn fight for the throne; the former defeated and banished.
	April-May	Yi Pang-wŏn orders disbanding of private soldiers.
	November 28	Yi Pang-wŏn ascends the throne as the third monarch.
1401	July	Ming envoy brings the investiture and the golden seal.
	May-June	Yi Pang-wŏn orders the printing of paper money.
	August 27	*Sinmun'go* (complaint drum) placed at the palace gate so that anyone who has grievances may appeal directly to the throne.
1402	May 23	Slaves belonging to the monasteries turned over to the government.

1403	March 5	Yi Pang-wŏn orders the casting of new copper types.
1405		Yi Pang-wŏn finally makes Hansŏng the capital of the Yi dynasty. Slaves belonging to the monasteries reduced in number.
1406	May 27	Korean-Jürched trade centers established in the northeast.
1408	June 4	Policy of granting monk's certificate initiated.
	June 18	Yi Sŏng-gye d.
	October 18	Ming envoy brings the posthumous epithet for the deceased king.
1409	May 27	The *Shindo pi* erected for Yi Sŏng-gye.
1410	February 14	Ha Yun and others begin compilation of the *T'aejo sillok* (completed April 22, 1413).
	March-April	Raids of the Wu-liang-ho, Wu-ti-ho, and Odoli in Kyŏngwŏn.
1413	April 11	Yi Pang-wŏn orders the Haein monastery to run off another copy of the *Tripiṭaka*, the blocks of which had been cut between 1236–1251.
1414	February 18	Bureau of Royal Household Administration established.
1417	January 21	Yi Pang-wŏn orders burning of books on divination and geomancy.
1418	September 7	Yi Pang-wŏn abdicates in favor of Prince Ch'ungnyŏng (Sejong).
	September 9	Sejong ascends the throne at the Kyŏngbok Palace.
1420	April 28	Hall of Worthies established at court.
1422	May 30	Yi Pang-wŏn d.
1423	May 24	Ming envoy brings the posthumous epithet for Yi Pang-wŏn.
1424	March 31	Yun Hoe and others begin compilation of the *T'aejong sillok* (completed April 28, 1431).
1434	January	The Jürched Li Man-chu's cavalry raids the southwest of Yŏyŏn in North P'yŏng-an; Korean army of 15,500 routs the enemy on the T'ung-chia River.
		Nine garrisons established in the northwest.

1437	August 31	Governor of Hamgil province ordered to inspect the site of Chŏk Island.
1442	April 11	The court interrogates eye-witnesses to the 1380 battle on Mount Hwang.
1443–1444		Korean alphabet completed.
1445	May 11	Kwŏn Che and others present the draft of the *Songs of Flying Dragons*.
1446	September-October	Korean alphabet promulgated.
1446	November 26	Sejong orders the Institute of Korean Language to revise the cantos dealing with his four ancestors and Yi Sŏng-gye.
1447	February-March	Commentary on the *Songs* completed in ten chapters.
	July 17	Sejong regulates the court music, the royal compositions based on the *Songs* forming the nucleus.
	November 23	Five hundred and fifty copies of the *Songs* distributed.
1450	March 30	Sejong d.
	April 7	Munjong (fifth ruler) ascends the throne.
1452	March 11	Monument erected for King Sejong.
	June 1	Munjong d.
	June 5	Tanjong (sixth ruler) ascends the throne.
1455	July 25	Tanjong abdicates; Sejo (seventh ruler) ascends the throne.
1457	July 19	Yang Sŏng-ji presents the illustrations for the *Songs*.

Glossary

Agi-batur 阿其拔都
Allyŏmsa (*onch'alsa, kwanch'alsa*) 按廉使 (按察使, 觀察使)
An Chi 安止
An Kyŏn 安堅
An U-gyŏng 安遇慶
Ansi (fortress) 安市城

Chach'o (Muhak) 自超 (無學)
Chahŏn taebu 資憲大夫
Ch'ahyŏn 車峴
Ch'amji chŏngsa 參知政事
Changdan 長湍
Ch'angdŏk (palace) 昌德宮
Chao Wu 趙武
Chi chegyo 知製教
Chi Ch'unch'ugwan sa 知春秋館事
Ch'ihwap'yŏng 致和平
Chii (mount) 智異山
Chindan hakpo 震檀學報
Chinp'o 鎮浦
Chiphyŏnchŏn 集賢殿
—*pugyori* 副校理
—*taejehak* 大提學
—*ŭnggyo* 應教
Cho Chun 趙浚

Cho Min-su 曹敏修
Cho Pan 趙胖
Chobong taebu 朝奉大夫
Ch'oe Ch'i-wŏn 崔致遠
Ch'oe Chŏng-suk 崔貞淑
Ch'oe Hang 崔恒
Ch'oe Mu-sŏn 崔茂宣
Ch'oe Un 崔沄
Ch'oe Yŏng 崔瑩
Ch'oe Yu 崔濡
Chŏk (island) 赤島
Ch'ŏnbo (mount) 天寶山
Chŏng Ch'ŏl 鄭澈
Chŏng In-ji 鄭麟趾
Chŏng Ka-sin 鄭可臣
Chŏng Mong-ju 鄭夢周
Chŏng Se-un 鄭世雲
Chŏng To-jŏn 鄭道傳
chŏngdang munhak 政堂文學
Chŏngjong sillok 定宗實錄
Chongmyo pusŭng 宗廟副丞
Ch'ongsŏkchŏng 叢石亭
Chŏnju 全州
Ch'ŏnsu (monastery) 天壽寺 (天壽院, 天水寺)
Chorae (mount) 照浦山

303

Chosŏn 朝鮮
Chumong 朱蒙
Ch'ungdam (master) 忠談師
Ch'ungnyŏl (king) 忠烈王
Ch'up'ungo 追風烏
Chwa sagan 左司諫
Chwajungho 左中護
Ch'wip'unghyŏng 醉豐亨

"Early Brilliance" 早明

"graceful hang" (polo) 垂揚

Ha Yun 河崙
Haeju 海州
Haep'ung 海豐
Hakp'o (bridge) 鶴浦橋
Hamgil (province) 咸吉道
Hamhŭng 咸興
Hamju (Yŏnghŭng) 咸州 (永興)
Hamyang 咸陽
Han Ch'ung 韓忠
Han Sang-jil 韓尙質
Hanyang (Hansŏng) 漢陽 (漢城)
Hoengun'gol 橫雲鶻
Hong Yu 洪儒
Honggun 紅軍 (紅賊, 紅頭賊, 香軍)
Hongwŏn 洪原
hu (tree) 楛
Huang Yen 黃儼
Hwang (mount) 荒山
Hwang Sang 黃裳
Hwangju 黃州
Hwŏnjat 奚關城
Hyŏnp'yo 玄豹

Iryŏn (great master) 一然大師

Kaeguk changjŏl kong 開國狀節公
Kaemusŏng 蓋牟城
Kakhun 覺訓
Kang Hŭi-an 姜希顔
Kanghwa (island) 江華島
Karaeol 楸洞
Kasŏn taebu 嘉善大夫
Ki Ch'ŏl 奇轍
Kil Chae 吉再

Kil Sa-sun 吉師舜
Kilchu 吉州
Kim In-ch'an 金仁贊
Kim In-hu 金麟厚
Kim Kye-ran 金桂蘭
Kim Pu-sik 金富軾
Kim Sa-hyŏng 金士衡
Kim Si-u 金時遇
Kim Wi-je 金謂磾
Ko An-wi 高安尉
Ko Chŏng-ŭi 高正義
Ko Yŏn-su 高延壽
Koguryŏ 高句麗
Kongju (Kyŏngwŏn) 孔州 (慶源)
Kongjwi 公州
Kongmin (king) 恭愍王
Kongyang (king) 恭讓王
Koryŏ 高麗
Kŭmo sŏwŏn 金烏書院
Kŭmowi sangjanggun 金吾衞上將軍
Kungye (king of T'aebong) 弓裔 (泰封王)
Kwanggaet'o (king) 廣開土王
Kwanghwa (gate) 光化門
Kwŏn Che 權踶
Kwŏn Kŭn 權近
Kyeryong (mount) 雞龍山
Kyŏnghŭng 慶興
Kyŏnhwon 甄萱
Kyŏng Pok-hŭng 慶復興
kyŏngsin (keng-shen, kōshin) 庚申
Kyunyŏ 均如

Milchik pusa 密直副使
Milchiksa taeŏn 密直司代言
Min Che 閔霽
Min Chi 閔漬
Mogŭn sŏnsaeng yŏnbo 牧隱先生年譜
mok 牧
Mok In-hae 睦仁海
Moraeogae 沙峴
Muak 毋岳
Mun Sŏng-yun 文成允
Mugong 武恭
Mundŏk kok 文德曲
Munha ch'ansŏngsa 門下贊成事
Munha sijung 門下侍中

Na Se 羅世
Nak (mount) 洛山
Nam Chae 南在
Nam Su-mun 南秀文
Nam Ŭn 南誾
Nosan'gun ilgi 魯山君日記
Niu Niu 牛牛

Odong 斡東
Ogo tojejo 五庫都堤調
Okchŏ 沃沮
Ŏnmunch'ŏng 諺文廳

Pae Hyŏn-gyŏng 裵玄慶
Pae Kŭng-nyŏm 裵克廉
Paegam 白巖
Paekche 百濟
Palchŏnja 發電赭
Pak Cha-an 朴子安
Pak P'aeng-nyŏn 朴彭年
Pak Shil 朴實
paktu 樸頭
Panya 般若
P'an samsa sa 判三司事
Pisa 秘史
P'ojŏng (hall) 布政殿
Pok Chi-gyŏm 卜知謙
Pokchu (Andong) 福州 (安東)
Pomungak taeje 寶文閣待制
P'oŭn munjip 圃隱文集
P'oŭn sŏnsaeng chip songnok 圃隱先生集
　續錄
pu 府
"pushed-back tail" (polo) 防尾
Puyŏ 夫餘
Pyŏn Chung-nyang 卞仲良
Pyŏngnando 碧瀾渡
P'yŏngju 平州
p'yŏnjŏn 片箭

Saaek sŏwŏn 賜額書院
Sagong 司空
Sajahwang 獅子黃
Sakpangdo pyŏngmasa 朔方道兵馬使
Sal (river; P'aesu) 薩水 (浿水)
Sambong chip 三峰集
Samch'ŏk 三陟

Samgye 三介
Samsŏn 三善
Sangju 尙州
Seja ubin'gaek 世子右賓客
—*ububin'gaek* 世子右副賓客
Shin Ch'ang 辛昌
Shin Suk-chu 申叔舟
Shin Sung-gyŏm 申崇謙
Shin Ton 辛旽
Shin U 辛禑
Shin Yŏng-son 辛永孫
"sideway block" (polo) 橫防
Silla 新羅
Sim Tŏk-pu 沈德符
Sinhye (queen) 神惠王后
Sinji (sinji sŏnin) 神誌 (神誌仙人)
Sinjong 神宗
Sinŭi (queen) 神懿王后
Sŏch'ŏn 舒川
Sŏk (heir apparent) 奭
Sŏl Chang-su 偰長壽
Sŏllae 善來
Sŏlmetkol 所磨洞
Sŏng Sam-mun 成三問
Sŏnggyun taesasŏng 成均大司成
Sŏngjong sillok 成宗實錄
Sŏnju 善州
Sŏnsan 善山
Sŏnwŏn segye 璿源世系
Ssangsŏng (Yŏnghŭng) 雙城 (永興)
Su Chiphyŏnchŏn kyori 守集賢殿校理
Su munha sijung 守門下侍中
Su Tollyŏngbu p'angwan 守敦寧府判官
Such'an 修撰
Such'ang (palace) 壽昌宮
Sukchin 肅愼
Sukchong 肅宗
Sukchong sillok 肅宗實錄
Sŭngch'ŏnbu (Kaep'ung) 昇天府 (開
　豊)
Sŭngjŏng taebu 崇政大夫

Taedohobu 大都護府
T'aesa 太師
T'aesang paksa 太常博士
Tŏgwŏn 德源
Tŏkpahŭi 德巖

Tongbungmyŏn wŏnsu 東北面元帥
Tongji Ch'unch'ugwan sa 同知春秋館事
Tongnyŏngbu 東寧府
Tosŏn 道詵
Tumen (river) 豆滿江
Tŭngju (Anbyŏn) 登州 (安邊)

U Hyŏn-bo 禹玄寶
Ŭijŏngbu uch'amch'an 議政府右參贊
—uch'ansŏng 右贊成
Ŭlchi Mundŏk 乙支文德
Ŭmnu 挹婁
Unbong 雲峯
Ungsangbaek 凝霜白
Up'ilsŏn 右弼善
ŭrhae 乙亥

Wang Kŏn 王建
Wang Pang 王昉
Wihwa (island) 威化島
Wŏn'gwang 圓光
Wŏn'gyŏng (queen) 元敬王后
Wu-la (Ura) 兀剌 (亏羅, 五老, 五女山城)

Yalu (river) 鴨綠江
Yang Paeng-nyŏn 楊伯淵
Yang Sŏng-ji 梁誠之
Yat'un (village) 也頓 (屯)
Yaŭn chip 冶隱集
Yaŭn sŏnsaeng sokchip 冶隱先生續集
Yesŏng (river) 禮成江
Ye 濊
Yemungwan ŭnggyo 藝文館應敎
Yi An-sa (Mokcho) 李安社 (穆祖)
Yi Cha-ch'un (Hwanjo) 李子春 (桓祖)
Yi Cha-hŭng (Prince Wanch'ang) 李子興 (完昌大君)

Yi Cha-sŏn (Prince Wanwŏn) 李子宣 (完原大君)
Yi Che-hyŏn 李齊賢
Yi Ch'o 李初
Yi Ch'ŏn-gye (Prince Yŏngsŏng) 李天桂 (永城大君)
Yi Ch'un (Tojo) 李椿 (度祖)
Yi Haeng-ni (Ikcho) 李行里 (翼祖)
Yi Hoe 李薈
Yi Hyŏl-lo (Sŏl-lo) 李賢老 (善老)
Yi In-im 李仁任
Yi Kae 李塏
Yi Pang-gan (Prince Hoean) 李芳幹 (懷安大君)
Yi Pang-gwa(Chŏngjong) 李芳果 (定宗)
Yi Pang-sŏk(Prince Ŭian) 李芳碩 (宜安大君)
Yi Pang-wŏn (T'aejong, Great King Kongjŏng)李芳遠(太宗,恭定大王)
Yi Saek 李穡
Yi Sŏng-gye (T'aejo, Great King Kanghŏn) 李成桂 (太祖,康獻大王)
Yi Suk-pŏn 李叔蕃
Yi Tal-ch'ung 李達衷
Yi To (Sejong) 李祹 (世宗)
Yi Tu-ran (Chi-ran) 李豆蘭 (之蘭)
Yijo chawrang 吏曹佐郎
Yŏmillak 與民樂
Yongbi ŏch'ŏn ka 龍飛御天歌
Yongdŭngja 龍騰紫
Yŏngjo sillok 英祖實錄
Yŏnsan'gun 燕山君
Yu In-u 柳仁雨
Yuinch'ŏng 游麟靑
Yuksŏnsaeng yugo 六先生遺稿
Yun I 尹彝

Index